Sports Babylon

To Amalda ...
a man who knows his sport,
its glory and its vices.

Captions to prelim pictures: (page 2) Ben Johnson makes some last-minute adjustments; (page 3) Paul Gascoigne re-enacts his finest dentist's chair moments; (page 4) Vinnie introduces himself to Gazza; (page 5) Robbie Fowler acting the baboon.

THIS IS A CARLTON BOOK

This edition published in 1999

10 9 8 7 6 5 4 3 2 1

Copyright © Carlton Books Limited 1999

All rights reserved. No part of this publication may be reproduced, stored in a retrieval system, or transmitted in any form or by any means, electronic, mechanical, photocopying, recording or otherwise, without the prior permission of the copyright owner and the publishers.

A CIP catalogue record for this book is available from the British Library

ISBN 1 85868 750 0

Project editor: Martin Corteel
Project art direction: Trevor Newman
Picture research: Jeff Beasley
Production: Sarah Schuman

Printed in Italy

Sports Babylon

Mihir Bose

CARLTON

CONTENTS

Introduction 6

Chapter 1
Never Mind the Ball... 8

When you boil it down to the essentials, there are two types of foul. They are fouls of the heart and fouls of the head.

Chapter 2
The Violence in our Midst 46

Sport, whenever and wherever it has been played, has always aroused passion and no sport is more passionate than football. In football, when the passions boil over and overwhelm the crowd, then Pele's beautiful game gets close to becoming an instrument of evil.

Chapter 3
Performance-Enhancing Drugs 78

Drug-taking to enhance performance is highly scientific and clever lawyers make it harder to distinguish between the bad and the unfortunate. What is certain is that the cry of 'drug cheat' is almost always made against athletes who destroy world records or rise overnight from obscurity to win a gold medal.

Chapter 4
Sexual and Other Misdemeanours 100

The sportsman who is transformed from a highly trained, focused athlete on the field into an irresponsible hedonist off it is not a new phenomenon. The pernicious flattery of hero worship has derailed the express career of too many contenders to mention.

Chapter 5
Racism in Sport 116

Racism in sport is hardly a modern contagion. The ancient Greeks, who are credited with inventing the concept of sports, knew all about excluding people because of their race, but it was the United States and South Africa in the modern era that truly introduced institutionalized racism into sport.

Chapter 6
The Fix 130
Sport generally prides itself on being clean and above-board, with no place for cheating or match-fixing. Yet, like the serpent in the Garden of Eden, dishonesty is almost inseparable from sport. As long as organized sports have been played there have been attempts to fix the results.

Chapter 7
Cricket's Bribery Saga 148
In the history of cricket there is much talk of a dark chapter, when matches were bought and sold. But this is presented as ancient history, when the game was young and all sorts of things happened.

Chapter 8
The Bung/Used Five Pound Notes and Motorway Cafes 162
The history of professional football is littered with stories of illegal payments made by clubs and their officials in order to gain an advantage.

Chapter 9
The Bung/Fishing Trawlers Off Hull and Bars in Park Lane 184
When the word 'bung' was first brought to the public's attention, Brian Clough asked, "Bung; isn't that something you get from a plumber to stop up the bath?"

Chapter 10
Rings of Deceit 200
The Olympics may have long since sold their soul to Mammon, but they still cling to the myth that their games have an ideal higher than filthy lucre.

Index 220

Rogues' Gallery
Vinnie Jones: Folk Hero of the Battering Classes 40 • **O.J. Simpson:** The Juice Turns Sour 74 • **Dennis Rodman:** The Orgasmic Worm 96 • **Mike Tyson:** The Norman Bates of the Ring 112 • **Eric Cantona:** Ooh, Aah, Cantona! 126 • **Don King:** The Ghetto Einstein 144 • **Lester Piggott:** The Long Fellow and the Tax Man 158 • **Paul Gascoigne:** Daft as a Brush 178 • **Dennis Wise:** Dennis the Menace 196

Introduction

Sport has lost its innocence

Sport is the ultimate fantasy factory: that is and always has been its greatest appeal. In an age far removed from myth and magic, when the rise of mass communications and the arrival of Marshall McLuhan's global village have meant that little is totally unknown or completely unexpected, sport has the ability to produce moments so unpredictable that they seem the nearest to what our ancestors considered magical, gifts from the gods.

Watch your favourite team or favourite player and, through their success, you can have a vicarious thrill that no other activity can provide. A Tottenham Hotspur win does not mean money in my bank account. Quite the contrary – it often means it has cost me money – but Tottenham's victories give me such pleasure and such a lift that I would willingly see more of a dent in my bank balance if it meant I could ensure more successes for them.

The pleasure that Tottenham's triumphs give me has no side to it, I am not obligated to anybody as a result and, what is more, it instantly makes me part of the community that, like me, supports Tottenham. I become part of a happy family merely because 90 minutes of athletic endeavour has produced what we think is the right result. Such feelings are common to all those who have sporting loyalties. What Manchester United supporter, who did not have the good fortune to be in Barcelona last May, would not have paid as much as he possibly could – and some paid thousands for a trip that ordinarily costs no more than a few hundred – to see, in 90 amazing seconds, their team change a losing 1–0 scoreline into a fantastic 2–1 victory?

There is nothing else in life that can match that. It proves the theory put forward by Sam Chisholm, former chief executive of BSkyB, that sport has replaced Hollywood. That, in a way, is appropriate. The start of this century marked the arrival of the movies, first the silents, then the talkies, offering the world an opportunity to dream. Hollywood has been the greatest dream factory mankind has known, only lately threatened by the rise of Bollywood, the Hindi film industry based around Bombay. The movies produced there do much to make the life of millions of poor Indians a little more bearable. But now, as the century closes, movies have had to give way to sport as the activity that can best tickle our fantasy bone.

Sport has two massive advantages over movies. It does not need language – you do not have to know Portuguese to appreciate Brazilian football – and, what is more, unlike most movies the endings cannot be predicted. Can you imagine a screenwriter scripting the outcome of the recent matches between Manchester United and Arsenal in the FA Cup semi-final, or the semi-final of the cricket World Cup between Australia and South Africa which ended with a tie?

However, divine as such moments can be there is a dark side to sport, and it is this which this book sets out to chronicle. The idea that sportsmen and women can get up to dirty tricks, cheat, lie, take drugs, bend the rules or even throw matches in order to

Brandi Chastain does wonders for Nike sports bra sales after the 1999 Women's World Cup

Introduction

make money is not new. As we shall see, this has been going on almost as long as sports have been played; and unlike some other writers I do not believe that there was once a sporting Eden which has been corrupted by the serpent of commercialism and greed.

Yes, sport has changed, and the new thing is the money in sport and the media spotlight under which sportsmen and women now find themselves. Nothing illustrated this better than the Lawrence Dallaglio story, revealing the England rugby captain's drug "adventures". George Orwell, in one of his classic essays, mourned the decline of the English murder. His thesis was that an Englishman liked nothing better of a Sunday afternoon than to curl up after lunch with his *News of the World* and read about a murder trial, which the paper specialized in reporting. But if that was true of pre-war and early post-war Britain, such murder trials are now rare, and with the abolition of the death penalty, the trial does not have quite the same force.

Now the *News of the World*, which ran the Dallaglio story, is more inclined to entertain its readers with the "Decline of the Sportsman or Woman". Hardly a week goes by when a Sunday paper does not have some exposé or other about the doings of some sportsman. Some of these stories form part of the book. But one sort does not. I have deliberately kept away from stories such as Graham Rix being jailed for his illegal sexual activities, because they do not relate to his sporting life. He made the news because he had been a famous sportsman. The only exception to this was the O.J. Simpson story, but its inclusion can be justified because it illustrated the power of modern sports. What else can explain how the trial of an ex-American football player became such a global media event that the press secretary of Britain's future Prime Minister felt he had to ring the BBC to make sure Simpson did not eclipse his boss on that evening's TV news?

How different it was a quarter of a century ago. In 1974 when Paul Gardner wrote *Nice Guys Finish Last* – a book about sport and American life which is among those that ought to have become a classic but did not – he spent much of his introduction explaining why such a book had to be written. Gardner, an Englishman and an Arsenal supporter living in New York, explained that his book was about an aspect of American life that had "been given surprisingly little attention by those who would understand Americans; sport, and in particular the commercialized, professional brand of it."

Yet today, 25 years later, there would be no need for such an explanation. Not only is sport as seen on the field of play exhaustively covered, but so too are its wider aspects and the ways in which it reaches out to other parts of society.

Twenty-five years ago sport rarely got on to the front pages of newspapers, let alone became a top item on TV news. When I was growing up, a sports story on the front page was so rare that it always meant something very dramatic had happened: an Ashes series victory, perhaps. Nowadays, sports stories are often given such prominence. Whether it is Sky trying to buy Manchester United or the FA giving United an exemption from the FA Cup, editors seem ever-eager to put sport on their front pages.

The reasons are many and varied. As the great ideological and political debates that divided our century have been resolved with the collapse of communism, the agenda on the front pages is no longer driven by the fear that we all face extinction, and news other than the purely political has gained prominence. But it is also because sport has changed. Sport is now more than just a test of athletic skills. That is still at the centre of sporting activity: but in order for that test of athletic skill to happen, there is a need for so much money, marketing and publicity that sport is now an industry.

Yet, for all the talk that sport is now business and sportsmen and women more like pop stars, the way most sports are run has not changed in the century or more since the British invented modern sport. This dichotomy between the money, glamour and kudos sport can bring and the way sport is organized has produced a dangerous gap

(Left) Blair plays keepie-uppie with Keegan; (right) Posh and Becks announce engagement

leading not only to much corruption but also a growing cynicism. This is perhaps the most depressing aspect of modern sport: it is becoming like politics. Just as we are all ready to believe that no politician can be trusted, so we are coming close to believing that all sportsmen and women are susceptible to filthy lucre and would do anything to gain an advantage, however unfair. Even more depressing is that there is no sign that sports administrators understand this, let alone that they are doing anything to remedy matters.

Perhaps it is not surprising, therefore, that modern politicians are so fond of sport. The President throwing the first pitch at the first baseball game of the season has long been an American custom, but now every politician seems keen to get in on the sporting act, as illustrated by the way the British government is backing the Football Association's bid to stage the 2006 World Cup in England.

But there again there is nothing new in sport, and nor is this new. Back in 1905 Theodore Roosevelt, then in the White House, picked up a newspaper and saw a picture of an American football player, his face battered and bloody. During that season 18 players were killed and 159 others seriously injured playing the game in the USA. Roosevelt immediately summoned representatives of Yale, Princeton and Harvard – American football then was an upper-class college sport – and told them: "Brutality and foul play should receive the same summary punishment given to the man who cheats at cards."

American football took the President's advice, and changed. But many other sports still need to heed that warning. More than a century later Roosevelt's words continue to resonate. The fact that sport does not appear to be listening to them accounts for a large part of this book.

I could not have written it without the help and encouragement of several people. I must first of all thank Nigel Dudley and Richard Weekes without whose assistance this book would have been impossible. I am also deeply grateful to Daniel Mokades and Clare Davies for their research, help, encouragement and general good advice.

The errors and omissions, however, are mine alone.

MIHIR BOSE
London, July 1999

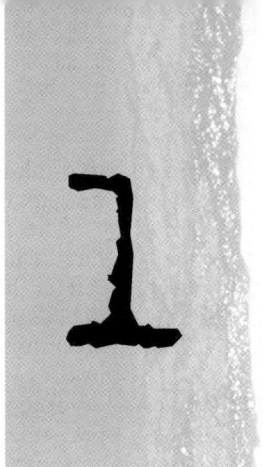

Never Mind the Ball ...

Sportsmen are fitter and faster than ever, and they are playing for ever higher financial stakes. The pressure to bend or break the rules increases every day. So too does the pressure on managers to defend or explain these misdemeanours. Conversely, sportsmen can now hardly bend their backsides without a slow-motion replay of the incident magnified three times. And that must mean that there are likely to be fewer crude fouls. But, until one can put a microchip into Michael Schumacher's or Duncan Ferguson's brain we will never be sure about their motivation. And that will keep the bars full of disputing fans until the end of time.

There are essentially two types of foul, whether committed on the pitch or in the stadiums. They are fouls of the heart and fouls of the head. A foul of the heart is easy enough to recognize – the flaring temper and the fact that it is invariably self-destructive give it away too easily.

Eric Cantona's kick at a fan chanting racist abuse from the stand, Mike Gatting's confrontation with Pakistani umpire Shakoor Rana, and Brian Clough's swing at a spectator who ran on to the pitch during a Nottingham Forest match were all examples of the heart ruling the head. And there are other actions that are just as clearly calculated, such as Mike Tyson's biting of Evander Holyfield's ear.

A more intriguing area, however, is the hinterland between the two. This includes those deeds which can't quite be classified as a misdemeanour, such as Michael Atherton's use of earth in his pocket to dry the ball, and the instruction to Trevor Chappell to bowl under-arm when Australia's opponents needed a six off the last ball – a crime against the spirit if not the letter of the laws of cricket.

Rutting season: Steve Staunton (left) and Fabrizio Ravanelli lock horns at the Riverside in 1997.

Here too are the actions which the perpetrators put down to an error of judgement. We will never know for certain the motivation for those collisions between Alain Prost and Ayrton Senna and between Michael Schumacher and Damon Hill – i.e. whether they were deliberate – but we can all work out who gained from them.

Then there are those calculated crimes which appear to masquerade as a real loss of temper. Just how calculated were John McEnroe's bouts of temper on the tennis court? – he always seemed to play better afterwards and his opponent worse. When rugby scrums start fighting, is it a natural release of tension, or is it deliberate provocation by one side to destabilize the other?

Finally, there are the defences put up by players and managers. And here it is the managers who are of most interest. A football manager will almost invariably condemn a referee for sending off his player. It is not so much an attempt to get that decision reversed as a warning to the referee to think twice about issuing a booking in the next match.

The reality is that violence has been a fact of life on the sports field since the first referee held his whistle to his mouth. And debate about what was foul play and what an unfortunate accident has filled the hours in bars wherever sports are played.

Today, thanks to mass communications – particularly television and its spectacular close-up camera – we see more violence. This does not necessarily mean that the sport itself has become more violent. What it does mean is that players' misdeeds can no longer be so easily dismissed as a slight slip of the ankle or a deliberate assault by a cheek on an elbow. It has also ensured that pictures are flashed round the world within seconds – contrast the time it took for Tyson's ear-biting to be seen with the time it took for real pictures of England's alleged bodyline bowling to be sent from Australia to London. And even then there were not live television pictures but, apart from the odd newsreel, mostly still camera shots.

Football

A century ago, when modern sports first developed, the battles were largely on the field. But now many take place off the field where sportsmen, and particularly managers, indulge in word-play that would do credit to a political spin-doctor. The master of this sort of psychological warfare is none other than one of the most successful managers ever of an English football club, Scotsman Alex Ferguson.

No one is better than Ferguson at finding an opposing manager's weak point; but even he must have been surprized at the response of Newcastle's Kevin Keegan as the 1995–96 English football season reached its climax.

Tensions between the two had risen steadily through the second half of the season as Manchester United chipped away at the 12-point lead held by Newcastle in early January. By the end of April, Ferguson's side was three points ahead.

After a match between Leeds United and Manchester United in which, despite losing their goalkeeper and going down to ten men, Leeds fought hard in defeat, Ferguson said he hoped Leeds would show the same will to win in the remaining games. Ferguson knew well enough that one of these was against Newcastle. Ferguson accused the Yorkshire side of letting down their manager and raising their game only when they played against United, and also doubted the level of commitment Nottingham Forest would show against Newcastle, as the two sides were also playing a testimonial match.

It is a football convention that managers, whatever they may think in private, do not comment on the opposition, and certainly do not criticize them in public. However, Ferguson had gone to quite exceptional lengths to do so, asking Leeds manager Howard Wilkinson if it would be all right to have a "pop" at his players. Wilkinson agreed, and it had the desired effect: Keegan lost his rag. He felt Ferguson had thrown the unwritten rules out of the window.

After Newcastle won a hard-fought game against Leeds by a single goal, Keegan was asked in a TV interview what level of tension he was under. In an emotional attack on Ferguson, he said: "Some of the comments I have heard over the last week have been close to slanderous. There is no doubt about it – the man has gone down a lot in my estimation. You'll have to send a tape of this game to Alex Ferguson, won't you? Isn't that what he has asked for – isn't that what he wants?...I would love it if we could beat them now. Football in this country is honest and we have kept quiet about this. But the battle is still on."

When Keegan climbed on to the team bus 45 minutes later he was still highly emotional and sat distraught, shaking his head. His team won that day, but the last laugh was with Ferguson: his psychology may have been cheap but it undoubtedly helped his side collect the championship.

There are some who would classify this as psychological warfare and view it as a new development in sport. However, what players from Manchester United and Arsenal – at present the country's two most successful teams – have been getting up to in the last decade has a fairly long pedigree.

Arsenal, under George Graham and now Arsène Wenger, gained a reputation as one of the hardest sides in English League football. During the 1986–87 season, which was Graham's first season as manager at Highbury and Ferguson's first at United, the feud between the two was ignited. In one match, which Arsenal lost 2–0, seven players were booked, Arsenal's David Rocastle was sent off and Graham and Ferguson glared at each other on the touchline and in the players' tunnel and exchanged what Graham called "industrial language".

But at the start of the 1990s, as Arsenal, having won their first championship since 1971, began to challenge the North's domination of the League title, signs emerged that the club which once transfer-listed a player because he had been sent off was now a very different animal. Arsenal under Graham not only won but often got involved in questioning referees' decisions. Four players were fined £1,000 each for dissent at Villa Park. In September 1988 cameras had caught an off-the-ball incident, missed by the referee, in which Paul Davis broke Glen Cockerill of Southampton's jaw. It appeared Cockerill had been baiting Davis. Davis was banned for nine games and the player seen as the midfield motivator for Arsenal and England never recovered to fulfil his promise.

Then on 4 November 1989, with Arsenal at home to Norwich, there was another flare-up. Arsenal were awarded a penalty in the last minute of a match which had already seen six goals. Lee Dixon's shot was saved, and in trying to get to the rebound Alan Smith was bundled into the goal by Norwich's Mark Bowen. This led to a fight involving Smith, another Arsenal player, Niall Quinn, and the Norwich team, which drew in the rest of the Arsenal side. Eventually, after the police had gone on to the pitch to break it up, Arsenal won the game 4–3.

But all this was overshadowed nearly a year later, on 20 October 1990, when Arsenal went up to Old Trafford. Arsenal, having won the championship the previous season, their first for 17 years, were now chasing their second under Graham. Manchester United at that stage had not won the championship since 1967 and their fans, having had to endure the triumphs of Liverpool, now had Arsenal to contend with. The result was a match of a kind never seen before on an English ground nor, thankfully, ever since.

Nigel Winterburn and Brian McClair had been going at each other throughout the match. At one stage Mark Hughes discovered he was the meat in a sandwich tackle by Winterburn and Anders Limpar. This was the cue for McClair to wade into Winterburn. Hughes also barged in, and Limpar then took a swing at McClair. Michael Thomas of Arsenal, the man who scored the goal that had so dramatically won Arsenal the championship with the last kick of the 1988–89 season, now grabbed McClair by the throat. By this time 21 of the 22 players were involved.

Ferguson went on to the pitch but was told to shut his face and go back to the dug-out – by Tony Adams, the Arsenal captain, who had run 50 yards to get involved and had pushed McClair over the touch-line.

In his autobiography, *Addicted*, Adams claims the press got it wrong: 16 of the players were trying to sort it out, and it was no more than what you would see any Sunday on Hackney Marshes. George Graham described it as "handbags at six paces".

When the FA asked Adams why he had got involved, he claimed that as captain it was his duty to sort it out. He also said that when players in training are told to stick together they can hardly stay away when one of their mates is in a fight. The FA found the excuses given totally unconvincing. Arsenal were deducted two points, United lost one, and both sides faced a £50,000 fine.

Before the FA announced their decision Arsenal, chasing the championship, were very nervous and worried about the punishment the FA might impose – they feared a hefty points deduction. The chairman Peter Hill-Wood, vice-chairman David Dein and managing director Ken Friar met in Dein's office with Graham.

What, they wondered, could Arsenal do that would take the heat off the Highbury club? Graham came up with the solution. Arsenal should announce that they were taking strong internal disciplinary action, fine each of the five players at the heart of the trouble and impose a fine on Graham. By suggesting that Arsenal fine him, Graham hoped the Board could distance itself from the turmoil at Old Trafford and thus escape punishment. So each of the five players at the heart of the trouble – Rocastle, Davis, Winterburn, Thomas and Limpar – was fined two weeks' wages, and Graham was fined £10,000. The public were told that as manager he was responsible for the behaviour of the players, but they were not told that he had suggested it himself as a way of softening any FA punishment.

The way Arsenal dealt with the incident shows how sophisticated sporting clubs had become in dealing with violence and dirty play. Not surprisingly, however, this did nothing to change Arsenal's reputation as a hard and possibly dirty team, a reputation that grew as the decade progressed. Thereafter there was potential for flare-ups whenever Arsenal met United, often centred round clashes between the Arsenal forward Ian Wright and the United goalkeeper Peter Schmeichel, with the Dane complaining about Wright and Wright protesting that Schmeichel had racially baited him. In the end it did not lead to anything – except that Wright, Arsenal's most prolific-ever goal-scorer, never scored for them against United. Did Schmeichel play mind-games with Wright? If so, he certainly succeeded.

Arsenal, aware of how crucial Wright was, did nothing to temper his tendency to explode, and in 1995 he had to apologize to the FA for calling referees "incompetent little Hitlers". In 1996 Sheffield Wednesday manager David Pleat wrote to the Football Association to complain that Wright had grabbed a handful of winger Regi Blinker's dreadlocks and pulled so hard that he had screamed in agony. Later Pleat claimed that Wright had stamped on Dejan Stefanovic's foot and forced him to limp off.

A year later Wright made unflattering comments about referee Mike Riley and got into more trouble when he referred to Pleat's alleged personal problems, which had attracted such publicity that he had been forced to resign as Tottenham manager in 1987. The FA took a dim view of Wright's comments and fined him £15,000 for both incidents. Wright then confessed he suffered from a rage he could not control and needed therapy. He went to rage therapy classes.

How much good they did is debatable. On 1 May 1999, as the 1998–99 season came to a close, Upton Park saw probably the most explosive of Wright's rages. By now with West Ham, he was playing in a match in which they were reduced to eight men, while four other Hammers and three Leeds players were booked by referee Ron Harris. Wright was sent off after 16 minutes. He started the match game by elbowing Alf Haaland: this went unseen and unpunished. Six minutes later an identical offence got him his first yellow card, and ten minutes later came a third elbowing, on Ian Harte off the ball, which linesman Paul Norman brought to Harris's attention. The second yellow card meant a very early bath for Wright, who had to be restrained by his colleagues as he was sent off, and a West Ham fan later tried to attack a linesman.

As Wright made his exit, instead of making his way to the home dressing-room, he headed for the referee's room. There he kicked in the door and proceeded to hurl all the referee's clothes on to the floor. For good measure he also threw a TV set on to the floor.

A contrite Wright would later say, " I was so upset that I behaved in an unacceptable manner. I don't even remember properly what I did, only that I was in the ref's room. I hope and pray to God that I can be forgiven for this stupid and reckless act by the match officials, the club, the fans and the authorities."

The authorities were far from forgiving: Wright was banned for three matches and fined £17,000.

The advent of Arsène Wenger, the Frenchman who could easily pass for an academic rather than a manager, has if anything increased Arsenal's reputation for the sort of play that many consider beyond the pale. While on the field Arsenal have started producing the type of stylish attacking play once considered the preserve of Tottenham and United, and won the Double in Wenger's first full season in 1997–98, this has been accompanied by a level of illegal and foul play from the Highbury men which has set new and dubious records.

In April 1999, during the first FA Cup semi-final match against Manchester United, the Argentinian Nelson Vivas, who was playing only because Emmanuel Petit had been suspended, got the red card for elbowing Nicky Butt after the ball had gone and with such force that he flattened the player. This meant that Arsenal had had nine players dismissed in the 1998–99 season, a joint record for the top flight, and a total of 22 red cards in the 30 months since Wenger had taken over. In spite of this, however, chairman Peter Hill-Wood insisted that Arsenal did not have a single dirty player.

"It's annoying when people assume we are the dirtiest side in the Premiership. Ten red cards is nothing to shout about, but it's not as if we keep having players sent off for kicking their opponents up in the air."

As far as Hill-Wood is concerned, the 1999 episode was nothing compared with the mass brawl with United in 1990, when he had to fine Graham: "I tried to put my foot down once when George was here, but I've never been inclined to repeat that episode since Arsène came to the club."

Hill-Wood did not mention that it was Graham who had suggested the punishment to take the heat off the club. Hill-Wood's insistence that his players were not dirty is valid only if we accept that the 1960s and 1970s, which saw some of the worst fouls committed, were the norm against which football is to be judged. That was the decade when, in the Charity Shield in 1974 between League champions Leeds and Cup-winners Liverpool, Johnny Giles of Leeds punched Kevin Keegan and then scurried back into a crowd of players. Keegan, thinking the offender was Billy Bremner, tried to get his own back, and as Bremner tried to protect himself Norman "Bite Yer Legs" Hunter stopped a confrontation, but only by putting his hands round Keegan's throat.

The result was that both Keegan and Bremner were sent off, and they reacted by throwing their shirts away in disgust as they left the field. A year later it was the turn of Hunter to be sent off in a match involving Leeds and Derby played in November 1975 at Derby's old home, the Baseball Ground. Francis Lee of Derby found himself subject to one of Hunter's crunching tackles. Hunter followed this up with a blow to Lee's head. Lee would have retaliated but four Leeds players held him back. The referee decided to send both players off, and as they walked away Hunter baited Lee some more, Lee swung at Hunter and other players had to come and separate the two. Lee would later recall, "Norman threw a punch at me when

Opening scraps: Kevin Keegan and Billy Bremner are sent off in the 1974 Charity Shield.

I wasn't looking. The referee sent us both off, yet I hadn't thrown a punch, so I just lost my temper as I was walking off. Fortunately, all I got was a split lip."

Yes, unlike the 1970s, players are not being kicked in the air. Almost all the players of that era agree that the game has been cleaned up since then. Certainly life is a little better for the forwards, now that the tackle from behind has been banned. Nevertheless, the way Hill-Wood justifies Arsenal's disciplinary record makes it hard not to see this as a cynical acceptance of foul play, with the Arsenal board well aware that this may be the necessary price to pay for success in the modern game. But regrettable as such cynicism may be, it is at least more understandable than the shaming, craven way the then-Everton board greeted the return of Duncan Ferguson after he became the first international player in Britain to be sentenced for an on-the-field offence. This had resulted in Ferguson receiving a three-month prison sentence in 1995 for butting an opponent. He was also suspended for 12 games by the Scottish FA.

Ferguson, who was an Everton player at the time of his appeal, but was at Glasgow Rangers when he committed the offence, was sent to prison for assaulting Raith Rovers player John McStay during the match. Ferguson lunged at McStay, grabbed his shirt and butted him to the ground.

Three appeal court judges said the sentence should stand because Ferguson was idolized by thousands of fans and could not be seen to get away with such an attack. Lord Hope, Scotland's most senior judge, said: "Criminal acts cannot be tolerated on the field of play any more than they can be tolerated in any place in the country."

A contributing factor, said the judges, was that Ferguson had three previous convictions for assault and was on probation when he assaulted McStay. In 1991 he had been fined £125 for butting a policeman in Stirling. Two years later he was fined £200 for kicking a Hearts supporter – on crutches – in an argument over a taxi: Ferguson claimed provocation. He used a similar defence six months later when he was put on 12 months' probation after being found guilty of assaulting a Pittenweem fisherwoman.

But what left the sourest taste in the mouth was the reception Ferguson received when he reached Everton after serving his prison sentence. A Rolls-Royce was laid on to collect him from prison. The then-Everton chairman Peter Johnson said Ferguson was "no danger to society", the then-manager Joe Royle spoke of witchhunts, at the ground there was a band to welcome him and the fans greeted him as if he were a soldier returning from the battlefront rather than a convicted criminal.

It is unlikely that Ferguson would have received anything like such treatment if Brian Clough had been the manager at Everton. Clough's teams always had a very good reputation, partly because they feared what Clough would do to them, and he was not averse to taking action against fans who he felt overstepped the mark. This led to deep trouble with the Football Association when he struck a spectator at a League Cup match between Nottingham Forest and Queen's Park Rangers. He was fined £5,000 and banned from the touchline for a season. Justifying his decision to clip one of the Forest fans who had invaded the pitch, he likened it to people coming into his kitchen without being invited.

Clough was also proud of the way he dealt with Kenny Burns, a player with a reputation for being dirty, soon after he joined Forest. He seized Burns by the collar with both hands and told him that if he misbehaved he would find himself back on the dog track at Perry Barr in Birmingham, from where he had worked his way into professional football. After that Clough had no problems with Burns, who was voted Footballer of the Year while at Forest.

Nor would Clough have used the sort of weasel words West Ham employed when they tried first to cover up and then to play down what one of their players, John Hartson, did to team-mate Eyal Berkovic.

John Hartson had earned himself a reputation as one of the bad boys of English football soon after he joined West Ham for £3.3 million from Arsenal. In 18 months, he was suspended three times, including two sendings-off, which ruined his club's FA Cup run in 1997. In October 1997, eight months after he signed for West Ham, he accused referee Mike Reed of being "an absolute joke, a homer and a shithouse" after a defeat at Leicester. The FA fined him £1,000 and warned him about future conduct. A month later he spent the night in a police cell after an evening out in Hertfordshire.

In April 1998 Hartson was banned for five games and fined £1,500 after a sending-off for elbowing Bolton's Per Frandsen.

In September that year he was arrested after using a pub hanging basket as a football while walking down a street in Swansea. For this he was given a conditional discharge, adding a criminal conviction to his catalogue of footballing offences.

Soon afterwards he achieved his greatest notoriety when he decided to use a human head as a football. This was when he assaulted his colleague Eyal Berkovic on the West Ham training ground by kicking him in the face.

As it happens, Sky TV cameras were present at the time, filming routine training shots. Initially the incident did not lead to any action by West Ham, but when the video of it was shown on television, club managing director Peter Storrie warned that Hartson had to "get his head round his football" and "stop getting involved in these incidents all the time".

However, West Ham tried hard to prevent any action from the FA. Harry Redknapp, the West Ham manager, said: "What have the FA got to get involved for? If they don't think that there are punches thrown at some training ground or other every week of the year then they're dreaming. Arguments and fights probably happen at every club once or twice a season, although not the sort of thing John did. I can't condone that because he was totally out of order."

Storrie added: "I don't know why this should be FA business. If they start looking at videos from training ground incidents then it will lead to cameras being banned by every club in the country."

But it did become FA business, even though, like Arsenal after the mass brawl with United, the club tried to draw the sting of any FA action by fining Hartson £10,000.

By the time of the FA hearing on 1 February 1999, Hartson had been sold to Wimbledon for £7.5m and had not only apologized personally to the commission but got his new employers to plead for him. Wimbledon pointed out that the two players had trained and played together since the incident and bore no grudges. Berkovic himself had confirmed this in a letter.

The FA also considered Redknapp's point that it was a training ground incident and nothing to do with the FA. However, FA spokesman Steve Double pointed out: " We regard it as clearly being in our jurisdiction on the grounds that John is a football player going about his duties and therefore subject to our rules. Berkovic's letter was noted and it was also pointed out on Wimbledon's behalf that the two players have subsequently trained and played together and no grudges were borne."

Nevertheless the FA decided to fine Hartson a record £20,000, the same fine as the one imposed on Vinnie Jones for promoting the video *Soccer's Hard Men* and on Patrick Vieira for a tunnel skirmish at the end of Arsenal's game at Sheffield Wednesday, where he was also alleged to have made a V-sign to Wednesday fans.

Redknapp confessed that he had not seen the fine coming but comforted himself with the thought that, had he not fined Hartson £10,000 – the money was donated to the Leukaemia Busters charity – Hartson might have been fined £100,000.

Hartson was also banned for three games. Wimbledon claimed Hartson had found it hard to live with himself, as if this was any excuse for what he had done. But by then he was part of the Crazy Gang. On his first day at the Wimbledon training ground he had been welcomed to his new club with the Wimbledon initiation rite. He was stripped of his £250 tracksuit and it was ceremonially burned. The fire set the dressing-room window frames alight and produced so much smoke that it set off alarms and prompted the arrival of police. Hartson was then thrown into a muddy puddle by his new team-mates before being given a pair of tracksuit bottoms that were more suitable for a 12-year-old and only came up to his backside. Hartson had expected all this and left his car at home, fearing that otherwise it would have ended up with no wheels.

The Hartson incident prompted Gordon Taylor, chairman of the Professional Footballers Association, as well as some lawyers, to predict that England would follow the Scottish example, meaning that players could be prosecuted for violence on the field. This is what had happened to Duncan Ferguson and former England players Terry Butcher and Chris Woods, who were convicted and fined for disorderly behaviour in an Old Firm game when playing for Rangers against Celtic in 1987.

Taylor warned: "When footballers are on the field of play they are not existing in an oasis away from the rules of law and order. They have a duty of care for their fellow-professionals and if they go beyond that and wilfully or recklessly injure another player, nothing in the world will protect them from the consequences.

"It would be the worst thing possible for football to be dragged through the courts. If there is a bad incident and the police see it, they have the right to get involved and we can't stop them We're not above the law. This is about sport, not war."

However, one of the PFA's most prominent members was soon indicating that he felt that sport, and particularly football, was a special case where a certain kind of war was very natural.

Shortly after the Hartson incident, Ian Wright used his ghosted column in the *Sun* to provide a defence of Hartson which revealed how the modern players feel: "We are not ballet dancers or chess players. Football is an aggressive game and these things happen, even involving nice blokes like Hartson." Wright, a team-mate of Hartson at West Ham, had not spoken to Hartson about the incident or tried to discuss it in any way. "What's the point? He knows he has done wrong, so I won't drone on telling him he's been a bad boy. I'm hardly squeaky clean."

He then let the cat out of the bag by blaming the presence of the television cameras at the ground for the whole thing. "It was purely bad luck that a television crew happened to be there. So it is disgraceful that a player will be disciplined because of something that is down to pure chance."

Aside from the depressing conclusion that Wright, like a lot of people in football, was really arguing that it was all right to commit such violence if you could get away it, the incident emphasized the increasing role played by television cameras in detecting the sort of violence commonplace in football. When television does not intervene, the human beings in charge can often come to amazingly different conclusions over very similar situations.

This was vividly illustrated by two matches, refereed by Richard Poulain and David Elleray, marked by almost identical outbreaks of mass violence on the pitch.

Poulain, the referee of a match between Chesterfield and Plymouth on 22 February 1997 that has come to be known as the Battle of Saltergate, went into the history books as the first Football League official to send off five players in a match. He dismissed Plymouth's Ronnie Mauge after 36 minutes, but it was later that the real mayhem started.

At a corner kick Chesterfield's Darren Carr slid into Bruce Grobbelaar, in the Plymouth goal, with such ferocity that he was concussed. Kevin Davies of Chesterfield exchanged blows with Plymouth's Richard Logan, Carr jostled with Plymouth's Tony James in the goal, and in all 14 players were involved. By the time it was brought under control Poulain had shown red cards to Carr, Davies, Logan and James. He later said he had just flown back from a holiday and now felt he needed another, while Mick Jones, the Plymouth manager, confessed he might have pumped up his players a bit too much.

Yet when a similar mass brawl took place just under a year later, on 3 January 1998, during a match between Barnsley and Bolton at Oakwell, referee David Elleray claimed he had seen nothing and it was a typical English cup tie which he had enjoyed. The enjoyable fare included an incident when Neil Cox of Bolton chased a ball that had gone out of play. The Barnsley bench was slow to return it and he shoved the person nearest to him. Eric Winstanley of Barnsley shoved Cox back, and soon not only players on the field but substitutes and management of both teams were in the middle of the mêlée. One player, Jamie Pollock, even received a right hook from a steward, who was arrested but released. But this did nothing to spoil Elleray's enjoyment, and in the absence of television inquests no action was taken.

The 1998–99 season was to see violence by players take a new turn. Such attacks are hardly new, but while it is one thing for a player to strike another player, the idea of a player striking a referee is completely unacceptable. Yet this is exactly what happened early in the 1998–99 season, and to complicate matters it was an Italian who did the striking.

Sheffield Wednesday's Paolo di Canio had begun the calendar year 1998 with a sending-off for abusing a linesman during an FA Cup replay at Hillsborough. Eight months later, on 26 September, when Arsenal were the visitors to Hillsborough, di Canio went one better, or rather sank even lower. On a day in which a record 15 players were sent off in England, and a further seven in Scotland, di Canio made the headlines for attacking match referee Paul Alcock.

After a brawl involved several players, including di Canio and Arsenal's Patrick

Vieira, di Canio was sent off. As he went, he reacted by pushing Alcock to the ground. For once, TV pictures captured the moment vividly. The referee, still clutching the red card he had just shown di Canio, was seen stumbling to the ground while the Italian, mouthing rage and, no doubt, obscenities, walked off. So what might have been a bad incident became an extraordinary one.

The Italian was virtually friendless after the game. He was immediately suspended by his club, whose manager Danny Wilson commented, "I don't know what was going through his head. He totally lost it. We will suspend him for as long as it takes." Sports Minister Tony Banks immediately demanded that the Football Association "chuck the book" at di Canio. The situation was hardly helped when the Italian accused the referee, who was later offered stress counselling, of taking a dive.

The pundits were confident that di Canio would never again play in English football. When the FA considered its punishment, however, di Canio was not banned, but suspended for 11 matches. Even this was considered outrageous on the continent, particularly in Italy, where there were allegations that his treatment was racist. That was an unfair charge to make. However, it is probably truer to say that the FA was compensating for its feebleness in dealing with earlier offenders. David Batty, Steve Lomas, Emmanuel Petit and Samassi Abou had all received no more than one-match bans for offences against the referee that to many seemed no less heinous.

Di Canio was in even deeper trouble with Sheffield Wednesday towards the end of the year when the club suspended him for 14 days without pay after his late return from a period of compassionate leave. He was infuriated by the suspension, which brought relations between him and the club to breaking-point. By that stage he had been fined £78,000 by his club and was facing a £12,000 legal bill for his disciplinary hearing.

He claimed he was suffering from stress and depression and blamed Wednesday for not loving him. "They never", he said, "gave me love when I needed it." In the weeks during which he refused to play for Wednesday he also refused to come back to England from his home in Turin, saying he needed a shrink and was suffering from depression.

It all seemed to follow a predictable pattern. His move to Sheffield Wednesday had come about because of problems with Celtic, his previous club, where he had refused to return for pre-season training and then gone on strike. This led to his transfer

Unthinkable: Sheffield Wednesday's Paolo di Canio pushes over referee Paul Alcock.

to Wednesday in the 1997–98 season.

Then, in January 1999, when it seemed that di Canio was frozen out of English football, West Ham came in. Just as Aston Villa's Stan Collymore was going to a shrink, saying he could not cope with stress, West Ham were signing di Canio, the move coming a day after the Villa announcement. Shane Barber, editor of West Ham fanzine *On a Mission*, claimed: "All fans love to see a complete lunatic on the pitch and that's what we've got with di Canio. West Ham have traded a player [John Hartson] who kicked his own team-mate in the head for a player who attacked referees. I don't know if that is progress."

After his move to West Ham, di Canio criticized his former Wednesday colleagues, saying they were jealous of him, and complaining that the masseur, a Dutch woman called Maggie, massaged like a woman when what he wanted was not an aesthetic massage but one to make him fit to play.

Di Canio also heaped abuse on referee Paul Alcock, particularly for Alcock's claims that after being pushed over by di Canio he could not sleep, that he had pins and needles in his legs and that he had suffered a slipped disc. But, thundered di Canio, after the same referee was butted by Frank Sinclair, then on loan to West Bromwich, he was able to officiate for eight seasons without problems. Now he is suddenly suffering from insomnia. Why?

Alcock responded by saying he had never received an apology from di Canio and that he had lost sleep as a result of physical injury. "I have the scan to prove that I slipped a disc and I was out of football for ten weeks, which is nearly as long as di Canio was."

Next to a player attacking a referee, one of the most unusual and deplorable sights in soccer must be a manager attacking a player. This unexpected twist of soccer violence occurred on 10 February 1996 and again it involved an Italian, although this time he was the victim. Grimsby's Ivano Bonetti went into hospital for an operation to repair a fractured cheek-bone and free a trapped nerve in his face. The act of a vicious opponent on the pitch or a drunken fan? No, the injury was inflicted by his own manager, Brian Laws, in the visitors' dressing-room at Luton, where Grimsby were playing that day.

Bonetti had signed for Grimsby on a free transfer, after the Bosman judgement had given players the freedom to move across the continent at the end of their contracts. Before that a player of Bonetti's class would not have ended up at Grimsby, and initially he had been hailed as the great saviour of the club. But at Luton that day something took place between Bonetti and Laws which the club described as a "regrettable incident". Laws initially admitted only to throwing a plate of sandwiches, insisting that he had not punched anyone. In court he would claim that he acted in self-defence.

According to one witness present in the dressing-room, it began as the sort of managerial lecture delivered to players in dressing-rooms up and down the land but degenerated into something very different. Grimsby had lost 3–2 and Laws was not best pleased. The spark for this appears to have been Laws noticing that Bonetti was more interested in eating his chicken leg rather than in listening to Laws. Bonetti is then believed to have denied that the defeat was due to him.

"Yes, it fucking is," retorted Laws, "it's every single one of you." This developed into a shouting match, and Laws struck Bonetti with either one or several punches.

Bonetti, who missed 19 matches at the end of the season and then moved to Tranmere, upset that Grimsby had merely fined the manager, filed a case against Laws for assault and battery. In September Bonetti got judgement in default when Laws failed to notify the court that he intended to contest the case. Laws then applied to have the judgement set aside, but on 20 November the High Court decided that his defence had no realistic prospect of success.

Laws, arguing that he was acting in self-defence, went on to lodge an appeal against the High Court judgement. On 16 January 1997 Mr Justice Buckley dismissed the appeal, saying that he found Laws' allegation that he acted in self-defence had no credibility and that eyewitnesses did not support his case.

Bonetti's lawyer, Steven Maier of Manches & Co., commented: "Ivano is relieved the issue of Mr Laws' liability is now finally concluded. The allegation of self-defence added insult to a very painful injury which severely damaged Ivano's career."

In a sense this incident is comparable to the one in which a referee punched a player, an incident that took place in March 1998 in a game between Southampton Arms and Hurstbourne Tarrant British Legion in the Andover and District Sunday League. The referee, Martin Sylvester, hit a player, Richard Curd, several times in the face and head and gave him a black eye. Sylvester, manager of Southampton Arms, had stepped in because the original official fell ill.

He admitted that he had punched Curd several times but explained that he was sorely provoked, as Curd had pushed him from behind and sworn at him. Curd denied this. Sylvester decided to give himself a red card and give up refereeing, having officiated in 40 games over two years.

As for the club mascots, who are supposed to provide some fun and entertainment before a game and at half-time, it is difficult to know whether to laugh or cry when their antics land the club in trouble. In March 1998 Aston Villa had to sack their mascot, who was known as Hercules the Lion but beneath the masquerade was plain Gavin Lucas. At half-time during the match between Villa and Crystal Palace he had grabbed Debbie Robins, Miss Aston Villa, and proceeded to give her a bear hug and kiss her. Defending himself, he said there was nothing sexual about it, and with his lion's head on he could hardly give her much of a kiss. An Aston Villa spokesman said that the heat inside the lion's head had probably turned his head, but with the incident caught on cameras he had to go.

While this was an internal Villa matter, the antics of Cyril the Swan, the mascot of Swansea City, landed his club in a lot of bother. Cyril, whose real identity has never been disclosed, had become a much-loved mascot at Swansea, but during the club's Cup game with Millwall in November 1998 he got so carried away that in kicking back a ball which had gone into touch he hit it at a Millwall player, and then, when Swansea scored, he ran on to the pitch to celebrate with the players.

On 23 April 1999, the Football Association of Wales held a hearing at which Cyril was represented by Maurice Watkins, the senior partner of the Manchester law firm James Chapman & Co. and a non-executive director of Manchester United. But despite Watkins' undoubted legal skills he could not save Cyril. The Welsh FA decided that while kicking the football was not a deliberate act, going on to the pitch to celebrate the goal was not acceptable. The club was fined £1,000 and told that Cyril could not be on the touch-line or the pitch while the players or the officials were still on the field of play.

In many ways the worst examples of the sort of violence that the beautiful game can lead to have occurred in international football.

Matches in South America have always carried the threat of violence, not only between players on the field but also between players and spectators. The classic of this genre was provided in the Uruguay-Argentina matches. The rivalry between the two nations is deep, and Uruguay appeared to have stolen a lead by winning the gold medal for football at the 1924 Olympics. Argentina had often beaten Uruguay, and there followed a series of matches between the two countries, the last of these beng the World Cup Final of 1930. When this resulted in a Uruguay victory there was serious rioting in Buenos Aires: a woman was stoned for waving a Uruguayan flag, and the Uruguayan consulate and the Oriental Club were stoned. Two people were shot dead.

British clubs found themselves on the receiving end of violence when they travelled to Argentina to contest the World Club Championship in the late 1960s. The Argentinians were still smarting from their controversial elimination in the World Cup quarter-final in England the previous year when the European Cup winners Celtic took on Racing Club in 1967. A bitterly contested two-leg tie went to a play-off, where five players were sent off when a brawl developed after Celtic's Bobby Lennox was spat at by Racing's Alfio Basile – later to manage the Argentine national team.

The following year Estudiantes, another Buenos Aires club, set about Manchester United with a vengeance, and George Best and Nobby Stiles were both ejected for rising to the bait. Sir Stanley Rous, president of FIFA, wrote a letter of complaint to Estudiantes, to no avail, and when AC Milan received equally violent treatment at the hands – or rather feet – of Estudiantes in 1969, several of Europe's champion clubs later refused to take part in the fixture.

Nobody died in the England–Italy match at Highbury in 1934, but the English players knew they had been in a war, and the match has come to be known as the Battle of Highbury. Italy had come as World Cup holders, while England, who in those days thought the World Cup was beneath them and did not participate, had not been beaten at home by a foreign side. Early on the Italian player Luis Monti had a toe broken in a crunching challenge by Ted Drake, winning his first cap for England. Italy felt it

Never Mind the Ball ...

In a flap: Swansea mascot Cyril the Swan.

was a foul, and they were incensed when it was not given. Skipper Eddie Hapgood had his nose broken and the game got increasingly violent as it went on. While England won 3–2, every English player ended up carrying some kind of injury.

However, this was tame stuff compared with what became known as the Battle of Berne almost exactly 20 years later, during the World Cup in Switzerland, when Brazil played Hungary for a place in the semi-finals. The Hungarians, led by Ferenc Puskas and Nandor Hidegkuti, were the most skilful side of their generation, having come to Wembley the previous year and demolished England 6–3 before beating them 7–1 in Budapest. The World Cup, it seemed, was theirs for the taking.

Brazil, having failed to win the World Cup in Rio in 1950, now sought to become the first team to win it in another continent – a goal they would achieve four years later in Sweden.

The match displayed the skills of both sides, but violence was always lurking beneath the surface. Nilton Santos of Brazil and Joszef Boszik of Hungary were sent off for trying to throttle each other; then, with Hungary 4–2 up having scored a fourth goal in the last minute, Humbert Pozzi became the second Brazilian to be sent off.

But all this was merely a prelude to the carnage in the dressing-room. The Brazilians were so incensed by the celebrations of the Hungarians that they kicked down the door of their dressing-room and invaded it. A mob of Brazilians kicked one Hungarian player, Mihaly Toth, unconscious. A soda siphon was thrown at the Hungarians, dressing-room lights were broken and bottles rained down on the hapless victors. The Brazilians alleged that one of the Hungarians had attacked their centre-half Pinheiro with a bottle, which left him with a deep five-inch gash on his head. It was some ten minutes before the fighting was stopped, by which time several players had been injured. The most amazing thing was that FIFA took no action and referee Arthur Ellis filed no report of the incident.

The 1962 World Cup in Chile was so marred by violence and controversy that, by the end of the first round of the 16-team tournament, 50 players had been injured, of whom four were in hospital. They had sustained a whole range of broken bones as the teams spent most of their time getting the man and ignoring the ball.

Worst of all was the match, inevitably dubbed the Battle of Santiago, in which Chile beat Italy 2–0. Players punched and kicked each other and argued with the English referee, Ken Aston. When Aston sent off the Italian Giorgio Ferrini for kicking Honorino Landa of Chile, Ferrini refused to leave and Aston had to call the police to take him off.

Unfortunately, Aston and his linesman missed Chile's retaliation when just before half-time Leonel Sanchez, with a punch described by commentator David Coleman as the neatest left hook he had ever seen, broke Limberto Maschio's nose. However, Aston did see Mario David try to kick Sanchez in the head, and he was sent off.

The Italians, who had suffered considerable provocation from the crowds, were singled out by correspondents as the worst offenders. Their game against Germany also disintegrated into a brawl.

In general the five communist countries were seen as the best behaved, with Yugoslavia taking the lead in trying to end the rough play which was destroying the tournament. They summoned inside-right Muhamed Mujic to explain one incident which culminated in a player being sent off.

Since then in each succeeding World Cup the violence level has decreased. FIFA have made greater efforts to protect the player of flair, but not always very successfully, and with some dreadful failures to punish the wrongdoer. The most glaring incident of this kind took place in the 1982 semi-final between France and West Germany. France were leading 3–1, and with Patrick Battiston of France bearing down on goal the German goalkeeper Harald Schumacher decided to take him out by lunging at him at head height. He prevented a goal, Battiston was rushed to the hospital, but Schumacher stayed on the field. He was not even booked, and in the penalty shoot-out his two saves helped to see Germany through to the final.

In 1986, when Uruguay arrived in Mexico for the World Cup, they were expected to play the most technically accomplished football. Instead the South American champions were branded the most violent team in the tournament, were fined for misconduct by their players and officials and were in danger of being thrown out.

After their first game against West Germany, some officials were reported to FIFA for misbehaving during the routine dope test. Not long after the start of their second game against Denmark, defender Miguel Bossi was sent off for a vicious foul. Even earlier in their match against Scotland – 50 seconds into the game, to be precise – José Batista, also a defender, was shown the red card for scything down Gordon Strachan.

Their manager, Omar Borras, was less than delighted at this turn of events. At a subsequent press conference, he turned his wrath on the French referee, Joel Quiniou, whom he described as "a murderer".

It is a measure of how far the game has come at the international level that such instances are no longer quite so common.

Yet as violence at matches between the major countries is controlled, incidents such as the one that took place as Jamaica was successfully trying to qualify for the 1998 World Cup showed how far the game has to go before it can claim to be remotely clean. This was in many ways the classic all-time international soccer brawl; the Battles of Highbury, Berne and Santiago rolled into one.

It took place when Jamaica played a friendly match in Mexico in March 1997 before the two sides met in a World Cup qualifier. The Jamaican team scored first against a local side called Toros Neza. But when a Toros Neza player over-reacted to a late tackle, a fight involving nearly all the 22 players developed. After about six minutes the fighting stopped as Jamaican players trooped off to the touchline. This was not because they were tired of fighting, however, but because they wanted to gather weapons such as lumps of wood, stones, bricks and bottles. Once they had done that they returned to the middle and resumed the fight. The match was abandoned, and the Jamaican coach, Rene Simoes, a Brazilian, blamed the whole thing on his players' lack of international experience. No doubt he thought of the Battle of Berne and how his own countrymen had behaved.

Even now to a great extent Eastern Europe and South America remain the outposts of soccer violence, where almost anything is possible and fact is often stranger than fiction.

In 1997 Yuri Pohrebnyak, coach of the Ukrainian team Metalurg Mariupol, led an angry mob into the hotel room of the referee Vadym Shevchenko in the small hours of the morning after his side, struggling to avoid relegation, had lost 2–1. The referee ended up with rib injuries and a broken nose, and Pohrebnyak was given a life ban for making a pre-planned attack on the official.

Colombia, where drug barons control the game, is even more of a wild frontier, where football and drugs produce a lethal cocktail of violence and death.

In August 1997, a Colombian police report stated that 80 of the 142 main shareholders in the country's 16 first division clubs were wanted on drugs charges. Drug barons had moved into Colombian soccer in the 1970s, when most of Colombian football was facing financial ruin. Medellin, the drugs capital of the world, also became the centre of Colombian football, and by 1989 things had deteriorated to such an extent that the football season was stopped after 20 football-related murders. The victims included three players and a referee. Not that this was uncommon. Back in 1982, just as Uriel de Jesus was about to score, he was shot dead by a rival fan.

However, it was the death in 1994 of Andres Escobar, after his own goal gave the

Fatal error: Andres Escobar of Colombia scores the own goal in the World Cup of 1994 that cost him his life.

USA a 1–0 victory over Colombia in the crucial World Cup match in Pasadena's Rose Bowl, that shocked the world.

Escobar, a defender, accidentally toed the ball into his own net, and the Colombian team who had arrived in the United States hailed as possible champions – they had received the endorsement of no less a man than Pele – returned home early, having failed to qualify for the knock-out stages. A week later Escobar went for a late-night drink at a bar in his home town of Medellin, an argument followed and then, as he got into his car to drive home, he was shot dead. Two small-time gangsters were arrested, but it was clear that it was a drugs-related killing, the suspicion being that Escobar was killed because the drug barons, who had bet heavily on Colombia winning in the United States, wanted revenge on the man they saw as responsible for their loss.

After that the Colombian authorities tried to clean up their game, particularly in 1995 when, after the arrest of the number three in the all-powerful Cali drug cartel, his address book was found to contain the home numbers of practically every leading football administrator. It forced the then-president of the Colombian Football Federation Juan Jose Bellini to resign a year later. However, just before the World Cup in France, the Colombian soccer federation suspended an investigation into the ownership of clubs amid allegations that it had been paid off. And as England prepared to meet Colombia in a crucial match to decide who qualified for the knock-out stages, the drug barons still seemed to be calling the shots. In the month leading up to the match Hernan Dario Gomez, the Colombian manager, and six of his players received messages from the drugs cartel. The words varied, but the message was the same: win or die.

One of the Colombian strikers against England, Anthony De Avila, was happy to acknowledge his debt to the drug barons, his godfathers Miguel and Gilberto Rodriguez, the gaoled founders of the Cali cocaine cartel. After his last-minute goal against Ecuador which helped Colombia qualify for France, he said, "I give this triumph to the two men who have been deprived of their liberty. I dedicate my goal with respect and love to Gilberto and Miguel."

The dedication was as grotesque as it was understandable. De Avila had been born in a ghetto consisting of metal sheds with no running water or toilet facilities and had been signed when he was 15 by America de Cali, the club owned by the Rodriguez family and run, with the brothers in gaol, by their sister, who acts as president. When De Avila became the club's star striker, he became the personal property of the Rodriguez family and had always to pay homage to them.

That Colombian players should always pay heed to the drug baron is hardly new.

One player missing from the side that lost to England was flamboyant goalkeeper Rene Higuita. He was considered for selection, despite the fact that in 1993 he had served seven months in gaol for acting as an intermediary in the kidnapping of a seven-year-old. It had been a "favour" to the same Medellin coke cartel that a year later was implicated in the killing of Escobar.

The player who knew English football best also missed the game. One-time Newcastle forward Faustino Asprilla stormed out of the Colombian camp in a fit of anger after he had been substituted shortly before the end of the game against Romania. But almost immediately he asked to be taken back, with the air full of rumours that this was because he had received death threats from the drug cartel. In the event he did not play and Colombia were beaten by England.

Asprilla, of course, had already made his mark as a player of great, even magical ability but also with a volatile temperament. In April 1997 he was involved in a clash with the Paraguayan goalkeeper Jose Luis Chilavert in a World Cup qualifying match between Colombia and Paraguay. Chilavert hit Asprilla in the mouth in an off-the-ball incident – the ball was in the centre circle at that time – with his team leading 1–0. Chilavert claimed he was provoked, both players were sent off and then, as the players left the pitch, Chilavert spat at Asprilla. A Colombian team-mate of Asprilla, Victor Aristizabal, barged into Chilavert and there followed an almighty punch-up involving several players and both benches. In the end Paraguay won 2–1 and both teams qualified for France, with Paraguay going on to shock Spain and qualify for the second round. FIFA banned Chilavert for four games, Aristizabal for three and Asprilla for two.

The Colombians were sure that Chilavert was the man responsible, a man whose reputation preceded him. In 1996 he hit someone at a stadium and received a suspended three-month gaol sentence. The following year, when the Presidential candidate and former general Leon Oviedo wanted to pay him his respects, Chilavert refused to meet him, accusing Oviedo of being responsible for putting Paraguayan democracy in danger. This led to a fight between the general's minders and Chilavert.

To an extent Asprilla's reputation also precedes him. He has kicked out a bus windscreen, fired guns in the air and been charged with possessing firearms illegally. In his home town in Colombia, while watching a rock concert in a football stadium, he started abusing the police. As he was being removed he headbutted someone and caused a general fight to flare up.

Rugby Union

There used to be a hackneyed old saying that, if football was a game for gentlemen played by thugs, then rugby was a game for thugs played by gentlemen. Today it might more accurately be said that rugby is a game viewed by video camera and ultimately refereed by highly-paid lawyers that the game can ill afford.

This has all been a direct consequence of the dramatic decision in the mid-1990s to transform rugby from an amateur to a professional sport. Both victim and perpetrator faced loss of income and career opportunity if they were unable to play as a result of injury or suspension. Meanwhile the plethora of television cameras uncovered violent actions that had previously been hidden from the referee, and m'learned friends were on hand to explain away the most dastardly deeds.

Ironically, both referees and players say that professionalism has not brought about the increase in violence that many predicted. As veteran international referee Ed Morrison noted, "They said that money would make the game dirtier. It proved to be anything but. In the late 1970s it was mayhem every other week. Most of the lads I knew then would be in prison these days for some of the things they did on a rugby field." Players agree, saying that the game is now so fast that there is no time to be dirty.

One down: Gregoire Lascubé becomes the first of two Frenchmen to be sent off in the same match, against England in 1992.

What is clear is that the violence which does take place is seen more widely. There is a growing realization that, in a sport that is desperately concerned about its image as it competes with other winter activities for sponsorship money and spectators, such indulgences can no longer be afforded. Even the ritual bout of fisticuffs that used to accompany the first scrum in a rugby international is now frowned upon.

But fundamental problems still remain in a contact sport that can produce as much blood and biting as world championship boxing but is also governed by complex and highly technical laws.

The margin between foul play and legitimate violence is often very narrow. To a New Zealander, a man on the wrong side of the ruck can legitimately be removed by the boot on the grounds that he should not have been there in the first place. To others, it is nothing more than illegal stamping. But, whatever the rules say, the sport has still to come to terms with the real issue of violence – should something that is technically legal be permitted if it can blind or disfigure an opponent?

There are still stomach-churning incidents in international and club rugby. The challenge to the sport is to ensure that they become few and far between by eliminating the thugs and ensuring that penalties for such offences are decided by the game's authorities and that the offences do not just become another opportunity for lawyers to make money.

Rugby is also, of course, the perfect game for the *agent provocateur*. For years England were able to tease French sides into giving away penalties and so infuriate them that they lost their discipline and occasionally members of their team. Modern French sides do not make the same mistakes.

The French rugby team of the early 1990s was renowned both for its sublime flashes of artistry and for a total lack of discipline, which was reflected in a less than detailed knowledge of the laws and a readiness to resort to fists that was frowned on by referees. During this period they could not beat an English team that knew how to strangle a game and had developed to a fine art the technique of provoking French forwards to lose their tempers.

The match between the two sides in February 1992 at Parc des Princes in Paris resulted in a convincing 31–13 victory to England. But the occasion was notable for the bravery of the Irish referee Steven Hilditch during a game that at times verged on anarchy. He sent off two front-row forwards, Gregoire Lascubé and Vincent Moscato, for stamping and butting respectively. He did so in the face of intimidating French forwards and a baying mob of a crowd.

It was the first time in the history of the Five Nations Championship that two people from the same team had been sent off, and they were duly suspended until September.

The seeds of the hostility between the two sides had been sown four months earlier during the quarter-finals of the Rugby World Cup. England won the game at Parc des Princes 19–10, with Pascal Ondarts ending the game in disgrace. England's tactics were the same – resolute single-mindedness triumphing over a French side that was riven by disarray and dissension.

There have been some disgracefully violent rugby internationals, and among the most notorious was the 1980 confrontation at Twickenham between Wales and England, which was described by one commentator as a "degrading war of attrition".

The crunch moment was the decision of the Irish referee, David Burnett, to send off the Welsh wing forward Paul Ringer – he became the first player since Cyril Brownlie of New Zealand in 1925 to be sent off in a Twickenham international. Ringer received his marching orders in the 13th minute of the match for a late and dangerous tackle on the England fly-half John Horton and was suspended for eight weeks.

The nastiness simmered throughout the game, with the referee twice speaking to the captains about foul play. Wales were clearly the better rugby side, scoring the only two tries. But the penalties, of which there were 34, went to England at a rate of two to one. Three late penalties, the last in the 41st minute of the second half, were enough to see England home by one point.

The victory by Wales over England at Cardiff Arms Park in 1987 was overshadowed by violence on the pitch that did much harm to the image of rugby. Four internationals, captain Richard Hill, Wade Dooley, Graham Dawe and Gareth Chilcott, were all suspended from England's next match.

Through the early 1990s, Leicester Rugby Club was renowned for the power of its forwards and its reluctance to let any three-quarter outside the fly half do much except tackle. They bored everyone except their own fanatical fans, tended to squeak home in games they should have won by a mile, and occasionally lost matches they should have won.

This was undoubtedly the case in the 1996 Pilkington Cup Final, which Bath won 16–15, having shown all the flair on a minuscule proportion of the possession. It was a game that Leicester should – and, in their later, more expansive period, probably would – have won easily. But the last few minutes cost them not only the game but also the services of their flanker Neil Back.

In the final moments of the game Bath were awarded a controversial match-winning penalty try when Back, who until then had had an exemplary disciplinary record, pushed over the referee, Steve Lander. Back insisted that he thought he was shoving his opposite number, Andy Robinson, but was suspended for six months for "conduct prejudicial to the interests of the game".

Back in the 1960s Colin Meads, a distinguished player, hit the headlines by becoming only the second All Black to be sent off during a tour of the British Isles. Now such sending-offs are more common, and judged very often on video evidence.

Perhaps the most glaring example of this was the case of Kevin Yates. The reputation of the England and Bath prop forward, already severely damaged by an ear-biting incident, was dealt a further blow when he was accused of stamping only a year later.

Yates, who was capped by England twice in 1997, was cited after an incident in Bath's match against Wasps in February 1999. Wasps took the decision after reviewing video evidence of the incident in which Paul Volley, their flank forward, received a gash in his head which required seven stitches. Yates received a four-week ban for "reckless play": the RFU decided he was not guilty of wilful stamping.

This incident came a year to the day after a tribunal had banned Yates for six months for biting the ear of the London Scottish flanker Simon Fenn in January 1998. Though he has consistently protested his innocence, Yates was also ordered to pay an estimated £23,000 in costs. In February 1999, London Scottish were claiming that they had not received any of that money. As it happened just before Yates tangled with Volley he had received an offer from a top New Zealand club to play for them, an offer he felt would end what was for him a nightmare year since the Fenn incident, a year in which he had spent more than £60,000 in an attempt to clear his name. Yates owed more than that amount, the costs were increasing as interest was being added and Yates told journalists how he was trying to cut every penny outside living expenses to pay off his debts.

Perhaps the abiding memory of the incident were the pictures, transmitted all over the world, of Fenn clutching his mangled left ear. Fenn ended up losing part of his ear lobe and carrying the scars from 28 stitches. That somebody had done something to Fenn's ear could not be doubted. However, Fenn never named Yates and the incident was never caught on film or videotape.

But what was also beyond doubt was that there were not adequate procedures to deal with such cases, particularly when the guilty individual was not shamed into coming forward quickly to admit his guilt.

Bath were unhappy at what they saw as pressure to railroad them into a quick judgement by a kangaroo court. They wanted more breathing time to resolve the issues, even bringing in a judge to investigate. London Scottish initially accused three players. Finally the issue became a protracted legal argument which enriched lawyers by an estimated six-figure sum. The Rugby Football Union held a protracted hearing over several days before describing the biting as an "abhorrent act" and suspending Yates for six months.

He insisted there was "no conclusive evidence against me", initially threatening to take the case to the High Court before opting to accept the suspension and stay with Bath. It was generally agreed that the sentence was a compromise. London Scottish had originally said they wanted a 12-month ban, while others said that two years would have been too short. Both players were happy enough to put the issue behind them. That proved to be harder for Yates, who has to endure jibes from opposing fans who constantly remind him of the ear-biting.

The convoluted logic of modern rugby management was demonstrated vividly by Leicester Rugby Club's decision to suspend their scrum-half Austin Healey for 21 days after television cameras had caught him stamping on the head of his London Irish opposite number Kevin Putt during a match in February 1999.

Leicester took their action in response to a citing by London Irish immediately after the game. In a somewhat elliptical judgement, the club said: "While accepting there was no wilful intent, it was considered other actions could have been taken to avoid the contact."

The ban was for the minimum three weeks and, even though it cost Healey two possible international caps, was considered inadequate by London Irish, who had wanted at least two months. The club pointed out that while Putt had only required six stitches and was back on the pitch in ten minutes, the stamp could as easily have been in his eye as his eyebrow.

As in the case of football clubs such as Arsenal and West Ham, this move by Leicester did not stop the Rugby Union taking action. A three-man disciplinary panel, chaired by the Sussex official Bob Rogers and consisting of Wakefield president Robin Foster and ex-England prop Jeff Probyn, held a disciplinary hearing on 8 March 1999 at that centre of rugby union gatherings, the East India Club in London's St James's.

Before the hearing Healey, who had 16 caps for England, had talked of giving up the game if the panel did not believe him. He mounted a strong defence, including video evidence, but could not convince the panel. After a two-hour hearing, they found Healey guilty of "recklessly" stamping on Putt. But they decided he had not done so "wilfully", and banned him for a total of eight weeks, including the three imposed by Leicester.

However, given that the recommended period of suspension for stamping on an opponent's head is three months, it meant Healey had not been treated as harshly as he might have been.

The punishment for South African international Johan Le Roux was much more severe. He received a 19-month ban for biting the ear of New Zealand captain Sean Fitzpatrick, though he claimed that he was retaliating after being provoked. He also pointed out that he was wearing a mouthguard so there were no scratches or stitches.

He maintained that the length of the ban was unfair, and said: "I was banned for 18 months, and for as long as I live I will feel that New Zealand treated me unfairly. It cost me a place in the World Cup-winning squad and about £375,000 in lost earnings."

He also maintained that there should be standard bans for offences, set by the International Rugby Board. On the basis of his punishment, whoever had bitten Fenn's ear could have expected a two-year ban.

Fritz Van Heerden, another South African international, was also banned for 18 months for sinking his teeth into Australian player Richard Harry.

Simon Devereux, the Gloucester player, faced criminal charges and was sentenced to nine months in prison for breaking an opponent's jaw. Devereux was convicted of inflicting grievous bodily harm after the court heard he had punched Rosslyn Park player James Cowie as a scrum broke up after the referee blew for a penalty. Cowie's jaw was broken: he spent five days in hospital, had his jaw wired with three plates and was out of the game for ten months.

A year before the Devereux case, Wales hooker Nigel Meek received a six-month sentence after breaking an opponent's jaw while representing his Fire Division XV.

Phil De Glanville, the Bath centre, needed ten stitches in a cut behind his left earlobe

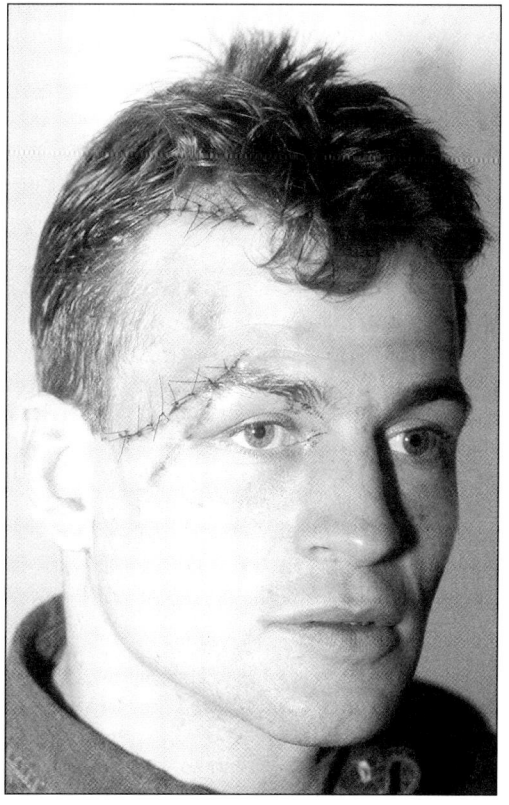

Damage done: Jon Callard's lacerated face.

after the 1996 match between England and New Zealand Barbarians. On this occasion the victim was quick to play down the injury, saying that it could have been a boot or elbow and that it was "nothing sinister".

He suffered a much more serious injury when he was booted off the pitch at Redruth while playing for Western Counties against the All Blacks. He was lucky not to lose an eye, having had his face ripped open by a New Zealand boot.

The Bath and England full-back Jon Callard came within an inch of losing his right eye in a brutal stamping episode in England's match against Eastern Province during their 1994 tour of South Africa. In all he needed 25 stitches to bring together the gaping wounds in his face and head inflicted when the boot was deliberately raked over him. The injuries were so severe that he was unable to take any further part in the tour.

What angered many rugby supporters was the failure of the referee to take any further action against the culprit, Eland van der Berg. He limited his sanctions to awarding England a penalty, even though the linesman told him he thought Callard had been deliberately kicked in the head.

From that point on, the game degenerated into a brawl, with England player Tim Rodber sent off five minutes later for punching. Speaking after the game, Callard said: "I was lucky. I wasn't blinded and I am still here. But how long before someone does lose their eyesight or suffers a more serious injury?"

Irish prop forward Peter Clohessy was banned for six months in 1996 after being found guilty of foul play by match commissioner Alan Hosie in the Five Nations international between France and Ireland in Paris.

Clohessy stamped on French lock Olivier Roumat's head during the match, which France won 45–10. The foul was missed by the referee but captured on television. This was the worst incident in an unpleasant match, in which two French players had to leave the pitch and a third, Christian Califano, suffered a damaged jaw and lost two teeth.

It was not Clohessy's first offence. Two years before he had been banned for 12 weeks after committing a similar offence while playing for Munster, and he was also strongly criticized by 1992 Wallabies coach Bob Dwyer over unspecified antics for Munster in a brutal clash with the tourists. In 1990 he was penalized for "remarks of a sectarian nature" apparently addressed to Willie Anderson during the game between Ulster and Munster.

In October 1995, New Zealand captain Sean Fitzpatrick was banned for eight days for punching during the provincial championship.

Rugby and football are, however, not the only games in which the actions of sportsmen and women violate all those principles that the Corinthian founders of modern sport held dear.

Athletics

When Mary Decker, the American favourite for the women's 3,000 metres at the 1984 Los Angeles Olympics, stumbled out of the race, she claimed that she had been tripped up from in front by Zola Budd.

Budd's very presence at the Olympics had already been controversial enough. The South African was only allowed to compete after she had received a British passport in a record-breaking 13 days with the connivance of the British government and the *Daily Mail*. Given what followed, she must have wished that the Home Office authorities had worked at their normal speed. In the race she committed the cardinal sin in the eyes of the highly partisan American crowd of being the means of Decker's departure.

Budd, 18, was roundly booed by the crowd and then disqualified for causing the incident. She was accused of cutting in too soon on Decker who then ran her spikes into Budd's calves. Budd nearly fell off the track with Decker.

After many replays, Budd, who finished seventh, was reinstated, and Decker received scant support from other competitors, who said the American should have avoided trouble instead of trying to slip through on the inside.

One year later, Budd and Decker met at Crystal Palace in London. Also present were American TV cameras. Budd's fee was $125,000, compared to Decker's $75,000, and – conveniently for the US networks, and no doubt to the delight of their viewers back home – Budd lost to her former rival.

Cricket

Cricket is billed as the ultimate gentleman's game. Not long ago a batsman would "walk" – that is to say, give himself out if he felt he was out. One celebrated case was seen when Don Kenyon was playing for England against Australia in the 1953 series, when England won back the Ashes after 20 years. Kenyon walked for a catch behind even though none of the Australians had appealed, because he knew he had edged the ball, the wicket-keeper had caught it and, according to his sense of honour, that was that.

Although this high moral standard has long since disappeared from the game, until recently its code of conduct was such that in all international matches, even in an Ashes series or between such bitter enemies as India and Pakistan, home-side umpires would officiate. Even now, despite the advent of neutral umpires, one of the umpires in every series is from the home country. To appreciate how remarkable this is, imagine a football match between England and Scotland having an English or Scottish linesman, let alone referee.

Yet in recent years incidents have happened which have sullied cricket's reputation as the fairest of games.

Perhaps no single incident revealed more clearly how cricket was changing then the last ball bowled in a one-day international between Australia and New Zealand. There can have been few more unsporting endings to a cricketing contest than the end of their World Series Cup match in Melbourne in 1981, which lent weight to the argument that the limited-overs game has corrupted the very soul of cricket.

New Zealand needed a six off the last ball to win the match. Greg Chappell, the Australian captain, instructed his brother Trevor to bowl it under-arm to ensure that the runs could not be scored. As required by the laws of cricket, Chappell informed the batsman, Jeremy Coney, who after playing it defensively threw his bat away in disgust. His anger was nothing compared with that of the other New Zealand players, the New Zealand nation and the cricketing world in general. The ensuing row brought the intervention of former Test players and leading politicians.

Robert Muldoon, the New Zealand Prime Minister, described it as "an act of cowardice", while former Australian captain and top sports commentator Richie Benaud said, "It was the most gutless thing I have ever seen on a cricket field."

Rarely can a sportsman have received so many differing verdicts on the same allegations in a such a short period of time as befell Michael Atherton, the England cricket captain, in the aftermath of the 1994 Lord's Test against South Africa.

First, the facts. Atherton undoubtedly had earth inside his trouser pocket – he had picked it up from the rough areas at the ends of the pitch – and he used the earth to dry the ball. Though it was highly unusual, in principle there was nothing illegal about doing this.

But his actions were picked up by the television cameras and came to the attention of the match referee, the former Australian Test batsman Peter Burge. He exonerated Atherton, accepting, as did the umpires and Ray Illingworth, the chairman of the England selectors, that the ball's condition had not been altered.

However, Illingworth decided to convict Atherton of two other "crimes" and promptly fined the England captain £2,000 for two offences. Atherton, who had until then a totally unblemished record, was punished firstly for using dirt inside his trousers to dry the ball and secondly for failing to reveal this to Burge.

The England captain insisted his conscience was clear. The sole purpose was to dry his fingers "in order not to dampen the ball. I did it to dry my fingers on a very hot and humid day in order to dry the ball and help my bowlers obtain reverse swing."

On the second charge, he said that if he had mentioned having dirt in his pocket, Burge might have misconstrued this as using an artificial substance to alter the ball's condition. Atherton paid a heavy financial price for not trusting the referee to come to a sensible conclusion. However, he was retained as team captain.

The confrontation between the Pakistani umpire Shakoor Rana and the English captain Mike Gatting in December 1987 began from such trivial origins that it is hard to imagine how it achieved such a status in the pantheon of cricketing misbehaviour.

However, it was a symptom of the powder-keg on which the three-match series sat and the near-certainty that it would not have survived a full five-match programme. The dispute, which began on the second day of the Second Test at Faisalabad, led to 65 hours of negotiations before it was resolved by an apology from the England captain.

Ironically, the day had been a productive one for England as Pakistan struggled to 106 for 5 in response to the tourists' 292. But Rana had, in the view of the English, given two dubious decisions against them, and Gatting was incensed when the umpire stopped Hemmings in mid-run-up. Rana said he believed Gatting was changing his field behind the back of the batsman Salim Malik.

Gatting, who had earlier urged his players to keep their heads in controversial circumstances, failed to live up to his own standards as he became involved in a finger-wagging row with Rana. The pair exchanged words eyeball to eyeball during the final over before Bill Athey ushered his captain away.

Gatting insisted that he had done nothing wrong. "I had already informed Salim that I was bringing in Capel, the deep square leg fielder, and when Hemmings was running in I indicated to Capel with my hand that he had come in far enough. Obviously the umpire thought I was cheating. A few words passed between us, but I am not saying what. I don't want a slanging match."

This remains the most explosive confrontation ever between a player and umpire, but by no means the only one. In the Melbourne Test of 1981 between Australia and India, the Indian captain Sunil Gavaskar, incensed at being given out lbw when he felt he had played the ball, threatened to walk out with his team. As he made his way back to the pavilion he motioned to the other batsman, Chetan Chauhan, to accompany him. The reluctant Chauhan followed, but at the boundary edge they were met by the Indian manager, Wing Commander S.K. Durani, who ordered Chauhan to continue the innings.

It was not only the proper thing to do but also paid off, as India, after being 182 behind on the first innings, came back dramatically to win by 59 runs.

Nearly twenty years later another cricket captain taking his team to Australia, this time the Sri Lankan Arjuna Ranatunga, also threatened to abandon a match. This time it was a one-day international during the triangular series played in January 1999 between Australia, England and Sri Lanka. The incident took place as Sri Lanka battled with England. During the England innings the Sri Lankan off-spinner Murali Muralitharan was called for throwing by the Australian umpire Ross Emerson. Three years previously, when Sri Lanka were touring Australia, another umpire, Darrell Hair, had called Muralitharan for throwing and this had led to an investigation of his bowling action by the International Cricket Council, the game's governing body. He had then been cleared.

Even before the 1999 match the Sri Lankans had been incensed by suggestions in the Australian press that Muralitharan's actions were suspect. When Emerson again called him for throwing Ranatunga, a combative cricketer, led his entire team off the field. Then, after a conference lasting several minutes with his own team management and ICC match officials, he walked back to resume play. Throughout the match, however, he treated Emerson with scant respect.

The ICC held an inquiry and suspended Ranatunga, but with Sri Lanka bringing in high-priced lawyers the suspension was itself suspended, demonstrating that the ICC was among the weakest international governing bodies in sport.

This match also saw cricket, which is not a contact sport, threaten to become one. With Sri Lanka's batsmen chasing victory, Tillekeratne went for a very short run, having just pushed the ball in front of him. Darren Gough in his follow-through tried to run him out. But before he could reach the ball he found the Sri Lankan batsman swerving into his path, obstructing him as he did so. It seemed a clear case of impeding but the umpire, probably already cowed by the Sri Lankans, took no action and Sri Lanka went on to win.

Later in the over Alec Stewart, the England captain, brushed past a Sri Lankan batsman and afterwards commented that it was the most unpleasant cricket match he had ever taken part in.

A similar incident took place many years earlier in July 1971 but here the cricket authorities did take action. India were chasing victory at Lord's and Gavaskar was called for a quick single by Faroukh Engineer. However, as he ran to the striker's end John Snow, the bowler, ran across Gavaskar and shoulder-charged him. The contrast between the 5ft 4in Gavaskar and the 6ft-plus, burly Snow could not have been more vivid and as Gavaskar

Arguing the toss: Ranatunga and Muralitharan contest umpire Ross Emerson's ruling that the Sri Lankan spinner is a chucker.

sprawled to the turf Snow compounded it by throwing the bat that had slipped from Gavaskar's hands at the prone Indian. The whole of Lord's had a sharp intake of breath. It did not take the authorities long to decide Snow had to be punished: he was suspended from the Second Test at Old Trafford.

The incident of physical contact that did most to scar the game of cricket occurred between two of its greatest protagonists, Javed Miandad of Pakistan and Australia's Dennis Lillee.

Although Ian Chappell had by then retired and his brother Greg was captain, this was still an Australian side shaped by Ian. The elder Chappell was the master of the art of sledging, the practice whereby a cricketer baits an opponent with verbal taunts in order to get a reaction and thus gain an advantage. Lillee was quite an expert in this, but Miandad was no slouch either.

While batting in one match involving Pakistan and India, Miandad was standing at the bowler's end and just as the Indian spinner Dilip Doshi was about to run in and bowl he shouted, "Hit him for six!" – completely ruining Doshi's concentration. On another occasion, as he faced up to Doshi himself, he shouted out, "Dilip, what's your room number?" The bowler ignored the calls a couple of times, then asked Miandad why he wanted to know. "Because I want to hit you for a six into your room."

In the same match there was another incident with Miandad which showed the humour of the man. Doshi decided to go round the wicket to Miandad. The left arm spinner wanted to use the rough round the leg stump. This immediately tied down Miandad and he could not score. He knew that as Doshi was bowling round the wicket and landing the ball outside the leg stump he could not be out lbw. So Miandad started using his pads and kicking the ball away to make sure it did not spin back and hit his stumps. However, as he kicked each ball, he would make a noise like a dog barking. This went on for sometime and Doshi, chastened by Miandad's wit earlier in the match, did not say anything. But the umpire could not stand it any longer and finally asked in Hindi, "What is this bow-wow noise you are making?" Miandad replied, "He is like a dog bowling in such a way, snapping at my legs all the time. Ask him to bowl properly outside the off stump and I will stop the bow-wowing."

Miandad was also involved in a famous altercation with Lillee during the First Test in Perth between Australia and Pakistan in November 1981. Miandad was facing Lillee, and after turning the bowler to the on side he was in the course of completing a comfortable single when he was obstructed by Lillee. In the ensuing fracas Lillee kicked Miandad, who responded by shaping to strike him with his bat. The Australian team imposed a $200 fine on Lillee and sought an apology from Miandad. Subsequently the Australian Cricket Board held a hearing in Melbourne at which Lillee was suspended for two one-day internationals. Miandad never apologized.

Lillee's own bat had got him into a rather different sort of trouble when he appeared at the crease in the 1980 Ashes series against England, sporting a revolutionary bat made of aluminium. When he was told he could not use it and had to use a traditional willow one, he flung it angrily to the ground. The episode probably backfired on England, as Lillee took 26 wickets in the series.

Motor Racing

British racing driver Damon Hill's career has been haunted by his German rival Michael Schumacher. The German's greater skills and the Briton's better Williams car left them very evenly matched through the mid-1990s and there were times when it appeared that it was not just the direction of the track which determined how the steering wheel was turned.

Their most controversial coming-together was in the 1994 Australian Grand Prix in Adelaide, the last race of a closely-fought season. When it began, Schumacher, driving a Benetton, was one point ahead of Hill in the drivers' championship.

The race ended for both of them after a crash which many observers felt had been deliberately caused by the German to prevent Hill from passing him and winning the race and the title. The incident happened on the 36th out of 81 laps when Hill, in second place, was putting intense pressure on Schumacher. The German made a mistake, went off the circuit and hit a wall. As he bounced back on to the track and tried to regain the racing line he succeeded only in colliding with Hill, who was trying to pass him at the next corner. As a result first Schumacher and then Hill were forced to retire from the race, and the title went to the German.

Four years earlier, a month before the final race at Japan's Suzuka circuit which was to decide the 1990 championship, Ayrton Senna and Alain Prost shook hands on an agreement to contest it honourably and fairly. It was always a long shot that this would hold in the face of the most acrimonious feud in motor sport, and in the heat of battle that commitment was only the first thing to be thrown out of the cockpit.

Only seconds after the start of the race, Senna's McLaren-Honda and Prost's Ferrari disappeared in a cloud of dust and debris, leaving the Brazilian driver world champion. Prost was in no doubt about what had happened.

was the defending world champion and – in name at least – his McLaren-Honda teammate. They were on the 47th lap out of 53 as he led Senna towards the chicane. As the Frenchman approached the first wide bend, he had no idea that Senna would try to force his way through on the inside. Inevitably they collided and ran off. Prost abandoned his car, but Senna restarted with the help of a marshal and cut across the chicane. That manoeuvre cost him both the race and the championship in the stewards' room.

Road rage: Ayrton Senna's and Alain Prost's decisive collision at Suzuka in 1990.

The Frenchman said: "He did it on purpose. He knew that if I made a good start my car was better than his and he would have no chance to win the race. So he pushed me out. I have no problem with losing the world championship. I have lost many. But not this way...the outcome is no good from the sporting point of view."

The collision was less of a surprise than it might have been, because the previous year's championship race had ended in similar circumstances. Prost was in the lead and looked set to win the title from Senna, who

But there was another twist to the saga, as Prost's own team appealed against Senna's disqualification. Senna himself stated that the result as it stood did not reflect either "the truth of the race in either the sporting sense or the sense of the regulations... As to the incident, that was the only place where I could overtake and somebody who should not have been there just closed the door and that was that." However, the International Automobile Federation confirmed the verdict of the local stewards and the title was Prost's.

Tennis

Tennis used to have the cosy image of a tea-and-cucumber-sandwiches game where everyone behaved impeccably and ladies were always addressed as Miss. The image has changed radically in recent years, with John McEnroe, dubbed the Superbrat by the British tabloids, more responsible for the change than any other player.

However, nearly 60 years before that, tennis did produce the odd controversy. In 1926, for example, Suzanne Lenglen, who had won six Wimbledon singles championships between 1919 and 1925 and had just won the French Open for the second time in succession, left Wimbledon in a huff after what was seen as a snub to Queen Mary and King George V. She had come to Wimbledon that year as reigning champion, and the problem began when she arrived late for a doubles match with her partner Diddie Blastow, keeping the Royal visitors waiting. Lenglen was not in the best of moods as Blastow was not her normal partner; she had been ordered by the French tennis federation to play with her instead of her regular partner, Elizabeth Ryan. That afternoon Ryan was to be on the other side of the net.

Lenglen had told the referee's office that she did not want to play a singles match as she was due to play the doubles. But this message did not reach the referee's office and on arrival at Wimbledon she found she was due to play the singles. She refused to play either singles or doubles. She ought to have been scratched, but she was allowed to play the doubles the next day, a match she lost. She played a mixed doubles match two days later, by which time the public at large had learned of her supposed snub to the Queen and gave her a hostile reception.

Lenglen took this badly and decided not to take any further part in the tournament, returning to Paris almost immediately. She never played at Wimbledon again.

Lenglen's record of six championships stood until 1986, when it was finally broken by Martina Navratilova.

John Parsons, the noted tennis writer, has commented that the real scandals in tennis "have either been covered up, brushed aside, or not been more than generally discussed because of the legal implications which might otherwise have been involved".

However there have been many incidents on the tennis courts which have been quite remarkable and done much to destroy the image of tennis as a genteel sport where the victor is always graceful and the vanquished always generous. The Romanian Ilie Nastase was as highly-charged emotionally as he was talented and, when his temper boiled over, the results could be disastrous. He was also playing at the same time as a number of other very volatile performers, and the authorities' response oscillated between excessive discipline and helplessness.

Nastase came close to being disqualified from the US Open in 1976 when playing against the German Hans-Joachim Pohmann. Nastase was up to his tricks, swearing and acting up. He carried on using abusive language even when Pohmann had cramps, and for good measure carried on his tirade into the locker room. He was fined $1,000, and because this took him above the $3,000 fine limit he was automatically suspended for three weeks. But the suspension applied only to Grand Prix tournaments, and he was free to play in exhibition matches and other non-Grand Prix matches, earning himself $50,000 in that three-week period.

Nastase put on one of his worst exhibitions during the 1979 US Open, while playing against the master of the structured tantrum, John McEnroe. The match had been hyped up with an advertizement in the New York Post urging fans to "come see the fight of the century". The first two sets were shared and the high quality of the tennis gave little indication of what was to come.

During the third set, Nastase began having interchanges with the crowd, and the situation deteriorated until, during the fourth set, the umpire Frank Hammond imposed first a penalty point and then a penalty game against the Romanian. At one stage Hammond asked plaintively, "What are you trying to do to me, Ilie?" The crowd took Nastase's side and turned against the umpire who, in the early hours of the morning, reacted to yet another delay by awarding the match to McEnroe.

There was total chaos, and beer cans, plastic popcorn buckets and various other objects were thrown on to the court. The response of the tournament referee was to reverse the decision, replace the umpire and allow the game to resume. McEnroe, who was leading 3–1 and by two sets to one, duly finished off the match for the loss of only one more game.

McEnroe, who could be a magical player, has the dubious distinction of being the first player to be disqualified from a Grand Slam tournament. He was thrown out of the Australian Open in January 1990 for what the chief supervisor called the worst abuse directed at him in 11 years. McEnroe had rained four-letter words on the officials for what he felt were bad decisions, and the Australian television channel showing the match had been flooded with irate phone calls. However, the crowd watching the match on the Centre Court did not see it that way at all. They booed the decision and for 15 minutes kept chanting, "We want McEnroe back."

McEnroe's Melbourne tantrums had involved smashing his racket, for the fourth time, after an error put him break point down, and it cracked. The mandatory point penalty for such behaviour took the game score to 2–4. McEnroe ingeniously tried to convince the umpire that it was only a small crack, meaning he would use the racket again. It was after this that verbal obscenities started to flow, but even here there was something calculating about it. After he had been disqualified he said he did not know the change in the rules, which had come in on 1 January that year, meant that a player was disqualified after two warnings and not one as previously. This suggested that had he known this he would have moderated his behaviour so as to avoid the third penalty point and disqualification.

It summed up the complex McEnroe – magical one moment with the racket, devilish the other with his mouth.

The words "You cannot be serious", addressed to a linesman and accompanied by a ferocious glare, were as much a part of John McEnroe's image as his supreme artistry with the racket. As he marched around the court, wearing a red headband and a ferocious scowl with equal enthusiasm, the tantrums, often at key moments of the game, were as much a certainty as his matchless shots. He was never slow to seek an advantage through his verbal assaults. Once, when playing doubles against the Indian Amritraj brothers, he saw a linesman in a turban give a point to them and said, "You are Indian so you must be biased." Yet the next moment he could play a shot beyond the powers of any other player.

McEnroe felt that the British press, particularly the tabloid press, set about trying to paint him in lurid colours. In 1981, when he was at the height of his tennis powers, and ended Bjorn Borg's five-year reign as Wimbledon champion, a fight broke out between an American radio reporter and Nigel Clarke, the tennis correspondent of the *Daily Mirror*, following questions in the press about McEnroe's private life and his behaviour. The American felt that the British tabloids were asking questions that had nothing to do with the game.

Other players had been disqualified before McEnroe, but that was in the days before the Open era began. In 1950 Earl Cochell was disqualified for life for his behaviour during the US championships, persistently arguing with the umpires and spectators. At one point he tried to climb the umpire's chair and seize the microphone to lecture the crowd. He then threw several games and, despite being a right-hander, played left-handed. Cochell's life ban was eventually lifted, but the reprieve came too late for him to resume his career. In 1963 the Spaniard Wille Pato Alvarez was thrown out of the French championships for bad behaviour.

What was different with McEnroe was that his behaviour, years before his disqualification in Melbourne in 1990, set a trend in tennis of players always questioning decisions and throwing tantrums if they did not get their way. It heralded the introduction of mechanical aids such as the electronic eye for line calls, but it also made the game more confrontational. In the decade since McEnroe became the first player in the Open era to be disqualified, such disqualifications have become all too common.

In 1995 three players were disqualified. Tim Henman, when hitting a ball in anger, accidentally struck a ball girl and was disqualified. The American Murphy Jensen went missing from a mixed doubles match and was also disqualified.

And then there was Jeff Tarango and his wife Benedicte. The previous October in Tokyo, after losing his serve in the third set of a match against Michael Chang which he was eventually to lose, he dropped his shorts to the crowd. Tarango explained, "I thought people were concerned because tennis isn't entertaining enough. People complain that tennis is boring. I played my heart out against Chang and after losing my serve against a guy I'd been a set and a break up against maybe four times I just lost my head.

My shorts came down. And that was that. The gig was up."

The gig really was up when, the following June, he came to Wimbledon and met Germany's Alexander Mronz in the third round on Court 13. Tarango disputed a line call; the crowd, getting restless, began barracking him and Tarango shouted back.

Rebeuh. Tarango roared at Rebeuh, "You are the most corrupt official in the game." Rebeuh awarded a point penalty and Tarango shouted, "That's it. I'm not playing – no way." He threw down the two tennis balls he was holding, collected his things and walked off the court, thus avoiding the disqualification that would undoubtedly have followed.

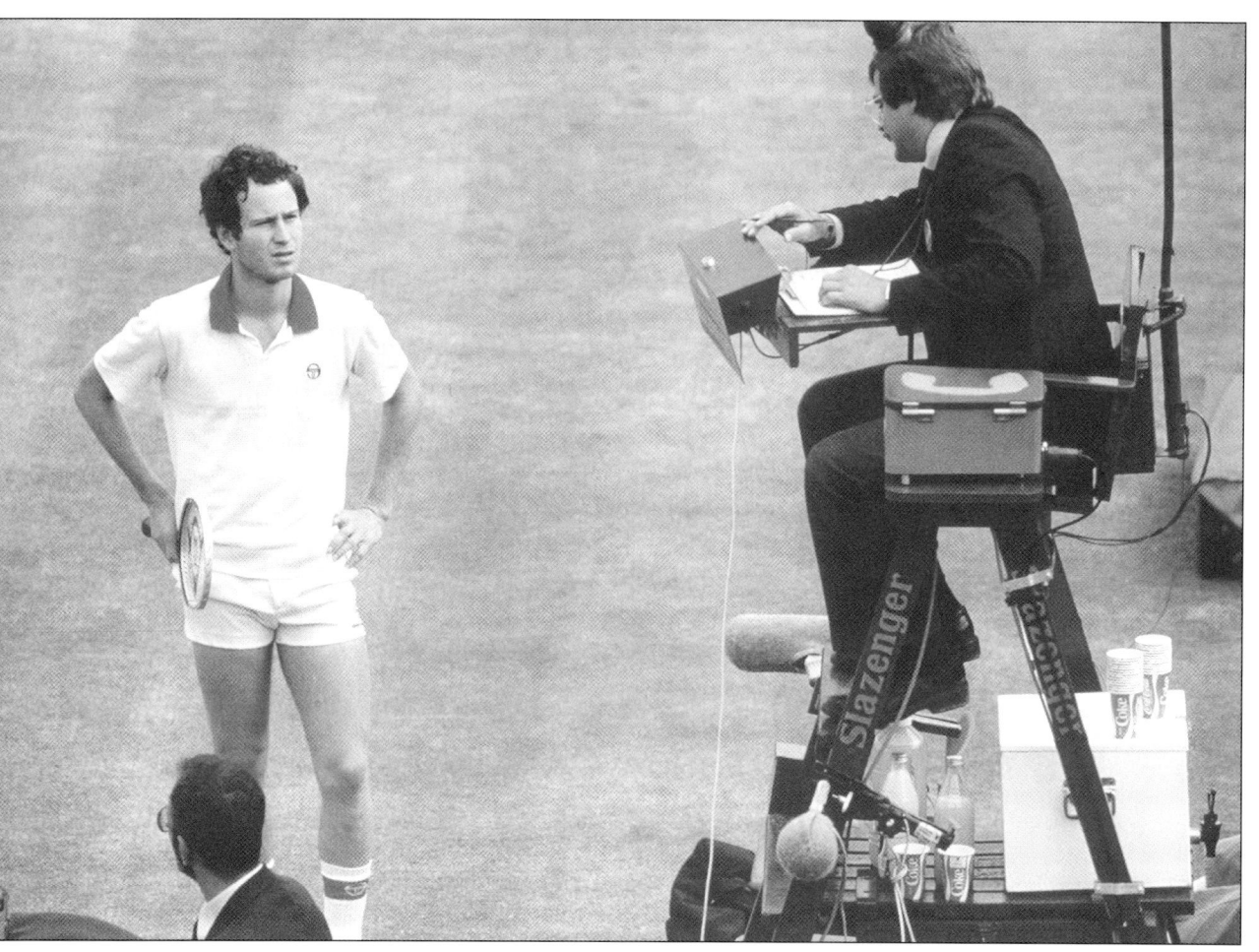

Getting the ump: John McEnroe suggests that the official "cannot be serious" in his ruling.

The umpire, Bruno Rebeuh from France, issued a warning for audible obscenity. Tarango, claiming he had only told them to shut up, said "I'm not having that" and demanded to see the supervisor, saying he had a "big beef". Tarango had long nursed a belief that Rebeuh, a highly regarded umpire, was less than even-handed when it came to non-French players.

The supervisor, a Swede called Stefan Fransson, heard both sides and agreed with

His wife then got into the act. Benedicte caught up with Rebeuh as he was going to report the incident to officials and slapped him. When Tarango and his wife came to the press conference, Benedicte justified herself by saying, "This guy deserves a lesson", and Tarango, sitting next to her, said, "I'm glad you did that." Tarango was suspended from the next Grand Slam tournament and Wimbledon the following year, but his fine of $15,000 was suspended subject to his offering a written apology.

Tarango's behaviour made the headlines because it was still quite unusual for a tennis player to behave like that. By 1999, however, Andre Agassi's abusive behaviour in the Sybasse Open in California raised few eyebrows and even fewer headlines, despite the fact that Agassi was a former No. 1 while Tarango, who was ranked 80 in 1995, was very much a bit player.

Agassi was about to be taken to a third set by a little-known American qualifier called Cecil Mamiit in their second-round encounter in San Jose. Agassi had romped through the first set, winning it 6–0, but was trailing 0–4 in the second when he began cursing. The first time he made an abusive comment the linesman walked across to talk to the umpire. As he walked back, Agassi made two more abusive comments. He claimed these were directed at himself, not the official, but two of them were heard distinctly by the crowd. After the third he was defaulted. It was the second time this had happened, the first being in 1996 during a first-round match against Daniel Nestor in Indianapolis.

After his disqualification Agassi seemed to be fed up not only with what he had done but with tennis itself, saying, "I'm tired of battles."

Boxing

In 1972 the Scot, Ken Buchanan, lost his world lightweight crown to an after-the-bell punch or kick in the groin from the Panamanian Roberto Duran. It would have been a travesty, however, if this had enabled Buchanan to win, as he was way behind the challenger on points when the incident happened at the end of the 13th round.

In a chaotic and undignified climax, Buchanan's corner and supporters were convinced he had been kneed in the groin by Duran, who counter-claimed that it was a punch to the groin. What was incontrovertible was that the punch was thrown after the bell as the referee tried to wrestle the two fighters apart.

Buchanan begged the referee to let him continue, but the referee was adamant that he was in no fit state. The controversial ending was the only thing that Buchanan had to complain about. He had been given a thrashing by Duran, who had won at least nine rounds with one even.

Racing

What can one say of a sportsman who claims to be someone else in order to gain an unfair, illegal advantage? In most sports it is not very easy to do, but Angel Monserrate did it in racing and even prospered for a time before being exposed.

The 29-year-old Puerto Rican came to England from New York in September 1998 and started riding in amateur races. He proved a very good rider, winning five races on the Flat in the 1998 season. However, what he did not tell his connections was that he was riding under a false name and that in America he had been a professional jockey before being banned in 1995 when he failed a drugs test. In order to continue riding he changed his name to Carlos Castro, and when this was discovered he was charged with criminal trespass, forgery and tampering with a sporting event. He then decided to try his luck and his deception skills in England.

There he settled in Soham, Cambridgeshire, and took his wife's maiden name, Jacobs, as his new surname. But Jacobs', or rather Monserrate's polished style stood out in the amateur races and soon his photograph was being sent to Dick Milburn, secretary of the Amateur Riders Club of America. Eventually Jacobs was proved to be Monserrate, his real identity unearthed by an exposé in the *Daily Telegraph*.

After a lengthy investigation the Jockey Club decided to ban Monserrate for ten years, a ban that applies in all 70 countries where racing takes place.

Monserrate, who now works in a Cambridge restaurant, said, "I regret what I did. I don't know if the punishment is harsh, but I will not appeal."

Vinnie Jones

Folk Hero of the Battering classes

Vinnie Jones is the sort of footballer who in another age would hardly have merited any attention. When Jones retired, Tommy Docherty said, "He couldn't play to save his life and I'm amazed he lasted so long in the game. He was so bad, he couldn't pass water, let alone the ball."

Typical Docherty: the quote was a bit over the top but not that far off the mark. Jones's playing record was undistinguished and splattered with the sort of violence on and off the field that would have made him a pariah in any other age.

His disciplinary record in football included: the quickest booking (five seconds after kick-off), 13 red cards (one rescinded), fines of £26,250 and a six-month suspended ban for appearing in a video entitled *Soccer's Hard Men*, which was an advertizement not for the beautiful game but for the ugly one, and designed to "glorify on-pitch violence".

Not satisfied with violence on the field, he also bit *Daily Mirror* photographer Ted Oliver on the nose in a Dublin hotel, while he was in that city for England's match against Ireland. That match was abandoned following the violence orchestrated by English soccer thugs. Jones said his actions were a joke, but admitted, "I behaved like a prat on too much champagne."

He was also ordered to do 100 hours' community service as a painter and decorator, following his conviction for assaulting a neighbour near his home in Hertfordshire. When he asked if he could coach young players instead, as Eric Cantona had following his conviction for assaulting a fan, Jones was turned down by probation officers on the grounds that he might be a "bad influence".

Yet within weeks this one-time hod carrier, hard man and professional footballer was getting the kind of invitations social climbers fight over. Just one weekend of many will illustrate how sought-after Jones was. On a Friday night he flew off to Milan to attend a party thrown by dress designer Donatella Versace. On Monday it was the Brit Awards nominations bash at a West End night club. And then there was the charity ball in London where he danced with a princess.

When attending the charity night, he sauntered over to the guest of honour, Princess Michael of Kent, and casually asked her to dance. "I asked the Prince for permission first," he said. "She was very nice, a caring lady. What did I call her? Princess, of course. She called me Vinnie. I know what people have said, that I shouldn't have approached her and all that. Why not? She appeared just a normal human being, just like I am."

Jones went on to say, "It's said royalty are this and that, arrogant, whatever. I've met all sorts like that throughout my football career. They have never impressed me. The only people I'm in awe of is my nan and my wife. I've known the Princess for a couple of years. You'd be surprized by the phone calls we get. I admire her for her interest in the charity we both support, we get along very well."

Jones was also invited to the launch of a Tibetan peace garden in London, organized by Trudi Styler and attended by Mick Jagger and others. His crowning social moment came when he shared a stage at the Lyceum with Stephen Fry, Rowan Atkinson, Clive James, Ulrika Jonsson et al, at one of the Prince of Wales's various 50th birthday celebrations. Vinnie duly traded on his hard-

Rogues' Gallery

man image in some dismal skit. Then there followed a fawning interview on Radio 4's *Midweek* programme and similar treatment in several newspapers.

When asked how he felt about mixing with lords and ladies, Jones said, "They are more inquisitive about me. They know I'm – what's the word? – they know I've got something about me. I think I excite people."

In view of all this, it is hardly surprising that while as a player he was one most people in football wanted to disown, off the field he has addressed students at Eton and Oxford and made a very successful acting debut in the film *Lock, Stock and Two Smoking Barrels*. Within weeks of its release Jones had not only had offers to do a sequel but an invitation to appear in a $100 million remake of *Spartacus*. He has since made his way to Hollywood as Britain's latest export to the fantasy land.

As one writer put it, Jones had transformed himself from a man feared on and off the football field for his violence to "a lovable thug in the English pantheon". The English tend to like thugs who are either not real thugs or whose thuggery took place so long ago, as with John McVicar and Frankie Fraser, that they can be forgiven. Present-day thugs on the other hand, such as Mike Tyson, Stan Collymore, even Geoffrey Boycott, are shunned. Vinnie Jones's status as a much sought-after celebrity suggests he has crossed this divide. He is making a living out of a reputation for violence while still having recourse to it.

A *Times* profile writer asked: "So what is it about Vinnie that redeems him, that earns him respect, fame and fortune in spite of his charmless behaviour on and off the football field? He is not a massively talented player, like, say, George Best. Far from it. He is a decent actor with a face full of the broad planes, acute angles and deep shadows that the camera likes. He does a lot of charity work for sick children. He is devoted to his wife, Tanya, to her daughter, Kalpy, and to his son, Aaron, by a previous girlfriend. He has made his own way in life. His violence is only directed at the other man. This is all laudable enough in its way.

"But, surely, he must have some other quality to justify his transgressions being so thoroughly and so swiftly overlooked. Am I missing something? Or do we now admire violence for its own sake?"

The conclusion the writer came to was:

Typecasting: Vinnie Jones in *Lock Stock & Two Smoking Barrels*.

"Vinnie, the folk hero of the battering classes...has realized that his reputation for violence can make him a living. He has realized that, yes, we do now seem to get off on violence, provided it is male-on-male and spiced with bogus proletarian authenticity. You cannot really blame Vinnie for his insight – he has precious little else to offer. But the film, newspaper, television and now royal establishments are co-operating with him, and that is a disgrace."

It is also a revealing commentary on modern sport that a man with such limited and even dubious sporting ability as Vinnie Jones should now be held up as some sort of folk hero, with headlines in the press such as "Hard Man's Heart of Gold". The report underneath this headline described him as "without doubt the biggest character in his era" and tried to arouse sympathy for Jones by saying that there was a side of his life which most people did not know about. This was the fact that his wife Tanya is under supervision at Harefield Hospital after having had a heart transplant operation in her teens and that, because of this, the pair cannot have children of their own.

So how has Jones pulled it off? He has done so through the distinctive and successful ploy of linking violent actions on the field with violent words off it.

Part of the ploy was that anybody who questioned him was immediately abused as a lesser human being. The classic example of this Jones tactic came in the 1995–96 season when he was sent off in a Boxing Day match against Chelsea for fouling Ruud Gullit. Claiming that Gullit had dived, Jones said, "I own two pot-bellied pigs, yet they don't yelp as much as Gullit." Then in his ghosted column he called Gullit a money-grabbing cockroach, shrewdly exploiting the resentment felt for high-earning foreign players.

Jones was fined £2,000, yet the whole episode illustrates the way in which his actions on and off the field have often been more calculating than his simple image as a hard man may suggest.

It was in the 1987–88 season, the year Wimbledon won the FA Cup by beating Liverpool, that Jones first realized how violent action, which at other times would have been considered unacceptable, could earn him a certain kind of fame.

Wimbledon played Newcastle, whose line-up included Paul Gascoigne, already showing signs that he would be a great player of the future. Jones marked him, and marked him so closely that as they lined up for a free kick he squeezed Gascoigne's balls very hard. Jones later said, "There was nothing serious in it, though. He was tugging at my shirt so I thought I'd make him stop. I squeezed his ego; you can do that against the big players." The picture, with the pain and surprize etched on Gascoigne's face, told the story vividly and was shown round the world. It was the first time Jones was noticed by the wider public.

After that Jones made a career of being violent, and making sure everyone knew he was violent. He told Kenny Dalgish that he would "rip your head off and crap in the hole". This was said to have inspired Quentin Tarantino to include a similar scene featuring Michael Madsen and a kidnapped cop in *Reservoir Dogs*. In the 1988 Cup Final against Liverpool, Jones took on Steve McMahon fairly early on in the game and fouled him so cynically and violently that McMahon, the hard man of Liverpool, did not want to know any more. In the notorious video in praise of soccer's "hard men", he advised viewers on elbowing behind the ear, poking in the eye, raking studs down the calf and Achilles tendon, treading on toes, grabbing testicles and abusing players' wives. It also revealed that one way of helping a fouled opponent to his feet was by yanking on the hairs of his armpit.

Jones used the ghetto-blaster as a psychological weapon to intimidate the opposition. In October 1992, when Wimbledon won at Manchester United, he turned it up full blast and danced naked in the corridor with a cigar in his mouth.

Jones's autobiography, *Vinnie*, reveals that violence has always been part of Jones's life and, as it takes the reader from the schoolboy thug to the fully-grown thug, that he fairly revelled in it.

He recalls how, as a schoolboy, "I gave the bully a good pasting and bust his nose", and made no secret of how much he loved violence. "There was always a ruck...we were fighting all the time. I have to confess that, yeah, I loved it." He seems to have grown up amid violence: "Dad, Uncle Martin, Dave and I set about them in no uncertain terms."

How much this violence was still part of

him when he had became a grown man was underlined in June 1998 when he was found guilty of assault causing actual bodily harm – to Tim Gear, his former neighbour. The two men had a dispute which culminated in Jones breaking into Gear's caravan.

Jones bit, punched and kicked Gear, who told the *News of the World*, "He kept on calling me a fat coward. I was pleading with him, 'Please stop', but every time I went to speak he stamped on my face. He was revelling in it."

Jones was fined and given 100 hours' community service. He was later given an extra 40 hours for not properly serving the initial order.

Jones would later explain, "I just snapped. Everyone makes a slip-up sometime. But it also cost me around £500,000 in lost earnings and opportunities and now I have to be whiter than white. I cannot afford to put a foot wrong."

Such is Jones's celebrity status that in talking to reporters he could convert his community punishment into something worthy which he might well have done voluntarily for the good of the community. "I have to go around the homes of old people and pensioners in the area, delivering commodes, mattresses and beds. It saddens me to witness their deprivation, sick people just waiting to die while my life is only just beginning. It's very sad. I try to be as cheerful as possible, exchange a few light-hearted comments to keep their spirits up. They don't know me from Adam, but it doesn't hurt for me to give them a couple of minutes of my time. After all, they don't have much left."

The court case did nothing to dent either his image or his marketability as the hard man the world desires, and the day he left court he was summoned to begin shooting for the hit movie *Lock, Stock and Two Smoking Barrels*.

In the film Jones played Big Chris, the debt collector, a part made with him in mind. When the writer and director Guy Ritchie began making notes for this darkly comic thriller set in London's gangland, one of them read: "Big Chris should be like the footballer Vinnie Jones."

Lock, Stock and Two Smoking Barrels is Britpop's closest answer to *Reservoir Dogs*. Big Chris is an "enforcer" for Harry the Hatchet and, in his own words, a "very cool

Mixing it: Vinnie in trouble for QPR v. Wolves in 1998 *(left)*, **and Wimbledon v. Spurs in 1996.**

dude who's feared and respected throughout the East End". Big Chris kills a man by banging his head in a car door. When he's not "doing someone over", Big Chris is a devoted dad to Little Chris, whom he dresses in a junior version of his own wardrobe and takes everywhere, even out on the job.

For Jones, "It wasn't acting. It was just me. After all, I had been involved in most of the situations in real life. When I started to act, the director shouted: 'Stop. Just be natural.'"

It was soon after this that Jones brought out his successful autobiography, which sold nearly 100,000 copies. He was now forced to take on not only a personal assistant, to deal with a constantly-ringing telephone and dozens of requests, but also a minder named Phil, just to make sure the peace is kept.

Jones said, "You still get the odd nutter who wants to have a go when I'm in a pub. If anyone wants to have a go at me, then Phil just steps in and sorts it out.

"But you know me; if I'm pushed I can step up and look after myself with the best of them."

It was reported that when Jones arrived for a photo session for the soccer mag *FourFourTwo* he was watched by the photographer David Bailey, who said: "Who's this fella, then? Does he think he's hard?" As someone who had photographed enough bad boys in his time, Bailey recognized The Hard when he saw it. Bailey's portrait of Jones, his face as obdurate as a pit bull terrier's, his torso naked except for a smudgy tattoo, was chosen to appear on the cover, over those of Alan Shearer and Teddy Sheringham, and the issue was a sell-out.

What makes Jones very interesting and the ultimate bad sportsman of our time is how he can now look back on his football career and mock the very people who took up acres of newsprint building up his media image as the hard man.

For Jones, such descriptions are a joke and tell us more about the writers than about him. "It is all comical really. They wrote as if I had raped their missus." Jones's contempt for sportswriters who devoted so much space to him and made him famous is total: "Sportswriters are bitter because they are wannabe footballers who were never allowed to play because they were too wimpish."

As for the wimpish writers being the ones who built him up as the hod carrier-turned-footballer, Jones can now just dismiss it: "It was an angle; it was all part of the Attila the Hun image."

An image that helped him get a lifestyle which would be the envy of many. Jones's parents split up when he was 14. He went with his dad. The divorce was a catastrophe for the boy, who was already temperamental and hyperactive.

For a while he fell out with both his parents, felt rejected and even went off the rails. Now everyone is reconciled. His father lives in St Albans, his mother "up the road", and he is the ultimate working-class lad made good.

The evidence of Jones's prosperity is in the driveway, where you can see a Range Rover, a Mercedes, a Toyota pick-up and Tanya's sporty BMW.

In the Range Rover, his dream car, he has a television and the windows are tinted because people are constantly bipping him on the motorway. "They're only being friendly, but sometimes you're concentrating on other things. You have to be on the phone and everything." He sighed. "That's what it's all about."

Had Jones not become such a celebrity, his decision to seek international recognition by playing for Wales, at a time when the Principality have been tremendously short of football talent, would be seen as cynical. But it is presented as an act of supreme pragmatism. He was born in Watford and has always lived in Hertfordshire, apart from a spell in Swedish football and his seasons in Yorkshire. Yet he was capped by Wales in 1994 on the basis that his grandfather was Welsh. In his book he declares, "I feel Welsh and regard myself as Welsh." But as a child he had supported England. Asked to explain this change in sporting nationalism, Jones said, "But it's like anything. You can have your loyalties to one woman and then divorce her, then your loyalties are to your next wife." Truly, Jones is a law unto himself – or perhaps part of his problem is that he speaks before he thinks.

But for Jones all this is very much part of what makes him so popular. "I just think people sort of relate to me. I try and be honest. I'm not slimy, I'm not a backstabber. I've worked for everything I've got. I think people appreciate that."

Squeeze play: Vinnie Jones gives Paul Gascoigne a feel for the "Crazy Gang's" antics in 1987.

The Violence in our Midst

It is tempting to believe that it is modern sport, with its love of money and commercialism, and modern society, with its under-class and ill-educated young men looking for thrills, that have combined to breed the monster of spectator violence.

Yet, if we look back nearly 2,000 years, to the very beginning of the Christian era, what do we find? We find a team of Nucerian athletes coming to compete in Pompeii. A brawl developed between athletes which led to a riot involving the spectators. Several people were killed and the city was damaged before troops managed to assert control. Pompeii's answer was to ban all athletic contests for ten years, and no games took place between AD 59 and 69.

This suggests that sport, whenever and wherever it has been played, has always had the power to arouse passions.

Terrace of death: the Heysel Stadium, 1985, after 39 people died before the European Cup Final.

Football

No sport is more passionate than football, and when the passions boil over and overwhelm the crowd, then Pele's beautiful game can almost become an instrument of evil.

One such evil day was 27 December 1948 when religion and sport combined to produce a real devil's brew. Its roots lay in Ireland's bitter politics of gun and religion, but the violence which nearly killed a player and did kill a team took place on a football pitch after Belfast Celtic, a club with a Catholic identity, met Linfield, the city's other major club, which was just as strongly Protestant.

A couple of months before, Celtic 'keeper Kevin McAlinden had punched Linfield's Billy Simpson. McAlinden received hate mail and there were ominous warnings of what would happen during the return match at Linfield's Windsor Park ground. McAlinden was nonetheless selected, and 33,000 people turned up for the game. The supporters had always been divided along sectarian lines: in 1920 a Celtic–Linfield match had ended with four fans being shot and wounded.

The game itself was ferocious. Linfield's Bob Bryson broke a leg in a challenge with Jimmy Jones, the Celtic centre-forward. This was announced to the crowd at half-time, an act many saw as deliberately provocative. In the second half each side had a player sent off and scored in the last ten minutes. At the final whistle, the crowd erupted.

Harry Walker, Celtic's captain, knew what to expect and had chosen ends knowing McAlinden would be a target for the crowd and should finish the match at the end nearest the tunnel. He told his players, "When the final whistle goes, all go for Kevin, for he's the one they're going to pick on." Walker and his team pushed, or rather fought, their way to the dressing-room to find they were missing not McAlinden but Jones, the player who had clashed with Bryson. At that moment, Jones – who would not even have been there had a proposed transfer to Newcastle gone ahead several months earlier – was still in the crowd, being beaten and kicked almost to death.

Jones would later recall: "I was chasing a long ball as the referee blew the final whistle and just proceeded to go off the ground like the rest of the players. But a whole crowd had come on from the Kop end. I was watching to see what was going on, but in next to no time I was amongst them, thousands of them. Somebody hit me on the back of the head with his fist and I turned around."

Knowing he could not argue or fight, Jones tried to reach the players' entrance:

"I tried to run down the track beside the pitch, but someone came and pushed me right off the pitch on to the terracing – there was no perimeter wire then. I landed on my hands and knees. I remember that, for I cut my right knee. That was the leg that got broke, too. I got up to run, but everyone was kicking me. I fell; somebody kicked me or tripped me. And then some boyo – my leg was just lying like a piece of wood – jumped off [the edge of the pitch] – he jumped on my leg.

"It was sore but I wasn't thinking about that, just thought of getting myself out of the way. I got up to run, but my leg was just wobbling about. So there was nothing I could do. I just had to lie down."

As Jones lay there, expecting to die, his life was saved by the swift action of Sean McCann, who played in goal for Ballymena. Racing out from the main stand McCann jumped into the thick of the violence and threw himself on top of Jones. McCann had a hat on, and the crowd, thinking he might be a police detective, eased off, at which point a uniformed policeman with a baton arrived.

There were all sorts of ironies here. McCann, a Catholic, was trying to save Jones, a Protestant, from being beaten up by a Protestant mob who either didn't care or weren't aware that he was a Protestant and saw only that he was wore the green hoops of Celtic, the Catholic team they hated.

Jones survived, but within six months Celtic, the most successful club in Irish history, was disbanded by its directors in response to the violence.

This was a special kind of football violence, but sectarian conflict has also occurred in other parts of the United Kingdom, particularly in Glasgow, another city with a Catholic–Protestant divide.

There, the two teams which dominate Scottish football – the 'Old Firm' of Rangers and Celtic – represent the two religious communities, Rangers being supported by Protestants and Celtic by Catholics. Both have their roots in the city's working-class communities, with Celtic drawing its support and inspiration from the migration of Irish Catholics to Glasgow.

While Celtic had many Protestant players and its greatest manager, Jock Stein, was a Protestant, Rangers did not field a Catholic until Graeme Souness (a Scot but, significantly, one whose football was nurtured south of the border) bought Mo Johnstone in 1985. The decision created such a storm that for a time it seemed many season ticket-holders and other supporters would desert the club. They did not, but it illustrated how deep the roots of bigotry go.

It first made its disgraceful mark on Scottish football history at the beginning of the century. The riot after the 1909 Scottish Cup Final replay between Rangers and Celtic in 1909 was described by reporters as "one of the most disgraceful blots disfiguring the annals of the game" – a status it retains even after nearly a century.

The first match had ended in a 2–2 draw, and when the replay at Hampden was also drawn, this time 1–1, it was widely assumed half an hour of extra time would be played. But after the referee had blown the final whistle and Rangers had left the field, soon followed by Celtic, it was announced that the game would not be continued.

The 60–70,000 spectators were incensed. Suspecting the authorities of collusion in trying to get a draw, they embarked on two and half hours of furious confrontation with the police. Some 60 people were treated for wounds and more than 100 were injured.

The crowd set fire to everything that would burn before invading the pitch and venting their rage on the police, who were pelted with stones, bottles and brickbats. Overwhelmed, the police drew their batons and in the hand-to-hand fighting which followed many officers were badly injured.

The mob uprooted the goal-posts, tore the net to pieces and ripped out woodwork to use as weapons. Surrounding the mounted police, they tried to drag the riders to the ground and furiously beat police and animals alike. Even after they were driven from the ground the mob continued to bombard the police with fusillades of bricks.

In the event everyone lost, because the Cup was withheld from both sides.

Nothing like this has been seen since, but there have been periodic bouts of violence, and even now Old Firm matches always contain the potential for a conflagration.

This was sickeningly demonstrated when, on 2 May 1999, Rangers won their tenth Scottish title in 11 seasons. For the first time ever they clinched it at Celtic Park, and this, plus the old demon drink, sparked scenes not seen in Scotland for 20 years.

The demands of TV meant the match kicked off at 6.05pm, allowing many hours of drinking on a long Sunday afternoon. In the 41st minute, with Celtic a man down and trailing 1–0, referee Hugh Dallas was struck by a coin and fell to the ground with blood pumping from the wound. Play was held up for several minutes while he was treated. Dallas had four stitches inserted at half-time and came out for the second half, in which he sent off two more players, one from Rangers and another from Celtic.

At the final whistle the Rangers team, who won 3–1, went over to the 7,000 Rangers fans amid the Celtic crowd of 53,000 to celebrate, taunting the home fans with a mocking copy of Celtic's huddle. This provoked more fury, and as they headed for the tunnel they were pelted with missiles.

There was more trouble outside the ground, with fans fighting in the streets near Parkhead and in rival bars. The police had to use riot gear, and in one incident more than 100 officers came under attack from 150 Rangers fans. Strathclyde Police made 100 arrests for public order offences, and the Scottish football authorities, lulled into complacency by years of largely trouble-free football, were forced to reconsider their assumption that Scottish football, unlike English, had beaten the hooligans.

At the police's insistence it was agreed 'high-risk' – for which read 'Old Firm' – matches would no longer be staged on Sunday evenings. Their immediate concern was that the teams were to meet again in the Scottish Cup final at Hampden Park on May 29, with Dallas once more putting his head on the block as referee. The message seemed to get through: in a low-key match, Rangers completed the treble with a 1–0 victory, with the players on their best behaviour.

The same could not be said of some club officials. Rangers' vice-chairman Donald Findlay was filmed by a tabloid newspaper at a post-match party singing anti-Catholic songs, and was forced to resign. His repertoire included 'The Sash', the unofficial Protestant anthem, 'The Billy Boys' and a football chant insulting the Pope and including the line, "We're up to our knees in Fenian blood". Such overtly sectarian displays were clearly at odds with chairman

David Murray's efforts to attract corporate support by presenting Rangers as a modern club worthy of a place among the giants of European football. His is an unenviable task: too many of those involved in football in Glasgow football seem all too happy to embrace the ancient hatreds in their midst.

Football violence south of the border, though not born of religious bigotry, has a long pedigree. In the 1970s, however, it took a more vicious turn. No one seems to know quite why, in the decade following England's one and only World Cup victory in 1966, football violence became synonymous with English, and for a time British, football fans. All too soon, 'the English disease' of violence began to be found whenever an English or British side visited foreign parts. Among the first to carry this deadly disease abroad were the fans of Glasgow Rangers.

Sectarian hatred: Referee Hugh Dallas is felled during the Old Firm clash in May 1999.

Their behaviour in Barcelona in 1972 took much of the gilt off Rangers' victory in the Cup Winners Cup final that year. The match, in which they beat Moscow Dynamo 3–2, ended with riots in which one person died and hundreds more were injured.

Rangers were banned for a year, and there was much sympathy for Moscow Dynamo's protest that drunken Scottish fans broke the match up deliberately. The pitch was invaded four times: at the start; in the 24th minute, when Rangers scored their first goal; two minutes before the end, when the fans thought the referee had blown for full time; and at the final whistle. On each occasion Russian players were manhandled, one was struck by a bottle and another knocked cold. At least Rangers' players were innocent, but the police veered from laxity at the start to wild clubbing of innocent and guilty alike as the situation deteriorated.

At English club level the first serious sign of hooliganism had come from Leeds. This was on 17 April 1971, when Leeds, one of the great teams of the period, were involved in a championship race with Arsenal. Leeds had to beat West Bromwich Albion to make sure Arsenal, two points behind with two games in hand, were kept at bay.

With 28 minutes left Leeds, already 1–0 down, were incensed when Albion were allowed to score when two of their players, according to Leeds, were offside. The linesman had flagged Albion's Colin Suggett offside but the referee ignored this, saying he was not interfering with play, and when Jeff Astle scored neither linesman nor referee agreed with Leeds that he, too, was offside.

The Leeds players surrounded referee Ray Tinkler, pushing and shoving him, but had to protect Tinkler when some 40 angry fans got on to the pitch. Thirty-two people were arrested. After play was resumed Leeds did manage to score, but they still lost 2–1 and Arsenal took the title by one point.

Most telling, in the context of violence, is that Leeds manager Don Revie and the club chairman condoned the fans' actions and blamed the match officials. This set the pattern of future behaviour by the clubs: we shall never find fault with our own. The FA fined Leeds £750 and ordered them to play their first four home games of the following season away from Elland Road.

Soon Manchester United fans were following Leeds' awful example, and by the mid-1970s were in the forefront of football hooliganism. Their fans seemed to have the idea, copied by others, that if their team was losing, a riot could force the match to be abandoned, resulting in a replay.

During the last-but-one game of the 1973–74 season, against neighbours Manchester City, and with Manchester United losing 1–0 with just eight minutes left – a result that would send them down to the old Second Division – United fans invaded the pitch. The game had to be abandoned, but their tactics failed because the score was allowed to stand.

United fans were to extend their actions abroad when, in the 1977–78 season, having won the FA Cup, they qualified for the Cup Winners Cup. Before the first match at St Etienne, in France, fighting broke out and riot police took half an hour to quell it. The skirmishes continued all night and UEFA initially banned United from Europe. However, they were reinstated on appeal but ordered to play the home leg 300 kilometres from Old Trafford. Since the League did not want to risk United supporters in London, the match was played in Plymouth, without further incident.

Three years earlier, in 1974, Newcastle had received a similar punishment from the FA, who annulled the result of their FA Cup sixth-round match against Nottingham Forest and forced Newcastle to play the following season's Cup ties away. The match had been won 4–3 by Newcastle, but only after it had been interrupted by a pitch invasion and an eight-minute delay. The FA ordered the match to be replayed at neutral Goodison Park: when that finished in a goalless draw, a second replay was also staged at Everton's ground which Newcastle won 1–0.

The start of the 1975 football season produced some of the worst scenes ever seen on English grounds. In one match at Luton, Chelsea supporters, seeing their side losing 3–0, attacked players, police and ground staff. Violence spilled out on the streets, a train was wrecked on the way back to London and 100 people were arrested. Disturbances also took place at Ibrox Park, the home of Glasgow Rangers, and at Stoke City's ground. At Crewe hooligans set a train on fire, and British Rail stopped running football specials for the rest of the season and refused to sell cheap tickets until after 3 p.m.

Soon there were other ideas to contain hooliganism, including one from the Police

Superintendents' Association which suggested that matches should be classified in the same way as films, with fans under the age of 16 banned from "X" rated matches unless accompanied by an adult. Chelsea, with already one of the worst records, could see no sense in it.

By the mid-1970s such violence was not only common throughout grounds in Britain but had spread to international matches. In 1975 Leeds got to the final of the European Cup, at Parc des Princes in Paris, where they lost to Bayern Munich. Leeds had a goal disallowed, two penalty appeals not given and, with every decision that went against them, their fans rioted. The French riot police had to struggle to contain the fans, who were determined to wreck the stadium. After the match the rioting continued in the centre of Paris, and Leeds were banned from Europe for four years.

Generally speaking these incidents were, and remain, a wretched story of English fans or, as the media like to put it, "so-called fans" spreading mayhem and violence in foreign fields. However, it was not always the English: the Welsh were at it too. In the 1975–76 season Wales played a two-legged European Championships quarter-final against Yugoslavia and, having lost the away leg 2–0, were drawing 1–1 in the return leg at Ninian Park when the East German referee disallowed a goal. Spectators invaded the pitch, beer cans were thrown and play was halted for five minutes. When play was resumed, another Welsh goal was disallowed and then a Terry Yorath penalty was saved. Four players were booked and the police had to escort the referee off the field as Wales went out of the competition.

Two years later violence was also brought to English grounds by visiting fans from Scotland.

There are few things in life which excite a Scottish football fan more than a victory over England. But the emotional excesses which followed the 2–1 victory at Wembley in 1977 unleashed an orgy of violence that led to the arrest of 289 Scottish fans. Many more would have suffered a similar fate but for the shortage of police on duty.

The misbehaviour began with massive gatecrashing and noisy whistling during the National Anthem. It continued with fans invading the pitch at the end of the game, pulling down the goal-posts and tearing up the pitch. Those parts of the pitch that were not carried away by the Scots as souvenirs were left deep in broken glass and other missiles. This incident contributed to the eventual death of the oldest international fixture in football, England's match against Scotland having launched international football in Glasgow on 30 November 1872.

Within a few years of the Wembley mayhem of 1977, the annual England–Scotland matches had been cancelled, crowd security being given as one of the reasons, and since 1988 England have played Scotland only once at Wembley, during Euro 96. By then, however, Scottish fans had done much to improve their image, and hooliganism was seen as a purely English disease.

Through the 1970s and 1980s, as violence by football supporters grew unchecked, the game's ruling bodies tried to blame everyone but themselves for the problems. After the Scottish riot at Wembley, Ted Croker, then the secretary of the FA, warned that by November the ground would be fenced in, and this was seen as football's answer to the problem of hooliganism.

The football authorities felt that if grounds were fenced in, so as to stop fans going on to the pitch, that would solve the problem as far as football was concerned. As to why there was violence in the first place, football blamed everyone and everything except for the game itself. What the football authorities did not realize was that such shirking of responsibility was merely stoking the problem, not solving it, and it is not surprising that the awful denouement was not long in coming.

Through the 1980s English football violence steadily increased at both club and international level. In the opening match of the European Championships of 1980, held in Italy, after Belgium had equalized an early Ray Wilkins goal fighting broke out between English and Italian fans – the English being the worse for drink and upset by the taunting of the Italians. The Italian police had to use tear-gas to stop the fighting, but the gas spread on to the pitch and play was held up for five minutes. More than 70 fans were taken to hospital, and UEFA fined the FA £8,000

It was during two years in the mid-1980s, however, that the problems of English football hooliganism and crowd behaviour were to reach their horrible climax. The start of the 1983–84 season saw violence at club matches when

Middlesbrough played Leeds and Chelsea visited Brighton, where seven policemen were injured. Official inquiries cleared the clubs of any blame, but it proved that the authorities were powerless.

In November England played a European championship qualifier in Luxembourg, a city which had bitter memories of what English fans had done in 1977. Now, with England failing to qualify, the fans went wild, rioting in the city centre causing thousands of pounds' worth of damage. Although only 13 were arrested, nine of them were fined and sentenced to four months in jail.

That season a referee was hit by a missile in a match between Notts County and Bristol City in the FA Cup, and the same competition also saw West Ham fans, when their team were losing 3–0 to Birmingham, make several attempts to have the game abandoned. West Ham were threatened with a two-year ban but reinstated on appeal.

Hans Bangerter, general secretary of UEFA, threatened to ban English clubs from Europe, a threat that was brushed aside at the time but which unfortunately proved to be prophetic.

Hooliganism hit the headlines again the following season thanks to the supporters of a club with one of the worst disciplinary records in the game: Millwall.

Millwall fans' misbehaviour had forced the closure of its ground, the Den, in 1934, 1947 and 1950. In 1967 the club had been fined £1,000 when spectators at the Den attacked the referee, and in 1978 Millwall was fined £1,500 and the ground closed for two weeks after crowd trouble during their FA Cup tie with Ipswich.

The 1984–85 season saw Millwall fans behave as if they were a medieval army bent on pillage when their team played Luton in the Cup. They rioted not only on the pitch but in the town, which led to the by now usual damage to houses, cars and also a train, which was wrecked. Forty-seven people, including 31 policemen, were injured.

For the first time the riot at the Luton ground was shown live on television, and Prime Minister Margaret Thatcher, appalled, summoned the football chiefs to Downing Street. They came on 1 April and it was on this occasion that Ted Croker, the FA secretary, made his now infamous comment: "These people's are society's problems. We don't want your hooligans at our sport."

Luton banned away supporters and Ken Bates, chairman of Chelsea, had an electrified fence erected to prevent pitch invasions and talked of introducing ID cards. As it happened, the electrified fence fell foul of the then-Greater London Council.

The wisdom of not having fences, let alone electrified fences, was demonstrated at the end of the 1984–85 season, when it was clear that the tragedy at Bradford would have been even worse had there been such fences. Bradford City were playing their last league match of the season and looking forward to celebrating their promotion from the old Third Division. Just before half-time a fire started in the old wooden main stand. Many escaped by jumping on to the pitch, but 56 people died in one of England's worst sporting disasters, which also demonstrated how antiquated and dangerous English football stadiums were.

Two weeks later the hooligans demonstrated the real wretchedness of their attitude. This was on 24 May 1985 at Heysel stadium in Brussels, just before the European Cup Final between Juventus and Liverpool, when English football violence reached its nadir. For more than a decade English football had been journeying down this path, inflicting destruction and violence, often on bystanders, and almost always in a foreign city or stadium. But in the litany of grotesque acts by English football fans, few have plumbed the depths of the events at Heysel.

In previous years Liverpool's triumphs in Europe had given warning signs of the trouble that might come. In 1981, when they beat Real Madrid in the 1981 European Cup Final at Parc des Princes in Paris, fans threw missiles at police outside the stadium and then faced a baton charge.

In 1984 Liverpool fans travelled to Rome to play Roma for the European Cup. They won, but incurred the wrath of the Roman supporters, some of whom ambushed Liverpool fans. This led to a comical aftermath in which two English football journalists, Hugh McIlvanney and Colin Malam, were rounded up by the Roman police for their own protection along with two thoroughly bemused American homosexuals. According to some Liverpool fans, it also created a burning hatred of the Italians among the Liverpool fans and shaped their attitude towards them.

The Heysel was a run-down, antiquated stadium and should never have been chosen for the final. But this in no way excuses what happened. Many of the Liverpool fans were very drunk, and security and policing were virtually non-existent. The fans inside could easily hand their tickets over the wire to those outside, while some just crawled under the fence.

The police, not anticipating violence, made no attempt to search spectators and took no notice of fans bringing more alcohol into the ground. Besides bottles, they also carried in sticks and iron bars.

The Liverpool fans were in the X and Y sections. The Z section was supposed to be neutral, but Juventus fans got in there. The corner of the Z terrace was a death-trap, with two adjacent walls at one end preventing a safe exit.

Following the by now traditional bout of taunts and insults, the Liverpool fans made their first charge at 6.30pm. As they charged from the X and Y sections into the Z section, eight policemen looked on. It was the third charge, at about 7pm, that was to prove the most deadly. Many of the Liverpool fans were using flagpoles and metal torn from safety barriers as weapons.

The police, in trying to control the situation, made matters worse. The Italian fans trying to escape were trapped by an old wall, which then collapsed, and in the panic Italian fans fell over each other and many were crushed to death.

By the time the horrific evening was over, 39 people had died – one more died later in hospital – and six hundred were injured. Among the dead, 33 were Juventus supporters and six were Belgians. Bodies were piled in two tents outside the stadium's main gates, and after the game supporters of both sides walked around looking for their friends among the dead and the wounded. Nobody from Liverpool was killed.

The result of the match was academic, but Juventus eventually triumphed 1–0 through a dubious penalty – neither team was told before the game that so many had died.

The next day Belgium banned English teams: a day later the FA took English clubs out of Europe. They did not return for five years – six, in Liverpool's case.

As for the Liverpool fans responsible; in April 1989, four years later, 14 of the 24 charged were found guilty and sentenced to three years, with half the term suspended, and fines of £1,000. They were given two weeks to appeal and in the end did not serve their sentences. The fans' argument was that it was all the fault of the Belgians and their rotten stadium and the rotten police.

Indeed, even as the dead bodies littered the Heysel stadium, senior Liverpool club officials were claiming that it was all the fault of the National Front. John Smith, the then-Liverpool chairman, claimed to have evidence of such infiltration. He said that he and Bob Paisley, the former Liverpool manager, had been confronted in the VIP area of the stadium by right-wing elements from England. Six members of the Chelsea National Front had boasted to him of their part in provoking the violence.

Paisley said he was forced to leave the directors' box at the start of the game as dozens of fans poured over the dividing wall, and that the person next to him claimed he was a Chelsea supporter and was wearing a National Front badge. A number of banners decorated with swastikas were recovered after the match, including one marked "Liverpool Edgehill". A banner with "England for the English" and "Europe for the English" was observed, and contingents of National Front were clearly seen in blocks X and Y. One party leaving Brussels main station consisted of Londoners wearing Liverpool colours, carrying Union flags and sporting National Front swastika tattoos.

Malcolm McDonald, a BBC producer and a Liverpool fan, recalls that he arrived at the stadium to find the approach littered with hundreds of posters from the National Front, making a very straightforward racist appeal to the Liverpool fans and blaming blacks for white unemployment.

The fact that there were National Front agitators at the Heysel should come as no surprise. The NF had long targeted football and Liverpool fans, coming from an area of high unemployment, were an obvious choice. The climate was right for the National Front to operate. However, Mr Justice Popplewell, who examined the evidence, did not conclude that the National Front was responsible for Heysel, and the whole tragedy illustrated how hooliganism had gripped English football and led to this black day.

Now for the intriguing question: did the city, the club or English football do anything to discourage this climate or in any way change it?

In the immediate aftermath of Heysel it seemed that the English game would be completely revolutionized. Mrs Thatcher called the soccer writers who had been at Heysel to No. 10 Downing Street to discuss the issue, and it was soon clear that the Government would impose ID cards, which everybody going to football would have to carry. Despite many objections – from inside and outside the game – Mrs Thatcher persisted, and it was only the much greater carnage of Hillsborough and Justice Taylor's report that finally slew this Thatcherite dragon.

Nevertheless, there was one immediate consequence of Heysel which remains with us to this day. The Liverpool fans in Heysel had been extraordinarily drunk – on this everyone is agreed – and drink was considered the main cause of hooliganism. So drink was banned from English football grounds or, rather more accurately, nobody was permitted to drink within sight of the pitch. This led to some rather comical arrangements for those who had executive boxes. In the Thatcherite yuppie Eighties these boxes had appeared on our football grounds for the purpose of providing their occupants an opportunity to eat and drink in great comfort – and in great quantity – while watching a football match. The boxholders could hardly go without their gin and tonics, and the ban meant that they had to be served in an anteroom – a place from where they could not see the pitch – and this could be done only when the game was not in progress.

The result was that at football grounds with boxes a new phenomenon emerged after Heysel: a crush in the allotted anteroom before the start of the match and a near stampede to get to the room and the drinks during half-time and at the end of the match.

Yet while drink may have played a part in Heysel, in 25 years of reporting I have never seen football crowds drink like the crowds during the Varsity match between Oxford and Cambridge at Twickenham. That is the nearest thing to a midwinter sporting Bacchanalia.

An hour before the kick-off, the car park at Twickenham is awash with wine, champagne and all kinds of spirits and drinks. Car boots seem to be stuffed full of bottles, which are produced throughout the match. I had long been accustomed to seeing foaming pints of bitter at cricket or football matches, but cricket or footballer supporters have never given me the impression that they go to the match with the object of getting drunk. At Twickenham, rugby supporters do. Bottles of wine are openly taken into the stand and drunk with an unrestrained enthusiasm.

The match is now so famous or notorious for drinking that the police have been known to set up breathalyser testing units outside the car park at Twickenham. confident of a rich haul. Yet, despite the incredible amount of drink, there is never any suggestion of hooliganism and there never has been any hint of trouble at these matches.

There are many explanations for this. The Tuesday in December when the Varsity match is played – and it's always a Tuesday – is the occasion for the brokers and other people in the City of London to travel down to Twickenham and use the excuse of a rather poor rugby match to relive their university days. There is also a big class factor: rugby supporters are middle-class, drink wine instead of beer, can handle their drink better and know how to behave at sporting occasions. Most football supporters, not having had the privileges of a public school education, cannot handle drink – or so the theory goes. Possibly so.

A more plausible explanation may be that when, back in 1974, there was the first hint of trouble, the rugby authorities took a very firm stand. Incidents at the end of the 1974 England vs. Wales international at Twickenham caused the Rugby Union to introduce measures to counter hooliganism in an attempt to stop their game being disfigured as much as football. They introduced closed-circuit radio to guide a team of crowd controllers specially recruited to help the police. It meant the end of a rather benevolent system of stewarding that had previously prevailed at the headquarters of rugby.

Football, on the other hand, mistook the symptom of drinking for the problem itself, and the eagerness with which drink has always been blamed for football's troubles shows how quickly football clutches at straws. And the way that foreigners and their inadequacies were blamed for Heysel and later Dublin indicates the other inevitable crutch for which English football always reaches when yet another bout of hooliganism makes for unwelcome headlines.

An unpublished book on Heysel written by two Liverpool-based authors came to the remarkable conclusion that everyone else was to blame for Heysel, but not the Liverpool fans.

The authorities in Brussels should have taken due notice and been warned by what took place in Rome in 1984.

The stadium was hopelessly inadequate as we have already stated and was the responsibility of the Brussels municipality who owned the ground.

The organization of the Belgian FA was hopeless as we have clearly indicated.

The supervision by the various police forces was pathetic.

And last, but by no means least, a great deal of responsibility lies with UEFA, whose representatives cleared the ground as fit for this European Cup Final.

It is perfectly true, as the Belgian Public Prosecutor said in his submission to the court, that if the defendants had not been on the terraces, no disaster might have occurred, but that is begging the question.

If all the authorities had done their job properly and the match been organized on a proper basis, it might not have prevented some fighting – which we hasten to say we would deplore in any event – but it would not have resulted in disaster.

But this has been the constant refrain not merely of Liverpool fans but all English football – don't blame English football. The excuses are many and varied: it's only a minority, and an unrepresentative minority, that causes problems; in any case it's society's problem, it's not a football problem; even if it is, it's not confined to England. Football hooliganism, so the apologists say, affects the whole world. And then there is the last excuse: it has all been got up by the press seeking to sell newspapers.

Such attitudes mean there is no attempt to address the peculiar atmosphere in English football grounds that those who watch English football day in and day out see as nothing odd, but leaves the outsider coming fresh to English football bewildered and confused.

The American writer Bill Buford is one such observer and has described his first encounter with the chant that resounds around English stadiums whenever a black player has the ball:

"The first time I heard the ape grunt – the barking sound that supporters make when a black player gets the ball – it was so foreign I couldn't figure out what it was. It was a deep, low rumbling, and I had trouble placing where it was coming from: from underneath the ground perhaps? That such a sound could be coming up from the ground was frightening. I thought: it's an earthquake, if only because that was the only sound – that low, bass drumming – that seemed to be comparable."

Buford eventually worked out who was making it. Later he took a friend visiting him from America to watch a match at Queen's Park Rangers. "The moment a black player touched the ball, the grunt started: uggh, uggh, uggh, uggh, uggh. My friend turned to me and said: 'What is that curious sound?'"

When Buford explained it was because a black player had the ball, "The looks that crossed my friend's face were so genuine and so unpremeditated – bewilderment, outrage, disgust, but mainly incomprehension: he couldn't understand it. The grunts continued: uggh, uggh, uggh, uggh, uggh. Both of us looked round. The grunt was coming not from a few lads but, it seemed, from everyone on the terraces – old, young, fathers, whole families. Everywhere we looked we saw the ugly faces of men grunting, sticking out their lower jaw in their crude imitations of apes…My friend's face was still fixed in an expression of intense incomprehension. I couldn't explain it. I was embarrassed to be living in this country. 'It's England,' I said."

Hostility towards black players is not the only evidence of this. There is the even older hostility to Jews, which I experienced at first hand in January 1991, the very night the Gulf War broke out and when Chelsea played Tottenham in a League Cup quarter-final.

I had been invited to Stamford Bridge as a guest of one of the pools companies, but owing to some mix-up, or negligence, found myself not in one of the chic executive boxes – as I had hoped and anticipated – but in the West Stand with the Chelsea supporters. The result was that the three of us, a PR man, a PR women and myself, sat amid the great mass of the Chelsea supporters for whom Tottenham and its supporters were not only the enemy but, worse still, the Yiddish enemy.

The match would have been bad enough for me; Chelsea so completely dominated

Tottenham that Spurs were lucky to escape with a 0–0 draw. But it was made much worse by the fact that every time a Tottenham player managed to get to the ball – which was not very often – the whole mass of Chelsea supporters bayed, "Kill the Yids!"

The only Tottenham player who looked remotely Yiddish was Vinny Samways – he is actually of Italian stock – and there was be the footballing equivalent of Nuremberg was probably right. I prayed that Spurs would not score, for I could not be sure of what my own reaction would be, and the thought of what might happen if I were suddenly to jump with joy at a Spurs goal did not bear thinking about.

However, thoughts about my own safety were overshadowed by the reaction of the PR

Heysel hooliganism: Belgian police launch a baton charge against Liverpool supporters.

nothing rational about the murderous shouts. But as the entire stand and the adjoining shed reverberated with such shouts through the night, and with the floodlights that dark, cold January night giving Stamford Bridge the sort of eerie quality to be seen in grainy 1950s movies, I began to think that Brian Glanville's remark that on such occasions Stamford Bridge can lady, who had clearly never experienced anything like it. She was so frightened and bewildered that she could not be consoled: not until we had hurried away from Stamford Bridge at the end of the match and retreated to a restaurant, some three miles away, and she was on her third glass of Chardonnay.

The anti-Jewish prejudice in English football is all the more important because this is a subject little discussed in English sport, even by Jews.

The Jewish support for Tottenham is well known, including the practice of waving the Star of David after Tottenham have scored a goal. However, Irving Scholar and his associates were the first Jews to get on the board in the 1980s. Before their arrival in the boardroom there was something like an unofficial apartheid: the supporters were mainly Jewish, the board was always gentile. Scholar himself had been subjected to horrific anti-Semitic abuse at Luton.

It had come in the wake of the nastiness that had crept into relations between the clubs following manager David Pleat's move from Luton to Tottenham in the summer of 1986. Scholar held David Evans, Luton's then-chairman, responsible for this. Evans had agreed to Pleat's move, negotiated a £100,000 compensation fee, then tried to prevent Pleat going by whipping up a press campaign against Tottenham. Pleat in Luton's eyes compounded matters by going back to the club and luring some players and coaches away: something which all managers do but which never fails to infuriate supporters. As a result, both Spurs–Luton matches had an unpleasant edge that season. When Spurs played at Luton a supporter walked past the directors' box and, looking Scholar in the eye, sang:

The yids are on their way to Auschwitz
Hitler is going to gas them again
No one can stop them
The yids are on the way to Auschwitz.

The song was a cruel anti-Semitic version of the one Spurs fans had sung when Tottenham had gone to Wembley to win the FA Cup in successive seasons, 1981 and 1982.

If Scholar was the first Jew in the Tottenham boardroom, then Pleat was the first Jew in the Tottenham dug-out, the first to be appointed its manager. But while anti-Semitism worried Scholar, Pleat was horrified by exuberant displays of Jewishness by supporters, notably when, in 1986–87, his only full season as Tottenham manager, Spurs supporters waved the Star of David after a goal – and Tottenham's performances that season meant they had plenty of opportunities. He even complained to Scholar, who tried to reassure him. Pleat was later to say, "I suppose Irving is middle-class, therefore does not mind. I found it disturbing."

In their different ways both Scholar and Pleat were trying to do the same thing: they just wished that any talk of Jews and how football reacts to them would simply go away.

To an extent they reflected English football as a whole, which never tried to tackle the roots of hooliganism, merely its manifestation. So it tried to contain violence at least within football grounds by fencing the ground. Away supporters were penned in a section like caged animals and not allowed out until the rest of the ground had emptied and the home supporters had left. A regular feature of matches would be an announcement just before the end of the match asking away supporters to remain in their caged area and wait for the home supporters to leave before police escorted them to their coaches or the railway station. English football was confident that such policing and security measures would curb what was described as a menace. In fact the very measures and the mentality that dictated it led, in April 1989, three years after Heysel, to the greatest tragedy ever seen in an English football ground.

Leading up to it there had been sporadic acts of hooliganism at various grounds. In the 1984–85 season Chelsea fans invaded the pitch after losing to Millwall in the FA Cup at Stamford Bridge. In 1988 there had been serious crowd trouble during the play-offs between Chelsea and Middlesbrough, which resulted in Chelsea being fined a record £75,000.

Hillsborough was different. The fans were blameless, but the measures to combat hooliganism and the thinking behind them made the disaster inevitable.

On a bright spring day, with clear skies and weather warm enough for T-shirts, 54,000 fans from Liverpool and Nottingham Forest travelled to Hillsborough, Sheffield, for an FA Cup semi-final. The Liverpool supporters were at the Leppings Lane end of the ground, the Forest fans at the other end, the East Terrace. Leppings Lane was the smaller end of the ground and it had a mere 23 turnstiles through which to filter just under 25,000 people, while at the other end there were 60 turnstiles to cater for just under 30,000 people.

The police had closed 12 turnstiles at the Leppings Lane end because they were close

The Violence in our Midst

to areas occupied by Forest fans and they feared a clash between Liverpool and Forest fans. The Sheffield club seemed to have assumed that each turnstile at the Leppings Lane end would filter through 1,450 people, when in most grounds they work on about 400 – and this, interestingly, is what the turnstiles at the other end were doing.

They also made the fatal assumption that people come through at regular intervals, whereas football crowds normally come in some numbers when the ground is first opened, after which the flow of spectators slows to a trickle before growing to a flood in the 15 minutes leading up to the start of the match.

The inevitable result was a crush. Thirty-five minutes before the match a crush had developed and a police officer tried unsuccessfully to open one of the outer gates to relieve the pressure. A police horse sowed panic, spectators had begun to scream, and children were being held above their parents' heads. Fans close to the edge of the crush climbed up on to the turnstiles, some jumping down into the area beyond.

Chief Superintendent David Duckenfield, who was in command of the 1,122 police officers at the ground, accepted that there was a difficulty but refused to delay the kick-off.

The terracing at the Leppings Lane end was soon showing signs of overcrowding. It was divided by iron railings into seven sections, but in the absence of any proper signs telling fans where to go, most of the fans converged on to the terrace and crowded into pens 3 and 4, leaving quite a bit of space in the other pens.

The overcrowding outside was even more terrible. Superintendent Roger Marshall asked if exit gates outside either side of the turnstiles could be opened. Duckenfield said no, fearing "drunken fans" or that those without tickets would get in. After more requests from Marshall, Duckenfield ordered the gates to be opened. The 2,000 fans who poured in also went into pens 3 and 4, doubling the numbers inside them.

By this time the game had kicked off. Forest won a corner. Two fans who had escaped the crush came on to the pitch and

Day of tragedy: the Hillsborough disaster forced a change in the policy of fencing in fans.

appealed to Bruce Grobbelaar, the Liverpool goalkeeper. He screamed at a policewoman to "open the fucking gates". Another supporter, known to the Liverpool player Steve McMahon, also came on to the pitch, shouting, "There are people dying."

At 3.06pm a policeman advised the referee to take the players off. They went to the players' lounge and watched the television pictures of the tragedy unfolding on the pitch and in the stadium, within yards of where they sat. They could see police still treating the situation as if it was a hooligan problem, with 150 officers lined up in front of the North Stand terrace to prevent fans from entering the playing area. The officers thought they were facing a possible pitch invasion. The fans attempting to pour on to the ground were just trying to find oxygen to breathe, and to get away from the deadly crush.

But by now television was already carrying pictures of the fans dying, perimeter advertising boards were being used as emergency stretchers and the gymnasium had been turned into a mortuary.

In the end 96 fans died, and the report by Lord Justice Taylor blamed the police for opening gate C but failing to close off the tunnel into pens 3 and 4, which he called "a blunder of the first magnitude". Taylor's final report also laid out a blueprint for safe, all-seat grounds.

However, the families of the bereaved have to this day failed to receive justice. In 1991 they were incensed when, after the longest hearing in British legal history, the Hillsborough inquest returned a verdict of accidental death.

After Labour came to power Jack Straw, the Home Secretary, set up a judicial review, but this found insufficient evidence to justify a new public inquiry. The families decided to pursue a private prosecution against retired police officers Chief Superintendent David Duckenfield and Superintendent Bernard Murray, which was given leave to proceed at Leeds Crown Court in August 1999.

Since then, investigations by *The Sunday Telegraph* have shown that policemen were forced to change their statements so as to try to avoid any blame.

The paper reported: "A detailed comparison by *The Sunday Telegraph* of the original written recollections and the altered statements shows that hundreds of sentences were removed or changed. In particular references critical of the South Yorkshire force and its senior officers policing the Sheffield ground, and comparisons with crowd control at the FA Cup semi-final at Hillsborough a year earlier, were deleted or altered. It was the amended statements which were presented to successive inquiries, including inquests in 1991 at which the jury returned verdicts of accidental death on the victims by a majority of nine to two." Ian Daines, Assistant Chief Constable of South Yorkshire Police, conceded that the amendments to statements, which were carried out on the advice of solicitors acting for the force, had been unwise. The amendments contributed to an erroneous myth that evidence had been suppressed.

By the early 1990s it did seem that the tragedy of Hillsborough was changing English football. The recommendations of the Taylor Report led to stadiums being remodelled, doing away with terracing and the traditional standing, and forced football authorities to accept that fans could not be treated like caged animals.

The police and clubs had also become extremely effective in treating the symptoms of crowd violence, even if doubts remained as to whether the underlying attitudes had been changed.

But the violence persisted.

During the 1992 match between Birmingham and Stoke at St Andrews, the pitch was invaded and the game was completed in an empty ground. Birmingham were fined £50,000 and forced to play two games behind closed doors.

Birmingham, of course, have the distinction of being one of the few clubs where Millwall fans, who normally dish out the violence, have found themselves on the receiving end.

In November 1995 Millwall substitute Dave Savage was punched by a Birmingham fan while warming up at St Andrews. Meanwhile fans from the two sides pelted each other with seats. After the game, the Millwall team coach was attacked by dozens of Birmingham fans and the inside showered in glass after several windows had been broken.

In 1995, two Millwall fans invaded the pitch and issued a death threat against Sheffield Wednesday goalkeeper Kevin Pressman. They were charged under the Football Offences Act and received a life ban from the club.

Pressman said that one fan had told him he would not get out of the ground alive, and the second remonstrated with the goalkeeper at the end of the game.

The previous September the club had also issued a life ban on a fan who had thrown a spanner during a match at Reading. The spanner had landed near the home goalkeeper Simon Sheppard.

Some two years before that Derby goalkeeper Martin Taylor had been assaulted and punched to the ground by Millwall fans in a First Division promotion play-off game. The penalty imposed on Millwall – considered inadequate by Taylor – was a suspended £100,000 fine coupled with the threat of having to play two games behind closed doors.

In 1998, hundreds of fans clashed with riot police after the club's 1–1 draw with Manchester City. Three dog handlers were injured, and the police described the scenes as the worst in years. The unrest off the pitch was partly provoked by a clash on the field which led to an 18-man brawl. After the match the violence continued outside, with the windows of cars and shops being smashed and 18 fans arrested.

Millwall fans, far from being repentant, merely made it a badge of honour, lustily singing, "Nobody likes us but we don't care."

Meanwhile, even as the spectre of violence in this country was being contained, whenever England played abroad the host country's riot police would get ready to deal with the English hordes and the trouble they knew they would cause.

In the summer of 1988 it was a grim European Championships on the pitch as England lost three matches, but the position was made even worse by the usual display of crowd hooliganism, with several hundred fans arrested. As a result, the Football Association withdrew the application from English clubs to return to European soccer.

In November 1993, when England failed to qualify for the 1994 World Cup in the United States after losing to Holland in Rotterdam, it was another shameful night for English fans. They terrorized ordinary decent Dutch people, caused hundreds of thousands to be spent on policing, and convinced the few remaining doubters that England fans are little more than thugs.

The scenes were bad enough for one senior British policeman to say they were some of the worst he had seen. It is hard to imagine how bad they would have been if the Dutch police had not taken unprecedented powers to round up groups of potential trouble-makers, including 1,200 English fans.

However, for all the violence and mayhem English fans had visited on foreign soil, none of the English matches had yet been abandoned. But that was exactly what English fans achieved in February 1995 as Terry Venables took his team to Dublin for his first overseas match, a friendly with the Republic of Ireland. The match was less than half an hour old when, with England trailing 1–0, a group of their supporters rioted. They tore up seats and, from their advantageous position in the upper tiers of the stands, started raining objects on the Irish fans below.

Ireland had just scored, and their fans were celebrating, but this soon turned to horror, as they became dartboards for the English. The Irish fans were forced to take shelter and the match was called off. It remains the one and only time an England international has been cancelled as a result of crowd violence. It soon emerged that the violence was orchestrated by a far-right group called Combat 18, which used football hooligans to spread its racist views. In this case its neo-Nazism was combined with its hatred of the IRA – "No surrender to the IRA" was a cry heard frequently during the Dublin match – and they proved a potent brew.

In Dublin, unlike Heysel, nobody was killed or even seriously injured – possibly the worst injury was that suffered by a *Daily Mirror* photographer whose nose was bitten by Vinnie Jones in a Dublin hotel. Yet both Heysel and Lansdowne Road, as well as providing wretchedly vivid exhibitions of English football hooliganism at work on foreign fields, provoked almost identical responses: at first there were general expressions of outrage and shock, then after a time the whole episode was forgotten.

Both incidents took place against a similar background. As television showed pictures of the violence, confused studio guests – mostly former footballing greats who were there to commentate on the game – tried to make sense of it and ended up expressing inarticulate shock, horror and outrage that the fair name of England had once again been besmirched by an unrepresentative minority.

The next day's papers carried articles

expressing a sense of guilt. The most eloquent of these came from Martin Samuel, then chief soccer writer of the *Sun*, who wrote:

Do not talk to me about being English today. I do not want to be English. I want to be a citizen of another country, any country. Tinpot African dictatorships, South American dictatorships, tiny European republics where the President goes to work on a bicycle.

I want to hand in my passport, renounce my nationality, hang my head in shame. Just do not ask me to associate with this scum. Do not ask me to share a flag or a common bond with the low-life who have shamed the nation at Dublin's Lansdowne Road. These bastards – I will not call them men, or anything normally associated with the merest scrap of dignity or self-respect – have left me sick to the stomach. As I sit here, I'm angry and confused and uncertain as to whether I want to watch another England international again...As Lansdowne Road cleared, a voice from the tannoy thanked the Irish fans for their impeccable behaviour, and the English around me applauded. How we wanted to swap nationalities, how we wanted to switch our passports and cite Dublin as a city of our birth. But there was no escape from the English last night. For the first time I'm ashamed of my accent. I do not want to open my mouth and reveal my guilty secret, but I will do for one last phrase: May those bastards rot in hell.

This was in the great tradition of English polemical writing: clear, direct, powerful. But readers barely had time to take it in before this sense of shame being displayed by the press was replaced by another, more enduring emotion: anger at the failure of the foreign authorities to police these events properly. Such anger surfaced within 24 hours of the Dublin riots, with Heysel it had taken a bit longer, but in both instances it was articulated with energy and conviction and provided a depressing insight into one variety of the English sporting mind.

By the time the Dublin riot took place, Euro 96, the first major football tournament in England since 1966 and the World Cup

National shame: England fans hurl debris from the stands in Dublin in February 1995.

victory, was little more than a year away, and there were fears that UEFA, the governing body for European football, might take Euro 96 away from England. However, following assurances from the FA that on English soil the English police knew how to control the fans, UEFA allowed Euro 96 to go ahead.

After reporting a decline in arrests related to the sport for the fourth year in a row, the police were able to claim that soccer hooliganism was on the wane, and their optimism about Euro 96 was justified. Far from ending in a violent debacle, it was for the most part good-natured. During the 31 matches at eight grounds there were only 1,148 arrests, mostly for drunkenness, ticket touting and disorderly or threatening behaviour. Much of the credit for this lay with the police, who had mounted pre-emptive strikes against known hooligans.

There was not one major incident at a ground, and the only serious trouble came after Germany's semi-final victory against England following a penalty shoot-out.

Then England supporters, most of whom had watched the game on television in pubs, ran amok in central London, attacking police, motorists and, for reasons of their own, the National Gallery. Elsewhere one Russian student, who had been mistaken for a German, was stabbed almost fatally in Sussex.

According to the police, the trouble in Trafalgar Square, where there was a crowd of about 2,000, was orchestrated by four of the most dangerous hooligan gangs. These gangs, from London, both north and south, whipped the crowd up into a violent frenzy, burning cars and encouraging assaults on the police. On the Wednesday, the police, who answered 2,500 emergency calls in the capital compared with the average for a Friday of 150, made 200 arrests.

The comparatively peaceful conduct of Euro 96 was achieved despite the best xenophobic intentions of the British tabloid press during the tournament. The only thing that excites them more than trying to destroy the England manager is the opportunity to be rude to foreigners. So the less subtle tabloids had a field day when it came to taking on the Spanish and Germans during the climax of Euro 96.

England played Spain in the quarter-final and then Germany in the semi-finals. Half a week of Spaniard-bashing was followed by some of the most repellent headlines even the British tabloids have been able to think up.

"Blitz Fritz" and "Filthy Hun" were accompanied by subtle digs at Chancellor Kohl – "the fattest and ugliest of all the Euro-politicians" – and the Germans – "they all wear stupid little leather shorts and daft hats".

But the *pièce de résistance* was a diatribe from the *Daily Mirror*, which likened the football match to the Second World War. Perhaps the only saving grace about this barrage of mockery and insult was that popular opinion came to its senses and, for the most part, English supporters told the press where to put its xenophobia.

As the World Cup in France approached in the summer of 1998 there were grave worries that English fans would cause trouble. France was easily accessible; the French, with their very different attitude to football, were planning to have giant screens in parks where people could watch – which to an English hooligan was an invitation to riot – while the availability of cheap booze and difficulty in obtaining tickets made for a hooligan cocktail.

And so it proved. Just before the World Cup there was indeed a riot, but this was caused by local French North Africans attacking Scottish travelling fans, who, in the two decades since their Wembley horrors of 1977, had so improved their behaviour that they were now among the most popular visitors: loud, boisterous, fun, but never any trouble. The attack by the North Africans caused the intervention of a hundred riot police wielding batons.

But then came the first of the England matches, against Tunisia in Marseilles, and the familiar refrain of England against the world on a foreign street. It began on the night before the match, when people in the old port area saw English fans attack Tunisian fans, burn the Tunisian flag, set cars alight and even attack pavement cafés as local people ran for safety. The police had to use tear-gas, and over 50 people, most of them English, were arrested. At least one petrol bomb was thrown, a number of people were beaten or stabbed, and several were seriously hurt.

On the day of the match, which England won, the French courts were quick to administer justice and gaoled three thugs, including one James Shayler, who had the cross of St George tattooed on his beer belly. Shayler, who was quickly dubbed the "suburban soccer thug", turned out to live in a £80,000 semi-detached home in

Wellingborough and always seemed to have money, although he had no regular employment.

As the English team travelled around France playing their group matches, visiting Toulouse and then Lens, so did the fans, spreading mayhem. Richard Pendlebury, of the *Daily Mail*, was in central Toulouse when hooligan trouble forced the French to use riot gas. As he struggled to recover, three English fans, total strangers, came to his assistance and could not have been more helpful to an Englishman in distress. Then they saw two Arab youths coming towards them. Immediately Pendlebury's friends turned into thugs, and one them landed a vicious punch on one of the Arabs, laying him out. As he lay there the other English thugs joined in, kicking him in the head. They only ran away when they saw a police van approaching, and as they ran they shouted, "Fucking black bastards!"

Pendlebury wrote, describing the mindset of the English football hooligan: "The hooligans are drawn together by a self-perceived patriotism which all too frequently manifests itself in ugly nationalism. The most popular chant among the more vociferous supporters was, 'Give me St George in my heart. Keep me English. Give me St George in my heart. Keep me English to my dying day. No surrender, no surrender to the IRA scum' which some altered to the more racist standpoint of imploring God to keep them 'white'. Frequently in response to perceived slights from the locals the chant went up, 'If it wasn't for the English, you'd be Krauts.'"

By the time the English fans went to Lens for the last qualifying match, against Colombia, the World Cup had seen even more shocking football violence, this time from the

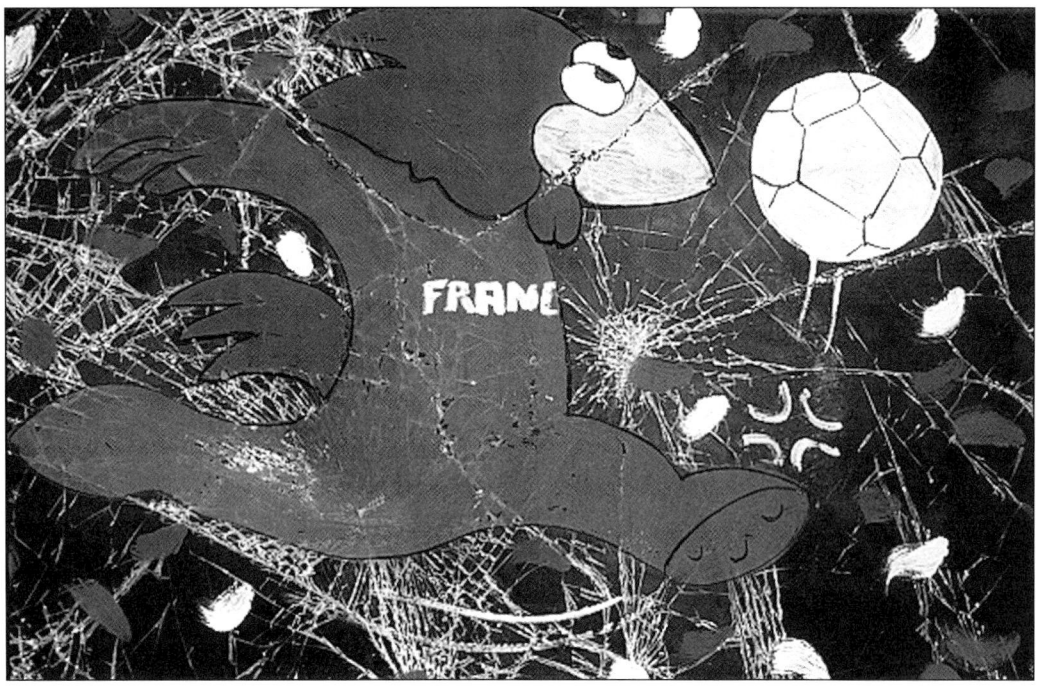

Hooligans' calling card: a window is smashed in Marseilles before England's first World Cup match in 1998.

German hooligans. When Germany played Yugoslavia, German hooligans, organized in military-style neo-Nazi gangs and driven more by political activism and the thrill of the fight than by drink – which is not seen as the driving force with the Germans – had displayed their evil face. They had so viciously beaten a gendarme, Daniel Nivel, a father of two, that he was in a coma. He was to survive, but was left with permanent injuries. In all, 93 fans were arrested, and for a time the Germans came close to pulling out of the World Cup in mortification.

For the visit of the English to Lens, a little

town whose population of 35,000 would double by match day, the French banned drinks for 70 miles around. Shops, restaurants and hypermarkets were ordered not to sell drinks to the thousands of English fans as they arrived for the match. Lens feared there would be another Agincourt, that bloody battle having been fought not far away. If Lens 1998 did not prove to be quite another Agincourt, it was still a bloody night.

But worse was to come.

On the night that England went out to Argentina in the second round, on penalties, an English fan named Paul Birch stabbed to death Eric Faschet, a Frenchman. This was the only fatality of the World Cup and Birch was gaoled.

However, it showed up the very different attitudes of the German and English authorities.

Unlike the German Football Federation, which supported the family of the policeman Nivel, beaten into a coma by German thugs, and the government which tracked down the four responsible and gaoled them, both the FA and the British government tried to distance themselves from Birch.

The British and the French tried to present the killing as the work of a deranged individual and not in any way related to football.

But in January 1999 Jeff Powell revealed in the *Daily Mail* the existence of a letter from Birch to Faschet's half-sister, which showed that Birch was in France solely as an England supporter. Rejecting the official line, Powell wrote: "Birch's handwritten apology to Miss Virginie Lentin, which also implicated the English National Front hooligans who were the ugly core of World Cup rioting in Marseilles, reveals that callous stance as nothing less than a national scandal."

As always, many pious statements were made after the World Cup about how this would never be allowed to happen again. Two months after the World Cup they were shown to be worthless when, as England lost to Sweden in Stockholm in the first of their qualifying matches for Euro 2000, English fans rioted, smashing plate-glass windows at the back of a stand and hurling objects including chairs, metal beer barrels and even a hot-dog stand on to the car park 80 feet below, a few yards from where Swedish fans were leaving the stadium. One of the English fans, Cameron Calhoun, had been in France and was known to the police, but had still made his way freely to Stockholm, where he urged English fans to attack the police and himself threw a coffee machine through a window.

The FA were eventually fined for the fans' behaviour. By then the government had recognized that the legislation was not tough enough and they supported a private member's bill which strengthened many of the measures which it was hoped would allow the police to stop the hooligan before he left these shores.

All this showed that English football could never relax and think it had beaten the hooligan. A bit of that mentality seems to be part of the make-up of most fans, as was demonstrated on 31 January 1998 when Portsmouth played Sheffield United at Fratton Park. Linesman Edward Martin had just been consulted by referee Mark Halsey as to whether United goalkeeper Simon Tracey should be sent off for his foul on Portsmouth midfielder Sammy Igoe. After the consultation Halsey decided to show Tracey the red card. Martin remembers being aware of some unrest in the crowd behind him, and the goalkeeper taking off his jersey – after which the next thing he remembers is waking up on a stretcher and being taken to an ambulance.

The reason was that a Sheffield United supporter named John Corker had run on to the pitch and punched him. Martin spent a night in Portsmouth's Queen Alexandra Hospital, and it was clear that Corker would have to be severely punished both by football and by the law.

Portsmouth magistrates found him guilty of assault with actual bodily harm, he was gaoled for three months and United banned him from attending any matches at Bramall Lane for life.

Corker's act was more like the ones that by now had become quite common on the continent, where the English disease of hooliganism appeared to have taken firm root. It has manifested itself in various unsavoury ways.

In October 1998, Dino Baggio, while playing for Parma against Wisla Krakow in Poland, was hit by on the head by a knife. He had five stitches in a head wound after the match. A 16-year-old Parma fan was also stabbed in a scuffle.

Towards the end of the 1998–99 season there was violence in the UEFA Cup semi-final between Bologna and Marseille.

Then, when Feyenoord won the Dutch championships, 250,000 supporters took to the streets of Rotterdam and, while the majority of fans were peaceful, a small hard core turned violent. Roaming gangs hurled bottles and stones, smashed dozens of shop windows, wrecked cars and looted shops, causing a total bill for damage estimated at £3m. At one point the Hilton Hotel was attacked and guests in the lobby dived to the floor as plate-glass windows shattered. It was suggested the hooligans had co-ordinated their attacks using mobile phones, and their actions surprized most of the Feyenoord supporters.

The police initially used water cannon. Then six policemen found themselves under attack by hundreds of youths and were forced to take out their guns and open fire, which led to four people being taken to hospital with gunshot wounds. One victim was hit in the stomach, another was shot in the neck, and two received leg wounds. There was a suspicion that the mobs had fired back at the police, support for which came from the fact that bullet holes were found in a window of the Hilton Hotel.

The Rotterdam police spokesman Ger de Jongh stated, "A small group of policemen were suddenly attacked by between 75 to 150 hooligans. They were in the street with thousands of other people about, but there was no way they could escape. They were cornered and they followed the procedure which is laid down when police feel their lives are in danger."

Just a few days earlier Moroccan fans had done damage in Rotterdam after their team had played Holland in Arnhem. Some of their fans had stolen money from a petrol station and then, as the match went on, more than 100 of them had invaded the pitch.

These incidents in Holland darkened the national mood and raised fears about potential violence when Holland, along with Belgium, will co-host Euro 2000. Violence between Feyenoord and their bitter enemies Ajax has been a feature of Dutch football for some time, and in recent years it has acquired a very ugly anti-Semitic overtone. Two years ago an Ajax fan named Carlo Picpornie was beaten to death by Feyenoord thugs with knives, bicycle chains and hammers.

Ajax fans identify themselves with the Jews and sing, "We are Superjews". Also, to the tune of "Tulips from Amsterdam", they sing "What my heart can't say, say bombs on Rotterdam" – a reference to the Luftwaffe's bombing of the city in May 1940.

Feyenoord fans sing songs praising Hitler, Josef Mengele and the Palestinian group Hamas.

Of the Rotterdam shooting incident, Dutch Interior Minister Bram Peper, a former Mayor of Rotterdam, said: "I've never seen anything so terrible. It's frightening to see the police harassed like that and forced to take out arms. When that happens the world has turned upside down."

The soccer world has often threatened to turn upside down on the continent, particularly in Italy where, after England, soccer violence has been most prevalent. But whereas English administrators and coaches at least always condemn it, in Naples, after fans reacted violently following a 4–0 home defeat by Parma, the then-Napoli coach Giovanni Galeone is reported to have said, "I can understand their anger. The fans who care behave like a lover who has been betrayed. When that happens, people insult each other and it can lead to shooting or stabbing."

Some of the acts of fan violence in Italy and elsewhere can be marked with humour.

In February 1997, following a 0–0 draw against Parma, the Reggiana fans, angered by the way their team was playing, hurled metal pipes into the Parma keeper's goalmouth. Not long after this the former Italian national coach Arrigo Sacchi, managing AC Milan, had a sack of rubbish hurled at him when he went with his team to Naples but just managed to avoid being hit.

Had Sacchi been hit by the rubbish he could hardly have been expected to see the funny side of things. Nor were Udinese fans being very witty when in December 1996 they threw snowballs after Verona scored a winning goal in injury time. The Vicenza fans who threw coins were being malicious, for they injured a referee and his assistant.

Just as English football hooligans have their own specialized gangs, the Italians have their Ultras, die-hard fans who are capable of extreme violence.

Ultra violence can take many forms, including racism. When Verona signed Marc Ferrier, the black Dutch national team player, Verona fans cut out a cardboard figure of a black player in a Verona kit and hanged him on a gallows.

In February 1998, when Verona and

Salernitana's Ultras clashed, the game had to be stopped for several minutes and police with tear-gas were required to restore order.

A Lazio fan was accidentally killed during a Roma–Lazio match when a flare fired by Roma Ultras hit him. But when Milan Ultras knifed a fan to death outside Genoa's stadium, Italy was so shocked that the following weekend all sporting fixtures were suspended.

The fans in South America, especially in Brazil, have been fortunate enough to enjoy some of the greatest football ever played. Indeed their passion for soccer helps to produce the glorious football that is Pele's "beautiful game". Like any passion, however, it also has its dark side. This is when it becomes violent – so violent that it cannot be controlled.

In March 1997, when the Rio de Janeiro club Flamengo were having a bad run, their coach Paulo Autuori offered to resign but was persuaded to stay. However, when Flamengo lost again the fans invaded the pitch and threw wooden sticks at the players. Then they shot up the club's headquarters and one fan threw a grenade into the trophy-room.

When, again in Rio, Botafogo drew with Parana, thus damaging their chances of winning the championship, it was not merely the fans who wanted to take it out on the referee – the directors did too. The match referee Dias Lima had to lock himself in the dressing-room to escape the angry Botafogo directors. He was only able to leave an hour later under police escort, and then had to run the gauntlet of beer cans. The police drove him straight to the airport for a quick getaway from Rio de Janeiro.

The referee is not the only person on whom Brazilian fans are liable to vent their anger. In 1996, when Guarani were struggling against relegation, the goalkeeper Pitarelli was stoned by supporters as he drove home from a match, and required medical attention. His team-mate Ailton was unable to go outside for a week as angry fans surrounded his home. Ailton was philosophical about it: "I don't like to go outside as I don't know what will happen to me."

Fans could argue that the behaviour of players hardly provides them with the right role model to emulate. One of the worst examples of player misbehaviour was the extremely cynical use, by the Chilean goalie Roberto Rojas, of fake crowd violence.

In a World Cup qualifying match in 1989, with Chile losing 1–0 to Brazil, a scoreline that would have eliminated Chile, Rojas was carried off after having apparently been struck by a flare. An inquiry showed that he had deliberately cut himself and, what is more, that he had the assistance of the Chilean manager, physio and team doctors. Chile were disqualified and Rojas and his accomplices banned.

In Latin America violence in the stadiums has led to tragedies that dwarf anything seen in Europe. In 1964 a disallowed goal in the match between Peru and Argentina in Lima led to crowd riots, which culminated in the worst-ever soccer disaster, with 318 people killed and 500 injured, most of them trampled in a stampede.

Latin America also provides the ultimate soccer violence story, the one that astonished the world back in 1969, when a series of matches led to war between two central American republics.

On 7 June 1969, the El Salvador team arrived in Tegucigalpa, the Honduran capital, for a World Cup play-off to decide who would qualify for the 1970 World Cup Finals in Mexico. The night before the match the Honduran fans laid siege to the Salvadorian team's hotel, honking their car horns, throwing stones at the windows and banging on drums. They also set off firecrackers and whistled and screamed all night. In the match El Salvador managed to hold out until the last minute, when Honduras scored through Roberto Cardona. In El Salvador the grief was so great that one 18-year-old girl, Amelia Bolanios, who had been watching the match on television, shot herself in the heart in front of her father, just after the final whistle.

A week later the Honduran team arrived in San Salvador. This time it was the turn of the El Salvador fans, who surrounded the Hondurans' hotel, throwing rotten eggs and dead rats and breaking windows. The team were driven to the stadium in armoured cars. The army surrounded the ground, and before the match the Honduran flag was ceremonially burned. El Salvador won 3–0 and the Honduran coach expressed relief that his team had lost. The consequences if they had won would have been unimaginable.

With a police escort the team got back safely, but the Honduran fans were attacked, hundreds were injured and two killed. More than 150 Honduran cars were burnt, and within hours the border between the two countries had been closed.

Just before the third and deciding match El Salvador broke off diplomatic relations and the match was played in Mexico City. Mexico drafted in 5,000 policemen to control the situation. This time El Salvador won 3–2 and qualified for the World Cup.

Two weeks later El Salvador invaded Honduras. Relations between the two countries had been potentially explosive owing to many land disputes, and the football matches provided the spark. Fighting raged for four days, Honduran bombers attacked Salvadorian oil refineries, and it required the intervention of the Organization of American States to negotiate a cease-fire.

By then more than 3,000 people had been killed and over 100,000 made homeless. In the 1970 World Cup, as it happens, El Salvador made no impression.

Almost 25 years later, a match took place in Zagreb, which showed that Latin America was not the only part of the world where soccer violence can be a prelude to military action. This was the cup match on 13 May 1990 between Dinamo Zagreb, a Croatian team, and Red Star Belgrade, a Serb team. With the state of Yugoslavia threatening to come apart, this quickly became a highly symbolic contest between the Serb and Croat nations.

Even before the match started there was a riot, in which the hatred between Serbs and Croats was clear. Red Star fans fought Dinamo fans, and the mainly Croat police joined in, which only incensed the Red Star players, who attacked the police. This clash between players and police can be seen as the first battle in the latest of the region's bitter conflicts. Within days of the match the Yugoslavian Football League was abolished, and within hours the real war had started.

Cricket

On the face of it cricket seems a peaceful game, incapable of arousing violence. However, its history has included numerous outbreaks of violence, not only in its early years in England when the game was developing in the eighteenth and nineteenth centuries, but also in more recent years, mainly in other parts of the world.

Back in 1884 a crowd at the Oval turned violent. The visiting Australians led by W.L. Murdoch were on the verge of victory against Surrey, needing just 11 runs to win, when two o'clock came. Instead of carrying on to a finish the players came off for lunch, which angered the crowd. When the bell sounded at 2.30pm for resumption of play, the crowd invaded the field and uprooted the stumps. The Australian players had to explain that they had stopped not in order to get more gate money from people coming in after lunch but to prevent the caterers from suffering a heavy loss.

Surrey officials asked Yorkshireman Edmund Peate to help calm the fans, but he declined, saying, "Naw, sir. Ah didn't coom 'ere t'quell riot; ah coom to play cricket."

It was only after the police arrived and cleared the ground that play resumed and the Australians won the match.

In the past two decades there have been two major disturbances at Test matches in England, one of which ruined what would probably have been a great finish. In August 1973, on the Saturday of the Third Test against the West Indies, the ground was evacuated as a result of a bomb threat, but of the 89 minutes lost an hour was made up and England lost by an innings.

Two years later, in August 1975, the last day's play at Headingley was abandoned after vandals campaigning for the release of a convicted criminal sabotaged the Rugby Ground end of the pitch with knives and oil. The day had promised interesting cricket, with Australia requiring 225 to win and England a further seven wickets.

Since then no Test match in England has been affected, although Headingley has caused other problems. As the drink takes its toll, late afternoons and early evenings at cricket matches there can become at best noisy and at worst violent. The Yorkshire cricket authorities responded in 1996 by banning alcohol on the notorious western terrace. Recent international matches had been marred by foul and abusive language, and they announced that anyone indulging in obscene chanting or racial abuse would be ejected. Yorkshire has also removed 3,000 seats to make it easier to deal with hooligans.

Lord's is normally a haven of decorous behaviour. However, the Centenary Test in 1980, which should have been a joyful celebration of 100 years of Anglo-Australian cricketing rivalry, showed the rather more modern phenomenon of hooliganism, albeit of the cricketing variety. On the Saturday of the rain-affected Test, MCC members, angered by five pitch inspections, jostled umpire David Constant in the Long Room. Police were required to escort the umpires back through the Long Room to the pitch and the MCC apologized for the behaviour of its members.

The most explosive Test series ever played was the bodyline series of 1932–33, when the decision of the English captain Douglas Jardine to use leg theory bowling – short-pitched balls delivered to a packed leg-side field – so incensed the Australians that it nearly ended Test cricket between England and Australia. In the Third Test at Adelaide two Australian batsmen, Bert Woodfull and Bill Oldfield, were hit and the crowd got very angry. However, although the English players – Jardine in particular – were mercilessly booed and for a time it even seemed, as cables flew between Australia and England, that diplomatic relations might be strained, there was no crowd violence. Had somebody jumped over the fence at Adelaide then, it might well have sparked a riot, but nobody did and the anger of the Australians was contained.

The one occasion when a riot did ensue on an Australian ground was also during an Ashes series, at Sydney in February 1971. England won the Ashes through the pace bowling of John Snow, but his bouncers to the Australian batsmen did not go down well with the crowd. Bouncers bowled at Terry Jenner, a tail-ender, led to a sharp exchange between Ray Illingworth, the England captain, and Lou Rowan, the Australian umpire. Irate fans started throwing beer cans, and when Snow walked back to the boundary a man in an orange shirt and a white towel hat grabbed his shirt and pulled him against the pickets. The man was drunk, and other spectators had to drag him away from Snow. Then, as Snow turned to face the cricket, more beer cans landed near him, one of them near his right boot. Soon bottles were raining in, some of them flying past the heads of Snow and Illingworth and, concerned about his players' safety, Illingworth took them off the field. Rowan threatened to forfeit the match in

Vandals stop play: the 1975 Test at Headingley fell victim to the "Free George Davis" campaign.

favour of Australia, but eventually the ground was cleared and England claimed a great victory.

The man in the orange shirt melted away in the confusion and remained undetected until February 1999, when a book about the Sydney Cricket Ground unearthed his identity. Now an 80-year-old pensioner, he wanted to apologize to Snow, who as it happened was in Australia on behalf of his sports travel business, promoting the Ashes tour of Australia.

There has been more persistent violence on the Indian subcontinent and in the West Indies.

In Pakistan in the 1960s and 70s two successive series against England were severely disrupted by crowd violence. In February 1969, with the country sliding towards chaos – it was eventually to lose its eastern wing, which became the independent country of Bangladesh – there were numerous crowd interruptions in the First Test at Lahore, led by students who were making a political point. The Third Test at Karachi was abandoned shortly before lunch on the third day. A mob several hundred strong stormed across the field of play carrying banners, and Alan Knott, who was then on 96 not out, had to abandon any hopes of making his first Test century.

The only riot-free Test on the tour was the Second Test at Dacca, where the students, then emerging as a powerful force – they were to play a major part in the creation of Bangladesh – policed the ground and made sure there was no trouble.

In December 1997, the Lahore Test between England and Pakistan was disrupted by two serious crowd disturbances, again reflecting the explosive situation developing in the country.

Through the 1950s and '60s every English tour of the West Indies led to some crowd violence. The West Indies were then seeking independence from Britain, and on the cricket field they were trying to overcome the racial prejudice of the West Indian cricket establishment, which at that time would still not allow a black player, however gifted, to be captain.

In January 1954, during the First Test in Jamaica between England and the West Indies, umpire Burke's wife and son were threatened after he gave the local man, Holt, run out six runs short of his century on his first Test appearance, though his team went on to win. In the Third Test at Georgetown, Guyana, Holt was again involved. He and the tail-ender McWatt were trying to rescue the West Indies when McWatt was run out. This led to a riot, with the crowd hurling missiles and bottles on to the field of play. But the Test continued and England won.

In January 1960, the Second Test at Port of Spain contained a more serious riot when a local player called Singh was given run out on the third day. Again the West Indies were struggling on the field, and the decision did not please a crowd of 30,000 – the highest ever in the Caribbean. The rioting and bottle-throwing were so serious that the day's play ended prematurely; but this did not prevent an England victory.

It was also in the 1960s that cricket violence manifested itself in India. On New Year's Day 1967 there was a terrible riot in Calcutta's Eden Gardens. But the causes had nothing to do with the cricket – the day's play had not even started – and everything to do with the greed and incompetence of the local Bengali cricket officials.

Cricket was now an extremely popular and profitable sport. But in trying to make more money, the authorities sold far too many tickets. Some of the tickets were forgeries, the ticket distribution system deliberately creating artificial shortages, encouraging black market sales and inflated prices.

Eden Gardens then had a capacity of 50,000, and decent facilities for less than half that number. Yet 70,000 people crowded in. The first day's play in the Test between India and the West Indies had already seen some crowd problems.

New Year's Day produced a full-scale riot. The players had taken the field but, with the spectators unable to find places in the stands, the crowd spilled on to the grass and the Calcutta police, always keen to flex their muscles, waded in with *lathis* – short, wooden batons. With the police clubbing them, the spectators retaliated with bricks, and the police came back with tear-gas.

The battle between the crowd and the police had been stoked by a whole host of issues, few of which had anything to do with cricket. Calcutta was then in its Maoist phase of left-wing politics, and the mixture of official incompetence, police heavy-handedness and a certain militant Maoist philosophy was combustible. On such occasions the crowd can be overwhelming, and on that New Year's morning they

Scoreboard problems: Crowd disruption at Georgetown, Guyana in April 1999.

overcame the police, invaded the whole ground, dug up the pitch and set fire to the stands.

The players fled, the West Indians fearing for their lives. In fact the crowd meant them no harm, but were after their own officials, some of whom took shelter with the Indian players, pleading with them for protection from the fury of the mob. A commission of inquiry eventually found the officials guilty. The West Indians were so traumatized that they wanted to withdraw from the Test series and fly home. But they were persuaded to carry on with the tour, and as it happened the Indians, caught on a wicket badly damaged by the rioters, were easily beaten.

No one died on New Year's Day 1967, but lives were lost two years later in a Test against Australia in the same city. On the morning of the fourth day, as 20,000 people waited patiently for their tickets, a rumour went round that there were no more seats. In the riot this caused, six people were killed and more than 100 injured. When play did eventually start the Indian batting collapsed, setting off another short riot which held up play for 15 minutes.

Later that day the Australian captain Bill Lawry clashed with an Indian photographer, who was knocked to the ground and claimed he had been hit with a bat, while Lawry insisted he had just pushed him away with his open palm.

Calcutta was to mend its ways and build a floodlit stadium which houses 100,000 and is probably the grandest cricket stadium in the world. However, in recent years crowd violence has come back to haunt the city. In 1996, as India unexpectedly lost a semi-final of the World Cup to Sri Lanka, the crowd rioted and the match was awarded to Sri Lanka, who were on the verge of winning in any case.

In February 1999, as Pakistan visited India for the first time since 1987, the unfortunate running-out of Sachin Tendulkar, when India were seeking victory, provoked a riot which held up play. The next day, as India slid to inevitable defeat, there was another riot. These incidents raised doubts about whether the world's greatest cricket ground deserved to host international matches.

Similar questions were asked about the West Indies in April 1999 when, in a matter of days, violence erupted again at two cricket grounds. It was no surprize that Georgetown, Guyana, was one of them. In 1972 a Test against New Zealand had been interrupted for 20 minutes by bottle-throwing when the crowd were incensed by the running-out of local hero Clive Lloyd. In April 1978 the Fifth Test against Australia in Jamaica had to be abandoned as a draw when, with the West Indies on 258 for 8, chasing 368, the dismissal of the No. 9 batsman sparked a riot. Another 38 balls of the mandatory 20 overs in the last hour remained to be bowled, but could not be. The West Indian authorities hoped that the match could be extended to a sixth day, but one umpire refused to help out and the Test was abandoned.

Now, on 21 April 1999, as the one-day international between the West Indies and Australia at Georgetown neared its close, the crowd invaded the pitch. An error on the scoreboard had made them think that the match was over and that the West Indies had won. But one over still remained to be bowled, and the ground was cleared, with Australia needing six runs to win with three wickets in hand. As the last ball was bowled Australia needed four to win and three to tie. Waugh hit the ball towards the boundary and he and his partner completed two runs. By this time the crowd had started invading and, as the Australians went for the third run, the crowd were in the middle of the wicket uprooting the stumps. After some consultation the referee Raman Subba Row declared the match a tie on the basis that the batsmen were turning to complete the third run and there were no stumps in the ground by which they could have been run out. Coincidentally, this was the same decision he had made on the same ground six years earlier, when in similar circumstances, and with the series standing 2–2, he declared a tie between West Indies and Pakistan.

A few days later in Barbados, after the West Indian batsman Sherwin Campbell collided with the Australian bowler Brendon Julian as he went for a single and was run out – shades of Sachin Tendulkar in Calcutta – the crowd rioted. The Australian captain Steve Waugh and his team-mates felt it was an accident and the umpire and match referee were satisfied, although Clive Lloyd, the West Indian manager, implied that Julian had acted wilfully. The crowd certainly seemed to think so. Bottles rained down, one of which narrowly missed Steve Waugh. For 45 minutes the riot raged, and although attempts were made to calm them, they kept throwing bottles and singing, "Bring back, bring back my Campbell to me".

Waugh had two options. He could either recall Campbell or not lead his team back on, in which case the game would be called off. He agreed to call Campbell back and the West Indians, chasing a revised target, went on to win. Waugh made it very clear that he had taken his decision because he feared for his own and his team's safety, saying, "We decided that going back is better than getting killed on the way home." His comments suggested that the police could not guarantee law and order, and this did not go down well with the island authorities. The local police chief sued Waugh, and the Australian team required diplomatic assistance to leave Barbados.

Dennis Lillee called on the international cricket authorities to take action, saying, "The ICC can count itself lucky it doesn't have blood on its hands."

Steve Waugh knew how lucky they were. As the mob stormed on to the field at Georgetown his mind had gone back to what had happened to Monica Seles and how a madman with a knife had changed the course of her tennis career.

Tennis

At the age of 19, Monica Seles was at the peak of her powers, the best woman tennis player in the world.

At a Hamburg tennis tournament in 1993, however, her world was destroyed when a spectator stabbed her as she rested between games.

The spectator, Gunther Parsche, lunged at her from the crowd, inflicting a single stab wound, one to two centimetres deep, between the shoulders.

Seles ran to the middle of the court before collapsing. Looking woozy but still conscious, she was comforted as she sat there, her face contorted with pain.

Her assailant Parsche, a 38-year-old East German, was wrestled to the ground by security guards.

Initial press reports suggested Parsche had attacked Seles to reduce the chances of her beating the German player Steffi Graf, with whom he was alleged to be infatuated.

However, Seles had also been a target of abuse because of the barbaric behaviour of the Serbian government in former Yugoslavia during the previous two years. The previous year a bomb threat had been received at the house where she was staying the night before the Wimbledon final – a factor that she claimed had contributed to her defeat.

It was a tragic end to a period of two and a half years in which Seles, despite being widely criticized for grunting after every shot in a way many opponents claimed was off-putting, had ruled the tennis world, winning seven grand slam tournaments in just 13 attempts. On her return to the game two years later, she was never as compelling or successful again.

Ice Skating

Tonya Harding shot to infamy just before the Winter Games in Lillehammer in January 1994 in circumstances which revealed that underneath the glitter of ice skating with beautiful bodies performing incredible feats on ice to the accompaniment of classical music there lurked some of the deadliest and most primitive of struggles.

Harding was the darling of the US figure skating world when in January 1994 won the US Ladies Figure Skating Championships. But even as she was winning she was involved in actions which showed the darkest side of sport. Jeff Gillooly, her ex-husband, and two of his associates were involved in an attack on Harding's greatest rival Nancy Kerrigan. On 6 January, as Kerrigan practised for the US championships in Detroit, she was clubbed about the knee with a metal bar. Gillooly and his accomplices were later jailed for their roles in the attack.

Harding was implicated in the attack by Gillooly, but at first denied any involvement. The Winter Games was about to start and for a time it seemed the US Olympic Committee might stop her skating there, but Harding filed a £25 million law suit and just a week before the Games began the USOC cleared her to compete despite police investigation into her role in the affair. Meanwhile a television station in Portland, Oregon, her homestate, reported that she had failed two out of three lie detector tests when asked about her involvement in the attack.

Kerrigan and Harding both took part in the Winter Games and the whole episode was so bizarre that they quite dominated the coverage of the Games. Normally ice skating is for the aficionado, now it made front page news with hundreds of media people crowding into press conferences to question Kerrigan and Harding. There was a media scrum when the two practised on the ice for the first time since Kerrigan had been attacked.

At Lillehammer Kerrigan won silver while Harding was involved in a farcical false start. As her name was announced she failed to appear and the camera shots on the television display showed confused movement behind the large blue curtain. The announcer then gave her two minutes to appear. Then with 20 seconds left she came into view bent double and tying up her lace. She started skating but it lasted only 20 seconds and included one abortive attempt at the triple lutz. She stopped and wavered and seemed to be crying. She then skated over to the referee and then returned to the ringside where she shouted to her coach Diane Rawlinson to re-tie her boots. It turned out she had broken a lace in her skating shoe. She did skate at the end of the group and finished eight.

The following month, back in America, she admitted to help cover up the crime committed by her ex-husband and his associates was fined $100,000 and ordered to perform community service. The US Figure Skating Association then decided to strip her of her title saying, "Miss Harding's actions as they related to the assault on Nancy Kerrigan evidence a clear disregard for fairness, good sportsmanship and ethical behaviour."

Harding said she was disappointed but not surprised. However, in the following year Harding underwent what American writers called a Nixonesque rehabilitation, confirming that Americans always love a bad guy or in this case a bad gal. Esquire magazine named her as one of the women Americans love, while People magazine identified her as one of the year's 25 most intriguing personalities. She appeared on television playing Santa's wife in an ice show and was shown taking meals to the snow-bound. She also played a waitress in a film, and a year after being the villain of the piece it was Harding rather than Kerrigan, the victim of the original attack, who won popular acclaim, demonstrating yet again that in America infamy is often perversely fashionable.

O.J. Simpson

The Juice Turns Sour

The story of O.J. Simpson is the classic story of the American hero turned to tragedy: a hero made by sport, given his status in life by his achievement on the sports field, but then brought down by forces that were shaped well beyond sport's boundaries.

The rise of Simpson to the status of an American hero is a testimony to the power of sport. It was his athletic prowess as an American footballer that propelled him from poverty, helped him overcome rickets and allowed him to attain the American dream.

Born in a poor family in San Francisco's Potrero Hill neighbourhood, he was called Pencil Legs because of his skinny calves and pigeon-toed gait that resulted from rickets, a calcium deficiency.

Then he found American football. It began in the little-known City College of San Francisco, where he had to wear a special white helmet because his head was too big for his team's red ones. But such was his ability and performance as a running back that he transferred to the University of Southern California, where he twice helped his team reach the Rose Bowl. He also won a Heisman Trophy as the top collegiate football player.

Soon nicknamed the Juice because of the initials of his name, Orenthal James Simpson, he became one of the greatest running backs of the National Football League and broke many records. He was the first back to gain 2,000 yards in a season. He finished his 11-year career in his native San Francisco, playing for the 49ers, with a total of 11,236 yards – the second best in league history. In 1985 he was inducted into the NFL Hall of Fame.

By then he was the all-American hero, but with one important difference. In the past such heroes had been blond and blue-eyed, but Simpson was black, suggesting that he had broken through the colour barrier. He was used in advertizements to promote Hertz cars, in which he was shown running and hurdling over barriers, to prove Hertz's ability to meet their clients' needs. He played golf with Presidents, including Bill Clinton, and he had that ultimate status symbol, a stunning blonde wife. In a still very race-conscious American society, there could be no more powerful statement of how far and how fast Simpson, a child of the ghetto, had come.

As Simpson was growing up he would say, "One of these days you are going to read about me", and his sister would reply, "In the police record." As Simpson became one of the most sought-after celebrities in America this became a joke in the Simpson household.

Film director Michael Winner described meeting Simpson in 1977: "He was a black man who presented no threat to the whites. He was ever-jolly, he was a sports star, already a bit on the wane, but with a place so firmly in American hearts it could never be erased. He took me to lunch in a restaurant with photos of him on an American football field adorning the walls. Every step of the way Americans greeted him and smiled."

Simpson was a sports star and an all-American hero with a film career and lucrative film contracts. He had divorced his black first wife and then, as the papers put it, "lived white". His was a world of affluence, respect and social status.

Simpson was presented as having a squeaky-clean image, although occasionally he allowed the mask to slip and admitted to under-age drinking binges, thefts from liquor stores when he was 13 or 14, as well

Rogues' Gallery

74

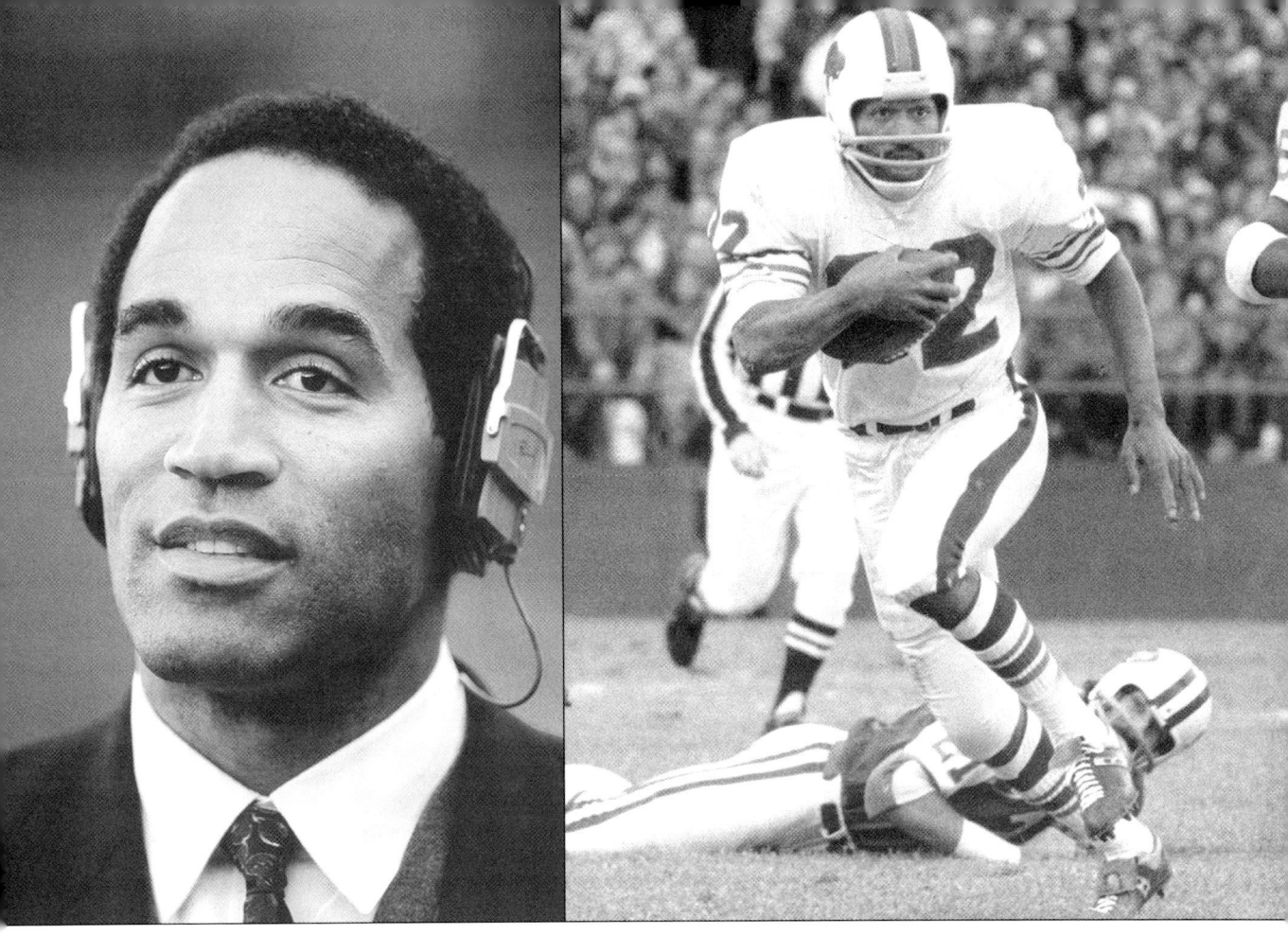

All American success story: O.J. Simpson's feats as a Buffalo Bill (right) made him a natural as a broadcaster.

as general shop-lifting. But the mask did not truly slip until the night of 12 June 1994 when, in the Los Angeles suburb of Brentwood, situated in the poshest section of the city not far from Beverly Hills and Rodeo Drive, outside a Spanish-style, split-level town house, were found the bodies of Nicole Simpson, Simpson's ex-wife, and her friend Ronald Lyle Goldman.

The police immediately suspected Simpson. Some six months earlier Nicole Simpson had had to call the police out as he threatened her and, in her words, was "going nuts". He had broken the back door to get into the house, his jealousy inflamed, it seemed, by what he saw as her dalliances.

As a result of that night Nicole needed hospital treatment and Simpson eventually pleaded no contest to a charge of spousal abuse. But instead of serving time in jail – a penalty such offences can carry – he was fined $200, ordered to pay $500 to a battered women's shelter, and did not even have to serve his 120 hours' community service in California. At the time he was taking part in several sports broadcasts from New York and served it there. There was more than a hint that this was special treatment for a great American sporting hero.

In June 1994, after the murders of Nicole Simpson and Ronald Goldman, the police informed Simpson's lawyers that he was to be arrested. Simpson then got into a Bronco driven by his former football colleague Al Cowlings, and there followed perhaps the most famous live televized car chase in American history. With Cowlings driving, Simpson led police along 60 miles of freeway and city streets, holding a gun to his head suggesting he might kill himself.

That week in June the eyes of the sporting world turned to America, where football's World Cup was due to be held, and as the Simpson car chase was taking place in LA, President Clinton and Chancellor Kohl had attended the opening match of the World Cup in Chicago, featuring Germany and Bolivia, which Germany won 1–0.

But now, as the Bronco drove around LA followed by several police cars, Americans forgot what little interest they had in this strange game called soccer and all of America sat riveted as they watched the car chase on television. America's numerous stations broke into their normal scheduling to show it live. Simpson eventually surrendered and was charged with murder. The trial, which lasted nine months, was televized round the world and demonstrated both the power of the medium and also how the public image of Simpson had changed from sports hero to villain.

There was one other aspect of the trial. Simpson, in using sport to make it in American society, had become, what a lot of blacks called a "coconut": black outside but white inside. But now, in the most profound irony of the O.J. Simpson trial, the black power salute was given by one of the jurors who acquitted him. Over the course of a few courtroom hearings the sporting hero, rich, talented and able to build a new and equally successful career as an actor, was converted from America's safest black man – a rich man who drove a Bentley and had a beautiful, blonde, white wife – into an icon of the black community.

When Simpson was first arrested it was headline news on American television and in the newspapers. But to non-Americans Simpson was only vaguely identifiable – a sportsman who had also got medium star billing in movies. To the sports reporters who had just arrived for the World Cup it was all a bit confusing. As the headline in the *Los Angeles Times* put it: "Who's O.J. Ask Foreign Media in U.S. for Soccer".

In the article that followed the paper noted: "The story of O.J. Simpson that has captivated Americans for the past week is hardly recognized by the 10,000 broadcasters and print journalists who have come to the United States to cover World Cup 94." When they were told what the story was about, they replied, according to the paper, "Oh, never mind. It's not important."

Amazing chase: Simpson's pick-up leads the police on a tour of the LA freeways.

What a difference a trial makes. By the time Simpson was acquitted 18 months later a global audience, slaked on hour after hour of trial coverage, had been told every detail of his life story. Every dinner table and pub debated his guilt. So familiar did Simpson become that the British tabloid the *Sun* was able to put just the letters O.J. in its headlines. Everyone knew that they went with Simpson. America stopped in its tracks as the Simpson verdict came and so did the rest of the world, in scenes not witnessed since the death of John F. Kennedy.

That transformation, extraordinary though it was, was nothing compared with the achievement of his defence team in converting Simpson into a symbol of routine black oppression at the hands of a racist white police force. In their attempt to present him as a man who had been framed, they were helped to a considerable extent by the performance in the witness box of some members of the Los Angeles police force, one of whom was shown to be a racist. So the trial changed from one about Simpson's guilt or innocence to one about whether the Los Angeles police force was racist.

The defence team's victory was achieved in the full glare of television lights. It occupied more news time than the war in Bosnia and the Oklahoma City bombing combined. Networks round the world ran hours of live court hearings of which every detail was dissected by legal analysts.

In Britain the power of the O.J. Simpson story to eclipse even the most important domestic news was demonstrated in a remarkable way. The day on which his verdict was due was also the day that Tony Blair was making his speech to the Labour Party about the "new Labour" he was producing to govern the "new Britain". Blair's press spokesman and chief spin doctor Alistair Campbell found it necessary to fax the BBC to make sure that the top story on its *Six O'Clock News* that day was to be Blair's speech and not the verdict from Los Angeles.

The not-guilty verdict was beamed round the world. Simpson found himself a villain in the communities that had once welcomed him, and could scarcely live up to the black victim status which his lawyers had so studiously created.

The response to the civil trial, which he lost, was much the same as to the original case, but feelings were expressed to a much

Split decision: the OJ verdict compounded America's racial divisions.

more limited degree because the television cameras were kept well away from the courtroom. There could be no more vivid demonstration of the power of television, nor for that matter of a personality shaped by modern sport and modern media, even one who many Americans believe did kill his ex-wife and her friend, as the guilty verdict in the civil suit suggested.

Talented black sportsmen will still make fortunes in the United States. But will they ever be welcomed into wealthy white America as O.J. Simpson was? Will they, indeed, want to be?

3

Performance-Enhancing Drugs

Athletics

Performance-enhancing drugs have been with us since Greek athletes used mushrooms in the third century BC, as Barrie Houlihan notes in his book *Dying to Win*. Egyptians had confidence in asses' hooves, specifically the ground rear hooves of the Abyssinian ass. By the nineteenth century athletes were using everything from strychnine to opium. Ether-soaked tablets were used to increase endurance during 144-hour cycling endurance races.

Today it is more scientific, and clever lawyers make it harder to distinguish between the bad and the unfortunate. What is certain is that the cry of "drug cheat" is almost always directed at athletes who destroy world records or rise overnight from obscurity to win a gold medal. What is still uncertain, however, is whose records have been won by hard work and talent and whose by recourse to the laboratory.

Year by year, the evidence has mounted that cynics were right and that the authorities were happy to turn a blind eye as sport, particularly athletics, became a multi-million-dollar business. While the Soviet Bloc states had a policy of using their chemically-enhanced heroes to boost communism, Western sportsmen and women were not as innocent as they tried to present themselves. Nor was it just that Western scientists were happy to develop the use of steroids as a Cold War duty in response to the growing evidence

Testcase: Mary Slaney tested positive for testosterone in 1996.

Performance-Enhancing Drugs

that they were being used by Soviet sportsmen and women. It was the use of drugs by American bodybuilders in the 1950s that first started this modern drug cycle.

Athletes today are pursuing money and fame rather than ideological victory. Indeed, the collapse of the Soviet empire exposed just how low the sport had sunk. Worst of all, surely, was the revelation that young gymnasts were forced to become pregnant, often by their coaches, and then to have an abortion – because this caused a hormone surge which improved performances.

Despite the millions of dollars now spent every year trying to stop runners, throwers and swimmers from gaining an illegal advantage by taking performance-enhancing drugs, there is little doubt that some known cheats are not reported, because administrators either do not want to see their sport getting a bad name or are frightened of being sued by the athletes they prosecute. Indeed, it is hard enough to obtain any form of agreement on what should be banned and how it should be tested. As a result, many are still drugging their way to the winning tape.

Hardly an event goes by without allegations being made against some leading performer. Invariably it is the sport which loses and the lawyers who line their pockets.

Some Olympic sports, such as weightlifting, have been dogged by controversy for many years, but it is in the glamour sports, running and swimming, whose greatest talents have presented themselves as role models – and been well paid for doing so – that the falls from grace have been most dramatic.

The real losers are the honest athletes who are increasingly frustrated at the weakness of their governing groups. A survey by the *Independent* newspaper of Britain's top sportsmen and women revealed that there was a groundswell of opinion in favour of improved testing and harsher penalties.

According to one respondent, "Drugs are widely used in rugby union, and officials – I have a feeling this is so – turn a blind eye." There were calls for random tests on rugby players and fines for clubs as well as players, as this would encourage officials to address the problem seriously.

A common complaint was that testing was virtually non-existent. One footballer said he had been tested once in 12 years, while one female tennis player said she had taken part in 20 tournaments without seeing a tester.

According to Sports England, as the English Sports Council is now called, there were 602 out-of-competition tests on athletes in 1997, while the total for football was two and there were one each for cricket and rugby league. There were none at all for rugby union, tennis or swimming.

It is naïve to pretend that the problem is easily solved. The jobsworths and freeloaders who run international sport are no match for the combination of highly-skilled scientists and lawyers who are prepared to connive with cheating athletes.

One example of the problems lies with the food substance creatine. It has been lauded and marketed as the safe, legal alternative to anabolic steroids, but a group of leading Italian sports scientists argued that it should be considered a doping substance because it can have positive effects on sports performances. Some doctors have also argued that it can harm kidneys and other organs. Meanwhile it has been widely taken by sportsmen and women, including Linford Christie and the 400 metres sprinter Iwan Thomas and England footballers such as Ian Wright and Sol Campbell.

However, these difficult calls do not excuse the way the authorities have failed to react, like rabbits caught in headlights, when faced with the problem of catching drug cheats. Do they admit that the prevalence of drugs was so rife that many of the records of the last 20 years are worth no more than the price of the drugs that made them possible? Do they challenge the athletes whom they suspect, or run a mile at the first whiff of legal grapeshot? Ultimately, do they risk losing sponsors as they try to clean up their sports?

Perhaps their inability to come up with solutions was best demonstrated by the IOC Congress on Drugs in Lausanne in February 1999, which failed to produce a cohesive strategy. Indeed, just when it needed all its resources to try to lift the terrible cloud of corruption and bribery that hangs over it, the IOC scored a spectacular own goal.

Four months earlier it had announced that it would hold an anti-doping conference, giving the impression that the IOC was prepared to step in where other sports federations and even governments feared to tread.

But after three days of talking the IOC had its toes firmly trodden on, both by the politicians and even by some of the sports federations who are supposed to belong to the much-vaunted Olympic family.

Nothing illustrated this better than the ending of the conference. Then Juan Antonio Samaranch, the IOC President, presented a two-page declaration entitled "The Lausanne Declaration on Doping in Sport". "All approved?" he asked the delegates, and they applauded in the sort of scene not witnessed since the stage-managed congresses of the old Soviet Union. It was a great victory for clean sport, declared Samaranch, who half-smiled and prepared to celebrate a moment of glory for the IOC.

Within minutes, however, it was clear this was the hollowest of victories. Delegates, led by European ministers and politicians from many countries, stormed out of the conference hall to tell the press that they had not agreed with the Lausanne Declaration and had severe reservations about it.

It also emerged that the IOC could not even carry with it all the sports federations, some of which made it clear they had no desire to accept even a two-year ban on a first offender for drugs. As for a life ban on subsequent offenders, which has been IOC policy, there was no mention of that in the declaration. When Samaranch was asked about it later he said lamely, "We didn't put it in the declaration because we know it very well."

In order to keep football and cycling sweet, individual sports federations would be able to modify the two-year ban in "exceptional circumstances", which, as politicians such as Britain's sports minister Tony Banks pointed out, was following the line of least resistance – a dangerous course. The result was that the only vote was on a declaration which was accepted "with all the reservations" expressed by the delegates. This essentially made it meaningless even as a statement of intent. It is as if international sport wants to be rid of drug-takers, but not just yet.

The IOC Congress had come exactly a decade after drugs in sport had emerged as the most serious issue. The *annus horribilis* had been 1988. That is when the extent of the involvement of drugs in sport become very evident, particularly when 34 people, including the British Olympic medallist David Jenkins, were indicted by the United States drug enforcement agencies on 110 counts relating to conspiracy to manufacture, smuggle and distribute enormous quantities of anabolic steroids.

Jenkins, who had studied chemical engineering at Edinburgh University, was found guilty on four counts of involvement in smuggling more than $70 million worth of steroids into the United States. Plea bargaining reduced his theoretical sentence of 100 years to seven, which he began serving in December 1988.

Sentencing the former golden boy of British athletics, who had won European gold, Judge Irving said: "You had it all. Brains, education, apparently in the upper ten per cent academically of the British population, able to speak French and Spanish, great health and God-given fantastic athletic ability. Then entered greed..."

The trial dented even the image of Jenkins's glory days. He admits now that, though he was never caught, he started taking steroids at the end of 1975 when he was number one in the world. It was, he said, all due to the insecurity he had felt when going to the 1976 Olympics with such expectations on his shoulders.

1988 was also the year of the Seoul Olympics, which opened to one of the most spectacular pageants in the Games' history. There was so much invested in these Games. They symbolized the booming success of the Asian 'tiger economies', which at that time seemed to show the way ahead to every moribund Western nation. A dynamic nation would show the world how to make the Games really profitable, with Asian efficiency and elegant culture spun seamlessly together.

More than that, it was designed to show that the Olympic family was back together again after the major boycotts of the three previous Games. The television stations had shelled out their millions of dollars, events had been timed to ensure maximum viewing figures in the United States, and to cap every marketing man's dream, there was to be an epic confrontation, including a clean-cut, black, all-American star, in the blue riband event.

But instead of a glorious hymn to man's sporting endeavour, the aftermath of the 100 metres exposed only the sordid underbelly of a sport that was never to be quite the same again. For when people recall the 1988 Olympics, they remember only one name... Ben Johnson. Rarely can a sportsman and his sport have risen so high and fallen so low in so short a time in front of so many people.

The men's Olympic 100 metres final is

arguably the most dramatic event in world sport. Four years of training is concentrated into ten seconds of action in front of a global audience of millions. There is no second chance; the minutest error means failure. When, as in the 1988 Seoul Olympics final, it was a showdown between two great runners, the Canadian Ben Johnson and the American Carl Lewis, the world held its breath.

Johnson, the stockier athlete, muscles bulging like the winner of a Mr Atlas competition, won the race, finger wagging in delight at the crowd. But that was the last smile in Seoul. The Canadian, whose physique since his arrival in top athletics had attracted allegations of drug-taking, was stripped of his medal when anabolic steroids were found in his urine sample. Never had such a prominent athlete been caught out so dramatically at an event watched by so many people round the world.

As officials and athletes fended off allegations that this was only the tip of the drugging iceberg, and journalists sought steroids in every winner's track bag, Johnson was hustled off to the airport in a blaze of flashbulbs and television cameras. Amazingly, he was allowed to return for the Barcelona Olympics in 1992, but a second doping offence led to a lifetime ban. The sporting world was stunned. Some naïvely hoped that the success in catching Johnson would send out a message that athletics was not only determined to fight drug abuse but was determined to do so successfully.

This proved to be a false dawn. Far from cleansing the sport, the episode cast a stain on athletics that it has never really removed. Johnson, who is reckoned to have lost £10 million in endorsements as a result of his exposure as a drug cheat, has done little to help the process. He claims that the sport is now driven by the money men who want the attention that only comes when records are broken. Consequently a blind eye is turned to positive drug tests.

In an interview with the *Sunday Mirror* just before the 1996 Atlanta centenary Games, he said: "If they caught every athlete on drugs, that would be the end of professional track and field...You've got a multi-million dollar industry that would collapse because no one would want to watch it if the times went into reverse."

Johnson, who made a film of his life, is unrepentant, cannot understand how he was caught and believes that the rules should be changed to allow for the legal use of drugs by athletes.

Canada responded by holding a major investigation, the Dubin Inquiry, into drugs. More than 15,000 pages of evidence were taken from 122 witnesses and, for a brief period before the lawyers got involved, it looked as if athletics might be able to cleanse its soul as a new programme of out-of-competition testing was introduced.

Johnson was not the only sprinter tested at the Seoul Olympics. The British sprinter Linford Christie tested positive for an extremely small trace of pseudoephedrine. He argued successfully that this was caused by a cold-cure remedy which did not mention pseudoephedrine among its ingredients.

For a time it seemed that the women's 100 metres had restored some faith in the Corinthian spirit of fair play. But as the years passed, the allegations grew more open that Florence Griffith-Joyner, the gold medallist, was extremely lucky not to have had to follow Johnson home...

Florence Griffith-Joyner should have been the answer to athletics' prayers. Dressed in multicoloured leotards and sporting talon-like finger nails painted in all colours of the rainbow, she was a marketing dream.

And she was very fast. Flo Jo, or Cash Flo as she came to be known when the endorsements came pouring in, was the outstanding woman sprinter of 1988. She won three gold medals at the Seoul Olympics, smashing world records both before and during the games.

But her progress from obscurity to Olympic stardom seemed just too fast to be true, and from that moment up, until and even beyond her tragically early death from a heart attack in 1998 at the age of 38, there were persistent allegations that her performances owed more to drugs than talent.

She vehemently denied the charges and to the relief of the Games authorities did not suffer the same fate in Seoul as Ben Johnson by failing the drug test. To lose one Olympic champion in the drug testing room had been unfortunate; to lose a second at the Seoul Olympics in 1988 could have destroyed the Games for ever.

But her critics were never convinced. To them, she showed the classic symptoms of drug-enhanced performance. For a start there was the dramatic improvement in form in the months before the Seoul Games. In

Performance-Enhancing Drugs

four successive 100-metre races, she ran the four fastest times in history. On one occasion she broke the record by a quarter of a second, whereas in the previous 75 years no one had done so by more than one-tenth of a second. Her world records for the 100 and 200 metres still stand.

Her physique also changed dramatically from one that was very feminine to a masculinity that her glamorous attire could not entirely disguise or distract attention from. Her voice deepened, and as Carl Lewis wrote in his autobiography, *The Year of the Steroids*, "Steroids often affect a woman's voice that way."

Even her death added further fuel to the suspicions. A heart attack is the all-too-common early death for those who have taken performance-enhancing steroids.

For many, the conclusive evidence was her decision to retire at the start of 1989, when her powers and earning potential were at their peak. As the sport had moved into the professional era, she had multiplied by 25 times her fee for competing in events. She insisted that she wanted to spend more time writing and acting. Others noted that year-round drugs testing was about to be introduced.

Johnson was, of course, not the first to have used performance-enhancing drugs to gain Olympic success. Had he been a few years older and able to compete at the Moscow Olympics, he could have got away with almost everything courtesy of the KGB.

The one certainty about the 1980 Moscow Olympics was that the KGB would not allow anything to spoil further an event that had already been hard-hit by a boycott by the United States and many other Western countries. There were certainly not going to be any drugs scandals – but for the Soviets this did not mean keeping the Games clean; it meant turning a blind eye to anything and everything.

It was hardly surprising that the less scrupulous athletes took full advantage to the extent that the Games were dubbed the "Junkie Olympics" by one observer, who claimed: "There is hardly a medal winner at the Moscow Olympics, certainly not a gold medal winner, who is not on one sort of drug or another; usually several kinds. The Moscow Games might as well be called the Chemists' Games."

There were of course no positive drug tests – the KGB saw to that. Today they would probably just provide free legal insurance to each performer. For, interestingly, when some of the samples were later retested there was evidence that a large number of athletes had used steroids.

The one certainty in the murky world of performance-enhancing drugs is that the East Germans would have been well and truly drugged up for the Moscow Olympics, where they collected 47 gold medals, as they were for most of the sporting events of that decade.

East Germany, home of the most rigidly-policed form of communism and supplier of the most effective secret police in the Soviet Bloc, decided in the late 1950s to create a sporting élite that would demonstrate to the world the superiority of Marxism. The collapse of the communist world in the late 1980s would show, however, that the sporting successes of the 1970s and '80s owed more to chemistry than political science.

The record was certainly remarkable. At the Olympics of 1976, 1980 and 1988 East Germany won respectively 40, 47 and 37 gold medals (communist countries boycotted the 1984 Los Angeles Games) and were consistently in the top three countries. On this basis the reunified Germany should have been unbeatable, but after unification the performances of the East Germans, particularly their women, plunged out of all recognition.

The only explanation was the systematic, state-managed use of performance-enhancing drugs. It was possibly the only area in which the planned economy really worked.

Nowhere was the impact of the East Germans felt more strongly than in women's international swimming and athletics in the 1970s and '80s. Inevitably, rumours that their success was due to drugs were dismissed in politically correct circles as Cold War jealousy, but gradually the evidence built up, first from the testimony of defectors and later from the more concrete proof that emerged after the Iron Curtain came down.

For the East German team, ironically, the main concern at the time was not the drugs but working out who were the political informers. Heiki Dreschler, winner of two Olympic bronze medals in 1988 and her fourth European long jump gold medal a decade later, lost a high-profile court case in which she tried to prove she was not a Stasi informer.

One who did inform was throwing coach Ekhart Arbeit, who reported Marlies Goehr,

Performance-Enhancing Drugs

the 100 metres champion, for showing dangerous signs of "materialistic interests".

Not everyone could be silenced or controlled. Renate Vogel, who held the 100-metres world breast-stroke record in 1974, gave evidence of the systematic use of anabolic steroids when she defected to the West.

The tragedy for the athletes is that the health damage from steroids only appears in later life, when they suffer from heart disease and premature ageing.

Further evidence is now coming from the courts. Coaches and doctors from two clubs, Dynamo Berlin and TSC, were prosecuted for forcing their charges to take performance-enhancing drugs which have left them physically and psychologically damaged. One swimmer, the triple gold medallist Rica Reinisch, said she started receiving pills at the age of 12 and now suffers from ovarian cysts and an enlarged muscle in her heart.

Details also emerged in court about other physical effects ranging from a benign liver tumour and other liver damage to deepening voices and extra body hair – one woman grew a beard. Among the horror stories was that of Heidi Krieger, the former women's shot put champion, who is now called Andreas after the side-effects of steroids had left no alternative to a sex-change operation. Roland Schmidt was one of 12 male athletes who developed breasts and had to have them surgically removed.

Nor did the scandals end with the collapse of the Berlin Wall. In 1992 Katrin Krabbe, Grit Breuer and Silke Moeller were suspended for four years by the German Athletic Federation for attempting to manipulate the results of urine tests. This could only have been done, said the German authorities, by the athletes or with their agreement, with the intention of falsifying tests to establish whether illegal performance-enhancing means had been used. In fact, the suspensions were subsequently lifted on a technicality, though in the same year, Katrin Krabbe tested

She became he: the side effects of steroids forced Heidi Krieger to undergo a sex change.

Performance-Enhancing Drugs

positive for the anabolic agent clenbuterol.

In the summer of 1998 a courtroom in Berlin began hearing about the secret doping that was part of the state-sponsored sports scene in East Germany.

At the heart of the system were coaches working for the SC Dynamo Berlin swimming club, who administered drugs to young swimmers and other sportsmen and women. This was part of the system run by the German Institute for Physical Culture and Sport in Leipzig, which had developed anabolic steroids as "supportive treatment" for athletes as early as 1973. The East German aim was to find a course of treatment, as well as masking drugs, that would protect the athlete from pre-tournament testing. Athletes such as Katrin Krabbe were also encouraged to use special vaginal bags containing somebody else's urine, so they would test clean before a race.

The natural heirs to the East German legacy are the Chinese. Desperate to use sport to gain international credibility and respectability for their political system, they have even resorted to hiring East German coaches associated with that country's swimming teams of the 1980s.

Consequently alarm bells should have started to ring in the brains of the International Olympic Committee when the Chinese women's swimming team leapt from the occasional appearance on the lower levels of the podium to a virtual monopoly of the gold medals. Instead, however, the instinctive response from the IOC, from its President Juan Antonio Samaranch downwards, was to insist that nothing was wrong. Only when the scientists provided incontrovertible evidence was action considered.

In the 1994 World Swimming Championships in Rome, the People's Republic of China women's team took 12 out of 16 gold medals, a dramatic improvement on the 1988 Olympics, when they managed only four medals, none of them gold. Equally dramatic was the change in their physique, which had clearly become more masculine, and the fact that their success was concentrated in the power events rather than those which emphasized technique.

There was also the ubiquitous presence of former East German coaches. The final element for most independent observers was that the improvement was confined to the women's team event and not the men's, even though the two squads were said to use

Katrin Krabbe: manipulated a urine test.

similar training techniques.

At first the allegations were dismissed as racism and jealousy, but scientific analysis was to provide compelling evidence of Chinese guilt. Between the time of the World Championships in 1994 and March 1995, 19 positive tests were recorded, all bar one being for steroids. The culprits were only caught by a combination of early testing and sophisticated analysis.

The Chinese swimmers, comfortable that the international sporting authorities were

Out of this world: the dramatic improvement in the times recorded by Chinese women swimmers was linked to drug use.

reluctant to confront the real problem, have still not mended their ways. At the 1998 World Championships in Perth, Australia, one Chinese swimmer was found with a flask containing 13 phials of human growth hormone. This would have been enough to supply the whole squad.

Allegations of dramatic improvements have not just been made against the Chinese. The pool-side debates at the 1996 Olympics in Atlanta were all about how one woman had improved so much so quickly. Her name was Michelle Smith.

Questions will always be asked about an athlete who appears from nowhere to win Olympic gold medals. When the swimmer happens to beat Americans on their own territory, the speculation is certain to be particularly intense.

Probably the only element that saved swimmer Michelle Smith from a more savage dismantling by the American press during the 1996 Olympics was that she was Irish – even President Clinton, conscious of the importance of the Irish-American vote at the 1996 presidential election, sent his congratulations after she had won three gold medals and one bronze.

Even that could not save Smith from a non-stop stream of rumour and innuendo which suggested her surprize victories were only achieved by drugs. Although she had tested negative on many earlier tests, more attention was paid to her rapid improvement and the fact that her husband and trainer, Erik de Bruin, had received a four-year ban after testing positive in 1993.

Two years later she was banned for four years for allegedly trying to manipulate a drug test. The charge was that she mixed whisky with her urine sample as a masking agent. Although Smith denied the charge and took her appeal to the Lausanne-based Court of Arbitration in Sport, this upheld the ban in June 1999, effectively bringing her career to an end.

British athletics has liked to claim the moral high ground when it comes to drug testing. In fact British athletes have faced allegations too, although in most cases they have vigorously, and often successfully, fought the charges.

The first to test positive was a woman who was believed by most people in the British athletics world to be one of the least likely to use drugs.

Diane Modahl was the first British woman to test positive for drugs. But, instead of accepting the four-year ban imposed by the British Athletic Federation, she protested her innocence and eventually cleared her name.

Modahl's nightmare began on 24 August 1994, when the 800-metre Commonwealth gold medallist was preparing to defend her title in Victoria. The authorities dismissed claims that the high level of testosterone – 42 times greater than normal – could have been caused because the urine sample had been mishandled by the Portuguese laboratory which analysed it.

The British athletics world was stunned to see the finger pointed at Modahl, who was widely regarded as the athlete least likely to take drugs. A popular, ever-smiling figure on the circuit, she had said that the increase in random drug testing was weeding out cheats and enabling her to compete with her rivals on level terms.

Despite her protestations of innocence, the five-strong British Athletics Federation disciplinary panel banned Modahl for four years after a one-day hearing in December 1994. They dismissed claims from her lawyers, who argued that the urine samples had been inadequately stored in hot conditions and that it was possible for bacteria in the sample to be distorted to such an extent that it produced a positive test.

Dr Martin Lucking, the panel chairman, stated: "Having heard all the evidence and considered all the documents, the committee was satisfied unanimously that a doping offence had been committed by Mrs Modahl."

Modahl, who is married to her coach Vicente, vowed to clear her name. Her case was helped by the sheer amount of testosterone in the sample, which one official described as "unbelievable".

It was many times higher than that found in Ben Johnson, who received a lifetime ban for a level of 10.3 units of testosterone to one unit of epitestosterone – the normal ratio is 1:1.

Further doubts were raised by the length of time between the test and the passing-on of the results. The story was first published by a Russian journalist who had received the information from a Dutch source.

Even so, it took the better part of two years before the International Amateur Athletics Federation (IAAF), ruling on the recommendation of their doping commission, judged that the case against Modahl could not be proven. They did not, however, offer any financial compensation.

The case revealed flaws in the testing procedure and led some in the ruling bodies to question whether the evidence of laboratories would in future be blindly accepted.

As for Modahl, she resumed her athletics career, though without the success that had taken her to fourth place in the 1993 World Championships, and has issued a writ against the British Athletic Federation for £500,000 to compensate for emotional stress and financial ruin. The case is being pursued through the courts.

In January 1999 came another shock. On the very day that British athletics was trying to relaunch itself in a new form, after the British Athletics Federation had gone bankrupt, came further revelations that a top British athlete had failed a drugs test.

The athlete was Dougie Walker, a Scottish sprinter who protested his innocence when drugs tests revealed traces of the banned anabolic steroid nandroline in his urine sample. Walker has vowed to clear his name, insisting that he had not taken a banned substance.

"I have never taken any banned substance and will be contesting the findings," he stated as his coach and other athletes rallied to his support. He is likely to claim that the test showed a false positive.

One theory is that this result could be caused by his use of a supplement like those marketed by Maximuscle UK, the company which sponsored Walker when he was an up-and-coming sprinter on Scotland's professional circuit. The product could be similar to androstenedione, which contains an offshoot of the compound nandrolone.

Walker, who won the European 200 metres in 1998 and was in the world's top ten for the distance, immediately felt the impact

Unworthy champions: those who backed Michelle Smith after she won three Olympic gold medals in 1996 were later to feel duped.

of the test. His lottery grant was suspended and his Reebok contract, estimated to be worth £50,000 a year, was put on hold.

One athlete who served the four-year ban for taking drugs was sprinter Jason Livingston. This, ironically, was a man who had regarded Ben Johnson as a role model, to the extent that he shaved his head in an attempt to look exactly like the Canadian.

"Baby Ben", as he was known, tested positive for a performance-enhancing drug in an out-of-competition test just before the 1992 Barcelona Olympics.

He protested his innocence but lost an appeal against his suspension by two votes to one. Livingston has since returned to racing.

Over the years there have been other British athletes who have failed drugs tests. Solomon Wariso was sent home from the European Championships in 1994 when a test result revealed that he had traces of the stimulant ephedrine in his system. He admitted taking a stimulant called Up Your Gas, but protested his innocence and is now racing again.

The British shot-putter Paul Edwards tested positive for drugs in the 1994 Commonwealth Games. He came back on the same flight as Diana Modahl, looking like a criminal in custody with his head covered in a blanket. He got a four-year ban and has tried to prove his innocence but without success. In June 1997 he requested another drugs test, only for the sample to show a high level of testosterone, which resulted in a life ban. However, in February 1999 he was allowed to compete in a Southern Open League meeting at Crystal Palace after being told he could have another disciplinary hearing, and he vowed to clear his name.

The British judo competitor Kerrith Brown took part in the 1988 Seoul Olympics but later tested positive for diuretics. These can be used to produce rapid weight loss, to make detection of other drugs more difficult or to overcome some of the side-effects of anabolic steroids.

Colin Mackenzie, the javelin-thrower, was banned for three months after testing positive for a stimulant, but has since returned to competition.

If so far the use of drugs since 1988 has been highlighted, it must be emphasized that performance-enhancing drugs are not just a feature of recent years. They have been around for a long time, as have the protestations of innocence. Indeed some athletes have probably received rough justice, while others will have escaped altogether. Here are some of those who made the headlines.

Tom Hicks collapsed following the use of a strychnine-brandy cocktail in the marathon at the 1904 St Louis Olympics. Hicks was refuelled with this mixture at various stages during the race, and pictures show him looking extremely dazed at the finish line.

Ironically, he had only been awarded the gold medal following the disqualification of Fred Lorz, who, after suffering cramp, hitched a lift in a passing car.

The American swimmer Rick DeMont was stripped of his gold medal for the 400 metres freestyle and prevented from competing further in the 1972 Olympics after testing positive for ephedrine. This happened even though he told officials he was using an anti-asthma drug, Marex.

However, there were consistent rumours that athletes were using blood-doping – in other words taking, storing and re-injecting their own blood to boost the red oxygen-carrying cells, thereby increasing their stamina. This was finally revealed in a remarkable way.

Martti Vainio, a Finnish distance runner, was stunned when he found himself disqualified for steroid use after finishing second in the 10,000 metres at the Los Angeles Olympics. He had not apparently used the banned drug for months before the Games.

However, he had also tried to improve his performance by blood-doping. He had failed to realize that when his blood was originally taken, it still had traces of the steroid. He was banned for only 18 months, the minimum sentence at the time.

Eleven athletes were disqualified at the 1976 Montreal Olympics, eight of them for the use of anabolic steroids – these Games were the first occasion when reliable tests for their presence in urine were available.

As the new testing regimes were put in place and were, for a period at least, ahead of the ability of the bent athletes to disguise their crimes, so there was the odd flurry of panic. Many athletes withdrew from the 1983 Pan-American games in Caracas, Venezuela; even so 19, including ten from the United States and Canada, tested positive.

In 1984 the British Canadian judo competitor Ronald Angus was given a life ban after traces of a drug were found in his urine system.

However, the drug had come from Sudafed, a nasal decongestant which had been prescribed by his doctor. He appealed and was reinstated in time to compete in the 1984 Olympics.

The 1990s were to see many high-profile athletes test positive for anabolic steroids, including Harry "Butch" Reynolds and Randy Barnes. Both protested their innocence Reynolds sued the International Amateur Athletics Federation, winning his case and being awarded $17 million by the US courts.

However, the lower court's ruling was overturned by the US Supreme Court, though by this time Reynolds had missed the Barcelona Games.

Mary Slaney, née Decker, also followed the Reynolds route when in April 1999 the IAAF found her guilty of taking drugs.

Considered the greatest female distance runner in American track and field history, Slaney tested positive for testosterone in 1996 but was allowed to run at the Atlanta Olympics. The IAAF stepped in and suspended her, demanding that the US Track and Field take action. In October 1997 Slaney was cleared to compete after a USTF hearing. The IAAF was not convinced and sent the case to arbitration.

An IAAF arbitration panel looked at her case and three years later, on 26 April 1999, announced that she had taken testosterone, the muscle-building hormone.

The ruling has had no practical effect on Slaney. Her punishment was a retrospective two-year ban which had ended the previous June. She was set to lose her $20,000 prize-money she won in the 1997 World Indoor Championships, but was free to run again and can compete in the Sydney Olympics. According to IAAF rules the decision is final and binding but Slaney, who had failed to appear before the hearing in Monte Carlo, has started litigation.

Slaney's test had found the ratio of testosterone and epitestosterone to be 11.6:1, higher than that found in Ben Johnson when he was banned for life in 1993, while anything more than 6:1 is an offence. Slaney maintains that the excessive level of testosterone in her urine sample was the result of a number of factors including the contraceptive pill and medical problems she was suffering at the time.

The arbitrators said that Slaney had failed to establish pathological or physiological conditions which might have explained the readings. Jim Coleman, Slaney's lawyer said, "When we decided not to go to the hearing it was because it was clear the proceedings would go exactly as they have. We are going to kick the IAAF's butts."

The Slaney verdict prompted calls from Craig Masback, the USTF's chief executive, that the procedures for testing for testosterone in women be re-examined.

Human growth hormone has virtually the same effect as an anabolic steroid, with one significant difference – it is virtually undetectable. Consequently, although its use is thought to be widespread and increasing, there is little hard evidence to back this up. One of the few athletes to admit using it was the Canadian sprinter Angella Issajenko, who told Justice Dubin's investigation into the Ben Johnson affair that she had used it along with other substances.

Over the years there have been some remarkable explanations for failing a drugs test. The most exotic explanation was offered by Dennis Mitchell, the US sprinter. He was probably the first ever to escape a two-year ban for having excessive levels of the body-building hormone testosterone in his system by insisting they were the result of having sex and drinking the night before the race.

There was genuine surprise among his fellow athletes when Mitchell, bronze medallist at the 1992 Olympics and an outspoken anti-drugs campaigner, failed an out-of-competition drugs test in April 1998.

Mitchell was immediately suspended by the IAAF, pending an appeal to the USTF doping panel, which in conditions of the deepest secrecy, cleared Mitchell in December 1998. The panel argued that there was reasonable doubt surrounding his positive test. Mitchell had claimed that on the night before giving the urine sample he had had sex at least four times and had drunk five bottles of beer.

There are certain circumstances in which testosterone, a naturally occurring hormone which can enhance performance by assisting muscle building and recovery from training, will increase in the body. But the verdict caused considerable amusement among some experts, one of whom said, "Testosterone levels will rise after sex but only to the body's normal limits."

The IAAF arbitration panel considered the case and, "decided that the scientific evidence provided by Mitchell could not explain the high level of testosterone". He was banned for two years.

Dennis Mitchell may have been the first to claim sex as the cause for excess testosterone, but Astrid Strauss got there before him when it came to blaming alcohol. The East German swimmer claimed that her failed test was the result of drinking too much beer. The swimming ruling body, FINA, was not convinced and found her guilty.

There are other defences which have been used with more success. At the 1996 Olympics, four Russian athletes were found to have bromantan, which is a stimulant and masking agent, in their blood.

It was assumed that the athletes, including a wrestler, Zafar Guliyev, and swimmer, Andrei Korneyev, who had won bronze medals, would be disqualified. However, the Russians, who accepted that their athletes had used the drug, argued successfully that it was not a banned substance. Only in February 1997 was it added to the list.

The Australian sprinter Dean Capobianco was allowed to compete in the 1996 Olympics even though he had tested positive for steroids earlier in the year. He had been cleared by an Australian tribunal, and the challenge by the IAAF could not be heard before the Games, so Capobianco was allowed to take part.

The Italian high jumper Antonella Bevilacqua tested positive for the banned substance ephedrine in May 1996, but the Italian federation accepted her explanation that she had taken it unintentionally in a Chinese herbal medicine. The IAAF believed the case against her was compelling but, fearing a legal challenge, allowed her to compete at Atlanta.

Baseball

In the summer of 1998, sports fans in the United States were gripped by the 'Race for 61', the attempt by two baseball players, Mark McGwire of the St Louis Cardinals and Sammy Sosa of the Chicago Cubs, to reach the Holy Grail of the sport, the seasonal home run record. The previous mark of 61 had been set by Roger Maris of the New York Yankees in 1961, and the pair of sluggers traded blows throughout the season.

Shortly before McGwire broke Maris's record — eventually he established a new mark of 70 — it was revealed that his power hitting was fuelled by taking a muscle-boosting drug called androstenedione (known in locker rooms as 'andro', and legally and widely available in the USA in health food stores, pharmacies and via the Internet). First discovered by the East German sports machine, 'andro' is a 'pre-hormone' that raises testosterone levels. Strangely, though banned by the IOC and America's National Football League, it was not illegal in Major League Baseball.

McGwire admitted he takes the drug three or four times a week to help him "get a better pump" before his weight-training sessions. Ironically, while McGwire was earning himself a permanent place in the baseball record books with the help of 'andro', the drug earned Randy Barnes, the US shot putter who won gold at the Atlanta Olympics, a suspension when he tested positive for the substance. Doctors warned that those who wished to try some of McGwire's favourite potion risked liver and kidney damage, acne, stimulation of tumours, thrombosis and uncontrolled aggressive behaviour.

Cycling

If much of the drug-taking in athletics and swimming remains undiscovered, cycling has a long history of trying to ignore the evidence before its eyes.

According to Barrie Houlihan, the author of *Dying to Win*, at the end of the nineteenth century cyclists took virtually every combination of drugs and alcohol in an effort to improve stamina and performance. Coaches recommended heroin and cocaine, the French took caffeine, and the British added strychnine and brandy to heroin and cocaine. Arthur Linton's death in 1886 is thought to be the first recorded case of an athlete being killed by a drugs overdose, but it did little to deter users, who continued to test the limits of human tolerance.

During the 1950s, cycling was widely thought to be the sport most involved in the use of performance-enhancing drugs. But not until a series of deaths in the 1960s was serious attention paid to the problem.

Danish cyclist Knut Jensen collapsed and died during the 175 team time trial at the 1960 Olympics. He had been using amphetamines and nicotinic acid – as had his two team-mates, who also collapsed but later recovered.

During the 1966 Tour de France, cyclists staged a protest against random drug tests carried out overnight in Bordeaux. Three miles into the ninth stage, 122 riders got off and walked for 100 yards. One dissenting voice was that of British competitor Tommy Simpson, who said: "I think it was stupid. It is French law and it is pointless protesting."

Tragically, in the next year's Tour, Simpson died owing to a deadly combination of amphetamines, heat and physical strain. His death, seen on TV, awakened Britain to the problem.

Simpson, 29 years old and the most successful cyclist Britain had produced, collapsed on the 5,500-foot Ventoux mountain, known as the Giant of Provence. He twice had to be put back on his bike by British team mechanics but insisted on going on for a further half-mile under a scorching sun that had taken the temperature into the nineties. He fell again, and this time was unconscious when the doctor arrived. A year after Simpson's death, Yves Mottin died shortly after winning a cross-country event.

In 1984 eight members of the United

States cycling team admitted blood-doping a few days before the Los Angeles Olympics, at which they won nine medals. The doping had been carried out under the supervision of the team doctor and the trainer.

Recombinant erythropoietin (EPO) is an artificial stimulant which has the same effect as blood-doping and has been available for medical use since 1987. One risk associated with it is heart disease, and various magazines have drawn attention to the number of cyclists who have died in this way. One claimed 18 cyclists had died after taking the drug in the period up to 1991; another said 12 Dutch cyclists had died from heart disease.

All this should have alerted the cycling authorities, but even when the 1998 Tour de France revealed widespread drug use, it was the French police who played the leading role in investigating. So much money, romance and prestige is wrapped up in the Tour de France that the sport's authorities have always been reluctant to take action.

The cycling authorities give the impression of a total surrender to performance-enhancing drugs; and, in doing so, have the support of some distinguished members of the French press. When Pedro Delgado was thrown out of the 1988 Tour for taking diuretics, used as a masking agent, the French newspaper *Le Monde* insisted that the international authorities had "broken the heart of the Tour" by monitoring for drugs.

A decade later, this attitude was on display again – even after a car driven by Willy Voet, the Festina team's Belgian masseur, was stopped by customs officials on the Franco–Belgian border on 9 July 1998 and found to be carrying enough performance-enhancing drugs to fuel every single rider on the Tour. The scale of the haul in Voet's car – 234 doses of EPO, 80 bottles of growth hormone, 160 capsules of testosterone and 60 of Asaflow, an aspirin-based product for thinning the blood, not to mention amphetamines, caffeine, heroin and cocaine – staggered observers. Voet's initial story – that they were for his personal use – amused the French police, but once he realized the Festina team, led by their star rider Richard Virenque, were denying any connection with him, he decided to tell all.

A chain of arrests followed, starting with Festina's team director Bruno Roussel and team doctor Eric Rijckaert, who were charged with inciting the use of doping products. Characteristically, the Tour officials' response was denial: Jean-Claude Killy, the former French skier and now the Tour's president, dismissed Voet's arrest as a "mere sideshow", but once Roussel admitted under interrogation that "a concerted system for supplying drugs was organized between management, doctors, the masseur and the riders in the Festina team", the Tour had no alternative but to expel Festina from the race.

Roussel's admission confirmed what many had long suspected – that the cheats were one step ahead in sport's endless battle between pharmacist and analyst. Yet if the cycling authorities seemed powerless to take on the cheats, French police were more than ready. The 1998 race was punctuated by almost daily arrests: Cees Priem, manager of the Dutch team TVM, was quizzed about 104 vials of EPO found in a TVM car earlier in the year; Rodolfo Massi, leader of the King of the Mountains competition, was charged with importing, distributing and transferring "poisonous substances" when police found drugs in his hotel room in Chambéry; so too was Nicolas Terrados, doctor to the Spanish ONCE team. In all 60 cyclists and support personnel were questioned, and 13 people were charged.

The scandal infuriated the cycling establishment and supporters of the sport, but their anger was directed not against the cheats but against the French police and courts who had asked questions the sport's ruling body had not dared to. ONCE, the team of Laurent Jalabert, the French national champion and world number one, tried to organize a riders' demonstration against the police after a dawn raid on their hotel, and later withdrew from the race. Three other Spanish teams declared they were no longer prepared to race in France.

Voet, who worked with five other teams before joining Festina, said the problem was that the administrators were mostly former cyclists. "They are party to the system too," he said. "The people who make the rules and moral judgments have done it too."

The cyclists' response was typified by a remark from Stéphane Barthe, a former French national champion, who boycotted a world championship road race because of the treatment meted out to those who had been caught. "I do not want to represent a country that treats riders like dirt. To hear people say that bicycle racing is the most corrupt sport is pitiful," he said. Equally dismissive was American rider Chris Horner, who said that drugs were "just part of professional sports now. Every sport has some problems like that. You just have to deal with it, in one ear and out the other, and keep training and keep racing. It bothers you, of course, when your director is called in by the police, but what can you do?"

The cyclists went on strike, wept and pleaded that they were innocent. But there was still more absurdity to come, when the International Cycling Union handed out punishments which scarcely added up to a severe reprimand. Festina riders Alex Zuelle, Armin Meier and Laurent Dufaux, had been suspended for eight months, but in autumn 1998 this was reduced to six months and they were fined a paltry total of £1,346. In effect, they would be back in time to have a good two months' competition before taking part in the 1999 Tour de France.

Throughout the investigations two Festina riders, Pascal Hervé and team leader Richard Virenque, consistently protested their innocence. Virenque, France's most popular cyclist, issued tearful denials, even threatening to walk away from the sport. Willy Voet would later tell *L'Equipe*, the French sports daily, that 80 per cent of Festina riders, including Hervé and Virenque, asked for and took doping products. He also claimed Festina spent more than £60,000 each season on drugs, with riders taking dozens of growth hormones. Six of the team admitted a slush fund existed for buying drugs, which the riders topped up from their winnings.

The paranoia was scarcely eased when Mapei, the world's number one professional team, was formally investigated in the middle of the three-day De Panne stage race. Suspected doping led to the team manager, Patrick Lefèvre, and race leader Tom Steels being taken into custody: both were freed after the suspicions proved unfounded.

Lefèvre and the Mapei team were prevented from taking part in the third stage after a package addressed to their hotel was found to contain amphetamines. On their release, prosecutors said there was no evidence linking them to banned substances.

Yet there was to be no let-up in the police investigation, centred on Lille and involving four different forces. In March 1999 Virenque himself was charged with "complicity in the crime of facilitating and inciting the use of drugs, complicity in importing, possessing, offering and acquiring substances harmful to health and complicity in distribution, illegal possession and importation of prohibited goods".

An even more illustrious target was Roger Legeay, vice-president of the French Cycling Federation, who was charged with turning a blind eye to drug-taking while holding a position of responsibility.

In May 1999 Belgian rider Frank Vandenbroucke was arrested for doping offences, and promptly declared that he would not contest that year's Tour de France. Laurent Roux of France tested positive for amphetamines in the Flèche Wallone Classic. Marco Pantani, who had seemed beyond reproach when he took the 1998 Tour de France's final yellow jersey on the Champs-Elysées in Paris, claiming that he had won "the cleanest Tour" because police raids had made it so, was expelled from the 1999 Tour of Italy while leading after tests measured his red blood cell count at 52 per cent. Anything over 50 per cent is deemed prejudicial to health, and a sign the athlete has probably taken EPO. Pantani also declined to race in the 1999 Tour.

Tour organizers, meanwhile, keen to avoid a repetition of 1998's scandal, banned several top cyclists, including Virenque (who by now had moved to the Italian Polti team), Roux and the entire TVM team, as well as Manolo Saiz, director of the ONCE team, and its doctor Terrados. "Richard Virenque is not welcome at this year's Tour," said Tour director Jean-Marie Leblanc. "Since last July his name and image is the incarnation of doping...his presence is incompatible with the image and reputation of the event we want to preserve."

The news forced other withdrawals including that of Laurent Jalabert, who declared solidarity with his excluded ONCE boss. With Leblanc declaring that all 1999 Tour entrants would face mandatory drug tests when they assembled for the race prologue on July 3, the war against drugs in cycling was clearly still far from won.

The odds against the testers shifted yet again when only a week from the start of the 1999 race Hein Verbruggen, the president of cycling's ruling body, who had earlier all but admitted defeat in the battle against the blood-dopers, ordered Leblanc to readmit Virenque and Saiz on a technicality.

Tennis

Even tennis appears vulnerable to drugs, and the reaction of other professionals to the case of the Czech Peter Korda shows the damage they fear could be done to their sport if the threat is not addressed quickly.

Wimbledon has spent a century building up an image of elegance, good manners, strawberries and cream. In the time it took for Korda to give a urine sample, however, the idea that the All-England Championships offered a haven from the sordid world of performance-enhancing drugs was shattered.

It was a humiliating end to 1998, a year that began brilliantly for the 31-year-old Korda. Having previously just failed to climb the highest peaks, he had won his first grand slam title at the Australian Open.

Korda gave the drug sample after his Wimbledon quarter-final defeat at the hands of Tim Henman.

The British star noted that during the match Korda "obviously had some sort of problem with his ankle although it was a bit difficult to know exactly how bad it was.

"He appeared to be lame at some points, but I remember that in one game he went up for a smash like he was Michael Jordan and there did not seem to be much wrong."

When the test revealed nandrolone, Korda had his Wimbledon points and prize money deducted by the International Tennis Federation but escaped a ban owing to "exceptional circumstances", which at first were unexplained.

It seemed the Federation believed Korda and his character witnesses, even though experts said the drug could only enter the body through a large-bore needle.

As the year passed the anger of his fellow-professionals grew, peaking in Melbourne, just before Korda's defence of his title, when the first-ever mandatory players' meeting was held. Players quizzed Donna Young, head of the drug-testing programme, but her answers only revealed the rules' inadequacy. Since then, players have demanded more testing in an attempt to clean up their game before it is too late.

The Korda scandal was not the first. In 1995 Mats Wilander and his doubles partner, Karel Novacek, tested positive for cocaine at the French Open. For two years they fought the test findings but in 1997, by which time Wilander had retired, he accepted that the positive tests on him and Novacek were correct, although he claimed he had taken the substances unknowingly.

Peter Korda: his case led to calls for more tests.

Horse Racing

The 1980 Cheltenham Gold Cup was won by the Irish horse Tied Cottage, which later failed a drug test. Traces of theobromine, which can be traced back to an animal's food, were found in its blood.

How much drug-taking there is in horse racing is impossible to determine. However, just before the 1998 Breeders' Cup races in America, Willie Carson, the five-times British champion jockey, shocked the racing world by suggesting that the horses he wished to take to America should be pumped with Lasix and Bute. These are drugs which help horses withstand the pressure of riding on dirt and are banned in Europe, where no medication is permitted that will improve a horse's performance during a race. But the substances are allowed in the United States, and the episode showed how the different standards can complicate the efforts to stop drug-taking.

Beta Blockers

Most drugs in sport are used to enhance performance but some, such as beta blockers, are take to calm people down.

Beta blockers, a prescription tranquillizer, proved popular with modern pentathletes who could vary the dose to suit each of the various disciplines comprising their sport. At the 1972 Munich Olympics, more than a quarter of pentathletes were found to have taken them to control muscle tremor, giving them an advantage, for example, in the shooting element of the competition. Only after the 1984 Olympics were they banned.

In 1985 snooker player Silvino Francisco, complained that his rival in a final, Kirk Stevens, was "as high as a kite" on drugs. It was later revealed that several players, including WPBSA president Rex Williams, were taking beta blockers.

Snooker's authorities then came into conflict with the Sports Council, which offered grants and facilities for drug-testing. Initially they were not prepared to ban beta blockers, even though they were on the Sports Council's banned list.

Though players were using beta blockers for legitimate medical reasons – Williams compared it to taking a glass of scotch – the drug's ability to reduce stress and steady the arm was well-known in the athletics world. The tide was against them, and within two years beta blockers were banned in snooker.

Football

It used to be thought the only drug footballers would happily take was alcohol, and lots of it. However, in July 1998 drug-taking in football blew up as a major issue in Italy. Roma's coach Zdenek Zeman alleged in a magazine interview that certain players had achieved remarkable increases in muscle bulk by using drugs, and named Alessandro del Piero and Gianluca Vialli. Zeman offered no evidence other than their muscular appearance, and both players indignantly protested their innocence: Vialli called Zeman a "football terrorist".

Italy's National Olympic Committee, CONI, investigated, but within a month concluded there was no doping in the sport.

By this time, however, magistrates led by the Turin public prosecutor Raffaele Guarniello began a separate inquiry. Then the Bologna prosecutor Giovanni Spinosa opened a third inquiry after a chemist in the city admitted supplying stimulants to teams.

Questions were raised about CONI's anti-doping procedures, particularly its laboratories, which were alleged to be negligent and involved in a cover-up. The Rome laboratory, which was supposed to test the urine samples of footballers, confessed it did not have enough staff and that it could only analyse ten per cent of samples. Mario Pescante, head of CONI, resigned, protesting his innocence and claiming the issue had been blown out of proportion. All but three of the laboratory's other directors also quit or were fired.

By October Christian Pavone of Lecce had become the first player to be banned, having failed a drugs test. Pavone claimed he had fallen off his bicycle and needed urgent treatment. The investigation caused a furore: players threatened to go on strike but eventually backed down.

At the heart of the issue are the deaths of some 45 players which it is felt could have been caused by drug use.

They include Renato Curi, who dropped dead on the field from heart failure in 1977 during a Perugia–Juventus match; Andrea Fortunato and 38-year-old Bruno Beatrice, victims of leukaemia; the former Italian international Guido Vicenze, killed by a rare form of muscular degeneration; and 30-year-old Enrico Cucchi and 49-year-old Bruno Mora, both of whom died as a result of stomach tumours.

Guarniello is pursuing manslaughter charges against those who administered the substances: but his inquiry, expected to take two to three years, may be hampered by the fact that the archives of the Italian football federation are incomplete and unlikely to contain all the information he needs.

Dennis Rodman

The Orgasmic Worm

The American basketball player Dennis Rodman has been described as a cross between Paul Gascoigne and Dame Edna Everage, a rebellious athlete who likes dressing up as a girl. It would be more accurate to say that Rodman is Cantona, Gascoigne and Vinnie Jones rolled into one, but for good measure is black, stands 6ft 10ins tall, has been seen in gay clubs, likes wearing make-up and has called himself Denise.

As a basketball player he is a defensive specialist with super-fast reflexes; off the field he has been the supreme publicist and once had an affair with Madonna, who called him her Daddy Long Legs.

His nickname is Worm, although in his second autobiography he said he would like to change his name to Orgasms – not Dennis Orgasms or Rodman Orgasms but just plain Orgasms.

He often appears as a celebrity, and he can be paid as much as $1 million for doing half an hour's work.

He has butted a referee, insulted the Mormons of Utah and then suddenly vanished from the professional basketball circuit to make action movies with Jean-Claude Van Damme.

Rodman provokes both intense love and hate. At the end of every game Rodman tosses his sweaty shirt into the crowd and female fans, both black and white, line up near the players' tunnel to scream for the grubby garment.

Yet when Rodman took part in professional wrestling, a sport mainly for the not-so-smart section of American society but watched by some 22 million on cable television in the States every week, it was billed in the newspaper *USA Today* under the strapline, "Want to See Dennis Rodman Get His Butt Kicked?"

Rodman's showmanship often comes out through his hair, which at different times has been dyed orange, yellow with a reddish tint and silver. For good measure he also favours silver nail-polish and a feather boa.

A 6ft 10ins cross-dresser with 11 tattoos and a pierced navel and scrotum, Rodman catapulted to a superstar status that in the mid-1990s rivalled that of his then-Chicago Bulls team-mate Michael Jordan.

In a sports field where any non-conformist stands out, Rodman would always attract attention. But what makes Rodman part of the Babylon gallery is his behaviour not only on the field but off it – so much so that one American journalist has written of him: "Rodman isn't merely a disruption, he's *the* disruption – a walking, cruising, Las Vegas strip-clubbing nightmare." Rodman likes to portray himself as the baddest man in the land, the weird one in the ultimate freak show.

In June 1997, when the Chicago Bulls were going for yet another championship and played an away match against Utah Jazz, Rodman, who had a bad game, blamed it on lack of sex. Three times he had fled strait-laced Salt Lake City for the carnalities of Las Vegas. As if this was not enough to shock the ultra-conservative Mormons, he then added that he couldn't get his game flowing because "you've got a bunch of asshole Mormons out here".

The Anti-Defamation League instantly complained. That season Rodman had already been suspended twice from crucial games for the Chicago Bulls, once for swearing in front of millions on television, the second time for kicking a photographer. The previous season he had attacked and butted a referee, and been suspended for six games.

Now, for his Mormon remark, the NBA commissioner David Stern imposed a

Work hard, play hard: Rodman in action for the Chicago Bulls in 1996 *(left)* and with his former Playmate wife Carmen Electra.

$50,000 fine, the largest in NBA history. But for Rodman, who earned $19 million in the 1996 season, a $50,000 fine meant nothing.

This was made clear when he was asked for his comment on the fine. Rodman's reaction: he said he would like to kidnap Stern, "strip off all his clothes, rub lipstick all over him, dress him up like Frank Sinatra and sing to him". This was in keeping with the patented Rodman style, which is one that sports administrators accept. So when he posed naked on his Harley-Davidson for the cover of his autobiography, NBA executives merely shook their heads and said, "Dennis is just being Dennis."

Famous and successful as he now is, according to Rodman it could all have been very different: at one stage he claims to have thought seriously about ending his life. His autobiography begins: "On an April night in 1993 I sat in the cab of my pick-up truck with a rifle in my lap deciding whether to kill myself."

Brought up in a bleak Dallas housing

project, he was abandoned by his father at the age of three. Like many tall, young, athletic blacks, Rodman found his redemption in basketball. His background made him a natural rebel, not unlike many other black athletes. Where he has stood apart from other black athletes is in the way he has related to the wider white American world.

Rodman was once asked what he took at school: "Hubcaps, mostly," he replied. And, asked what he would he doing if he wasn't a basketball star, Rodman said, "About 30 years, I guess."

From there to dating Madonna is a big step, but for Rodman this has been a natural part of his journey and he glories in it. He described how Madonna once had a note delivered by hand to his locker-room after a game in Los Angeles. According to Rodman, "She'd wanted to get married; she said, 'Be in a bedroom in a specific hotel in Las Vegas on a specific day so you can get me pregnant.'"

In his autobiography Rodman gallantly went on to rate Madonna in bed, saying that while she wasn't exactly a sexual acrobat, she wasn't a dead fish either.

Unlike his one-time colleague Michael Jordan, who is graceful and the epitome of the best kind of sporting man, Rodman has gloried in saying things that were considered taboo in America. For instance, he claimed, "White women get into relationships with black men because they think the sex is going to be better."

Rodman can never stop being a showman, even when getting married or changing basketball clubs.

He married Carmen Electra in November 1998. The wedding to the former *Baywatch* babe, Prince backing singer and *Playboy* playmate took place in the Little Chapel of Flowers in Las Vegas. Carmen wore black leather, Rodman a baseball cap and Army fatigues – which for a man who likes to wear jangling earrings, gold bangles, a studded leather dog-collar, mascara, blusher, purple glitter, hot pants, a PVC halter-neck top and assorted chains was a serious case of under-dressing. Rodman must have been in a forgetful mood, for afterwards he confessed he could not remember a thing about it; he was too drunk. The wedding took place on a Sunday at eight in the morning.

In early February 1999 Rodman, Carmen Electra, his agent and his sister

Tattoo you: the Rodman insignia.

strode into the Beverly Hills branch of Planet Hollywood – not usually considered the ideal venue for sporting press conferences – and told the assembled journalists that he was to sign up with the LA Lakers.

In making the announcement he also specified the shirt number he would be wearing and cracked a joke about his favourite sexual position with his wife. But when reporters started quizzing him about why nobody from the Lakers was there and the specifics of the deal, he got angry, broke down, mumbled something about having very little money and stormed out. Yet within a couple of weeks, on 23 February, Rodman was indeed signing for the Lakers; a decision that led to a dispute within the club and the departure of the Lakers' coach, who was opposed to Rodman joining.

Neither Rodman's marriage nor his new club contract lasted long. He is separated from his wife, and in mid-April 1999 it was announced he would be leaving the Lakers, after a mere seven weeks.

The Lakers had won their first nine games with him; but then in March he went AWOL. He returned, but arrived late for a morning practice match and was then slow in getting ready because, he claimed, he could not find his shoes and socks. (Which could even be true: though he earns millions advertizing sports shoes Rodman prefers going barefoot around the house and does not even wear shoes to drive his pick-up or his Mercedes.)

Jerry West, the Lakers' vice-president, said, "This obviously didn't work out like we had hoped, but we would like to thank Dennis for the contributions he did make and wish him the best of luck."

None of this will dim Rodman's ability to cause a stir wherever he goes or to land in trouble: at present he is being sued for harassment by a waitress, who says he shoved a $100 bill down her blouse and tried to grab her breasts.

Dennis Rodman: he's one of a kind.

Career highlight: The Chicago Bulls celebrate their NBA championship in 1996.

4

Sexual and Other Misdemeanours

The highly-trained, focused athlete on the field who turns into a drunken slob off it is not a new phenomenon. In the days before intrusive tabloid newspapers, what sportsmen did in their own time rarely got into the public domain, often because they did it in the company of their journalist friends, who would think it a breach of ethics to reveal it to the world.

There can be little doubt that if Denis Compton and Keith Miller, two of the finest cricketers ever, were playing today, their exploits off the field would provide a year of tabloid front pages. The 1940s and '50s were a more discreet age and their escapades, passed around by word of mouth, merely added to their heroic status.

Stories are still told of how Compton arrived at Lord's on the morning of a Test match still in his dinner jacket from last night's revelry and then proceeded to score a century, or of how fast bowler Miller was often at his most devastating when nursing an awesome hangover. While ordinary mortals would need to lie down in a darkened room to recover, Miller did so with a cricket ball in front of a packed stadium, bowling a bouncer or two.

When, in the permissive 1960s, George Best emerged as the greatest footballer these isles have produced, the tales became more

Having it all: George Best with his girlfriend, then-Miss UK, Jennifer Lowe, plus Jaguar in 1996.

public, but Best still remained the sportsman everybody loved, partly because of his unique talent but also because his exploits were cast in such a kindly light. He became a legend for his boozing and bedding of innumerable women, including at least two Miss Worlds. Even when he went missing from his main occupation – playing for Manchester United – his exploits were viewed indulgently. The world seemed to see that, like all great talents, he had an instinct for self-destruction. Best the player seemed so perfect that Best the man must be flawed.

Once, on a pre-season trip to Copenhagen with United, he met a statuesque blonde whose breasts fascinated him. She was with her boyfriend, but on his return to England he put an ad in the Danish press for his "Danish dream girl". He received hundreds of letters; picked out Eva Haraldsted; brought her over to Manchester; proposed marriage; then tired of her and, when she sued for breach of promise, settled out of court for £500.

Even more spectacular was an escapade that made the BBC news for several nights in January 1971 – when he went missing. Eventually he was found holed up in the Islington flat of the actress Sinead Cusack.

Best, with his wild talent and wilder private life, could turn people's fantasies into reality. If only, we all said, he could control the drink – what Best called "the demon who keeps beating me". He attended drying-out clinics; once even went to Norway to have implants inserted to curb his need for drink. But they never really worked.

It was only in the 1990s, a very different, harder age, that people began to see Best for what he really was: a sad, drunken slob. Notoriously, he appeared on the Terry Wogan show drunk, having over-indulged in the BBC hospitality lounge. What followed was both painful and sad. Eventually Wogan asked about women: "I like screwing, all right", Best replied. Wogan, trying to change the subject, asked: "So what do you do with your time these days?" and Best replied, "Screw". It was at this point that Wogan, mercifully, brought the interview to a close.

In the 1970s and '80s, stories about sporting heroes and sex had glamour and humour. Peter Shilton, the then-England goalkeeper, was caught in his car at 5am with a married mother of three called Tina Street. His car was parked on a dirt road near Nottingham racecourse when Street's husband arrived, his suspicions having been aroused when Tina rang at 2.25am to say she was going for a meal with a girlfriend.

Colin Street followed Shilton's car as he and Tina left an Indian restaurant and, when Shilton parked, Street put his headlights on. Deciding Shilton was making love to his wife. he knocked on the window: a confrontation ensued and Shilton drove off, or tried to: instead he hit a lamp-post. Street called the police, and later said when the boys in blue had arrived Shilton was pulling up his trousers and Tina was hurriedly trying to get dressed.

Shilton subsequently failed a breath test, but probably his most sobering moment came when Nottingham Forest went to Highbury to play Arsenal a few days later. As he came on to the field, the North Bank shouted in unison: "Peter Shilton, Peter Shilton, does your missus know you're here? Does your missus know you're here?"

Shilton's lifestyle did not affect his playing abilities, but this could not be said of another gifted player of the 1970s, Frank Worthington. As he makes clear in his subtly-titled autobiography, *One Hump or Two*, he enjoyed the women and the drink that the game brought him: "My bed wasn't for sleeping, it was for birding. I was at it five nights a week, with rarely the same woman twice and often the odd quickie before a match...I never really minded who it was. Sometimes, though, I would wake up in the morning and look at the face next to me and wonder what the hell I was up to."

In his book, Worthington described joining the Mile High Club with the help of a married Frenchwoman, bedding both a mother and daughter while on tour in Sweden and a chambermaid just before leaving for a game. He also boasted of having made love to Mandy Rice-Davies, one of the decade's most notorious women: she had been a key figure in the famous scandal which ended the career of the government minister John Profumo. Frank met Mandy on a train during his time at Birmingham City, and their relationship was deep and meaningful enough for him to say in his book that he could understand why Cuban leader Fidel Castro had flown her to Havana for just a single night.

When Worthington was 23 Liverpool, then managed by the legendary Bill Shankly, had wanted to sign him, and he had to have his blood-pressure tested. The doctor found his pressure so high he advised Frank to take a holiday, try to relax and not even consider playing football. However, Frank had his own ideas. He went to his brother's wedding and ended up in bed with one of George Best's old girlfriends, Carolyn Moore.

The next day he left for his holiday in Majorca, where the friend in whose flat he was staying had two nubile Swedish girls waiting: Frank thoughtfully slept with both of them, and also had sex with a Belgian girl, temptingly called Knokke, whom he met later the same day. Not surprizingly, when he returned home his blood-pressure was still incredibly high and the transfer was cancelled.

A somewhat darker tale was that of Peter Storey of Arsenal, one of a number of hard-tackling players of the 1970s. Storey was good enough to play for England, but it was off the field that he attracted most attention.

As a player Storey lived the usual life of women and drink, including one three-in-a-bed romp with an air hostess and a team-mate. On another occasion he and a girl had sex while a team-mate hid in a wardrobe.

But it was after his playing days ended that Storey achieved real notoriety, as a professional in another, not unrelated field. He rented a flat in Leyton High Street, called it the Calypso Massage Parlour and allowed three prostitutes to ply their trade from the premises. This got him a fine of £700 and a three-month suspended sentence in 1979.

The following year he was gaoled for three years for trying to counterfeit gold coins: in 1982, he received two six-month gaol sentences for car theft. Declared bankrupt in 1983, Storey claimed he had spent all his money on women and drink. In 1990 came a 28-day sentence for illegally importing porn videos. By comparison, his 1991 conviction for swearing at a traffic warden, for which he got another 28 days, must have been light relief: the sort of high jinks sportsmen are supposed to get up to.

More lovable rogues were Ian Botham and Alex Higgins. Brilliant sportsmen both, their performances outside their chosen fields were at times shocking, more often amusing.

Botham was, arguably, the greatest all-round cricketer this country has produced since the war. His exploits in the 1981 Ashes series won him, but his deeds off the field also made the headlines.

In his autobiography Botham admitted smoking pot to relieve tension on the 1983–84 Test tour of New Zealand: he had tried it for the first time at a party, aged 18. During the tour the British tabloids claimed Botham and several other England players were using large quantities of both cannabis and heroin, although New Zealand police failed to find any evidence of this.

Botham sued the *Mail on Sunday*, and also publicly denied ever having used drugs; but as part of the libel settlement admitted in the paper that he had taken drugs after all. This was one of the reasons given by the TCCB for a decision to punish him in 1986.

On New Year's Eve 1984, after more media allegations, Botham's house was raided by police. Officers found cannabis and arrested Botham and his wife Kathy. She was released without charge, but Botham was charged with possession of 2.9 grams of cannabis and fined £100 at Scunthorpe Magistrates Court on 14 February 1985. Though this lost him a contract with Saab, his equipment manufacturer stood by him and a TCCB disciplinary hearing cleared him of bringing the game into disrepute. However, Botham does have the dubious honour of being the first professional cricketer convicted of a drugs offence.

During the 1986 England tour of the West Indies Botham again hit the headlines. At a party at Mick Jagger's home in Barbados he met Lindy Field, a former beauty queen and a friend of team-mate Bob Willis's sister-in-law. The *News of the World* ran a story involving Ian, Lindy, drugs and a broken bed. Botham insisted nothing had happened, pointing out that his father-in-law Gerry Walker had been a guest at the same party. Later he said he had learned Lindy had sold the story to fund a cocaine habit. However, his cause was not helped when a friend Tim Hudson, reportedly told a questing journalist: "I'm aware [Ian] smokes dope, but doesn't everyone?"

Back in the UK, Botham was again called before the TCCB. On 29 May 1986, while waiting for their verdict, he played brag with his then-lawyer Alan Herd, lost £375 to Herd and was then told he had been banned from the game for two months. He later discovered some members of the TCCB had pressed unsuccessfully for a life ban.

For much of the 1970s and '80s, as the snooker boom took off, Alex Higgins was the most charismatic player in the sport, but for all his brilliance with a cue he made as many headlines off the snooker table as he did on it.

Born in Belfast, the only son in a family of four children, it is perhaps no surprize Higgins turned out as he did. His father, brain-damaged as the result of an accident, was thus unable to read or write. Alex was very close to his mother, and she in turn supported him, including lying to the school welfare officer who called to discover why Alex had been absent for 34 days in a year.

The truth behind his truancy was that Alex was a self-confessed schoolboy hustler at the city's Jampot snooker club. Leaving school at 15 with no O-levels and unable to make a living from snooker, he answered a newspaper advert and left home for the first time to become a stable lad in Eddie Reavey's yard in Wantage, Berkshire. It was on the ferry to Liverpool that he had his first drink. But Alex's career as a prospective jockey was short-lived: he was dismissed for gambling.

After becoming a professional snooker player, Higgins won his first world title at the Crucible in Sheffield in 1972, and it was during his early career that allegations about his drug-taking and drinking first began to hit the headlines. The first stories originated from a source described by Higgins as a pusher and addict who made up stories to feed his own habit. Concerning one allegation – that Higgins, at a party in Marbella, was too stoned to have sex – he claims he threw out the young woman in question, who went to the press in a fit of pique. In his autobiography Higgins admits being offered and using cocaine, but insists he was never a serious addict and only ever used drugs socially. However, he is the first to admit that stories about his gambling were closer to the truth. His worst day at the races was at Wolverhampton in 1976, when he lost £13,000 in an afternoon.

After his second world championship win in 1982, Higgins was arrested after a disturbance at his Cheshire home which grew out of an argument with his wife, Lynn, who accused him of having an affair with Daniella, their Spanish *au pair*. After an evening together at a local pub, Alex and Daniella were in the snooker-room when Lynn came downstairs. His explanation – that he was showing Daniella his cue collection – did not go down at all well! Higgins was arrested, and by the time he was released out Lynn had left, taking their daughter Lauren and son Jordan with her.

Shortly afterwards, Higgins appeared at a tournament sporting a black eye, which he said was the result of a riding accident. In fact he had had a fight with a friend, Paul Medati, at the Potters club in Stockport. During a break in a practice session, Higgins decided to call Lynn and ask her to come back. Paul tried to stop him and they agreed to settle their differences in the matchroom. Higgins finally admitted the truth on ITV's *News at Ten* after Medati's girlfriend went to the papers.

After this incident, feeling unsupported by the WPBSA, snooker's governing body, Higgins went out to Dubai to recuperate. The break-up of his marriage, the relentless pressure of the professional circuit and the relentless media spotlight had brought him to the verge of a nervous breakdown. However, there was still no escape from the British tabloids, although Higgins claims a "mystery blonde" seen with him was an old girlfriend who came to his rescue when Lynn turned down the offer to join him.

As new stars emerged, Higgins slowly faded from the snooker scene. However, he remains one of the great names in the history of his sport – a man who could do wonderful things with a snooker ball but could not conquer his temperament.

One of the strangest cases involving sportsmen and drugs was that of England rugby captain Lawrence Dallaglio, who in May 1999 allegedly confessed to the *News of the World* that he had dealt drugs, had sex sessions with prostitutes in Amsterdam and snorted cocaine with fellow-British Lions after the victorious Test series against South Africa's Springboks in 1997.

Interest centred on the web of deception the tabloid created to elicit the alleged confession. Dallaglio's agent Ashley Woolfe was approached by a reporter calling himself Peter Simmons and claiming to be an executive of "CSR Partnership", supposedly a design and advertizing agency working on behalf of the shaving products firm Gillette. "Simmons" offered Woolfe £500,000 for Dallaglio to promote a new product and front an inner-city rugby promotion.

The scam was so convincing Woolfe agreed to bring the player to an introductory dinner at Langan's Brasserie in London. There Dallaglio was left alone with two *NoW* reporters, Phil Taylor and Louise Oswald, posing as Gillette UK's managing director and a public relations woman, while Woolfe and 'Simmons' discussed the deal elsewhere. After the meal, at which large quantities of champagne were drunk, Dallaglio was invited to a suite at the Park Lane Hilton. More champagne was drunk and the discussion turned to drugs and sex.

Dallaglio claimed the two reporters boasted of their drug-taking experiences, and he insisted it was this that led him to invent stories of his own drug adventures.

A month later, Dallaglio was summoned to a photographic session at the Conrad International hotel in the exclusive Chelsea Harbour area, where he posed with Gillette products. Later, alone with Taylor and Oswald, more champagne was produced and, Dallaglio said, the conversation was again steered round to sex and drugs. He alleged he was asked if he wanted to take drugs there, though none were produced.

Dallaglio also claimed his memory was hazy after drinking the champagne in both hotels, and that on the morning after he had a headache that could not be attributed to alcohol alone. Strangely, Sir John Hall, the former chairman of Newcastle United, reported that his son Douglas became unusually talkative after drinking a bottle of champagne produced by undercover *NoW* reporters in Marbella in 1998.

That incident resulted in a controversial front-page story in which Douglas Hall and fellow-director Freddie Shepherd were quoted as ridiculing Newcastle supporters and women from the city.

The Dallaglio story seemed to take an ominous turn for the player a fortnight later when the *Mail on Sunday* produced further

People's champion: for all his excesses Alex Higgins ws a genius at the snooker table.

allegations that he and fellow-Wasps players took cocaine during a club night out at a bar in south-west London. The allegations were based on sworn affidavits from Richard Nicholls, a chef at Harvey's Bar in Lavender Hill, and a female employee of the bar.

Dallaglio issued a complete denial: and within the week it emerged that the *Mail on Sunday* had been the victim of hoaxers, who had invented the follow-up story for money. One of Arsenal's biggest stars in the early 1990s, Paul Merson's talent should have earned him a regular place in the England team. However, rumours about excessive drinking and even drug use dogged the Highbury dressing-room, and few people who follow football were totally surprized when Merson called a press conference to admit his addictions to alcohol, cocaine and gambling. Merson chronicled all this in an autobiography, entitled *Rock Bottom*. Even then, there were some sports journalists who unsympathetically suggested Merson had added drug addiction to the list in a bid to win support from his club and the public.

During the mid-1980s Merson had hit the tabloid headlines for his drunken behaviour, particularly because of a one-night stand while on a binge. Through support group meetings, and with the backing of his wife and team-mates, Merson got his life under control again. He moved to Middlesbrough but did not stay, finding the dressing-room culture of drinking and gambling a danger to his new-found health. At the end of the 1997–98 season he moved to Aston Villa, and his turnaround was rewarded with a place in England's 1998 World Cup squad. But Merson remains a recovering alcoholic, drug addict and gambler who always seems to be fighting the demon drink.

What Stan Collymore is fighting within himself is difficult to say – perhaps he is too busy publicly fighting with his girlfriend – but his story shows how the media's treatment of modern sportsmen has changed.

The men discussed so far, with the possible exception of Paul Merson, were all great players – but even he is a footballing giant compared with Stan Collymore. As a player Collymore promised more than he ever delivered, and but for his behaviour off the field we might hardly have heard of him.

A brief look at Collymore the player, who was released by Walsall, the club he joined as a YTS trainee, shows how inflated both his value and his image are. His career to date has been one long catalogue of problems.

In January 1991 Collymore joined Crystal Palace, but left in November 1992 claiming he had been taunted at the training-ground by Ian Wright and Mark Bright on account of his Midlands accent. In January 1994, by now at Forest, he was fined £3,000 for a breach of club rules, although the club never disclosed what he did. In November that year he punched team-mate Alf-Inge Haaland during a training-ground practice match. In February 1995 he was cleared of assault after being racially abused outside a nightclub in his home town of Cannock. In October 1996, after joining Liverpool for £8.5 million, he was fined £20,000 – a club record – for missing training and failing to play in a reserve match. In February 1998, by then with Aston Villa, he alleged he had been racially abused by former Liverpool colleague Steve Harkness. Nothing came of it; but six months later, when Villa and Liverpool met again, Collymore's foul on Harkness was particularly brutal.

In this media-conscious, hype-infested age, however, Collymore has gained a high profile not because of his achievements on the field but largely because of his antics off it. In years to come, when his football has been long forgotten, he will be remembered as the man who made the World Cup in France a hooligan story even before it had begun, because of what he did to his girlfriend.

In a Paris pub called the Auld Alliance, where 500 Scottish fans had gathered before the Brazil–Scotland match which opened the World Cup match, Collymore punched and kicked the TV personality Ulrika Jonsson, leaving her in tears. Ulrika had been delighting the fans by pulling pints while they shouted, "There's only one Ulrika."

"It all happened so fast," said barman Stephen Dixon later. "The Tartan Army were all singing Ulrika's name as she was downing pints in one behind the bar. Collymore obviously couldn't handle it and kept saying, 'We are going, we are going.' But Ulrika wanted to stay another five minutes."

Collymore was even more upset when he found Ulrika chatting to movie star Ewan MacGregor, and that seemed to set him off. As Danny Farmer, another barman, recalled: "He was like a deranged animal. He jumped out of nowhere as Ulrika was drinking beer like he was some kind of mad stalker. There was real anger in his face and his eyes were staring as he hit her. Ulrika flashed past me and hit the deck. Then Collymore lashed out with his hands and feet. Ulrika was screaming for him to stop, but he kept on hitting and slapping her and grabbing her hair. At one point he shouted her name. I grabbed him by the arm with two other lads and one of them had to head-butt him to get him out of the door."

The barman who butted Collymore, Stephen Dixon, said, "He started pushing back, so I gave him the Glasgow Kiss. The rest of the staff were all shouting to get him away. I got him straight out of the door and locked it behind him."

Beside himself with remorse, Collymore later said in a statement: "A stupid and silly argument had developed throughout the day with myself and Ulrika, someone who I have realized is very special to me. My actions are totally reprehensible, something I am not proud of and finding it very difficult to come to terms with. In a fit of petulant temper I struck out at the girl I love and immediately regretted my action, but it was too late."

Months later, Collymore was still clearly besotted with Ulrika. According to one close friend, "Stan loves Ulrika but he says she is literally driving him around the bend. When he asked her to marry him for the first time she said 'No'. He asked her again and she said 'Yes'. Two days later she said she had changed her mind. The poor guy doesn't know what to do with himself."

Lyndsey Nicholas, who had an on-off friendship with Collymore, described how he once rang Ulrika at four in the morning. On another occasion he was on the phone to her while Lyndsey was at his home. "I suddenly heard him shout, 'You bitch; why are you doing this to me?' And then I heard something smashing. He came downstairs and he was sobbing uncontrollably."

During another conversation Ulrika had hung up on him, whereupon she again saw Collymore in tears. According to Lyndsey, he once said he thought he was on the verge of a breakdown. She later heard him tell Villa physio Jim Walker, "I really need psychiatric help."

Collymore's eventual crack-up took place in the last week of January 1999, on his 28th birthday. Instead of going out to celebrate he spent the day surfing the Internet, and later phoned Jim Walker to say he could not cope.

On the morning of Friday 29 January he was admitted to a London clinic where he spent two hours before being driven away, grim-faced, in a blacked-out Range Rover. Earlier Collymore had gone missing after being left on the substitutes' bench for Villa's 2–0 FA Cup defeat by Fulham. He also missed their 2–1 defeat at Newcastle on the Saturday, the day after he went to the clinic.

Villa issued a carefully neutral statement: "Stan Collymore has made it clear that pressures and stress have been building up for a long period of time which culminated in the decision by the club not to consider him fit to play on Saturday. Following this Stan has declared he is to seek further counselling to help him overcome his current difficulties."

Fellow-players such as Paul Merson have been sympathetic: Collymore, they say, is a loner. He comes for training: he goes home: he is quiet, not a mixer.

Ulrika Jonsson's mother had no such sympathy. She had no doubt that Collymore was a nutcase. Mrs Gun Brodie said, "He is the type of person who needs counselling and I just hope he is going to get some good help because he needs it. If he is in a clinic he should stay there. He isn't a very stable guy, and we don't want anything more to do with him."

The Paris incident was not the first time Collymore had been accused of hitting a woman. In April 1998, two months before, he had been cleared of assaulting former girlfriend Michele Green.

Apart from Ulrika, one of the reasons given for Collymore's crisis was that he had been a substitute for six of the previous eight matches before the cup defeat by Fulham.

Collymore was not the first player to find the stress of the professional game more than he could handle. As a young player, Brian Law was told by QPR that he would not make it in the top flight. His response was to set off walking round the world, living, as he put it himself, like a hippie. Returning to football with Wolverhampton Wanderers, he soon went off the rails, helped steal and crash a bus in the town centre and found himself in court. he was covicted of aggravated theft and taking a vehicle without permission, and was sentenced to 200 hours of community service, fined and given a driving ban. Since then he has settled down to captaining Millwall and is regarded as a solid centre-half.

However, no other player's personal problems have received such extensive media treatment as Collymore's, at least not since the days of Best, and Collymore is hardly in the Best class. John Gregory, the Villa manager, reflected the bewilderment felt by many when he confessed: "I'm gob-smacked by the whole issue and find it hard to accept.

"I find it difficult to understand how anyone in Stan's position, with the talent and the money he has, is stressed. I do often wonder how a 29-year-old at Rochdale, in the last three months of his contract with a mortgage and three kids, copes with stress. I wonder what they would be thinking, looking at this. And there are plenty of Aston Villa fans, too, who have their own worries and who will be looking at this and finding it hard to understand. I just can't see how players get stressed, or maybe I'm old-fashioned. I'm totally confused by it all; the issue is a new one to me."

As Collymore was talking to shrinks, there was talk of Villa signing the Brazilian Juninho from Atletico Madrid, and it emerged that Collymore, whether in a clinic or not, stood to gain financially if the deal went through. Because of a clause in his contract guaranteeing him parity with the highest-paid players, had Juninho joined then Collymore's wages would have gone up from £25,000 to £30,000 a week. His pay had already risen by £5,000 when Gareth Southgate and Dion Dublin overtook him in the wages league table at Villa.

As it turned out, the deal fell through; but it is a sober commentary on the state of the modern game that so much money and attention should be paid to such a player.

A few weeks after the Collymore saga, Graeme Le Saux and Robbie Fowler showed other ways in which modern footballers have been troubled by sex and drugs.

In the last week of February 1999, Liverpool visited Chelsea for a League match. Just after referee Paul Durkin had booked Le Saux for time-wasting, TV cameras picked up Le Saux felling Fowler with a blow to the head which Durkin didn't see (in fairness to his, the print journalists covering the match missed it too).

Both Le Saux and Fowler were hauled up by the FA on a charge of misconduct, and a rather unpleasant story began to emerge.

Within days, "friends" of Le Saux were telling the *Guardian* newspaper about the anguish and traumas that had made him strike out at Fowler. (The effect of this technique, favoured by royals and disgraced politicians, is that no intelligent reader is left in any doubt that the friend is really expressing the thoughts of the person in question).

Fowler, according to Le Saux's friends, had persistently abused him, calling him a "poof" and a "faggot". Midway through the second half, as Chelsea were about to take a free kick, Fowler bent over and pointed his bottom at him, shouting, "Come on, come on, give it to me up the arse."

Le Saux complained to the referee and the linesman, but they did not take any action. Le Saux was then booked for time-wasting. Le Saux told Fowler that he was a disgrace and that he had insulted his family. Fowler responded, "Fuck your family."

According to Le Saux's friends, as reported in the *Guardian*, "He had never been humiliated like that before. He's had abuse in the past, but last Saturday was the worst ever. Graeme just lost his cool. He has suffered a lot of provocation in the past, but he felt utterly humiliated, and the fact that it came from an England colleague made it harder for him to accept." So he hit him.

Le Saux, whose wife Marianna is an arts graduate and who recently became a father, has always maintained he is neither homosexual nor for that matter anti-homosexual, but sees no reason for him to prove anything. He feels what has happened to him is part of football's failure to deal with anything that is different.

English football has always hated nonconformity. When Hunter Davies wrote *The Glory Game*, his classic book about the Tottenham of the 1970s, he noticed Mike England stood out because he read the *Daily Telegraph*; all the other players read the *Daily Mirror*, then the most popular paper in the land. It is interesting to note that Mike England was Welsh: the rest of the team were all of traditional English stock.

Two decades ago, when West Bromwich Albion visited China, the only members of the team who took up the invitation to visit the Great Wall were the three black players, Laurie Cunningham, Brendon Batson and Cyrille Regis. Manchester United's Brian McClair was considered "odd" because on a visit to a place such as Kosice in Slovakia he would seek out an ancient church.

Le Saux, who comes from Jersey, grew up in a small community where he was encouraged to be open-minded. Chelsea signed him in December 1987, and from the start he stood apart from other new recruits to the game. While they lived in digs, he lived with family friends in Kingston, Surrey. His Sundays were spent visiting antique fairs, assembling a collection which included furniture and a grandfather clock.

Unlike the stereoyped modern player, popularly supposed to spend his time outside training either with the bookmaker or on the pool table, Le Saux preferred to hang out in a West End café or visit an art gallery.

His problems started when, aged 21 he

Raving Rovers: Blackburn skipper Tim Sherwood breaks up the fisticuffs between Graeme Le Saux and David Batty

went on a camping trip with three male friends. When he returned, his fellow-players were saying he was gay. A few months later, while playing against West Ham, he heard the jeering taunt, "Le Saux likes it up the arse."

All this may have contributed to his developing what is widely seen in the game as a fiery temper. In December 1997 he was reported to have made obscene gestures which incited a fight between Spurs and Chelsea players. Earlier in the 1998–99 season, too, when Chelsea went to Anfield to play Liverpool, he had clashed with Paul Ince. In September 1998 he was sent off against Blackburn after a scuffle with Sebastian Perez: TV pictures showed Le Saux throwing a punch. But it was his clash with his own team-mate in a European match that first set Le Saux apart.

There are times when even the most gentlemanly footballer feels like punching an opponent (though mercifully most resist the temptation): but to deliver a left hook to someone on your own side takes an unusual level of anger. This is exactly what Le Saux, by then with Blackburn, did in November 1995. In the fourth minute of their away match against Spartak Moscow, Le Saux lashed out at David Batty after they collided accidentally. Luckily for Le Saux the referee did not see the clash.

It appears Batty had been sniping at Le Saux, supposedly referring to his alleged homosexuality. Le Saux later apologized and revealed he had made his peace with Batty. "There were reasons why I did what I did, but I was unprofessional and I'm sorry for letting everyone down. It all happened, though, because of something that went on on the pitch and not before the game."

Le Saux faced a month out with a broken

hand, the result of his left hook to Batty's chin: he was also fined £12,000.

The Le Saux-Fowler incident prompted the press to address for the first time the question of homosexuality in the game. *Gay Times* editor David Smith told *BBC News Online* that while Le Saux was not gay, the "rule of averages" meant there must be many homosexuals in the Premiership, and possibly several in the England squad. But Smith, an Arsenal fan, said football's "pack mentality" tended to discourage gay teenagers, who preferred individual sports.

Britain's first openly gay footballer, Justin Fashanu, committed suicide in 1988, and Smith felt that sport, and football in particular, seemed to be lagging behind other sectors in coming to terms with homosexuality. He said: "Nowadays there are many openly gay people in showbusiness and even half a dozen gay MPs. Individual sports, such as tennis, do not have a problem with it. But, the late Justin Fashanu aside, football seems to be holding out."

David Allison, a spokesman for pressure group Outrage!, said he thought ten per cent of players were gay but that his organization, which has in the past "outed" politicians and clergy, would not seek to unmask secretly-gay footballers unless they hypocritically expressed homophobic views.

Gordon Taylor, chief executive of the Professional Footballers' Association, agreed Le Saux had a quick temper, but added: "On this occasion he deserves some sympathy. He was provoked...[had it been] a racist taunt we would want to eradicate it, and I think we should look at what we can do to avoid the lad having to put up with this. If we can't stop it from supporters we should be able to stop it from players, because clearly it presents a chance of damaging and ruining his career."

Taylor pointed out that taunts, be they racist, sexual or whatever, were common in boxing, rugby, ice-hockey and in cricket, where the practice is called 'sledging'. The idea is to goad a player into losing his temper or letting his concentration slip. "Sometimes players will latch on to something when they know a player is particularly sensitive and will react," he said.

Piara Powar, a co-ordinator with the anti-racist Kick It Out campaign, conceded that racist abuse was more common than sexual but added: "Something similar also needs to happen in terms of other forms of abuse, whether it is over the question of someone's alleged sexuality or whatever."

He was supported by David Mellor, the former Tory minister who is now head of the government's football taskforce. Calling for sledging to be stamped out, Mellor said: "The ridiculous situation where Fowler was waggling his backside at Le Saux and Le Saux protested and got a yellow card was not what the game is all about." All this led an FA spokeswoman to confirm that sexual taunting was included, along with racial abuse, in the FA's misconduct charge.

Within weeks of this incident, which was all about Le Saux's response to baseless charges of homosexuality, the spotlight had shifted back to Fowler who was now in even deeper trouble for trying to answer, albeit stupidly and mockingly, what he insisted were equally groundless charges of drug abuse.

After he scored for Liverpool against Everton in a Merseyside derby, he celebrated by running to the goal-line and crawling along it with his nose to the ground as if sniffing a line of coke. Colleagues tried to pull him away, but he repeated the gesture.

It was later explained that Fowler felt provoked by taunts from the Everton supporters – and by the endless jibes he kept hearing in Liverpool – to the effect that he was a cocaine addict.

The FA took a dim view of this and hauled him in on another misconduct charge. A hearing in Birmingham considered both his confrontation with Le Saux and his mimicking of a coke addict: he was banned for six matches and fined £20,000.

The FA were particularly sensitive to Fowler's coke-sniffing action, given the results of the introduction of random drug tests within English professional football in recent years. Although there is yet to be a single positive test for steroids, it has revealed players' use of 'recreational' drugs.

Chris Armstrong tested positive for cannabis while at Crystal Palace in 1995, and was obliged to undergo counselling sessions. Two Charlton players – Lee Bowyer, now with Leeds, and Dean Chandler – also showed traces of cannabis, as did Arsenal's David Hillier, who claimed he'd been offered a cigarette at a party and was unaware that it contained anything other than tobacco.

While the imposition of rehab and counselling sessions for cannabis use might seem excessive to some, more recent positive tests for cocaine and ecstasy resulted in harsher penalties from the FA.

Leyton Orient's Roger Stanislaus was banned for a year and sacked by his club after cocaine was found in a sample taken on the morning of a league match, while West Bromwich's Shane Nicholson, Barnsley's Dean Jones and Jamie Stuart of Charlton also received bans for using amphetamines or cocaine. Jay Notley, another young Charlton player, tested positive for a cocktail of ecstasy, cocaine and cannabis. Although to the players these indulgences might seem recreational, the authorities consider cocaine and amphetamine performance-enhancing.

"The use of drugs is growing within society and especially among young people," said the FA's spokesman Steve Double. "Footballers are young; some of them have a lot of money. If players do get caught, we have shown we come down hard on them. But to call it an epidemic in football is an exaggeration."

Crossing the line: Robbie Fowler's "coke-sniffing" goal celebration.

Mike Tyson
The Norman Bates of the Ring

Mike Tyson achieved fame, respect and glory by becoming the youngest ever world heavyweight boxing champion, but then proceeded to drag both himself and his sport through the gutter by his behaviour in and out of the ring. He has served one prison sentence for rape and assault, is serving another for road rage, and has been disqualified for biting off a chunk of his opponent's ear in a world championship fight.

After that, as he tried to get back his licence to fight, he was examined by therapists who told the Nevada State Athletic Commission that Tyson was "sort of desperate to feel touched and loved". Tyson himself said, "I feel like Norman Bates surrounded by all these doctors."

This vision of the boxer as psychopath seemed a thousand miles away in 1986, when Tyson became WBC world champion at the tender age of 20 years and five months by beating Trevor Berbick in Las Vegas. It took him only an additional ten months to become the undisputed champion by winning the WBA and IBF versions as well.

For the next two years, his blend of brute strength and considerable skill enabled him to rule the division in a class of his own. He was a popular and respected champion, who appeared genuinely modest and more interested in boxing than fame and fortune.

The change came, in the eyes of many boxing commentators, when he became involved with the promoter Don King. Still only 22, he suddenly stopped developing as a boxer; at the same time, his character started to deteriorate. The change was summed up by *Boxing Illustrated*, which in 1989 produced a cover story headed "Is Mike Tyson Becoming the Most Unpopular Heavyweight Champion in History?"

In the ring, he defeated the British fighter Frank Bruno in five rounds but looked a mere shadow of the boxer who had beaten Michael Spinks. He lacked the intensity that was his hallmark in earlier contests, and he fought only in spurts; he moved his head less frequently and had become an easier target.

The warning signs were there when Tyson pulled out of a fight with Razor Ruddock, claiming a lung infection but refusing to allow any hospital tests to prove the ailment. It was in February 1990, however, that the slow, lethargic, overweight Tyson paid the ultimate price for his failure to train or take any fight seriously.

On paper it was a mismatch: the 24-year-old undefeated champion against a mediocre journeyman called James "Buster" Douglas. While Douglas had lost only four of his 34 contests, many of his wins were lacklustre, and people talked of his notable defeat against Tony Tucker when, seemingly set for victory, he gave up and virtually allowed Tucker to hammer his motionless body at will. The referee stopped the fight and Tucker went on to win the IBF world heavyweight crown, eventually losing it to Tyson. Douglas's performance had so appalled his own father that he walked away and never attended another of his son's fights. So nobody questioned the bookies' odds of 35–1 against a Douglas win, which had risen to 42–1 by fight day.

But in the ring it was all very different. Only once did Tyson, behind for the first time in his life, find inspiration, knocking Douglas down with a right uppercut. Douglas was ready to rise at the count of two but waited until nine before getting up. Two rounds later a three-punch combination sent Tyson to his first defeat. It was after this fight that Muhammad Ali rang Thomas Hasseer, his biographer, and asked, "Do you think folks will now stop asking if I could have beaten Tyson in my prime?"

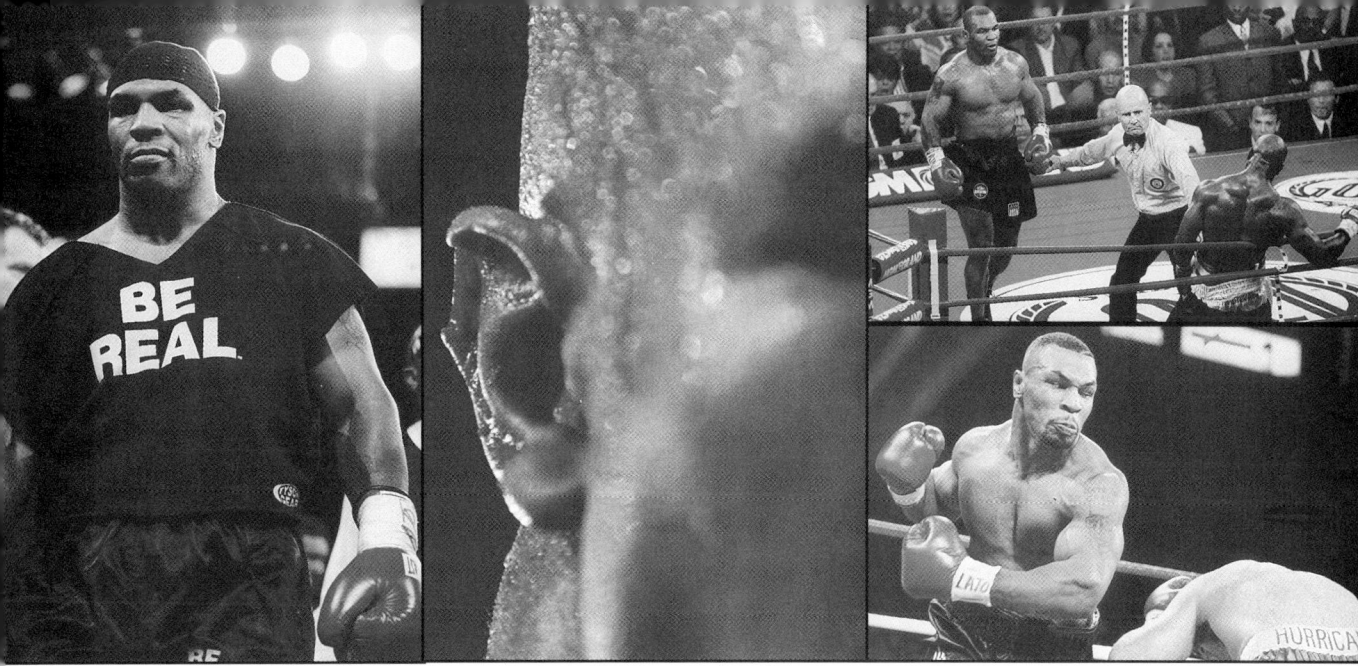

Courting controversy *(clockwise from left)*: Tyson has a message for his opponent before the fight against Frans Botha in January 1999; Holyfield's mutilated ear; Tyson harries his bloodied opponent at Las Vegas in June 1997; and his onslaught has McNeeley taking cover in August 1995.

The question is impossible to answer. Ali, for all his bravery and skill in absorbing George Foreman's monstrous attacks during 1975's "Rumble in the Jungle", might have found Tyson's ferocious assaults hard to take. However, one thing Tyson could never have was Ali's innate sportsmanship, and his actions from the moment he lost to Douglas showed that whatever his physical abilities, he was no sportsman.

Instead of accepting defeat and trying to analyse it Tyson, aided and abetted by Don King, claimed that Douglas had been down for 13 seconds, that he should have been counted out and that he, Tyson, should still be champion. It took the better part of two weeks to force Tyson to back down.

From then on Tyson's life went into a downward spiral from which it has never recovered. Nine months later Tyson was in court in Manhattan for a hearing to assess damages to a woman he had been found guilty of fondling in December 1988. And in 1992 he went on trial, accused of raping a contestant in the Miss Black America contest which he was attending in Indianapolis. Several of the contestants had complained that Tyson had molested them during the pageant, and the previous year's winner filed a $100 million lawsuit against him.

According to the prosecution, in the early hours of the morning, Tyson invited Diane Washington, one of the pageant contestants, to his hotel room. What followed was the basis of the charge. The next day Washington went to a local hospital, claiming she had been raped. By then Tyson had left Indianapolis, even though he had a number of engagements in the city. However, his hotel room had not yet been cleaned, and the police were able to gather forensic evidence from the bedsheets. He was indicted on rape charges in September and arrested almost two months later as he prepared to fight Evander Holyfield.

At the trial Tyson was charged with rape, confinement and criminally deviant behaviour. Both Tyson and Washington testified, the latter saying that if Tyson had apologized and sought help for his violent behaviour, she would not have gone to the police. The jury took less than ten hours to find Tyson guilty on all three charges. His appeal failed, and in March 1992 he was gaoled for six years. He should have been eligible for parole after three, but violent behaviour early in his sentence earned him an additional two months.

In fact Tyson was given an early release, and came out on 25 March 1995, after which he regained the WBC heavyweight title in 1996, stopping Bruno in the third round. Holyfield was a tougher proposition, however, and he defeated Tyson in a fight that was stopped in the 11th round.

But it was the rematch a year later that

was to create the biggest headlines and strip Tyson of what little dignity he had left. Tyson alleged that Holyfield had delivered a deliberate butt to his eye which had left it bleeding. Enraged, he bit off part of Holyfield's ear. Disqualification was inevitable, as was the revocation of his boxing licence, and he was fined $3 million by the Nevada State Athletic Commission.

Tyson would later show remorse, but he would also say, "I wanted to kill him, bite him. I was enraged and angry." As he waited for the Nevada State Athletic Commission to let him box again, he said in a revealing interview with *Playboy* magazine:

"No one gives a fuck about Mike Tyson. If some one accuses Mike Tyson of a horrible crime, they say, 'Yeah, he's capable of that, Mike probably did it.' Nobody's fighting a crusade for my black ass. I expect the worst to happen to me in my life. I expect that one day somebody will blow my fucking brains out over some bullshit, that his wife or girlfriend might like me and I don't even know that she exists."

Tyson's licence was restored in October 1998 after a plea from Muhammad Ali. In an emotional statement – delivered by Ali's wife, because Ali is suffering from Parkinson's disease – the former world champion said:

"I sit here today on Mike's behalf because I know he is ready to walk from this hearing and make his mark in history. I will be there for him to help and want nothing. There's a lot of work in the world for us to do: good work, helping people. But first Mike needs to go back to work. He needs to go back to what he knows best – boxing: something he has done from the age of 12."

The support of Ali and the American basketball legend Magic Johnson could help Tyson win his licence back, but they could not keep him out of trouble. Even as Tyson was filing a $100 million lawsuit against his former mentor King, his reputation was further savaged inside and outside the ring.

Tyson was pitted against the South African Francois Botha, a man whom he could have defeated in his prime with one hand tied behind his back.

Before the fight Tyson said he expected the South African to die. But he was barely matching Botha on points when he knocked him out in the fifth round. During the fight Tyson twice locked Botha's arm in a clinch and violently wrenched it. Tyson did not deny Botha's allegations that the aim had been to break his arm.

But this apology for a comeback was overshadowed by another assault charge – indeed, it was hanging over Tyson as he tried to win back his licence. In September 1988, Tyson's Mercedes was rear-ended by another vehicle in a minor accident. Tyson leapt out of the car and assaulted the other two drivers involved, punching one and kicking the other in the groin. They filed lawsuits against him, alleging assault. Tyson pleaded "no contest" and, shortly after his fight with Botha, he received two concurrent two-year gaol terms, one for each of the motorists involved, but with one year suspended. He was also fined $5,000 and ordered to undertake 200 hours' community service. His imprisonment is said to be costing the sport £150 million in lost revenue.

Tyson had paid compensation to the victims and hoped to get off. But Judge Stephen Johnson agreed with prosecutors that Tyson was "a time bomb waiting to explode and a danger to the public". He also said, "There is a lasting image of a violent, volatile personality. Tyson repeatedly acts compulsively and violently."

Tyson and his supporters were shocked by the decision, but its correctness is beyond question. This was underlined shortly afterwards when he had to be sent to the segregation unit of his Maryland prison after throwing a TV set at the bars of his cell. This time, it appears, the rage was triggered by the fact that he could not take his anti-depressants as he refused to allow the prison psychologist to examine him.

The greatest tragedy of Tyson's decline is that it also destroyed his reputation in boxing, the sport that saved him from a life of crime and violence. His parents were unmarried when he was born in New York in 1966, and his father, unable to work after a heart attack, left the family.

Small for his age, with a noticeable lisp and nicknamed "Fairy Boy", Tyson was an easy target for bullies, including his older brother; but the turning-point came when he fought back against a boy who killed one of his beloved racing pigeons. Later he admitted to enjoying the feeling of taking control and defending himself.

After joining a local gang, the "Jolly Stompers", he was soon in trouble with the police, and by the time he was 12 had graduated from petty theft and bag-snatching to store robberies. Tyson spent time in juvenile detention centres, but after being released or escaping he always returned to his mother's house to start the cycle again. By the time he met Muhammad Ali, then the heavyweight champion of the world, who was touring some of the deprived areas of the city, Tyson was involved with robberies using guns.

Eventually, with his behaviour continuing to spiral out of control, Tyson was sent to the Tryon school for boys in upstate New York. It was here that his interest in boxing began to develop.

Reacting badly to the discipline of the school system, he was quickly moved to a house for the most disruptive boys. One of the school's counsellors was a former professional boxer, Bobby Stewart, who had won the Golden Gloves championship as an amateur. He recognized Tyson's potential and set about working with him.

Stewart also realized Tyson could neither read nor write, and that this was contributing to his frustration and anger. He introduced Tyson to manager Cus D'Amato, who was to become one of the biggest influences in Tyson's early career. D'Amato had a home in the Catskills, and at the age of 14 Tyson moved in with Cus and his wife.

The couple had a real understanding of troubled youngsters, and Tyson improved in both his boxing abilities and his temper almost overnight, winning the Golden Gloves championship himself in 1984. He failed, however, in his attempt to get into the 1984 Los Angles Olympics squad when he lost in the trials to Henry Tillman. Tyson turned pro in 1985 aged 18 and in the first year of his professional career had 15 fights, all of which he won by a knock-out.

At this time he started dating the TV star Robin Givens who, like Tyson, came from a broken home, and had been pushed and encouraged by her mother Roper to be a success. Some of Tyson's friends felt that Roper was encouraging her daughter to go after Tyson as a way of increasing her own profile, as she had already had a string of famous boyfriends including the basketball player Michael Jordan.

Tyson and Givens eloped and married in February 1988, but within six months the marriage was already in trouble amid rumours of violence on Tyson's part. In October 1988 Robin filed for divorce in California, whose community property laws would entitle her to half Tyson's fortune. She cited verbal and physical abuse and irreconcilable breakdown, and appeared on talk-shows and news interviews describing "my hell with Mike Tyson". Tyson countersued, accusing Givens of defamation, manipulation and money-grubbing. The divorce was granted in 1989.

Many people trace Tyson's problems back to his involvement first with Robin Givens and then with Don King. But perhaps it is truer to say that Mike Tyson's story is that of a sportsman who sought redemption through the violence in the boxing ring, hoping it could save him from the violence he was born to but to which in the end he succumbed. His enemy was the violence within him, which sport could neither alter, shape, moderate nor lessen, but merely provide a world-wide platform to display.

Just before his latest gaol sentence Tyson said, "They keep talking about sending me back to prison. So get on with it and send me. Maybe I'd be better off inside than out here with everyone giving me a bunch of crap about how I'm supposed to behave."

It is a sad but sobering comment from the man who could have become the greatest boxer ever, but was defeated by the demons inside him.

5

Racism in Sport

Racism in sport is hardly a modern invention. The Ancient Greeks, who are credited with inventing the concept of sport, knew all about excluding people because of their race. Not only did they have slaves, many of them foreign, but they treated foreigners with great disdain. Sparta did admit foreigners, but only grudgingly, and from time to time expelled them. Athens was more liberal, but again there was no question of naturalizing foreigners. And as far as the Olympic Games were concerned, only men could take part – and only men of pure Greek blood.

It was in the United States and South Africa, however, that institutionalized racism was comprehensively introduced into sport.

Not until 1947, two years after the United States had participated in a war to fight the scourge of Nazism, that in its own homeland it allowed the first black player to play in the national game of baseball. Until the historic moment when Jackie Robinson stepped up to the plate in a Brooklyn Dodgers game America's black or, as they were then called, Negro players could not play major-league baseball and had to organize their own all-Negro leagues.

Such was the racism that even exhibition matches could not take place. In September 1887 an all-Negro team was due to play the St Louis Browns, an all-white team, and 7,000 people had gathered in the stadium at West Farms in New York State, when a telegram arrived from the Browns' owner saying that his team had too many injured players. The fact was that eight of the players did not want to play against blacks. They had told their owner, "We will cheerfully play against white people at any

Hitler's *bête noir*: Jesse Owens, the American sprinter, at the Berlin Olympics in 1936.

time and think, by refusing to play, we are only doing what is right."

This idea that it was somehow morally right not to play blacks was to be given even stronger force by the white South Africans, who carried the torch of racism in sport until the beginning of the 1990s, when the release of Nelson Mandela and the dismantling of the apartheid system finally killed off their rather novel concept of sport.

Sometimes an attempt to beat the American colour bar produced farcical results. In 1901 John McGraw, the manager of the New York Giants, found an exceptional black player called Charlie Grant. Because he was light-skinned, McGraw tried to pass him off as a Cherokee Indian called Tokohama, but the secret got out. Another owner said, "The Cherokee of McGraw is really Grant, the crack Negro second baseman from Cincinnati, fixed up with war-paint and a bunch of feathers."

Even in 1947, when Jackie Robinson finally broke the colour bar, it took a lot of artful dodging by the Brooklyn Dodgers' manager, Branch Rickey, who knew the other owners would oppose it. When he had suggested it in 1945 all but one of the owners of the then 15 major league baseball teams voted against. So Rickey sought out a symbolic man who could break the barrier. He found Robinson, aged 26, and coached him relentlessly for hours, telling him how he would have to put up with insults from opponents and supporters, bias from umpires and even racism from hotels and innkeepers who might refuse to let him stay with the rest of his white colleagues. He then packed him off to Montreal, one of the Dodgers' farm clubs. Robinson survived, and in 1947 Rickey brought him to the Dodgers.

Even then there was trouble. Rickey had to make sure that the blacks in Brooklyn would not be too triumphalist at this breaking of the colour bar and sought the help of Brooklyn's community leaders. One team, the St Louis Cardinals, refused to play but were told by the baseball authorities they had to; and although Robinson got plenty of abuse, particularly from Philadelphia players, he did finally make it. Even then, however, it was many years before the racial barrier was completely broken.

Just before Robinson played his first match at Montreal, Clay Hooper, the Montreal manager, asked Rickey, "You don't really think Nigrahs are human beings, do you?"

The question was very similar to the one the Nazis had raised exactly ten years earlier during the 1936 Olympics in Berlin.

Hitler had considered the Olympics the perfect opportunity to demonstrate the superiority of the blond Aryan Germans, but this plan was blown to smithereens when Jesse Owens, the son of black sharecroppers from Alabama, won four gold medals in track and field, setting new world records in the process. In five days of competition he raced ten times, in the 100 metres, the 200 metres and the 4 x 100 metres relay, and jumped twice in the long jump competitions. He won them all, in the process equalling the record for the 100 metres and setting new standards for the long jump and 200 metres.

Although Owens' achievements had exploded the Nazi myth of racial superiority, some Germans refused to accept them. The German press called Owens and the blacks in the American team "black auxiliaries", and Martha Dodd, the daughter of the American ambassador in Berlin, recorded a comment made to her by an aide to Joachim von Ribbentrop, who had just been appointed ambassador to Britain. The aide said blacks were animals and utterly unqualified to enter the Olympics, and that, "of course, if the Germans had had the bad sportsmanship to enter deer or another species of fleet-footed animals, they could have taken the honours from America in track events."

The inherent racial problems in American sport were highlighted in dramatic fashion during the 1968 Olympics in Mexico. The Olympics, that most political of all movements, has always taken a rather dim view of athletes who did anything that could damage the Games' carefully nurtured non-political image. But, given the volatile racial climate of the United States in the 1960s and the large number of black athletes in the American team, some confrontation looked inevitable.

As it turned out, the black American athletes supporting the militant Black Power movement chose to make their protests at the medal ceremonies. The first to do so were Tommie Smith and John Carlos, first and third respectively in the 200 metres, who gave the Black Power salute as they received their medals. The United States Olympic Committee reacted angrily, suspending them immediately from the

American team and ordering them out of the Olympic village. They were given 48 hours to leave Mexico.

Then the three black American athletes who had produced a clean sweep in the 400 metres, Lee Evans, Larry James and Ron Freeman, appeared in black berets and made the Black Power salute at their medal ceremony. Two of them removed their berets during the playing of "The Star-Spangled Banner", but Lee Evans, one of the leading advocates of the Black Power movement, kept his on.

Berlin in 1936, Brooklyn in 1947 and Mexico in 1968 were staging-posts on the route to tackling racism in sport and proving that sport was universal and race should have no part in it. Yet it is astonishing to consider that as recently as 1992 there was a regime in South Africa whose laws made it very clear that race still mattered. The struggle against white South Africa seeking to impose its racial sports theories on the world was one of the great moral issues of modern times, and it is amazing that even 30 years ago many people had to be convinced that it was a moral issue on which there could be no equivocation.

South Africa sent all-white teams to the Olympics until the 1960 Games in Rome, and tried to carry on in this fashion for the 1964 Olympics in Tokyo. It proposed sending two teams, one white, one black, selected from separate, racially-segregated trials. The two teams were to have travelled separately, and could not have competed in the same event, while the non-white team could not even have worn the South African uniform. Until this comparatively recent stage, the international bodies had done little about white South Africa. But this proposal proved too much: at last the world began to take note, and South Africa was not invited to the Olympics. This was the first step which eventually led to the great sporting boycott of South Africa – an event that played a part in the eventual dismantling of apartheid both in sport and in the country as a whole.

However, in several sports such as cricket, rugby, golf and tennis, South Africa continued to participate. The authorities of these sports, generally white middle-class people with strong family and other ties with white South Africa, saw nothing wrong in playing with their fellow-whites.

What is more, they allowed South Africa to dictate to them who should play in their teams. If South African racism was bad enough in South Africa, the racism it imposed on other countries was intolerable. For almost half a century white South Africa set an uncompromising racist agenda for its international sporting contests, deciding not only who would play for white South Africa but who could not play for its opponents. No other country in the history of international sport has been able to exercize such power; indeed, no other country has had the impudence to try.

When South Africa toured England in 1929, K.S. Duleepsinhji, then the finest batsman in England but also an Indian prince, was due to play against them. The South Africans objected, and he was dropped. Earlier in the same decade South Africa's rugby authorities forced New Zealand to drop the legendary Maori George Nepia, considered by many to be one of the country's greatest-ever rugby players, and he drifted out of the game. On the 1937 tour there was no fixture against the Maoris, and in 1948, when the All Blacks proposed to tour South Africa, the New Zealand Rugby Union announced that, much as it regretted it, "Players selected to tour South Africa cannot be other than wholly European."

On a previous tour of New Zealand, South Africans had played against Maoris, and one reporter cabled back home: "Bad enough having to play officially designated New Zealand natives but spectacle thousands Europeans frantically cheering on band of Coloured men to defeat members of own race was too much for Springboks who frankly disgusted."

The white South African trick was to get their fellow-whites in other countries implicitly to accept this view. And this situation lasted until 1968, when events finally proved too much for English cricket, which over the years had been strongly supportive of white South Africa.

English cricket, meanwhile, had long respected the West Indies, although series defeats by them have never quite hurt as much as those by Australia. There have been many West Indian cricketers who have brought their talents to the English county and league scenes. There was also much sympathy in England for the fact that until 1960, despite the many brilliant black West Indians, no black man had captained the West Indies.

Frank Worrell, on the history-making tour of Australia in 1960–61, was the first.

Yet those same English supporters were probably among the most diehard defenders of sporting links with South Africa. It was the decision of the selectors not to choose Basil d'Oliveira for the 1968 tour of South Africa that was a defining point for many – although that came only after a rather sharp prod from the Labour government.

In the 1960s, the English Test selectors allowed themselves to appear more concerned about appeasing the sensitivities of their South African hosts than choosing the best team. D'Oliveira had been born a coloured South African. In his native land he could not play cricket with whites, and as a spectator could only watch the game from segregated stands in the most uncomfortable part of the ground. He had come to England to play league cricket and then county cricket for Worcestershire, and qualified by residence for the England Test team. In 1968, however, he was not chosen for the touring side to South Africa that winter. According to the MCC, the decision was based on form, even though d'Oliveira had scored 158 in the final Test of the English summer against Australia, laying the foundation for England's victory.

The real reason for the decision remains hidden in the consciences of the selectors. One close observer has said: "If they were arses, they were cricketing arses." MCC had in fact written to the South Africans earlier in the year, asking for assurances that any team selected by them would be accepted. They had received no reply.

Whatever their motivation, it is certain d'Oliveira had been dropped to save the apartheid government any embarrassment. There was a flood of protest from MCC members and Labour politicians, including the sports minister Denis Howell, who said: "As a minister I am supposed to be speechless on the question of team selection – and I am."

Then Tom Cartwright withdrew from the tour because of an injury, and on 17 September d'Oliveira was brought into the touring party. Within hours the South African government cancelled the tour. The Prime Minister, John Vorster, claimed that the England side was "no longer a cricket

Turning point: South Africa's ban on Basil D'Oliveira swelled the ranks of anti-apartheid campaigners.

team but a team of trouble-makers for South Africa's separate development policies". He added that this is "no longer the team of the MCC, it is the team of the anti-apartheid movement".

This comment came from an Afrikaner leader who represented a section of the white South African community that did not even take cricket very seriously. The journalist Donald Woods tells the story of Vorster's response on being told that the English were 42 for 3. "Their English or our English?" he asked.

The d'Oliveira affair was the turning-point in the fight against apartheid in sport. By now South Africa had been excluded from the 1968 Olympics and at last the world woke up to the evil of sporting apartheid.

The South African rugby team, which toured the United Kingdom in 1969–70, was subjected to a barrage of protest on and off the pitch from anti-apartheid protestors. One of the more prominent anti-tour protestors was the Liberal politician Peter Hain, who would later switch his allegiance to Labour, the more prominent opposition party, and eventually become a government minister. During the tour Hain stepped up the protests, making sure they followed the South Africans wherever they went, after increased security at the grounds made it harder to disrupt matches.

The protests had their effect, however, and brought pressure to bear on the Labour government, which then requested the cricketing authorities to call off the summer tour by the South African cricket team.

Despite the cancellation of England's 1968 cricket tour, South Africa had been invited to visit England in 1970. They were still due to come less than a month before the scheduled date of the first Test. It was only owing to the intervention of the Home Secretary, James Callaghan, that the tour was eventually cancelled on 22 May. Callaghan had an election to worry about, and there were also fears that if the tour had gone ahead it would have split the Commonwealth, done untold damage to race relations in Britain and destroyed the Edinburgh Commonwealth Games. Twelve African countries had threatened to boycott the Games if the tour were not called off.

At the last moment, South Africa were replaced by a Rest of the World side in which the South Africans Eddie Barlow, Peter and Graeme Pollock, Barry Richards and Mike Procter played alongside five West Indians, two Pakistanis and an Indian.

The Rest of the World won a tense series, contested sadly in front of pitifully small crowds, by four matches to one. Perversely, however, the cricket authorities reneged on their original decision and declared these to be non-Tests. Hardest-hit was the Glamorgan batsman Alan Jones, who was forced to return his kit after his only England appearance in the first match.

The rugby and cricket authorities, like those of golf and tennis, still tried to pretend that nothing had changed, but the tide had turned against their cosy acceptance of racism in sport. In 1977 came the Gleneagles Agreement, which formalized the sporting boycott of South Africa. The South African rugby and cricket authorities tried to maintain sporting links with the lure of South African gold, the size of the cheques on offer easing the scruples of all but a few players such as Ian Botham and David Gower.

In all there were seven rebel cricket tours of South Africa, the first being that of 1982. It was headed by Graham Gooch, who was thought to have received £40,000 for the month-long tour. He and the 14 other tourists received a three-year ban for taking part in the tour, which took place directly after the 1982 MCC trip to India. Among those disqualified were Gooch, Geoffrey Boycott, Derek Underwood and John Emburey.

Mike Gatting's ill-fated tour of South Africa in 1990 – the last of the rebel tours – finally collapsed altogether with the release of Nelson Mandela. The violence and bombings which accompanied Mandela's release convinced the cricket authorities that it was simply too dangerous for the tour to continue. Even before then it had become clear that the tour was at best misjudged and at worst acting as a magnet for serious civil unrest. For once the threats by black activists that they would disrupt the matches were no longer empty ones.

After several days of speculation, the decision was taken to cancel the Cape Town "Test". The release of Mandela had been the deciding factor, which, said Ali Bacher, the South African Cricket Union's managing director, required a "gesture of conciliation and compromise".

Gatting, who, together with his players, was paid off and sent home, expressed the players' disappointment at not being able to continue playing cricket. He said: "We were invited out here to play cricket and earn a living, as do many other people who come to this country. But I have no regrets about coming. I now understand a lot more about South Africa."

Tours by the South African rugby team during the apartheid era were invariably accompanied by noisy and violent protests. The 1981 tour of New Zealand was no exception, starting with brawls involving police, rugby fans and anti-apartheid demonstrators and bringing the most vociferous protests since the Vietnam war. Before, during and after the first game there was violence in five cities. In Gisborne, where the South Africans beat Poverty Bay 24–6, police and protestors fought in mud as the game continued. There were also protests in Christchurch, Wellington and Auckland, and the day culminated with the police commissioners threatening a crackdown on demonstrators.

In 1976 New Zealand rugby's insistence on maintaining its links with South Africa had meant that the African and Arab nations boycotted the Montreal Olympics in protest at the refusal to ban New Zealand from the Games.

The Guyana leg of England's 1981 tour of the West Indies was called off after Robin Jackman was called into the side as a replacement for the injured Bob Willis. Guyana objected to Jackman's links with South Africa, where he had coached.

Among the more bizarre attempts by South Africa to counter world criticism of its apartheid policies was the decision in 1975 to allow a black team to take part in its one-day tournament, the Gillette Cup. However, the team could only compete on the condition that it played against Natal, the strongest state, and it was also told that, in the highly unlikely event of victory, it would not be allowed to progress to the next round.

Some of the spectators who go to watch sport, not surprisingly, are also infected with racism. In August 1995, the NatWest Trophy semi-final was marred by racist chanting by the Yorkshire crowd, directed at Northamptonshire's Indian spin bowler Anil Kumble, who was also pelted with tomatoes and other fruit. It was perhaps no surprise that this happened at Headingley, which had been singled out by players such as Viv Richards and David "Syd" Lawrence as a racist ground and had remained so even though the situation has improved as a result of intervention by the Yorkshire authorities. It was at Headingley in 1992 that a pig's head was hurled at Pakistani supporters. Lawrence recalled a game in 1982 when he was pelted with bananas, reduced to tears by abuse, called a black bastard many times and told to "go home", even though he comes from Gloucestershire.

Today sport has moved beyond white champions – "the Great White Hope" used to be a familiar phrase in boxing circles – and colour-counting. British sports reporters of the 1970s and '80s did refer to a player's colour and periodically commented on the number of coloured people in a national or club side. Nowadays it is usually only the name or a verbal inflection heard in radio interviews that gives any clue about colour before the player is seen live or on television. The exception is South Africa, where, because of its apartheid legacy, the lack of black cricketers or rugby players in the national team is a topic for political debate.

There is danger in trying to draw conclusions that apply to all sports and all nations. English cricket has welcomed such gloriously talented players from the subcontinent as K.S. Ranjitsinhji and K.S. Duleepsinhji, although to supporters their colour probably mattered less than whether they came out of the gentlemen's or the players' entrance.

Yet only a couple of years ago an article in *Wisden Cricket Monthly* could question the commitment of players of foreign origin to the English team, which led to Devon Malcolm and Phil de Freitas successfully suing the magazine for defamation of character. And in Yorkshire it was extraordinary how the definition of a true-born Yorkshireman seemed to exclude anyone with a dark skin. Even the appearance of Sachin Tendulkar and Richie Richardson, once Yorkshire had eased its rules, has not led to a significant shift in the colour balance of the county side – and this despite the huge presence of black and Asian cricketers in Bradford, Sheffield and Leeds.

The problem of race always seems to be bubbling away underneath the surface. Devon Malcolm denied that his dispute with the chairman of the England selectors, Ray Illingworth, during England's 1995–96 tour of South Africa had anything to do with race. He issued a statement clarifying his speculative remarks about whether he would have been treated the same way had he been a white bowler. Malcolm said this was one of several possible reasons for his treatment that he was considering. Illingworth had said that he was very upset about the remarks.

Nor are the problems restricted only to England. Until Sir Frank Worrell's appointment in 1960, the West Indies used always to have a white captain – now one wonders when we will see the next white West Indian playing for the Test side. Australian cricket may be more liberal today, but 30 years ago there was much speculation that Malcolm Franke, the leg-break bowler, might have made the national side had he been the right colour.

There are are just as many contradictions in football. No one refers any longer to the colour of a new young Premiership player, some of the most talented members of the English team are black, and at all levels it is probably the most multi-racial and class-free of all team sports. Yet the first black player did not make his debut until the late 1970s, and then managers wondered if the black players were tough enough. Even now, the Football Association distributes leaflets to spectators at national matches, warning them not to make racist chants, and players such as Andy Cole, Paul Ince and Ian Wright are regularly subjected to racist abuse.

Ince was acquitted of charges of assault and threatening behaviour after an incident with a Crystal Palace fan that followed Cantona's sending-off.

It emerged during his trial that the fan, Dennis Warren, 48, of Anerley in south London, had four convictions for football violence and drunkenness. He is alleged to have shouted to Palace players about an opponent: "Get the nigger." Asked whether his reputation was such that Millwall fans put up "wanted" posters for him, he said: "I don't know where you get that from."

If Ince thought that by going to Italy he would escape from racist taunts, he was mistaken. He had a far from easy time there and was again a victim of racism. A message on a wall near Milan's San Siro stadium read: "We don't want you here, you dirty negro Ince." This followed an away game at Cremonese, where the home fans hurled racist abuse at him.

Ian Wright has always taken on controversy as readily as central defenders, and it is perhaps on account of his high profile that he has attracted more racist abuse than any other black player. In 1995 Barnsley apologized to Wright and Arsenal after some of their stewards encouraged the "monkey" chants directed at the player. In the 1996 Coca-Cola Cup, Wright was cuffed round the ear and flattened by hooligans after Arsenal crashed out of the tournament in a match against Aston Villa.

Ruud Gullit, star Dutch player and a successful manager at Chelsea and Newcastle, says he still bears the scars from verbal assaults which have led him to label British fans as the most racist in the world. He once said he had only suffered racist abuse three times, and on each occasion it was in Britain. He said that people used to spit at him and call him a "fucking Rasta bastard". He has also had bananas thrown at him and had to suffer gorilla grunts.

Even now, when the United States has had a black Chief of Defence Staff in Colin Powell, Britain has no black Test selector and only one black manager in the Premiership. It will only be possible to believe that we are truly open-minded when a black England manager chooses the wrong team, fails at Wembley to qualify for the World Cup finals and is greeted with chants about the legitimacy of his parents rather than the colour of his skin.

It is a supreme irony that Tiger Woods's first major victory should be in the Masters at Augusta. For that institution, of all American golf clubs, believed until recently that black men had no role at the club beyond waiting and caddying. But what makes the story even more perverse is that of all the courses in the world this is probably the one best suited to Woods's power game. In the longer term he may force them to make as many changes on the course as they have in the clubhouse.

Augusta has hardly been at the forefront of American racial integration, and would probably be even further from it now were it not the venue for the Masters. Until 1975, when Lee Elder was admitted, no black golfer had ever played at the Masters, and no white man had ever caddied. Lee Trevino found the atmosphere so distasteful that he refused to change in the locker-room.

In 1995 Woods became only the fourth black player to have taken part in the tournament, which at least means that the players were ahead of the members. The first black member to be admitted, in 1990, was

Ronald Townsend, a wealthy Washington television station owner. The second was Bill Simms, a local businessman of considerable standing, who was invited to cross the threshold in 1995.

Rugby league has admitted that it had what it described as a "small" racial problem in the mid-1990s, but that was no consolation to Wigan's talented wingers Jason Robinson and Martin Offiah. While warming up before one game at Widnes, Robinson was subjected to what Wigan's New Zealand coach, Graeme West, called "mindless, disgraceful racial taunting" by Widnes supporters. Offiah, a former Widnes player who had gone to Wigan for a higher salary, was abused throughout the game. For a former Widnes player a lively reception was only to be expected, but the racial abuse came on top of that. Offiah said he hardly ever allowed his parents to watch him play, because the abuse was so degrading.

Linford Christie was a victim of a peculiarly British form of institutionalized racism. It was not so much direct abuse – though there was some of that – as the determination of the popular press first to speculate on the size of his sexual organs and then to go through his private life with a fine tooth-comb. Had he been a white rather than a black athlete, there is little doubt that his anatomy would not have been subjected to such mockery, nor his family to such scrutiny.

This is not to suggest that Christie was a candidate for sainthood. One black British athlete commented that Christie was Britain's best-balanced athlete as he had "a chip on both shoulders". In *The Voice*, the black columnist Tony Sewell noted that the start of summer was the time of year when black celebrities started whingeing. "It began with Linford Christie's usual outcry about not enough money, not enough praise from the media and not enough worship for his sacrifice as a Black role model," wrote Sewell.

The criticism has not stopped Christie from becoming a role model for millions of black – and white – athletes, who have been inspired by his triumphs. But it has meant that he has had to confront issues – the role of the media, white attitudes to black men, the obligations of absentee fathers – that no training on the track could have prepared him for. His high profile has also brought him into very public conflict with the British athletics establishment, leading to rows about appearance money in which he has rarely been portrayed sympathetically.

The result is that he has made it easy for those who want to see him as paranoid and obsessed with the desire to have "respect" for his achievements. He has not helped himself by statements such as, "The media is meant to be in your camp". But, in fairness, he certainly has suffered from gratuitous criticism. "Can we forgive Linford for sulking? No we can't...he doesn't deserve it," wrote Kate Battersby in the *Evening Standard*.

Christie's outbursts, which have been frequent throughout his career, have invariably been governed by emotion rather than calculation. In June 1995, for example, he assailed the press for disrespectful coverage of his career and threatened to retire before the Olympics – but didn't. When he saw a photographer at the airport on his way to Atlanta, he confronted him, saying: "I do not want to see any bloodshed on this airport, but if you want some..."

He is invariably seen in terms of his reaction to the publicity that surrounded his achievements rather than the achievements

Tiger Woods: forcing change upon Augusta.

Finest hour? After winning gold in Barcelona, Christie woke up to tabloid jokes about his "lunchbox".

themselves. And it meant that he, a Christian Fundamantalist, was put on the spot when Sir Roger Bannister, possibly still Britain's most famous athlete, suggested that black athletes owed their prowess to certain anatomical advantages. "Christie Rejects Darwin", mused the headline writers.

Perhaps the most grotesque example of what Christie, who remains a strong patriot despite it all, has to tolerate came on the morning after his 100 metres triumph at the 1992 Olympics in Barcelona. He had won probably the greatest prize in athletics, yet Britain's highest-selling daily paper, the *Sun*, instead focused its anthropometric attentions on the size and shape of what it called his "lunchbox".

Not surprisingly, Christie was furious. "I felt very humiliated, to be honest with you. My first instinct was that it was racist. There we are, stereotyping a black man. I can take a good joke, but it happened the day after I won the greatest accolade an athlete can win...I don't want to go through life being known for what I've got in my shorts...I want to be remembered for being one of the greatest athletes ever."

The press also focused on his private life, particularly on whether he was paying maintenance for two children by two women with whom he had had relationships – and there was even more attention when the 16-year-old son was himself to become a father. The unspoken assumption was that this would not have been happened to a white athlete. One headline said simply: "How Linford Christie Put His Family On the Fast Track to Handouts From the Welfare State".

There has also been the question of drugs. Christie has always campaigned vociferously against performance-enhancing drugs, and many believe that he is one of the sporting exceptions who owe their triumphs to hard work at muscle-building. But that has not stopped the incessant sniping at him by others.

The ultimate irony is that the final image of Christie as an athlete will not be his Olympic, World Championship, Commonwealth and European golds, but his disqualification from the 1996 Olympics for two false starts. Even here he could not escape the critics. Linford, they said, had been able to get away with such starts in Britain because he kept bullying the British athletics authorities.

He was not even allowed defeat with honour.

Eric Cantona

Ooh, aah, Cantona!

It was Gerard Houllier, a confidant of Eric Cantona, who probably best summed the Frenchman up when he said, "Eric is an island." He made the comment as Cantona was returning to English football after one of the most amazing incidents in the history of football, when a player attacked a fan.

That, the most notorious event of the 1994–95 football season – and there was plenty of competition in a particularly bad year – came when Cantona was playing for Manchester United against Crystal Palace in a midweek Premiership match at Selhurst Park on 25 January.

Cantona had been sent off in the 52nd minute of the game after kicking an opponent, Richard Shaw. On his way to the dressing-room, which at Selhurst Park involves walking round the touchline quite close to the home fans, the Frenchman was subjected to a stream of abuse from Palace supporters. One fan in particular called his parentage into question and insulted him in racial terms. Cantona, unable to contain his anger, jumped across the advertizing barriers that divided him from the fans and lunged with both feet at the supporter, who was standing behind the touchline barrier. The two then exchanged punches before police and stewards broke up the fight.

Alex Ferguson, the United manager, saw the sending-off incident thus: "In charting Eric's career everyone agrees he reacts when he feels an injustice. It wasn't really a kick at the guy [Shaw]. It was just a wee flick. We've seen guys do that before. It wasn't really a sending-off offence, but because he was Cantona he was sent off. There were two bad tackles on him in the first half and the referee didn't even speak to the opponents. Some referees would have clamped down immediately in that game at Crystal Palace. Others, as you saw, didn't. All we ask is that he gets the same fair treatment as anyone else."

It was a characteristic piece of special pleading by the man who had brought Cantona to United from Leeds and made him the centrepiece of his successful hunt for the Holy Grail of the championship which had eluded United for 26 years.

However, for some time after the kung-fu kick at Selhurst Park it seemed that even Ferguson thought that the offence would mean the end of Cantona in English or, for that matter, any football. This was certainly the opinion of many in the game. But the tide began to turn in Cantona's favour when details began to emerge about the man he had assaulted.

The Palace fan was one Matthew Simmons. He had a past, which was that of an undesirable petty criminal. In 1992 he had been convicted of attacking a petrol station attendant with a spanner. He pleaded guilty to assault with intention to rob and was sentenced to two years' probation.

During Cantona's court hearing, at which he faced charges of assault, witnesses who were at the match described how Simmons had shouted at Cantona, "Fuck off, French bastard!" and "Fuck off back to France, you mother-fucker!" Simmons had admitted he was shouting at Cantona and pointing to the dressing-room, but claimed he was only saying, "Off you go for an early shower."

Long after the Cantona hearing, Simmons was himself brought to court, charged with threatening behaviour with the intent to cause a person to believe that immediate unlawful violence would be used against him. At his hearing in Croydon, Simmons attacked the prosecuting counsel. No sooner had the chairman of the bench, Mrs Mary Richards, pronounced Simmons guilty than he leapt over a table and hurled himself at the back of Mr Jeffrey McCann,

Boiling point (clockwise from left): Cantona launches his kung-fu kick at Selhurst Park; squares up to the referee; and goes on the offensive in France.

ripping the lawyer's tie off and grabbing him by the throat. It took six prison and police officers to pull Simmons away as he kept yelling, "I'm innocent, I promise. I swear on the Bible." Police struggled to handcuff him and drag him from the court. Simmons was fined £500 with £200 costs and banned from football for a year for the original offence and sentenced to seven days in gaol for contempt of court. However, he was released after one night behind bars.

Cantona had neither been called as a witness nor asked to give a witness statement. And by then his own conviction was history.

Amid much publicity Cantona had been found guilty and given a prison sentence, which was commuted on appeal to 120 hours' community service. At the end of the court hearing he produced probably the most elliptical comment ever to come from the mouth of a football player. He said: "When seagulls follow the trawler, it is because they think sardines will be thrown into the sea."

There had been calls for a permanent ban from football, but the FA fined him and banned him until the end of September 1995.

But for a time it seemed that Cantona might not be able to keep this date. During his exile he had talked of quitting, and Ferguson had to fly to Paris to talk him out of it. This happened when the FA sent a warning letter to United after Cantona played in a practice match against Rochdale behind closed doors.

Ferguson said, "We made a representation to the FA to explain what we felt. I don't know exactly what happened in there. From what I can gather, somebody had a bee in their bonnet and they decided to send a silly letter to us. I think it was embarrassing to them at the end of the day. I mean we've had games many times against teams like Stoke, Rochdale, Bury and Oldham, you know, closed-door games where you've got suspended players or one coming back after injury. That goes on throughout the country, so to say all of a sudden you can't play in one because you are still suspended was a bit much. I think maybe Eric felt he couldn't win. They weren't going to allow him to win."

More interesting was the way in which Cantona, despite his misdeed and his punishment, was treated as an icon, particularly in the advertizing media. Whereas in another age a player who attacked a spectator would have carried the mark of Cain, Cantona now carried the mark of pounds sterling, as his notoriety helped sell the products promoted by marketing men and advertizers.

It started with Cantona's own sponsors Nike. What Cantona had done was presented as a reaction to extreme racist provocation. This was soon built up into a myth and was so readily accepted that within weeks Nike had a new advert featuring Cantona and Les Ferdinand protesting against racist abuse. The use of black-and-white film, evoking 1950s newsreels, made a powerful impact, and it further burnished the myth that Cantona had been racially abused.

Yet while Simmons was a wretch, and a racist to boot, it is arguable that Cantona had been abused by him as a Frenchman – and abusing the French has long been an English pastime. The words hurled at Cantona were not very different from what the Swiss linguist Ferdinand de Saussure heard in the streets of London back in the last century. In a letter to his family he recorded that the worst insult the English could throw at anyone was "French dog. This name is the most common, and evidently, according to popular idea, the greatest and most forcible insult that can be given to any man."

The marketing men were using race to promote Cantona and make sure he remained a very marketable icon. They knew the worth of their product. During his months of exile Cantona had hardly hidden away in shame. Just before his return he had teamed up in Paris with Diego Maradona to launch the International Association of Professional Footballers, with Maradona as President and Cantona as his deputy.

Meanwhile, market research by Unijet, a tour operator, revealed that 40 per cent of men said they would rather go on holiday with Cantona than with Claudia Schiffer or Cindy Crawford. These two, plus catwalk stars such as Naomi Campbell and Helena Christiansen, chalked up a combined score of only 28% with the men, while the women preferred Mel Gibson, Tom Cruise or Brad Pitt.

So Cantona, who had long been used to seeing his name exploited to sell products – his lawyer Jean-Jacques Bertrand complained about Cantona French Wines Limited, Cantona French Brandy and Cantona Pour Homme Limited – now saw his own sponsors make sure he remained the great iconic figure, the king over the water returning to his kingdom after a minor problem.

As Cantona's return approached, Nike ran a series of advertizements which cleverly suggested that Cantona was saying sorry but on careful reading turned out to be a no apology at all but a joke. There was one entitled "Apology", which saw Cantona mockingly saying sorry for a number of things, including scoring twice against Chelsea in the 1994 Cup Final and missing a late chance against Newcastle. He also said, "I apologize for only scoring once against Manchester City" in the 5–0 drubbing by United of their old rivals. City, who had apparently lost not only the match but also their sense of humour, complained, and the reference to City was removed.

Then, just before his return, a Nike advert showed Cantona standing in front of what looked like prison gates along Sir Matt Busby Way. Cantona was wearing his No. 7 shirt, and the words read: "He's been punished for his mistakes. Now it's someone else's turn."

And two United fans got into the act. At a personal cost of £1,200 they produced a poster which showed Cantona's face under the headline: "We'll never forget that night at Selhurst Park (when you buried that amazing volley against Wimbledon)."

But opinion remained divided as to whether Cantona should be welcomed back, and Brian Clough spoke for many when he said he should not. On the Sunday when Cantona was to return, the *News of the World* quoted Clough as saying: "I don't give a damn if I never see him again. I have been known to clip a few people, but what he did at Crystal Palace last season was completely over the top. If I had been his manager I would have done what Howard Wikinson did at Leeds: sold him without hesitation."

Then, comparing Cantona to the supporters he had clipped for invading the ground at Nottingham Forest, Clough said, "It's my view that Cantona did exactly what they did. He went somewhere he shouldn't have been – flying into the crowd feet first. He had been sent off and should have walked round the track, gone into the dressing-room, had a shower, put on his smart French designer clothes and waited to get on the coach."

Yes, said Clough, Cantona had brought sublime ability to the game, but "on occasions I don't think he is in his right mind. There's something wrong with the man."

Cantona eventually returned to United's team after eight months in a 2–2 draw against Liverpool in October 1995, when he made one goal and scored another from a penalty; and long before the end of the 1995–96 season his rehabilitation was complete. So much so that on the eve of the Cup Final, on 9 May 1996, he received the highest accolade: the football writers' Footballer of the Year award. The presentation provided another occasion for some Cantona verbal mystification when he said, "Some criticisms mean nothing, so I compare them to toilets and think 'Screw them'. It has been a long year but what a beautiful one."

Yet the passions which Cantona and United aroused were on display little over 24 hours later when United achieved their second double, beating Liverpool to add the Cup to the League they had already won.

The Cup victory was through a Cantona goal, the only redeeming feature of a very poor final. But as Cantona led his United team up the steps to collect their winners' medals he was spat on by three supporters, who also hurled insults at him. A Liverpool fan in a red wig then swung a punch at Alex Ferguson.

Cantona, clearly shocked, wiped the spit away with his hand, shaking his head in disbelief. In contrast to his reaction at Selhurst Park, however, he merely looked at the fan and then dismissed it, saying later, "The Liverpool fans were just very disappointed. But it did not spoil the team's victory." If this showed a new maturity for Cantona, it also emphasized what a complex and unlikely sports player he was.

Cantona had always stood out as a player, both for his ability on the field and his antics off it. Fairly early in his French career Cantona was dubbed "Le Brat". Among the reasons for the nickname were actions such as punching Bruno Martini, the French international goalkeeper, who was also Cantona's team-mate at Auxerre, the club he had signed for when he was 15.

He had hardly joined Olympique Marseille when there was further trouble. After being substituted he threw his shirt at the referee, and he called their manager Henri Michel *"un sac de merde"* – a shitbag. The club suggested he seek psychiatric help and banned him for a year. He was then loaned to Montpellier, where he had another fight with a team-mate.

On his transfer to Nîmes his reaction to a booking was to throw the ball at the referee's head. The French tribunal chairman confessed that Cantona was in a special category, saying to the player, "Behind you there's a trail of the smell of sulphur." On being given a month's suspension he called

Le Roi: Cantona lifts the Premiership trophy.

every member of the panel an idiot, and when this resulted in another ban he announced his retirement at the ripe old age of 25.

Before his inevitable move to England – to get away from France – he fell out with Trevor Francis, the manager of Sheffield Wednesday, over a possible move; and although he helped Howard Wilkinson clinch the league title for Leeds in 1992, the following season he was a Manchester United player, and Wilkinson was not unhappy to see the back of him.

Long before the Selhurst Park explosion, United too had problems with Cantona. He stamped on various opponents, spat at Leeds fans and got into an argy-bargy with Turkish police after defeat by Galatasaray in the Champions League. For good measure he accused the referee of being in the pay of the Turks. After the match, which put paid to United's hopes in the Champions League that season, Cantona told *L'Equipe*: "I am certain that referees have been bought in the European Cup. I ask myself whether Mr Roêthlisberger has not also been bought." These comments, considered outrageous by UEFA, were widely regarded as sour grapes at the time. Since then, however, Roethlisberger has received a life ban for "attempting to influence" the result of the 1996 Champions League match between Grasshoppers and Auxerre.

Alex Ferguson took a gamble on Cantona, first in signing him from Leeds, then in continuing to show faith in him after his conviction, but it was a gamble that paid off.

6

The Fix

Sport generally prides itself on being clean and above-board, with no place for cheating or match-fixing. Yet, like the serpent in the Garden of Eden, dishonesty is almost inseparable from sport. As long as organized sports have been played there have been attempts to fix the results.

The Baseball Fix

The classic case was, of course, the fixing of the 1919 World Series.

In 1919 the Chicago White Sox were playing some of the best baseball ever seen. Having already won the American League they were odds-on favourites to beat National League winners the Cincinnati Reds, and take the coveted World Series.

However, beneath their surface brilliance on the field bubbled player resentment and discontent about money – the factor n whic the fixer always feeds.

Earlier that season, Sox owner Charles Comiskey had cut the players' salaries, pleading poverty due to falling attendances. But though victories brought the crowds back, the salary cut remained. Comiskey also reduced the meal allowance from $4 to

In the dock: Bruce Grobelaar was found not guilty of corruption, but received a suspended FA ban.

$3 a day and often refused to pay laundry bills, which meant the players appeared in grubby uniforms.

In September 1919, as the World Series loomed, the White Sox looked enviously at their better-paid opponents. For example, while the Cincinnati Reds' first baseman got $9,000 a year his White Sox opposite number, Chick Gandil, was paid just $4,000.

Gandil set about doing something to rectify the situation. In his room at New York's Ansonia Hotel, he and seven teammates met and agreed that for $80,000 they would throw the World Series. Gandil had been in touch with gamblers who were willing to put up that sort of money. It would mean $10,000 for each man, and it would teach the tight-fisted Comiskey a lesson.

The deal was done in an amazingly off-hand way. Gandil did not plan which matches were to be thrown, nor how. Nor was there any agreement about how they were to get their money. Indeed, Gandil was talking to two sets of gamblers, of whom one promised $80,000, the other $100,000.

Although Gandil had only dealt with underlings, he was assured that Arnold Rothstein, a legendary East Coast gambler, was willing to back the offers. But before Rothstein, who had backed Cincinnati heavily to win, would commit his money he needed a signal that the fix was on.

Say it ain't so: the 1919 Chicago White Sox, were nicknamed "Black Sox" after match-fixing.

The signal was to be this: in the first innings of the opening match of the World Series, when the first Reds batter came to the plate, the pitcher would deliberately throw his first ball to hit the batter – and the White Sox would lose that opening game.

Rothstein received his signal. The batter was hit by what looked to the uninitiated like a wild throw from pitcher Eddie Cicotte. In fact it was deliberate, and Cincinnati won the game 9–1. They went on to win the series by five games to three.

The gamblers cleaned up, but the players got only $40,000 between them, unevenly split; four received $5,000 each, Gandil and Cicotte $10,000 apiece: two got nothing.

For a whole year the secret was kept and the conspirators played on. Not until the

1920 season did suspicions began to grow – because by then the fixing of games seemed to have become common. In September, a newspaper claimed $500,000 had been bet on a fixed game between the Philadelphia Phillies and the Chicago Cubs. Several players signed confessions. Cicotte told the Grand Jury: "I needed the money. I sold out the other boys for $10,000 to pay off a mortgage on a farm and for the wife and kids. I had to have the cash in advance. That night I found the money under my pillow."

"Shoeless" Joe Jackson also came to confess; a small boy reportedly approached Jackson as he left and uttered the soon-to-be-famous words, "Say it ain't so, Joe".

The players were charged with various conspiracies. But, as would often be the case, the gamblers – apart from some minor figures – escaped. When the trial began, the confessions signed by Cicotte, Jackson and Claude Williams were found to have mysteriously disappeared from the Illinois State Attorney's office. Rothstein is said to have paid $10,000 to get them. The players then repudiated their confessions, Jackson claiming he was half-drunk and thought the paper he signed contained only his address.

The players were defended by well-paid lawyers, suggesting baseball's authorities did not want the game's dirty linen washed in public. None of the accused players took the stand, so nothing emerged about how Comiskey managed his club. Stranger still, other White Sox players who were not involved in the fix but who knew a lot about it, gave evidence but revealed nothing.

After a trial lasting just over two weeks, the jury took less than two hours to reach a verdict of not guilty. Everybody – gamblers and players – went free. The very next day, however, the newly-appointed Baseball Commissioner, Kenesaw Mountain Landis, issued a statement saying, in effect, that despite the verdict, because the players had associated with gamblers, they were never to play professional baseball again.

For one player the decision was very harsh. Third baseman Buck Weaver had been at the Ansonia Hotel but then changed his mind and played honestly. He was implicated by the others' confessions, stood trial and should have been vindicated by the not guilty verdict. But Landis banned him as well, and he spent the rest of his life trying unsuccessfully to get the ban lifted.

The White Sox as a team never recovered and have never won the World Series since.

The whole episode showed, as one writer has said, the schizophrenia of baseball and the perennial attraction between sport and gambling. Everyone in sport wants it to be clean and free of gamblers, yet the people in it and those who watch it love to gamble. This creates the climate for the fix, stories of which resonate in all sports through all ages.

The Football Fix

Match-fixing in football is almost as old as the game itself. The Football League was barely ten years old when, in 1898, Stoke and Burnley, in a Test Match to decide who would stay in the First Division, agreed to play for a draw – the best result for both.

It was so contrived that the 40,000 spectators cottoned on, and angrily refused to return the ball when it went out of play. The authorities later replaced Test matches with automatic promotion and relegation.

In 1900 Burnley goalkeeper Jack Hilman was banned for a year for trying to bribe Nottingham Forest to lose. Forest in fact won 4-0 and Burnley were relegated.

In the period leading up to the First World War, Britain's most popular footballer was Billy Meredith. That is, until the end of the 1904–05 season, when Manchester City were making a championship challenge. Then Meredith was found to be at the centre of the country's first major football bribery scandal. The City captain and Welsh international outside-right was banned for a season after offering Aston Villa captain Alec Leake £10 to lose a game.

Manchester City's disgrace did not put an end to attempts to fix results. In 1911 Middlesbrough manager Andy Walker and chairman Thomas Gibson Poole, a prospective MP, were banned for trying to fix a home game against neighbours Sunderland, which Middlesbrough won 1-0.

On 29 November 1913 there was another attempted fix. Jesse Pennington of West Bromwich was offered £5, and his ten team-mates similar sums, to lose to Everton. They refused, the match was drawn and the fixer arrested and gaoled.

Then, a few months after the outbreak of war, Liverpool and Manchester United players had a go. They were due to play on Good Friday, 2 April 1915, with United facing relegation but Liverpool in mid-table safety. Two days beforehand, some players met in the Manchester's Dog and Partridge pub and decided Liverpool would lose 2–0. In the match, played in driving rain, an apathetic Liverpool allowed United to score twice and lost 2–0 as agreed.

Their fans were incensed and a bookie, smelling a rat, refused to pay out. The FA and the police investigated. Eventually Jackie Sheldon of Liverpool confessed and nine players were banned: United's Enoch "Knocker" West did not have his suspension lifted until 1945, when he was 62. Three others had their bans lifted more speedily but then went off to fight in the war: one, Sandy Turnbull, was killed.

The end of the war saw the resumption not only of football but of fixing. In 1924 John Browning, formerly of Scotland, and Archibald Kyle of Rangers, Blackburn and Airdrie, were given 60 days' hard labour for offering Bo'Ness players £30 to fix a Second Division match against Lochgelly.

Another British footballer to see the inside of a prison cell was former Montrose captain Gavin Hamilton. He received his 60-day sentence in 1932 for offering £40 or £50 to Montrose player David Mooney to fix a home match against Edinburgh City.

The English game's most dramatic match-fixing scandal broke on a spring Sunday, 12 April 1964, with allegations in the *Sunday People* of bribery. One of those accused called the story "a load of nonsense" – but it was to end with ten professional footballers serving prison terms of between four months and four years.

Rumours of match-fixing had been doing the rounds for years. Everton were said to have been involved in match-fixing in their championship-winning season of 1962–63, but there was no evidence. The Football League investigated other allegations but found no proof. Only when Jimmy Gauld, an inside-forward for Charlton, Everton, Plymouth, Swindon and Mansfield between 1955 and 1960, told all to a newspaper for £7,000 did the truth emerge.

Gauld's story was sensational. A match at Portman Road in December 1962 in which Ipswich beat Sheffield Wednesday 2–1 had been fixed, he said. Three Sheffield Wednesday players – the centre-half and captain Peter Swan, centre-forward David Layne and wing-half Tony Kay – had made sure of the result, and each of them had won £100 by backing their team to lose.

That, it turned out, was not the only betting coup that day. Gauld went on to reveal that on the same day the matches between Lincoln and Brentford in the Third Division and York and Oldham in the Fourth Division were also fixed.

The police investigation that followed led to more than 60 players being interviewed, and in the end ten were brought to trial at Nottingham Assizes in January 1965. Gauld received the heaviest sentence: four years' imprisonment and costs of £5,000. The three Sheffield Wednesday players, Kay, Layne and Swan, were also gaoled and banned from football for life, although these bans were lifted in 1972.

But in many ways the most tragic outcome was for Tony Kay. By the time the *Sunday People* story broke he had moved to Everton and had just won his first international cap. Instead he was sent to gaol, and his defence counsel sorrowfully recorded that for £100 he had given up what could have been a great career. But for this lapse he, rather than Nobby Stiles, might have played for England's World Cup-winning team of 1966.

After that the English game vowed to clean itself up, although it was not the end of such scandals. Frank Munro, the Wolverhampton Wanderers centre-half, revealed to the People that he had been the subject of an attempted bribe by Leeds's Scottish international Billy Bremner in 1972. Leeds, who had already won the FA Cup, needed to avoid defeat in their final League match of the season against Wolves at Molineux to clinch the Double. Bremner, acting at the behest of his manager Don Revie, approached Munro before the game with an offer of £5,000 for the Wolves man to give away a penalty, which Munro refused. Leeds lost the game 1-0.

Bremner sued over the allegations in *The People*, but before the case came to trial in 1982 he tried to back out, offering to accept no damages and pay his own costs on condition that the settlement be kept a secret. The newspaper, unwisely in view of

Tony Kay: gaoled and banned from football.

the hostility of judges and juries to newspapers faced with cases brought by stars, refused and the case went to trial. Munro's sworn statement failed to convince the jury, and Bremner netted an award of £100,000, a near-record sum for the time.

The next big match-fixing scandal broke in the 1994-95 season and, as in 1964 and 1982, it began with allegations in the press.

These followed a sting operation set up by the *Sun* newspaper with Christopher Vincent, a former business partner of Bruce Grobbelaar, the Liverpool goalkeeper. Grobbelaar and Vincent, who both came from Zimbabwe, had gone into business together after meeting in London. The business failed and in August 1994 Vincent approached the *Sun*.

The paper started its own investigations and then set up the sting. Vincent contacted Grobbelaar, suggesting a reconciliation, and they met in a hotel room bugged by the *Sun*. Grobbelaar was seen on video accepting £2,000 from Vincent, who claimed he was representing a Far Eastern syndicate which would pay more – as much as £100,000 – if he was prepared to chuck games.

The day before the *Sun* published on 9 November 1994 it contacted Grobbelaar, who was at Gatwick Airport. He denied the allegations. The *Sun* took its dossier to the police and the FA, and the allegations led to a police investigation codenamed Operation Navajo. It led to Grobbelaar suing the *Sun*, but before this case could proceed the police made dawn raids on the homes of Grobbelaar and three others. After an investigation lasting two and a half years, in which statements were taken from 700 witnesses, the four were brought to trial at Winchester Crown Court in January 1997.

Besides Grobbelaar they were Hans Segers, who had played in goal for Wimbledon, John Fashanu, who had played as a forward for Wimbledon, and a Malaysian businessman called Heng Suan Lim. They were charged with conspiring to corruptly give and receive money to influence football matches. Grobbelaar was also charged on his own with corruption – accepting £2,000 from Vincent to influence a football match. All the men denied the charges and Grobbelaar also denied his own individual corruption charge.

The Crown prosecutor, David Calvert-Smith QC, told the court that much of the evidence of the case came from Vincent and that the jury would have little sympathy for him as a witness. "His decision to expose Mr Grobbelaar was as a result of a business quarrel and he went to the Sun as a result of a desire to enrich himself." Despite this, said Calvert-Smith, Vincent's evidence was backed by other evidence, and some of the admissions made to him by Grobbelaar about matches he had fixed were borne out by videos of the games.

There were also files full of documentary evidence, many of which linked the four men. Calvert-Smith told the court that Vincent first learned of the alleged corruption in 1993, when Grobbelaar told him about a scheme to help Far Eastern betting syndicates. Grobbelaar reportedly told Vincent he was unhappy with his low level of pay at Liverpool and was determined to make as much money as possible over the next two years. Later that day Grobbelaar and Vincent went to a hotel at Manchester City Airport, where the player was allegedly given an envelope containing £1,000 by the "Short Man" – Heng Suan Lim. Grobbelaar then reportedly informed Vincent that the Far Eastern syndicate for which Lim acted as a go-between was now prepared to pay him between £40,000 and £60,000 per game if he would "do business".

Vincent later learned of a code system used by the players in which 'Wimbledon' stood for win, 'Leeds' for lose and 'Dundee' for draw. Mobile telephone records for Heng Suan Lim revealed extensive communication between himself and Grobbelaar, Fashanu and Segers. This key evidence, claimed the prosecution, backed up much of its case, including Chris Vincent's claim that he and Grobbelaar drove to London for a meeting with Lim – calls had been logged on the mobile phones of the men which showed this to be true.

The prosecution case was that Lim was the link between the players and a Far Eastern betting syndicate which allegedly masterminded the scam. Grobbelaar was accused of taking a £40,000 bribe to throw a game in November 1993 when Liverpool, for whom he was keeping goal, lost 3–0 to Newcastle. He could also have collected £125,000 for throwing a game against Man United, it was alleged, but this finished 3–3 after Grobbelaar made some instinctive saves.

Segers was accused of taking large sums of money to throw matches involving Wimbledon in deals set up by Fashanu. Fashanu was accused of handing £40,000 to Grobbelaar following the Liverpool–Newcastle match and receiving £20,000 from Indonesian sources. Heng Suan Lim was said to have contacted the three men on numerous occasions via mobile phone calls. The prosecution presented a list of 25 Liverpool, Southampton and Wimbledon games which they claimed were at the centre of the match-fixing allegations:

Focal point: Newcastle's 3–0 victory over Liverpool was central to the case against Grobelaar.

8 August 1992:	Wimbledon 0 – Ipswich Town 1
2 October 1993:	Leeds 4 – Wimbledon 0
25 October 1993:	Wimbledon 0 – Ipswich 2
30 October 1993:	Newcastle 4 – Wimbledon 0
21 November 1993:	Newcastle 3 – Liverpool 0
26 December 1993:	Wimbledon 1 – Coventry 2
1 January 1994:	Wimbledon 0 – Arsenal 3
4 January 1994:	Liverpool 3 – Manchester United 3
8 January 1994:	Wimbledon 3 – Scunthorpe 0
11 January 1994:	Wimbledon 1 – Sheffield Wednesday 2
15 January 1994:	Wimbledon 2 – Sheffield Wednesday 1
5 February 1994:	Norwich 2 – Liverpool 2
16 March 1994:	Chelsea 2 – Wimbledon 0
19 March 1994:	Queen's Park Rangers 1 – Wimbledon 0
29 March 1994:	Wimbledon 4 – Blackburn Rovers 1
2 April 1994:	Wimbledon 2 – Coventry City 0
4 April 1994:	Wimbledon 1 – Liverpool 1
7 May 1994:	Everton 3 – Wimbledon 2
24 September 1994:	Coventry City 1 – Southampton 0
1 October 1994:	Wimbledon 1 – Tottenham Hotspur 2
8 October 1994:	Wimbledon 1 – Arsenal 3
17 October 1994:	Nottingham Forest 3 – Wimbledon 1
22 October 1994:	Liverpool 3 – Wimbledon 0
5 November 1994:	Leeds United 3 – Wimbledon 1
5 November 1994:	Manchester City 3 – Southampton 3

For the defence, goalkeepers such as Bob Wilson and Gordon Banks, ex-England captain Jimmy Armfield, former World Cup star Alan Ball, the manager who had employed Grobbelaar at Southampton, and Liverpool colleague Alan Hansen all swore that Grobbelaar did not throw matches. Armfield found "no deliberate errors" in his goalkeeping and Wilson, after examining videos of the suspect games, said nothing untoward had happened. Grobbelaar, who had been secretly filmed by the *Sun* taking £2,000 from Vincent, denied corruption and claimed he was actually trying to trap Vincent into revealing who was behind the rigging racket. He admitted he knew Lim, but insisted that he was only supplying information which would help forecast the outcomes of matches, not fixing the results.

Fashanu claimed all he had done was to introduce Segers and Grobbelaar to Lim. He did not take the stand and his challenge to the prosecution was, as his counsel put it, that he "didn't do it – prove it if you can".

Segers likewise claimed he only helped forecast results, not fix them. His QC said soccer to Segers was "a shrine at which he worshipped". However, Segers was, in many ways, the weak link in the chain.

In the box he had to admit lying to the police. He had denied knowing Lim because he feared that helping Lim forecast the results of games would get him into trouble with the football authorities.

When the police asked him to explain the money in his various accounts, including some overseas, he had claimed it came from stealing cars in his native Holland. This, he told the court, was another lie: the money actually came from a tie business he ran in Holland, which he feared might get him into trouble with the tax man.

Segers also admitted lying to the police about his relationship with Fashanu. He told them he and Fashanu were only in contact once a month, but phone records showed numerous calls between them. These, Segers said, were to arrange alibis for one another: both were cheating on their wives and trying to conceal it from them. Fashanu's business associate John Mason corroborated Segers's story, and described keeping track of Fashanu's love-life and deflecting calls for him as "a routine part of [the] day".

Lim claimed he was a football fanatic who had done nothing more than predict match outcomes for his benefactor in Indonesia. The £800,000 paid into his Far East accounts came from a rich uncle.

The 'trial of the century', as the tabloids dubbed it, lasted 34 days. After ten hours and 59 minutes of deliberation, the jury could not reach a verdict. The judge then told them he was prepared to accept a majority verdict on which at least ten of them agreed, but this too proved impossible and the jury was discharged. The prosecution immediately called for a retrial, which began on 4 June, also in Winchester but before a different judge.

The second trial, which ended on 8 August after 45 days, covered nearly all the same ground as the first, but this time there was a result. The jury took 26 hours and 20 minutes to find Grobbelaar, Fashanu and Segers not guilty of conspiring with Lim to receive corrupt payments from a Far Eastern betting syndicate. On the separate charge against Grobbelaar, that of accepting £2,000 from Vincent, the jury could not decide and the judge entered a verdict of Not Guilty.

Fashanu and Segers asked for costs but the judge, Mr Justice McCullough, refused, saying, "Mr Fashanu brought suspicion on himself" and Segers had told "lie upon lie" when offered the chance to explain £104,000 paid into a Swiss bank account.

Britain's biggest soccer fix trials had cost the taxpayer £12 million and was, as the *Daily Mail* said, "the fix that never was".

However, Grobbelaar and Segers faced trouble from the FA. They were charged with breaking Rule 26a(iv), and in December 1997 both received six-month bans and £10,000 fines. The punishments were suspended for two years because the players had suffered, in the FA's words, "considerable financial hardship and a three-year blight on their careers" while facing the match-fixing allegations.

However that was not the end of the story. Grobbelaar pursued his libel action against the *Sun* and a month-long hearing took place in the High Court in July 1999. On 28 July 1999, nearly five years after the *Sun* had published the original allegations, Grobbelaar finally cleared his name, winning his libel action against the *Sun*. The jury awarded him damages of £85,000 plus costs, accepting that he had not received bribes to throw matches.

Outside the court, Grobbelaar said, "it is a day we can all relish. I have been through two criminal trials and an FA hearing. Today ends the slur on football, the game that I love. It was not the money I was after. I was only wanting to clear my name in football, which I have done today."

Nevertheless, if Grobbelaar had cleared his name, the shadow of the Far East continues to hang over football.

On 11 February 1999, the police and the FA announced they were investigating a suspected Far Eastern betting syndicate which had tried to sabotage floodlights at Premiership matches. Four men – three Malaysians and the head of security at Charlton – were later arrested for allegedly plotting to knock out the lights at that Saturday's game between Charlton and Liverpool using a firebomb.

It was claimed a Malaysian betting syndicate had paid a man £20,000 to plant the remote-controlled device in the floodlight power-room at Charlton's Valley stadium. Sources said the bomb would have completely disintegrated on detonating, destroying any evidence of the crime.

It also emerged that the police were now looking into four games which suffered sudden floodlight failure, of which three had to be abandoned. The suspect games were:

- West Ham versus Crystal Palace on 3 November 1997, when the lights went out in the 65th minute, moments after a Frank Lampard goal had made the score 2–2.
- Derby versus Wimbledon on 13 August 1997, when the lights went out after 56 minutes with the score at 2–1.
- Wimbledon versus Arsenal on 22 December 1997, when, with the score at 0–0 and just 13 seconds into the second half, the lights went out and the match was abandoned.
- Manchester United versus West Ham on 10 January 1999, when the start was delayed for 45 minutes after workers accidentally cut a mains cable outside the Old Trafford stadium.

English football is immensely popular in the Far East, where millions of pounds are wagered on matches. Some estimates suggest as much as £1 billion is gambled on English soccer in Malaysia, Indonesia, Thailand, Singapore and Hong Kong. It is significant that in the Far East, unlike Britain, the "result" of a match stands for betting purposes as long as the second half has started. It does not have to be finished. These factors were being considered as the detectives investigated the lights failures.

The whole episode also threw a fresh spotlight on betting syndicates in the Far East, particularly Malaysia.

Many a bookie must sometimes dream of taking in the bets, working out the most profitable result and then somehow making sure this is what happens. In Malaysia, Indonesia and Thailand was that this dream became a reality, and the game a near-farce, thanks to a £350 million-a-year scam.

The Malaysian allegations often seem too fanciful even for a movie plot, with bundles of notes wrapped up in newspapers being handed to middlemen at bus-stops late at night, destined for international players. The masterminds included one figure known as "the Blind Man", who made a fortune from a sport he had never seen.

Thanks to the bookmaking syndicates, many games in the 1994 Malaysian season were decided not on the pitch but in bars and coffee-shops. Men standing by the pitch would receive instructions by mobile phone and relay them to the players in their pay.

The bookmakers made a fortune from gambling in a Moslem country where, though it is technically outlawed on religious grounds, people will bet on anything from the time of the first yellow card to the number of corners awarded.

When the authorities were belatedly forced to take action, the extent of the corruption was revealed. Eighty footballers were banned, of whom 20 were internally exiled to far-flung villages in the interior. Among those convicted was the Australian-born Singapore international Abbass Saad, who was fined $36,000.

This is not to say that Britain and the Far East are the only places in the world where football matches have been fixed.

Every Brazilian remains convinced that Argentina's 6-0 victory over Peru in the 1978 World Cup, which took the hosts through to the final at Brazil's expense, was due to Peruvian goalkeeper Ramon Quiroga, a naturalized Argentinian, suddenly rediscovering his loyalty to the land of his birth. At the very least, it was unsatisfactory that Brazil's final group match against Poland kicked off in the afternoon, allowing Argentina to know exactly what would be required that evening against the Peruvians.

Recent allegations suggest Argentinian aid worth some £50 million later found its way into the Peruvian economy. Whatever the truth – Quiroga later published an open letter defending his and the team's honour – it left an unpleasant taste in the mouth.

In Greece and Yugoslavia in the 1960s and '70s, fixing reached farcical levels. In 1962 a German referee had to be flown in to oversee a domestic match between AEK Athens and Panathinaikos, while in 1979 in the former Yugoslavia one team beat another 134–1 in an end-of-season clash. Similarly, in South Africa in 1993, East Blackpool beat an opponent 68–0: the sports minister, tongue firmly in his cheek, said: "I think something fishy is going on."

It is Italy, however, which has the worst reputation. In the 1930s Juventus full-back Luigi Allemandi was offered the equivalent of £550 to play badly against Torino. He accepted the money, but even then stopped a certain Torino goal. However, he came under suspicion; accused, then suspended, he was later reinstated, going on to play for Italy in the 1934 World Cup Finals.

In the 1954–55 season, Udinese were found guilty of match-fixing and after finishing second in Serie A were relegated to Serie B. But they blithely carried on, even in Serie B, and a game against Pro Patria was so rigged that the referee later said he thought of putting his whistle away and letting the players do what they wanted.

In the same season Catania were also convicted, but they were only one of many involved: it was suggested that throughout Italian soccer in 1954–55, some 150 matches were fixed. In the 1957–58 season, it was estimated that between seven and 12 in Serie A alone had a suspicious result.

In 1958 Atalanta were relegated after being convicted of bribery. However, Gianni Azzini, Padova's international centre-back, who had been suspended, found himself back in the game when the main witness against him turned out to be a girlfriend he had promised to marry and later ditched.

In 1961 Bari were caught at it, relegated and then had ten points deducted to prevent an immediate return to the top flight.

Not surprisingly, Italy was widely suspected of spreading its match-fixing disease abroad. Internazionale, then under the control of wheeler-dealer Italo Allodi, employed Hungarian refugee Dezso Solti to offer sweeteners to referees in crucial European ties. In 1964 a Yugoslav referee called Tesanic, who had failed to send off an Inter player for kicking an opponent in a European Cup semi-final, was reported to be enjoying an Adriatic holiday at Inter's expense. The European football authorities investigated but ruled nothing was amiss.

The next year Liverpool also lost to Inter at the semi-final stage of the European Cup, going down 3-0 in Milan after a 3-1 win at Anfield. Liverpool manager Bill Shankly was convinced referee Ortiz de Mendibil had fixed the game, and defender Tommy Smith angrily pursued the referee all the way to the dressing-room after the final whistle.

Then, in October 1968, suspicions arose of a fix in an Inter Milan–Malmo game after many dubious decisions went Inter's way. Inter, on the verge of losing, won the tie.

In 1984, two spivs, who were subsequently gaoled, approached Dino Viola and said that for a payment of 100,000 Swiss Francs the referee could be bought. Viola gave the money, the referee was never approached. Roma won 3–0 (taking the tie 3–2) before losing the final to Liverpool. When the facts emerged Viola, who's now dead, was banned for four years, reduced to three on appeal. He was an Italian MP and lost the election.

Italy's greatest international football scandal occurred during the 1974 World Cup Finals when the Polish team accused Italy's players of offering them money to lose a crucial group match. Italy needed a draw to stay in the tournament, but lost 2–1. Years later football writer Brian Glanville of the *Sunday Times* was told by Polish captain Kazi Denya and other players that six Italians, who weren't on the bench that day, had offered them money in the grandstand. A further bribe was allegedly offered in the dressing-room during the match.

In the 1980s came Italy's biggest domestic scandal. A Rome magistrate began investigating allegations that players in Serie A had been paid upwards of £20,000 to fix games. AC Milan, Juventus and Lazio were the clubs said to be involved and the host of players named included one of Italy's greatest, the striker Paolo Rossi.

At the pinnacle of his career Rossi, then one of the world's most talented and highest-paid stars, was one of 30 footballers banned for fixing games for an illegal betting ring. Rossi was accused of fixing a match between Perugia and Avellino: he insisted that the

Zero to hero: after his match-fixing ban Paolo Rossi led Italy to victory in the 1982 World Cup.

presence of his name on a list was a mistake. He was suspended for three years but this was reduced to two which, it was noted, conveniently allowed him to lead the national side to World Cup success in 1982.

Among others punished, AC Milan were relegated and there were life suspensions for their president, Felice Columbo, as well as goalkeeper Ricky Albertosi and Lazio goalkeeper Massimo Caccitori. Lazio were fined £6,000, and Perugia and Avellino had five points deducted at the start of the next season. Eight other players were banned for periods ranging from three to five years.

At the height of the match-fixing there were some bizarre scenes. A match between Juventus and Bologna was supposed to be drawn 1–1 but when Juventus scored, the

Bologna goalkeeper fumbling a long-range shot, the scorer ran to the bench asking in panic, "What do we do now?" The answer was for Juventus to let in an amazing own goal which kept the scoreline as planned.

Bernard Tapie was a former French culture minister, mayor of Marseilles and once a confidant of President Mitterrand. But it was his role as president of Marseilles' football club that was to bring about his fall and imprisonment for match-fixing.

The scandal broke in 1993 when the Marseilles midfielder Jean-Jacques Eydelie was accused of trying to bribe three Valenciennes players to lose a league match. The match was six days before Marseilles won the European Cup, beating AC Milan in the final. The scandal deepened when general manager Jean-Pierre Bernes was charged and an envelope containing the equivalent of £30,000 was dug up in the garden of a house occupied by Valenciennes player Christophe Robert's mother-in-law.

This was too much even for European football's governing body UEFA (Union of European Football Associations), which barred Marseilles from defending their trophy. The net then closed on Tapie, who in 1994 was ordered to quit as president of Marseilles and then jailed for three years, with one year suspended. The court heard Marseilles had spent £1.2 million a year bribing opponents to throw matches; some of the money went on buying referees. Tapie, said Bernes, was "the godfather of match-fixing, who decided which match to buy".

As well as being stripped of their European title, which went to AC Milan, Marseilles were also stripped of their French title and relegated to the Second Division.

Marseilles' shame was not unique. In March 1999, Bordeaux officials stood trial for attempting to bribe referees in European matches during the 1980s. Claude Bez, the chairman, died before the case came to court, but ex-general manager Didier Couecou and former secretary Hervé Bizot, as well as Croatian scout Ljubomir Barin and Portuguese scout Licio d'Onofrio, faced charges of fraud and bribery.

Barin said the corruption had began after Bordeaux were beaten by Hamburg in a 1981 UEFA Cup tie, when the German side was given a controversial penalty. Barin said he told Bez that to achieve European status "we would have to act like the rest of them".

After Bordeaux had created a slush fund to curry favour with referees and linesmen, match officials "started falling over themselves to come to Bordeaux". They were taken to meals in the best French restaurants and given rooms in luxurious hotels. Acting on behalf of Bez, Barin said he hired Paris prostitutes at £2,000 a night. "We needed one for each of the four officials. When the refs were greedy, the girls stayed for two nights. We also had to think of the referees' wives. Officials went home with suitcases full of watches, perfume and fur coats," he said.

Barin further claimed that Real Madrid, who won the Champions League in 1998, always offered linesmen Rolex watches, costing between £1,500 and £4,000.

The court was shown a document dated on the day of an important match between Bordeaux and Naples, refereed by German officials. The document said: "50,000DM + 25,000DM + 25,000DM. Total 100,000DM = Fr342,000". Bizot said he had withdrawn the sum in cash from the club's bank account that evening. Bizot and Couecou said they never tried to find out the destination of money they handled. "You don't know anything and you don't ask questions," they said.

In 1988 more than 40 Hungarian players and officials were arrested on charges of match-fixing. They included former national team manager Kalman Meszoly and full-back Sandor Sallai. The Hungarians, of course, have a long history of match-fixing; so much so that in 1975 the communist government banned a book which described how a set sum was paid for important league points. In one case cash was paid as the team waited to go on to the field of play; when the players were questioned, they claimed they were collecting an old loan. In 1983, a total of 26 people were arrested for fixing matches to make a killing on the pools.

Other countries have also had their match-fixing sagas. In 1971 officials of the German club Arminia Bielefeld were found guilty of putting up £90,000 to fix four matches in the West German League. And in 1990 in Calcutta, a match between local football giants Mohammedan Sporting and Mohun Bagan was supposed to have been fixed. They drew 2–2 to make sure both teams qualified for the later rounds of a tournament and shut out a rival team. An inquiry established that a fix had taken place, and coaches, referee and linesmen were suspended.

Attempting to bribe the referee is the

classic way of fixing a football match, and is not unknown even in Britain. But it is the world-wide game that has provided the most startling examples, with British referees often the subject of bribes.

Howard King, a leading international referee of the 1980s, claimed clubs supplied him with hookers in the hope of winning favours on the field – but insisted he had taken what was on offer and then officiated impartially. King said he spent a night with a blonde supplied by Sporting Lisbon before their game with Dynamo Kiev: though Lisbon duly won, King said it was because they were too good for the opposition. King admitted being provided with women in his hotel room on 12 to 15 occasions, in European states from Russia to Portugal. He also admitted on one occasion threatening to ensure that the Russian national team lost unless he was able to bed a beautiful girl who did not speak a word of English.

Some Brazilian referees had always insisted that match-fixing had been going on since 1985, but it was still a shock when five referees and four directors, including the president of the Rio de Janeiro federation, Eduardo Viana, were arrested.

The referee bribery case that was never solved was the European Cup semi-final between Juventus and Derby in 1974. Juventus were accused of using the services of Dezso Solti, named in the Inter bribery scandal of ten years before, to bribe the Portuguese referee, Francisco Marques Lobo. UEFA accepted that Solti did attempt to bribe the referee, but also accepted Juventus's assertions that Solti was acting independently when he went to see Lobo. Juventus acknowledged Solti was their supporter but said they could not control his actions. UEFA took no action against Juventus, and there was some suggestion that Juventus would sue Solti, but it came to nothing.

Brian Glanville, who with *Sunday Times* colleague Keith Botsford tirelessly investigated the affair, wrote: "Do UEFA not know that it was an open secret that, for a decade, the big Italian clubs and probably (no, more than probably) the international team were wheeling and dealing in referees, bribing them rotten wherever they could, frequently manipulating matters so they had the referee of their choice appointed for the important games?"

Brian Clough, then manager of Derby County, was furious and said, "No cheating bastards will I talk to. I will not talk to any cheating bastards." Juventus, perhaps deservedly, lost the final 1–0 to Ajax.

More than a decade later, in 1984, Clough's Nottingham Forest team were victims of cheating when their opponents bribed the referee. This time, in contrast to Juventus, Forest's opponents admitted what they had done. Forest were playing the Belgium team Anderlecht in the UEFA Cup semi-finals. They had taken a 2–0 lead from the Forest ground, the sort of score that should have been good enough to see them through to the final.

But in Belgium, Forest lost 3–0. A Paul Hart goal was disallowed and a very dubious penalty given against Kenny Swain. Brian Clough and his players suspected the referee was on the opposing side, but could not prove anything. Anderlecht went on to the final, where they lost to Spurs.

Then, 13 years later, the Anderlecht president Roger van den Stock admitted that his father Constant, who was the president in 1984, had paid the Spanish referee Guruceta Muro a million Belgian francs (about £16,000) the day after the game.

According to Roger van den Stock, it was not a bribe but a loan, and one given to help a man in trouble. Muro, who has since died in a car crash, pestered his father for money. "He refused two, three, four times, and in the end, the day after the game, he eventually said, 'I'll give to this man who is in financial trouble, I'll give him a loan of one million francs.'"

UEFA banned Anderlecht from European competition for a year. However, Anderlecht went to the Court of Sports Arbitration, which held that UEFA's executive committee was not competent to rule on the bribery charge, and that since more than ten years had passed since the offence, no further action was possible. Forest, who wanted to take Anderlecht's place in the UEFA competition, launched a case against the club in Brussels claiming compensation, which presently remains unresolved.

So the cases roll on and, as UEFA president Lennart Johansson has said, "The more you dig, the more you find." There seems no solution to the problem.

If this is the state of soccer, which is a rich sport, what about other sports, where the honest rewards provided by the game are smaller, and dishonesty is therefore all the more attractive?

Don King

The Ghetto Einstein

Since two men first made fists of their hands and squared up to each other in a ring enclosed only by the crowd, boxing has attracted a host of characters whose actions have placed them on or beyond the margins of what is usually regarded as acceptable behaviour.

Don King, a man whose syntax is as surreal as his hair-style, and whose wheeler-dealing makes both of these look plausible, stands out even in the company of other fight promoters. It is deeply revealing about the mores of modern boxing that for a quarter of a century it has been dominated by, and earned a fortune for, a man with a record like King's.

He served time for killing a man in 1966. On two separate occasions he has been investigated by a grand jury, but neither was able to find sufficient evidence to indict him. He has also been investigated both by the FBI and the US Attorney's Organized Crime Strike Force unit. Many people in boxing, both inside and outside King's own camp, feel that King is beyond the law. And in many ways he has changed little from the man who in the mid-1960s had risen to the top of the hustlers' meritocracy and today is worth an estimated half a billion dollars.

In his book, *The Life and Crimes of Don King,* Jack Newfield says that even in the 1960s King was "a street Machiavelli, a ghetto Einstein" who "dressed like a pimp, talked like an evangelical storefront preacher and thought like a chess grand master". King was already "a force of nature. He possessed the alchemy of a brilliant strategic mind, working-class ambition and anger – and no conscience."

Boxing was made for King, just as an open hen-coop is made for a fox.

While boxers are not usually regarded as candidates for *Mastermind,* King has the sort of mind and personality that would probably take apart the leading members of many professions that rely more heavily on the intellect.

Boxers readily signed up to fight for King, some living to regret signing blank contracts. Many ended up with much less money than they expected, while King's riches continued to grow. The relationships with his boxers and his fellow-promoters seem inevitably to turn sour and litigious. And King has little time for those whose talents are waning.

One of his more ruthless tactics is to dump a large sum of cash on the table in front of a boxer – on the principle that this tends to make a bigger impact than a cheque. In that way a fighter will often accept a much smaller amount than he is actually owed.

At times he seems to be a real-life J.R. Ewing: a man we all love to hate, but who always comes back – in King's case, always finding someone else who will sign away his career. Only those who come into contact with King fully understand the spell he weaves.

The journalist Nigel Farndale, writing in the *Sunday Telegraph*, said that none of King's success made any sense "until you meet him. An hour in his company and you would sign anything just to shut him up. A typically demented answer of his will last 15-20 minutes – and it won't bear any relation to the question you have asked. In fact, in its deafening, syntax-mangling, stream-of-consciousness way, it won't resemble anything you could reasonably define as discourse at all."

There is a theory that King simply batters everyone into submission with waves of rhetoric. And he is undoubtedly an imposing

Teflon Don (clockwise from left): the electric hair; arriving for one of his many court appearances; before the controversial Lewis v. Holyfield fight.

presence. He is 6ft 3ins tall, his 250-pound body is crammed into a three-piece suit, the eyes are cold and the hair flies away in a style no barber would dare imitate.

The latest victim was the British boxing promoter Frank Warren, a man hardly known as a soft touch or shrinking violet. Warren is used to controversy himself. He was once shot and wounded, and is now barred from being a director of a company having been disqualified as a result of court action brought by the Department of Trade and Industry. Yet Warren ended up agreeing to pay King £7.2 million to make a clean break of their four-year partnership to promote British fighters.

This victory saw King at his most dangerously benevolent. "Whether I ever see the money is immaterial. I happen to be very fond of Frank Warren. He's sort of a likeable rogue. I can find no means, no method, no madness to formulate a theory to you about the propaganda as regards to my friend Frank Warren. When I arrived in the UK, he was at his lowest ebb; self-admittedly. And I reached out and touched him and he became a successful and wealthy man. Somewhere in the road, dust got in our eyes."

There was a time too not so long ago when he talked in similar vein about Mike Tyson, whom he still refers to as "that dear lad". There are many who blame King's stewardship for the decline of Tyson from the outstanding champion of his generation and potentially one of the greatest of all time into a convicted rapist who appears to have lost more talent than most heavyweights have ever been blessed with.

Not long after Tyson came under King's shadow at the tender age of 22, he ceased to develop as a boxer and became, equally quickly, one of the most unpopular heavyweight champions in boxing history. He continued to win, but his fighting lacked the intensity and hunger of his early years. It appeared there was no one to stop him believing his own propaganda, and he paid the price when he tried to fight once too often without training properly. He lost his title to the 42–1 outsider Buster Douglas and was never the same fighter again.

After serving time for rape, then losing a title fight for biting an opponent's ear, he was sent back to prison after a conviction for assault. The former friends and business partners are now suing each other, and King has moved on to boxers who are still fighting in the ring.

One of the most revealing aspects of Douglas's victory over Tyson was the behaviour of King once the fight was over. It demonstrated the extraordinary mixture of "front" and power that the man possesses.

Only once did Tyson find any form of inspiration during that fight, and that was when he knocked Douglas down. It was not a savage blow, and Douglas could have got to his feet on the count of two. Instead he did what most boxers do in these circumstances and waited for a count of nine. His state of well-being was demonstrated only two rounds later by the three-punch combination which knocked out Tyson.

Instead of asking for a rematch, King demanded a recount, claiming that Douglas had been down for a count of 13 seconds and had therefore effectively lost the match two rounds before he had won it. Extraordinarily, it seemed for a time as if the boxing authorities would accept his complaint and, against all logic and fairness, declare Tyson the winner. Eventually, however, public pressure proved too strong to resist and Douglas was confirmed as the victor.

In March 1999 King was the promoter of the championship fight between Lennox Lewis and Evander Holyfield, which also ended in controversy. In the view of most observers Lewis clearly won the fight, but one judge amazingly awarded it to the American, while the British judge declared it a draw. The judging of the fight is now the subject of several official inquiries. It would be a major surprise, however, if anything was pinned on the man who has earned his reputation as "Teflon Don" the hard way.

King was born in Cleveland, Ohio, in 1932. After his father died in an industrial accident, Mrs King used the compensation she received to help the family enjoy a better lifestyle and move to a nicer area.

King's career as a hustler began when he graduated from high school and began running a numbers game (an illegal lottery) to raise money for his college tuition. However, King never made it to college, and by the time he was out of his twenties he was one of the most successful numbers racketeers in Cleveland.

His first serious brush with the law came when he shot a man who was trying to rob one of his numbers establishments in 1954, but the killing was ruled a justifiable homicide. Twelve years later King was again involved in a violent incident which left Sam Garret, one of his runners, with brain damage. He died one week later. King was accused and found guilty of second-degree murder and sentenced to ten years in gaol. He was a model prisoner, used his time to improve his education, dabbling in philosophy and literature, and was released after serving only one-third of his sentence.

Within four years of leaving prison King had built himself a reputation as a boxing promoter. During the next 20 years King became the most powerful man in boxing, signing up top fighters and becoming better known than many of the fighters he represented. His greatest coup was to realize, early in the 1970s, the importance to boxing of television and the revenue it would bring. It was his understanding of the importance of TV exposure for his fights, allied to the dream world heavyweight championship bout between Muhammad Ali and George Foreman, that laid the basis of King's fortune.

That fight, which King with characteristic *chutzpah* christened "The Rumble in the Jungle", was a blueprint for the way he was to manage operations for the next two decades. Typical of his promotion activities was the way he got the two into the ring. Ali, it is said, was bored into submission, and a 90-minute walk with Foreman convinced the then-champion to sign a blank piece of paper which King filled in later. King offered Ali and Foreman $5 million each for the fight, making them the highest-paid boxers in history. However, he then had to guarantee the money. He was able to get $1 million from the British-based Hemdale Corporation, but it was a stroke of near-genius that enabled him to raise the rest of the money and create another piece of boxing history. King decided to promote the fight as a black event, capitalizing on the Black Consciousness movement of the times, and to stage the fight in Zaïre, now the Congo.

King, who also promoted the Ali/Joe Frazier "Thrilla in Manila", has turned the world heavyweight championship into a virtual monopoly. His tactics have been as single-minded as they have been controversial, and they have periodically got him into deep trouble, most notably in 1977 when he set up the United States Boxing Championship.

"Somewhere in the road, dust got in our eyes": King and Frank Warren with Frank Bruno in 1995.

King drew up a contract for all the entrants stating that if they won, King would have the right to promote their next three fights. This was a condition of their taking part – no contract with King, no place in the tournament. Marvin Hagler refused to accept the contract, which would also have committed him to accepting two of King's associates as his managers. Hagler told the press that he had been blacklisted from the event. A subsequent investigation by the broadcasters ABC revealed that there were unqualified fighters in the tournament and that others had been given false records to improve their image. However, the fighters' fake records had been published in *The Ring* magazine. According to Jack Newfield, it later emerged that the editor of the magazine, John Ort, had been paid $5,000 in cash by King.

Prosecutor Michael Armstrong was recruited by ABC to investigate and said the $5,000 cash payment seriously compromised the integrity of the selection process, but was unable to get the evidence he needed as the investigation was a private one with little real power. In response, King said that he was the victim of a racist conspiracy. Despite the fact that Armstrong found evidence of unethical conduct at the tournament, King was never prosecuted.

King also got into difficulties with the revenue authorities, and faced trial for tax evasion in 1984. King was indicted along with his personal assistant Connie Harper on 23 charges, including the filing of fraudulent tax returns and attempting to conceal unreported income. Harper was convicted while King left the court a free man. He had yet again lived up to his reputation as "Teflon Don".

7

Cricket's Bribery Saga

In the history of cricket there is much talk of a dark chapter, when matches were bought and sold. But this is presented as ancient history, when the game was young and all sorts of things happened. That time was the beginning of the nineteenth century. The following was written by cricket's early historian James Pycroft, after talking to two great cricketers of that age, William "Silver Billy" Beldham and William Lambert, the brilliant professional whose career came to an end because he was believed to have sold a match:

Hundreds of pounds were bet upon all the great matches, and other wagers laid on the scores of the finest players, and that too by men who had a book for every race and every match in the sporting world; men who lived by gambling; and as to honesty, gambling and honesty don't often go together. What was easier, then, for such gentleman to mix with the players, to take advantage of their difficulties, and to say, "Your backers, my Lord this, and the Duke of that, sell matches and over-rule all your good play, so why shouldn't you have a share in the plunder?" – that was their constant argument, "Serve them as they serve you."

On the spot: Pakistan's Salim Malik was alleged to have tried to bribe three Australian players.

To get an idea of the scale of the betting, and how it cast a dreadful shadow over the early nineteenth-century game, one only has to look at a match between England and Hampshire, played on 24 August 1823. During the course of the match – in which Hampshire, who made 319 and 38, beat England, who made 144 and 212, by one run – bets were frequently taken not merely on the result but on how many runs individual batsmen would make. The effect was recorded by Mary Russell Mitford, one of the finest female writers on the game:

I was never so disappointed in my life. But everything is spoiled when money puts its ugly nose in. To think of playing cricket for hard cash! Money and gentility would ruin any pastime under the sun. Much to my comfort (for the degrading my favourite sport into a "science", as they were pleased to call it, made me quite spiteful) the game ended unsatisfactorily to all parties, winners and losers. Old Lord Frederick, on some real or imaginary affront, took himself off in the middle of the second innings, so that the last two men played without him, by which means his side (meaning England) lost, and the other could scarcely be said to win. So be it always when men make the noble game of cricket an affair of betting and hedgings, and, maybe, of cheatings.

Cricket then was rife with rumours and stories of cheating and one day, as Pycroft records, a quarrel broke out between two players at Lord's, right in the pavilion, with blows being exchanged. One player said, "You had £20 to lose the Kent match, bowling leg long-hops and missing catches", and another asked, "Why did that game with Surrey turn about – three runs to get, and you didn't make them?"

But this quarrel opened the eyes of the authorities, and the bookmakers were banned. Cricket cleaned itself up and became a world game. Then, more than 150 years later, cricket saw the return of the scourge it thought it had banished for good.

Rumours of match-fixing taking place in subcontinental cricket had been rife for some time, but this seemed no more than bazaar talk. It took on a whole new meaning in the winter of 1994–95 after Australia's tour of Pakistan. Three of their leading players, Shane Warne, Tim May and Mark Waugh, alleged that Salim Malik, then Pakistan's captain, had offered them bribes of £130,000 to throw a Test match. He was also alleged to have visited May in his hotel room in Pakistan just before a one-day game and offered him money to throw it.

Even before this there had been a story of alleged match-fixing in England, with Don Topley, a former Essex player, claiming in a *Sunday Mirror* article that an encounter between Essex and Lancashire had been so arranged that Lancashire won the Sunday game played in the middle of a county championship match, and Essex went on to win the championship match played either side of it. However, the other players involved in the matches denied the allegations, and they were never proven.

The Australian charge against Malik was on an altogether different scale. Malik, of course, denied it vehemently, but it had opened up a veritable can of worms and stories started emerging from the Indian subcontinent of match-fixing on a massive scale. The allegations had surfaced just as Pakistan were touring Zimbabwe and South Africa, and soon fresh rumours emerged.

These gained credence when Pakistan unexpectedly lost a Test match in Zimbabwe – the first time Zimbabwe had won a Test match. Now the rumour-mills began grinding wildly. The stories of match-fixing got so insistent that just before Pakistan played South Africa in Johannesburg on that tour, their players were gathered together in the dressing-room by their manager Intikhab Alam, made to kneel, place their hands on a verse from the Koran and promise that they would not throw matches.

Imran Khan, the former Pakistan captain, also revealed how he had done something similar during a one-day tournament in Sharjah. Having heard rumours that certain players had agreed to throw a match, he gathered all the players together and made them pledge their match fee on a bet for Pakistan to win. They did, and Pakistan defeated the match-fixers by winning.

The Pakistanis had by then also launched an inquiry into the allegations against Salim Malik. On 20 February 1995 Javed Burki, then head of the *ad hoc* committee running Pakistan cricket, went to Lord's for a meeting with David Richards, chief executive of the International Cricket Council, the body responsible for running the game worldwide, and ICC lawyers Simmons and Simmons. At the meeting Burki was given sworn statements from the Australians describing how Malik had tried to bribe them. When Burki asked the ICC lawyers to evaluate the strength of the Australian charges, he was told they were strong and would probably stand up in a court of law.

The Pakistanis appointed Fakruddin G. Ibrahim, a former Pakistan Supreme Court judge, to conduct the inquiry. However, the three Australians, Warne, May and Waugh, refused to go to Pakistan to give evidence under oath. The Pakistanis did not take kindly to this and on 21 October 1995 Judge Ibrahim concluded that the allegations against Malik were "not worthy of any credence and must be rejected as unfounded". He also concluded that the Australian allegations "appear to have been concocted for reasons best known to the accusers".

This infuriated the Australian Board, which condemned the findings as "extraordinary and damaging". The Australians now asked the ICC to investigate the match-fixing allegations under Rule 2 of the Code of Conduct. This was an extremely ironic request, although the irony did not become evident until four years later when, on 8 December 1998, the bribery story was suddenly turned on its head.

The intervening period of four years saw more allegations of match-fixing emerge and the net of suspicion and rumour spread from Pakistan to India. But while there was no lack of stories suggesting that matches were being fixed, there was no definite proof. No cricketer was found guilty of any wrongdoing, and in all that time the only casualty, albeit an innocent one, was a cricket journalist. The bizarre way in which that happened showed how this story had taken on a life of its own.

The journalist concerned was Ramaswami Mohan, for 18 years the cricket correspondent of *The Hindu*, one of India's leading newspapers. In a country with few specialist cricket correspondents, Mohan had a position almost unique among cricket journalists. Neither Mohan nor *The Hindu* has ever officially commented, but according to one *Hindu* source Mohan lost his job because "*The Hindu* had to think of the credibility of the paper. It could not afford to be associated with allegations of match-fixing in any way."

The credibility problem arose in June 1997, when the Delhi-based magazine *Outlook* published allegations by former Indian cricketer Manoj Prabhakar that, just before the India vs. Pakistan match in Sri Lanka in 1994, he had been offered 2.5 million rupees (£41,666) by an Indian team-mate "to play below my usual standards". Prabhakar's response was: "I told him to get out of my room."

Prabhakar did not name his team-mate, but *Outlook* accompanied this bold Prabhakar claim with an article, the result of three months of investigation, which highlighted many other matches showing possible evidence of having been fixed. One of the matches under scrutiny was a one-day international in St Vincent between the West Indies and India in May. India, chasing 250, had reached 201 for 3 in the 42nd over with Azharuddin in charge, but contrived to lose by 18 runs. Mohan, writing about the match, had suggested that Azhar's batting could raise suspicions, although he exonerated the player, saying, "I don't believe he sold out to the forces of the grey world beyond the boundary."

However, *Outlook* used this match and others, and Mohan's own comment that he believed five per cent of matches were fixed, to turn the spotlight on journalists and in particular Mohan himself. It described how whenever India played an international match certain Indian journalists regularly got phone calls from Indian bookies seeking information about the state of the match. The magazine named Mohan as one of the journalists who were in regular contact with the bookies. Although *Outlook* did not specifically allege that he played any part in match-fixing, the strong implication of the article was that he acted as a conduit between players and Indian bookies, who are cricket illiterates and whose profession is illegal on the subcontinent. The magazine wondered how his newspaper could allow him to operate in this fashion.

Mohan, like many journalists, bets on cricket but there has never been any suggestion that he has acted as a conduit between players and bookies. In England, where betting is open, his actions would not be unusual, but in India, where there is no off-course betting – the only licensed bookies are on racecourses – his habit of betting aroused suspicion, however unfounded. Now, as *The Hindu* and Mohan were parting company, the Indian Board, which had looked on with a slightly smug, superior air when the allegations against

Salim Malik surfaced, were forced to act.

Mr Justice Chandrachud, former Chief Justice of India, was asked to report on whether there was any fire behind all the smoke. He not only spoke to Prabhakar and other players but also listened to a tape recording in the possession of a Bombay policeman.

The policeman had told *Outlook* that he had a tape recording of conversations between an Indian bookie and two Indian players before New Zealand and India played at Napier on 16 February 1995. The policeman had overheard a phone call between the bookie and the players. He then got the bookie to ring the players and recorded his calls. The bookie asked each player in Hindi, "Has everything been completed?" Each player replied, "Yes." India were bowled out for 160 in the 40th over and lost by four wickets with 17 overs to spare.

Mr Justice Chandrachud's inquiry was never likely to produce any startling revelations, and that even became even more evident when he questioned Prabhakar. The Indian Test cricketer refused to name the player who had offered him a bribe, and the result was that the Justice's conclusion was just as limp-wristed as the earlier Pakistani inquiry into Salim Malik.

However, even before Justice Chandrachud's inquiry reached its anti-climactic close, there were more allegations. As so often, newspapers led where the authorities appeared incapable of doing anything. In *Outlook* on 30 July 1997 Rashid Latif, a former Pakistan wicket-keeper, made wide-ranging accusations. They went from the seemingly trivial to grave allegations about his old nemesis Salim Malik, whose vice-captain he was during Pakistan's tours of South Africa and Zimbabwe in 1995. One charge was that Malik got regular phone calls from Indian players such as Mohammed Azharuddin, Ajay Jadeja, Navjot Siddhu and Raju asking him about the pitch and whether it would favour batsman or bowlers, and the strength of the opposing teams.

If this sounded innocent enough, Latif also showed *Outlook* what he claimed were seven bearer cheques made out in favour of Malik by Pakistani bookies, all post-dated and each a month apart, in payment for matches in 1994.

Latif was quoted as saying: "When Salim Malik was captain he would bowl himself at crucial stages of the match. He would set an off-side field and bowl on the leg-side. While batting, he would run out his colleagues. I escaped being run out by him in England last year. The third umpire gave me out but the match referee overruled the decision. Having said that, bookies like to have three to four players on their rolls because then they can control the outcome of a match better. For, if the result goes contrary to the bookies' expectations, they suffer huge losses."

Latif alleged that bookies had

Rashid Latif: fingered Salim Malik.

approached him twice. Once was during a Test match in England, when he was asked by an Indian bookie to make sure Pakistan's total did not pass 300. He was offered £20,000 if he did so. Pakistan were 290 for 9 overnight and Latif was batting with the No. 11 batsman Ata-ur-Rehman. Latif not only told the Pakistani management, but the next day made sure Pakistan reached 350. Latif also alleged that bookies tried to fix the third one-day international at Nottingham between England and Pakistan in 1996. Pakistan had lost the previous two, and the betting was on a 3–0 whitewash for England. Pakistan were chasing 250, and Latif, although going in to bat with Pakistan requiring more than seven runs an over, took his side to victory. "The players had to return more than 25 million rupees (nearly £500,000) to the bookies because this result wasn't to their [the bookies'] liking." Latif did not say who the players were, but again the implication was that Malik was involved.

But even as this edition of *Outlook* was hitting the Indian news-stands, Azharuddin and other Indian players were flourishing faxes from Latif denying that he had said they made phone calls to him.

As with all the previous allegations nothing was proven, but there was now a growing belief in the Indian subcontinent that their cricketers were bent. An opinion poll showed most Indians believed matches were fixed. The allegations had surfaced with the rise of one-day cricket. Once the subcontinent had been the home of Test cricket, and crowds flocked to see matches even if they ended in draws. But since the coming of the limited-overs game in the early 1980s, it was now the most favoured form of cricket.

However, the often unexpected finishes in one-day games were a phenomenon which the cricketing public of the subcontinent, brought up on tame draws in Tests, were still getting used to. Often, when unable to understand how what looked like a certain win had turned into defeat, it was easier for many of them to believe that the match must have been fixed.

The Pakistanis were still embroiled in their efforts to get to the truth about the match-fixing allegations. In the summer of 1998 an internal probe leaked to the press just before the Commonwealth Games in Kuala Lumpur alleged that there was evidence of match-fixing not only on the part of Salim Malik but also Wasim Akram, who had succeeded him as captain, and other players including Mushtaq Ahmed.

Akram was so incensed by the accusations that a few weeks later he dramatically announced his retirement from international cricket in order to fight what he termed "false charges". He soon changed his mind, and there were suggestions that some of the accusations reflected the perennial internecine battle inside Pakistani cricket.

The internal probe led to a full-scale judicial inquiry conducted by Justice Malik Mohammed Qayyum. The Pakistanis now began to question their players and almost everybody associated with their cricket. The evidence, some of it given behind closed doors, appeared to be damning, and now not only against Malik but also Wasim Akram, Mushtaq Mohammed and several other Pakistani players. Nearly all the great and good of Pakistani cricket trooped in front of Justice Qayyum's court and gave evidence, including coach Javed Miandad, Amir Sohail, a former captain and, of course, Rashid Latif.

Latif alleged that just before a one-day international in Christchurch in 1994 he was called to Malik's room. "Malik told me we had to lose the match as he had struck some deal with somebody about it. I was offered ten lakh rupees (around £15,000) by Malik. I told him I would think over the matter.

"There were also four or five other players and it was obvious that they must have been offered money. The next morning when I took a catch off a batsman from New Zealand, Malik came to me and reprimanded me and reiterated that we have to lose the match. During the water break, I told Malik I was not a party to the fixing, as I decided during the night not to accept any money."

In his evidence Latif went on to allege that Wasim was also involved. "In my view no-balls and wide balls were deliberately bowled by him [Wasim]. There was an imminent threat of the match being washed out due to rain, which led the bowlers to bowl deliberately in a way that the scoring rate could be accelerated."

The Qayyum Commission also took details of the Pakistani players' assets to check if any of them might have profited from money from the bookies.

With the Australians touring Pakistan again, four years after the tour that had started the whole saga, the Pakistanis took the opportunity of getting them to give evidence under oath. Tim May had retired but Mark Waugh was there and, while Shane Warne did not tour, Mark Taylor, the Australian captain, was prepared to give evidence on Warne's behalf. However, the Australians did not want to go to a court, so a special court was assembled in the house of the Chief Justice of Pakistan. The lawyer for the Pakistan Board, Ali Sibtain Fazli, himself administered the oath to Waugh and Taylor, and both players promised to tell the truth, the whole truth and nothing but the truth.

They repeated their allegations against Malik. During their evidence they were asked why they were bringing this charge against Malik, and they spoke eloquently of how shocked they were to hear that anyone would throw a match and how they as Australians played cricket for love of country, not money. Justice Qayyum was said to be much impressed by the credibility of Waugh. It seemed that at last, after four years, the wretched bribery saga would produce a result.

At this stage the belief in the rest of the cricketing world, which had viewed these allegations with some sardonic amusement, was that it was a subcontinental speciality, like a new form of Indian curry. Even the Bombay policeman who had investigated all this seemed to endorse the view when he said, "Every side with the exception of Australia and England can be purchased."

This smug belief regarding the English and the Australians lasted until 8 December 1998. On that day a Melbourne radio interview given by the former Australian cricketer David Hookes turned the whole story on its head. Hookes revealed that two Australian cricketers had themselves been involved with a bookmaker. The cricketers were Waugh and Warne.

They had allegedly became involved with an Indian bookie, whom they knew as John, during Australia's tour of Sri Lanka in September 1994, which preceded the now notorious Australian tour of Pakistan which had set off the whole controversy. They had provided John with information about the weather and the state of the pitch. For this Warne was paid 5,000 Australian dollars (around £2,500) and Waugh 6,000 Australian dollars (around £3,000). The players insisted that while they were naïve and stupid, they had not been involved in match-fixing and provided much less information than they would give freely to journalists.

The Australian Board had promptly found out about it and fined Waugh £5,000 and Warne £4,000 for their actions.

For the Pakistanis this revelation was like an incendiary device thrown into their carefully-prepared plans. Justice Qayyum, having placed great reliance on the evidence of Mark Waugh, given under oath, was now inclined to doubt his credibility for failing to disclose his own involvement with a bookmaker. "If he did not have a legal obligation, he had a moral duty to bring it to our notice, and it casts doubt on his credibility." Fazli, the Board's lawyer, wondered, "When they gave evidence and promised to tell the whole truth, was this the whole truth?"

As if this was not bad enough, what made the whole story worse and gave it a sinister edge was the discovery that the Australian Board had not only covered it up but, having informed the International Cricket Council, had told them to keep it a secret from the rest of the cricketing world.

It was this ICC involvement in the Australian cover-up that caused the most angst, and not merely for the Pakistanis. It now turned out that eight days after Richards and the ICC's lawyers had told the then-Pakistan cricket chief Javed Burki that the evidence against Malik was very strong, Richards had learned of Waugh and Warne's involvement with 'John'.

Richards and Clyde Walcott, then chairman of the ICC, had flown to Sydney and met the Australian Board at the Sheraton Hotel, where they were told what Warne and Waugh had done and that the Australians had fined the pair. Richards said, "The then-chairman Alan Crompton and then-chief executive Graham Halblish informed us what had happened. They were informing us as matter of courtesy and asked us to respect their confidentiality."

After the meeting with the Australians, Richards and Walcott discussed whether they could tell the Pakistanis but, according to Richards, "We felt the way the ICC were constituted we could not inform Pakistan. We were of the view that the onus was on the ACB to disseminate the information. We were informed after the event. You have got to look at the ICC in the historical context. It is changing, but it has always been a fundamental plank of the ICC – the

Biter bit: Shane Warne's admitted that he had received money from an Indian bookmaker.

sovereign right of member countries to deal with matters of player discipline and all manner of selection and all that sort of thing. At the time it was very much the responsibility of the ACB to deal with it, just as it was with Pakistan to go off and investigate allegations of match-fixing."

According to Richards, the Australians did not tell them why they wanted to keep the matter quiet: "The ACB made their own decision. People will make their judgement whether it is right or wrong."

People quickly began to form a view, and many thought not only that the Australians were wrong but also that the ICC was at fault. It was hardly surprising that Salim Malik, who had so far been the bad boy in the story, now claimed he was the victim of a frame-up. "They have," he said, "been lying all along. I have maintained all along that I was being framed by the Australians because I was in great form and because Pakistan had won a series against them."

There was also much sympathy for the view that the Australians had been quite contradictory in their response to the whole bribery saga. As we have seen, back in 1995, when Mr. Justice Fakruddin G. Ibrahim had dismissed the allegations against Malik and suggested that their accusers had concocted them, the Australians, incensed by the Pakistani comments, had demanded that the ICC hold its own inquiry under Rule 2 of the Code of Conduct.

Yet that was the very moment when they were asking the ICC to keep their own punishment of Waugh and Warne a secret. In the eyes of many, and not just Pakistanis, there seemed a glaring contradiction between how the Australians had viewed the powers of the ICC when investigating the Pakistanis and how they had asked the ICC to view their own players' involvement with an Indian bookie.

The revelation of the cover-up also put an entirely new focus on the bribery saga, and events quickly gathered fresh momentum. The Pakistanis demanded that Waugh and Warne return to Pakistan to give further evidence. There was talk of a video link between Pakistan and Australia to get evidence. It was eventually decided that the Pakistanis would travel to Australia to question the pair. The Australians, having tried for four years to cover up Waugh and Warne's involvement with an Indian bookmaker, were now determined to turn over a new leaf.

They arranged for a hearing in Court No. 1 of the Victorian Civil and Administrative Appeal Tribunal in Melbourne's King Street. It was conducted according to Pakistani law – in effect, a Pakistani court was sitting in Melbourne. The Australians also paid all the expenses of the Pakistanis.

The day before the hearing Brian Ward, the lawyer for the Australian Board, met Fazli to decide technical matters about the hearing. All this did much to smooth ruffled Pakistani feathers about the Australian cover-up, and Fazli told Ward: "We have a common interest. We are playing on a common wicket. We are both probing for the truth."

The search for truth began on 8 January 1999, when Justice Abdus Salaam Khawar, registrar of the Lahore High Court, sitting in for Justice Qayyum, heard evidence from Shane Warne and Mark Waugh.

Both men were closely questioned by Fazli, in particular about a match between Australia and Pakistan which Pakistani investigators felt held the key to this long-running match-fixing saga.

The match was played at the Singhalese Sports Club ground in Colombo on 7 September 1994 as part of the four-nation Singer World Series between India, Sri Lanka, Pakistan and Australia. That series resulted in many stories of match-fixing, and it was after this series that the Pakistanis banned mobile telephones from their players' dressing-room.

The match saw Australia, batting first, make 179 for 7 in 50 overs. Pakistan, who appeared to be cruising at 80 for 2, suddenly lost Saeed Anwar, who had been batting well, to a hamstring injury and collapsed so abjectly that they finished up on 151 for 9 and lost by 28 runs.

During the course of the match several things happened which in an ordinary match could just have been regarded as coincidence, but which, in the light of Waugh and Warne's involvement with the bookmaker, the Pakistanis began to look at again. For instance, just before Saeed Anwar hurt his hamstring the Pakistani 12th man went on and words were exchanged. Anwar did resume his innings later, but by then the Pakistani cause was lost.

Anwar had told a previous Pakistani inquiry into match-fixing that the behaviour of the Australians in the field had led him to believe the match was fixed.

As the Pakistani investigators saw it, the revelation of Australia's cover-up invested the match with dramatic significance. The reason was that it was information about the weather for this match, and the pitch conditions at the Singhalese Sports Club ground, that Waugh and Warne had given to the Indian bookie 'John' and for which they were paid. Yet even before the Australian involvement was revealed, the Pakistanis had heard evidence that bookies had paid Pakistani players to fix the match.

In testimony before the Pakistani judicial commission, a Pakistani bookmaker called Salim Pervez had said he gave money to Salim Malik and Mushtaq Mohammed, the Pakistani leg spinner, to fix this match.

Pervez claimed he gave the money at the request of another bookmaker. His evidence was given *in camera* but Mushtaq, when he was confronted in open court, denied it. Salim Malik had always maintained his innocence.

For the Pakistani investigators the question now was: if the bookies had already fixed the match with Pakistani players, as alleged, then why pay the Australians for routine information regarding the weather and the state of the pitch? Or were they paid for some other reason?

For all the grilling to which the Pakistani investigators subjected Waugh and Warne in Court No. 1 in Melbourne's King's Street, however, they could not find the sort of conclusive evidence on match-fixing, let alone the smoking gun, for which they were looking. Waugh and Warne denied they knew anything about the one-day match against Pakistan at the Singhalese Sports Club ground being fixed.

Warne came over as naïve rather than nefarious when he related how he had met 'John' in a casino and accepted money from the bookmaker to save the bookie's feelings.

This sense of anti-climax was heightened two days later, on 10 January 1999, when the ICC held its much-heralded meeting in Christchurch, New Zealand. This was billed as the meeting at which the ICC would at last come of age and finally assume some of the powers of policing wielded by comparable international organizations, such as FIFA in football.

However, with ICC president Jagmohan Dalmiya unable to attend because of his mother's death – though he was available via a conference telephone link-up – the ICC appeared to have come up with its traditional limp-wristed response. A three-man commission was set up to investigate such allegations, but with neither the names of the commissioners nor the exact scope of its power to investigate and punish being revealed, it seemed like another ICC cop-out.

Meanwhile the Pakistani investigation was stalled as the investigators waited to re-examine some of their own cricketers. All this led to the conclusion that, four years after cricket was rocked by the bribery allegations, the game had failed to come to grips with the problem. It is now commonly accepted that the sheer proliferation of one-day matches provides innumerable opportunities for bookies to try to fix matches. One problem is that one-day tournaments involving three or four nations often produce quite a few matches which are "dead" because they have no bearing on the overall result of the tournament. Such matches provide ideal opportunities for bookies.

The cricketers are always very susceptible. The sums of money paid to them for playing in these tournaments are often relatively small, and a bookie waving a large dollop of cash can easily tempt them to throw a match. What is also sobering is evidence that the virus of match-fixing, so long believed to be confined to the subcontinent, now seems to affect cricket world-wide.

This was demonstrated when, soon after the revelation of the Waugh–Warne link-up with an Indian bookie another Australian player, Ricky Ponting, disclosed that a bookie in Sydney, many thousands of miles from Bombay or Lahore, had offered him money for information about the pitch and weather conditions. Ponting had refused to help, but it showed the extent of the world-wide cricket bookie network.

A two-month Australian investigation, carried out in the wake of the Warne–Waugh revelations, reported on 24 February 1999 that while there was no evidence of the Australians throwing matches or taking bribes, the contact between Warne and the bookies was more extensive than had previously been known. The bookies had also made contact with several Australian players as far back as 1992.

Rob O'Reagan, the lawyer who conducted the inquiry, concluded that there was "a distinct possibility of a connection between the two matters [Warne and Waugh's contacts with the bookies and their allegations against Malik]. I don't know how the ACB concluded they were separate."

And so cricket, like football and other sports, remains surrounded with suspicion and mistrust. The fans cannot be sure that the players they have paid to watch are really trying to do their best, or that the result is not decided even before a ball is bowled because the players have taken money to fix the match.

And with modern cricket, unlike the game in the early part of the nineteenth century, unable to throw out the match-fixers, there seems little chance that this whole sorry chapter will ever end, let alone do so soon.

Lester Piggott
The Long Fellow and the Tax Man

Lester Piggott's 5,300 winners, including a record 30 Classic victories, were a testament to his brilliance in the saddle. But even his artistry as a jockey and ability to put money in the punters' pockets could not overcome his reputation for meanness and taking rides from other jockeys. Nor could it save him from the tax man – or from prison.

In his time at the top Piggott became Britain's richest-ever sportsman, but in court he was accused of illegally trying to ensure that as little as possible was handed over to the public purse. At the end of his trial in October 1987 he was sentenced to three years' imprisonment for a £2.8 million tax fraud. He was released one year later, but the sentence cost him the OBE that he had earlier been awarded, and removed any chance of the knighthood that he might reasonably have expected.

Ironically, that would have been a singularly inappropriate reward for a man who was congenitally incapable of being part of the Establishment and lived every aspect of his life outside its rules.

There was, in fact, scarcely a single convention of racing or social behaviour that he was not prepared to flout. He stole rides from other jockeys without blushing; he rode horses ruthlessly and was prepared to put himself and other riders at risk. He had over the years a quite appalling disciplinary record. In that context, dodging the tax bill was just another episode in his perpetual conflict with authority.

There was no denying his bravery, however. He took his share of falls – on one occasion at Epsom having one ear nearly torn off – and the bones in his back were scraped bare when a horse he was riding bolted from the starting-stalls. Despite these injuries he was back in the saddle within a month. He had a similar injury at the start of a race at Goodwood.

Apart from the jail sentence and regular suspensions by the stewards, Piggott's behaviour went unpunished to a surprising extent. The reason was his sublime riding ability. He was a master tactician and a superb judge of pace, equally at home waiting in front or dropping a non-stayer out before producing it to win in the last stride, and he had an uncanny ability to pick the right horse for a particular race.

That alone would have made him one of the top jockeys of his generation. What set Piggott apart was a singular ruthlessness and a fanatical determination to win. It was symbolized by the way in which he kept his weight down. At 5ft 7ins, he should have been two stone heavier than his riding weight of eight and a half stone. It was, said one commentator, as if Piggott had declared war on his body and kept his weight down by force of will.

If he wanted a ride, he would pester and pursue an owner until he agreed to replace the stable jockey with Piggott. Once on the horse, he would give no quarter to other jockeys and he would ride with power and a robust use of the whip that few horses would dare defy.

The result is that he won some big races that other jockeys, riding the same horse, might have lost. Few owners were prepared to risk living with the knowledge that their horse had lost by a nose because they had turned down Piggott's demand to ride. And, as long as he kept winning – which he did until the day he first retired – few punters questioned his methods or his morality. It is this that made him the housewife's favourite, and a Piggott ride always got the backing of the ordinary punter, who would be confident that whatever the horse did, the jockey would not fail.

The roots of this single-mindedness lay in

Special breed: Piggott's father instilled in his son a ruthless streak and a desire to win at all costs.

his childhood. Piggott was the only son of elderly parents, and he was born with speech and hearing impediments. His parents were both steeped in racing, and the whole ethos of his upbringing was to get on a horse – and to win.

The tuition of his father Keith instilled in Piggott a ruthless streak that the stewards' wrath and sanctions could never eliminate. He was taught that the way to remove a horse in front was to ride into its hindquarters. And when it came to boxing, Piggott was put in with the biggest and toughest stable-lads.

At the tender age of 18 Piggott, who had that year won his first Derby on Never Say Die, was suspended for the rest of the season after a race at Royal Ascot. He was also banned from riding for his father who, in the view of the authorities, was deemed to have

Point of contention: Piggott split with trainer Vincent O'Brien after a difference of opinion.

encouraged him to disregard the rules of racing.

After riding Never Say Die again in the King Edward VII Stakes, Piggott said he was unable to prevent the horse from hanging to the left. But television evidence showed another horse, Raleigh, ridden by Sir Gordon Richards, hanging sharply to the right just after Piggott's offence was alleged to have taken place.

Piggot then switched to one of the country's leading trainers, Sir Noel Murless, and at 21 he had his second Derby win on Crepello, giving him two wins in four years.

The winners kept coming in, and by the mid-1960s Piggott was the highest-paid sportsman in the country. But it was his behaviour off the track that was attracting increased attention. Although married, he was cited in a divorce case and, like many of his colleagues, he had plenty of friends who were prepared to place bets for him, which was technically a breach of racing rules.

By this time he had also built a reputation as a miser who would take anything for free. He was never invited to parties by his wealthy patron Charles St George – everyone knew he would turn up anyway – and he took a peculiar pleasure in not paying, even if it was for something as trivial as an ice-cream or a taxi ride.

All the conflicting desires within Piggott were allowed to thrive in the late 1960s, when he broke one of the last remaining racing conventions: that it was impossible to succeed as a freelance rider. He did not want to be on a poor horse and he did not want others jockeys to be on better ones than him.

For Piggott, the important thing was to be on the right horse in the Classics and other Group One races, or their equivalent. Other jockeys could ride the horses in the warm-up races, so Piggott could see how good they were. But for the important race he would do almost anything to get on board. Perhaps the most blatant example was the way he persuaded the owner of Commanche Run to remove the stable jockey and put him on for the St Leger: Piggott duly won the race in a driving finish.

By the mid-1970s, Vincent O'Brien – a genius of a trainer of horses, first over the fences and then on the flat – persuaded Piggott to become his stable jockey and ride horses owned by the millionaire Robert Sangster. He won his eighth Derby on The Minstrel – a race that probably no other rider could have won with this non-stayer – but he charged a high price for delivering such triumphs. He took 2.5 per cent of the breeding rights on any Classic-winner – and that made him an even wealthier miser.

Off the course, his financial fortunes ebbed as well as flowed as he lost money on syndicates at Lloyd's – though characteristically he was better at banking the cheques than he was at paying the bills.

Inevitably he split with O'Brien, who did not like the way Piggott used training gallops not to fine-tune the horse but to discover just how fast it would go. It was his return to the stables from which he had ridden for Sir Noel Murless – but this time to ride for Sir Noel's son-in-law Henry Cecil – which was to sow the seeds of his downfall.

Cecil's owners had to pay Piggott secret retainers, payments and breeding rights, details of which were spelt out in a letter. Extraordinarily, several of the recipients were members of the Jockey Club, racing's ruling body. The story inevitably found its way to Fleet Street and then, despite the best efforts of Piggott's friends, into one of the papers. But the ultimate irony was that the decision to print was taken by the *People's* proprietor Robert Maxwell, a man scarcely in a position to make a moral judgement.

Piggott was duly raided by the tax authorities, and when they offered him a deal he accepted it. Piggott coolly drew out a chequebook and wrote a cheque for £2 million – only for the Revenue to realize that this was from an undisclosed account.

In 1987 he was sentenced to three years in jail and stripped of his OBE. He was released the next year and returned to what he did best, riding Royal Academy to a brilliant victory in the Breeders' Cup.

Happier days: Piggott leaves Buckingham Palace after receiving his OBE, though he was stripped of the award after he was gaoled.

8

The Bung/Used Five-Pound Notes and Motorway Cafés

The history of professional football in this country is littered with stories of illegal payments made by clubs and their officials in order to gain an advantage. Back in 1884 Preston North End were banned from the FA Cup when their manager, Major William Sudell, admitted he was paying players for their services. Accrington Stanley were found to have done something similar and it was then that the FA finally agreed to allow payments to players.

But the introduction in 1900 of a maximum wage of £4 per week, just about the average for most people at the time, only led to more illegalities. In 1904 Sunderland, found to have made illegal payments to players, were fined £250 and their directors and secretary suspended for three years.

Manchester City were an ambitious club in the first decade of the century and this led them to bend and break the rules. Billy Meredith had been caught trying to bribe an opponent to lose a match, but the full extent of the corruption only became clear when Meredith fell out with the club and told all to the Football Association. In all 17 players, past and present, were found to have accepted illegal payments. They were fined, suspended for a year and banned from

Whistle blower: Billy Meredith of Manchester City exposed their systematic bribing.

The Bung/Used Five-Pound Notes and Motorway Cafés

playing for the club again. Manchester City were also found to have broken transfer rules for offences in 1904 involving second-division Glossop player Irving Thornley, who was banned for a season, and Frank Norgrove. The clubs were fined £250, the Hyde Road ground was shut for two games and five directors were suspended.

The "arrangements" with Manchester City were not Glossop's first brush with the authorities. Earlier in the year they had been fined £259 for mismanagement and deception. Four directors were suspended for three seasons, the secretary censured and six players suspended for three months.

In the same year, 1904, Middlesbrough were censured by the FA and fined £250 for making irregular, under-the-table payments to players. Then, the maximum wage players could earn in a year was still £208. Middlesbrough were keen to sign Alf Common from Sunderland in order to avoid relegation: Common had recently joined Sunderland from Sheffield United. United's chairman Charles Clegg, who was also the FA chairman, had reluctantly allowed Common to go back to his native North-East, accepting a fee of £375 from Sunderland. When, three months later, Common joined Middlesbrough for £1,000, Clegg was furious; all the more so as Common returned to Bramall Lane and scored the winning goal. Acting on a tip-off from a shareholder Clegg investigated Middlesbrough's accounts, and the result was that 11 of their directors were suspended for three years.

In many ways this was the classic football bung story involving player transfers, although the word 'bung' only came into the language in 1993, following a famous court case (of which more later). In the intervening 89 years football produced many examples of bungs large and small, dictated in almost every case by the clubs' need to get round what they saw as the game's restrictive laws.

On being transferred to a new club a player expected a signing-on fee, but the FA said this could not be more than £10. This maximum fee remained in force until 1958 and caused innumerable problems. There was also a maximum wage of £20, which lasted until 1961. Club after club fell foul of the football authorities' determination to keep a maximum wage and restrict signing-on fees. However, it was generally assumed that most clubs tried to get round football's ridiculous laws, and only relatively few were caught and punished.

In 1919 Leeds City, after refusing to hand over financial details of their payments to players, were expelled from the League for making illegal payments, and Port Vale played the remainder of City's fixtures. City's players were put up for auction, fetching £1,000, and eventually a new club, Leeds United, was formed to replace City. Herbert Chapman, City's manager, was implicated but denied any knowledge and went on to become one of the greatest managers in the history of the game, taking first Huddersfield and then Arsenal to glory in the 1920s and '30s.

In 1925 Sir Henry Norris, the man who created the modern Arsenal, was himself found guilty of financial irregularities and was forced to drop out of the game, having apparently made unlawful payments to a chauffeur.

Owing to the ridiculous £10 maximum signing-on fee, clubs seeking top-class players were almost forced to break the rules and pay the going rate, albeit illegally. Len Shackleton, one of the greats of English football, was given £500 on being transferred from Bradford Park Avenue to Newcastle. Shackleton wanted to put the money into a building society, but Newcastle's chairman Stan Seymour feared this would be discovered and told Shackleton he could take £20 out of the Newcastle safe every time he needed cash.

It was quite common for players to be offered hard cash by clubs wanting to sign them. England internationals George Hardwick and Wilf Mannion were offered £5,000 at King's Cross station, and when Jimmy O'Neill's wife wanted a new cooker on his transfer from Everton to Stoke she was duly given one.

In 1957 Sunderland were fined £5,000 for making illegal payments to players. In the 1967–68 season Peterborough were relegated from the Third Division to the Fourth and fined £500 for the same offence.

Having the legendary Stanley Matthews as club manager was no protection for Port Vale. The club were fined £4,000 and expelled from the League in 1968, also for making illegal payments. But they were back the next year after being re-elected.

In 1969 administrative irregularities cost Manchester United a £7,000 fine, and a year

The Bung/Used Five-Pound Notes and Motorway Cafés

later caused Derby to be fined £10,000 and banned from the Fairs Cup for a year. Such action was not uncommon, but it showed how inflation affected football. In 1958, Leyton Orient had been fined £2,000 for irregularities in their accounts; 20 years later, when Fulham were caught making illegal payments, they were fined £15,000.

In 1989, the players of Wimbledon probably appreciated the club's generosity when it gave them unauthorized loans. The football authorities took a different view and fined the club £10,000.

When Graham Roberts, the England defender, was signed by Chelsea from Rangers in 1991, he needed to sell his Scottish home. A company linked to Chelsea paid £100,000 over the odds. For this generosity and payments to two other players, the club was fined £105,000.

In 1993 Barnet were fined £25,000 for making irregular payments and warned that a repeat offence would lose them their League status. And so it has gone on, with almost every decade seeing some club or other getting into trouble for making irregular payments to players.

In the 1990s Swindon Town found themselves on the wrong side of the FA and ended up being fined and dropped down from Division One to Division Three. The problems started with the Newcastle vs. Swindon FA Cup tie in 1988, which the West Country club lost 5–0. Swindon found themselves in deep trouble when it was alleged they had breached a rule barring FA members from betting on football matches except through authorized and registered football pools.

Even though there was no suggestion that the result was affected, two years later the club was fined £7,500, while former manager Lou Macari, who by 1990 was West Ham boss, received a £1,000 fine and was censured. Chairman Brian Hillier, who admitted having a bet, was suspended from football administration for three years.

The decision to impose a £1,000 fine on Macari and censure him was seen by some as too lenient. The FA's chief executive replied that there was no evidence "of widespread abuse of this rule. We regarded the charges as serious and imposed the appropriate penalties." It seemed also that the authorities had accepted that, while Macari knew about the bet, he was not directly involved in it.

Mug's game: Lou Macari was fined for his part in a bet placed by Swindon Town players.

More serious were the illegal payments Swindon made to players, in violation not only of the laws of football but also of the law of the land. This led to the Inland Revenue bringing a case which resulted in the arrests on 1 May 1990 of Macari, Hillier, former chief accountant Vince Farrar and club captain Colin Calderwood. Macari, Hillier and Farrar were charged: Macari was acquitted, Farrar got a six-month suspended sentence and Hillier was sent to prison for a year, but this was reduced to six months on appeal.

The FA then went in to look at Swindon and decided that the club, which had just won promotion to the then-First Division, should be relegated to the Third over 36 counts of making illegal payments to players. On appeal, however, they were reinstated in the Second Division.

The Swindon example was much invoked when, on 12 May 1994, after an investigation by the *World in Action* television programme, the FA charged Tottenham with misconduct in relation to interest-free loans made to players between 1985 and 1989. Supporters of Swindon Town immediately demanded that Tottenham, who had just escaped relegation on the field, now be relegated for their activities off it.

Tottenham argued that their case was very different. For a start they, unlike Swindon, had not kept their lending a secret from the Inland Revenue. The Revenue were well aware of it. They had investigated Tottenham – many other clubs would also be investigated in due course – and Tottenham had settled all the dues owed to the tax man. So, again unlike Swindon, there was no question of any criminal charges.

But they had kept it a secret from the football authorities. In the Tottenham boardroom there had been much anguished debate as to what should be done about informing the powers-that-be, and QCs were consulted. But in the end nothing was done. Here again, in contrast to Swindon, the whole affair had come out only because Tottenham itself, in what proved to be a misguided public relations strategy, publicly disclosed all the loans. In the case of Swindon the football authorities had great difficulty dragging the details out of the club.

The Tottenham story came about like this. The row that broke out in May 1993 between chairman Alan Sugar and chief executive Terry Venables led Venables to take Sugar to court over Sugar's decision to sack him. The case attracted huge media coverage, and a lot of Tottenham's dirty linen – and eventually football's too – was washed in public.

Around this time both the BBC's *Panorama* and Channel 4's *Dispatches* programmes made documentaries about Tottenham, concentrating on the Sugar–Venables fight. ITV's *World in Action* were also interested, but then discovered the loans Tottenham had made to Ossie Ardiles, who by then had become the Tottenham manager, and turned their attention to that.

They went to interview Sugar about it. *World in Action* would later say that in trying to stop them Sugar had scored an own goal. Faced with dishonour for Ardiles, the man he had appointed to soothe fans after the Venables sacking, Sugar decided to pre-empt the programme by releasing everything Tottenham had on file about its loans.

The loans story had really started in 1978, when Ardiles and Ricky Villa arrived from Argentina. Since then, however, loans had been given to many other individuals besides Ardiles. Sugar, in his television interview with *World in Action* – he had his own cameras present as well – made a robust presentation of his case but did not succeed in discrediting the programme. Also, his oft-repeated pleas that the loans were all made before he took over as chairman, and that he had made a clean breast of them, cut little ice.

The five-man FA commission, charged with judging Tottenham, met at Wembley on 14 June, just before the start of the 1994 World Cup. After a day-long hearing they handed down their punishments. Tottenham were fined £600,000, were to have 12 points deducted in the 1994–95 season, and were booted out of that season's FA Cup.

Sugar refused to accept what he felt were monstrous punishments. He appealed and, although the fine was doubled, the points deduction was reduced to six. This appeared to be the end of the story, but Sugar fought on and forced the FA to go to arbitration, where Tottenham won the six points back, were reinstated in the FA Cup but still had to pay the original fine. On the Saturday following the triumph Sugar, for the first and only time, got a standing ovation at White Hart Lane. By this time Sugar and the entire football world were well involved in the bungs scandal, which had revealed for the first time the goings-on deep inside football and the

The Bung/Used Five-Pound Notes and Motorway Cafés

murky world of transfers.

The word bung first surfaced in May 1993 as a result of a court action brought by Terry Venables in an attempt to reverse his sacking as chief executive by Alan Sugar. The allegations heard in court resulted in a three-man Premier League inquiry headed by Rick Parry, then chief executive, Steve Coppell, until recently manager of Crystal Palace, and Robert Reid QC. The inquiry soon grew to encompass not just the initial transfer but many others involving numerous clubs.

As a result, the investigation eventually lasted nearly four years. By the time it finally reported it had examined 10,200 pages of written evidence and questioned 66 witnesses, 42 of them under oath and some of them more than once. The inquiry was also in touch with the Football League, the FA and 12 other FAs round the world, 21 clubs in the UK, 22 overseas clubs, and took in evidence from no fewer than six different sets of legal proceedings. In addition, inquiry members travelled to overseas places as far apart as Norway and Malta. The whole exercize probably cost more than £1,000,000.

The resulting report of more than 1,000 pages covered a whole host of transfers in the modern game. But the biggest section was devoted to the most intriguing transfer and the one that had started the whole thing off: the transfer of Teddy Sheringham from Nottingham Forest to Tottenham in August 1992. No single transfer in British football history – probably in the history of the game – has been more thoroughly analysed, and it is fascinating to study it. Even today, seven years after the transfer, aspects of the deal read like a whodunit, with plenty of clues but no definite answers.

In the summer of 1992 Terry Venables, then chief executive of Tottenham (the team management was in the hands of Ray Clemence and Doug Livermore), was looking for a striker.

He was initially keen on Dean Saunders, but felt that Liverpool's price was £250,000 too high, and his thoughts instead turned to Teddy Sheringham, then playing for Nottingham Forest. Ted Buxton, Tottenham's chief scout, was told by Ronnie Fenton, Brian Clough's assistant at Forest, that Sheringham might be available.

Before the start of the 1992–93 season, probably on Sunday 26 July, Sheringham arrived in London and met Venables at the

Alan Sugar: overturned the FA's Cup ban.

Royal Garden Hotel. Buxton was present, as was Graham Smith, who ran First Wave Sports Management in partnership with former Arsenal captain Frank McLintock.

McLintock was an old friend of Venables, who had known him for 30 years and had employed him as coach when he was at QPR. McLintock and Smith's company First Wave claimed to offer promotional merchandizing and marketing services. This was a grand way of saying that they acted as agents, but at that time the football authorities frowned on agents and pretended they did not exist. Since 6 February that year McLintock had had a contract with Tottenham to provide such services, and McLintock had acted as an agent for quite a few players purchased by Venables.

The negotiations about Sheringham did not go well. The sticking point was his demand that Tottenham come up with the unpaid portion of his signing-on fee with Forest – the fee was spread over the length of his contract at the City Ground – which Forest were refusing to pay.

On 27 July the Forest team went to Ireland for a pre-season tour. By 29 July it seemed Clough had changed his mind about selling Sheringham. Clough was not in Ireland, but that day Fred Reacher, the Forest chairman, told Sheringham he would not be transferred to Tottenham. Sheringham reacted by asking not to play against Shamrock Rovers that evening and Forest agreed. By the time the season started Sheringham was still a Forest player. Indeed, he scored in Forest's opening game, which resulted in a misleading 1–0 victory over Liverpool.

Venables had not given up on Sheringham, although by this time, if Sugar is to be believed, it was already clear that this was not going to be a straightforward deal. In Sugar's affidavit he alleged that Venables was conducting negotiations with Clough and had told Sugar that "Mr Clough 'likes a bung'. He [Venables] explained that Clough wished to receive a payment personally for selling Mr Sheringham. I told Mr Venables that it was absolutely out of the question and that I have never heard anything like this before and it is certainly not the way Tottenham Hotspur or I do business."

A few days later, according to Sugar, Venables returned to the subject. Now there was more detail about how Clough liked receiving the money. "What usually happened was that people would meet Mr Clough in a motorway café and Mr Clough would be handed a bag full of money. At this I told Mr Venables, 'I don't want to discuss this matter again', and that he should not even mention it to me again."

Venables not only denies all this but denies he ever had any contact with Clough on this transfer: "I tried to speak to Brian Clough but he would never take my calls...I had no direct contact with Brian Clough, since all my negotiations at that time were conducted with Mr Fred Reacher, the chairman of Nottingham Forest...The allegation that I told Mr Sugar that Brian Clough 'liked a bung' is untrue. I never used that expression and I've never used those words or words to that effect to Mr Sugar. As to what I am alleged to have said to Mr Sugar about Mr Clough meeting people in motorway cafés to collect his bags of money, it really is a lot of nonsense. I certainly never said any of that to Mr Sugar; he is either making it up or he is repeating something he heard from some other source."

Sugar's allegations and Venables' denials frame the story of this extraordinary transfer.

The Sheringham saga gathered pace in the first week of the season. On the pitch, Spurs had begun badly. Venables insisted this was another transitional year but the early results – an away draw followed by a home defeat – suggested it could be a doomed one.

Just after this, on Thursday 20 August, Venables had lunch with Tony Berry, a Tottenham director. This is either another clue or a red herring, depending on how you look at it. Berry's story is simple and consistent. The venue was Langan's. During lunch a call came for Venables. It could not be put through to the table, so Berry suggested the caller ring Berry's mobile phone. It was Ted Buxton.

After Venables had finished the call Berry asked him, "What was that about?" According to Berry, Venables replied, "You don't want to know." Then he said, "I've got the deal done, but now they want something." Berry asked, "What do you mean, 'want something'?" and Venables replied, "You know, you know, you know." Berry asked, "What, Cloughie?" Venables said, "Yes."

Then, according to the testimony Berry gave the Premier League inquiry, the telephone rang again.

"He [Venables] said, 'No, oh no, no, no, that's it – he's not going to do the deal' – then the phone rang again and it was Ted

The Bung/Used Five-Pound Notes and Motorway Cafés

Buxton and he said, 'Well he'll do the deal for –' I heard him mention Fenton and I heard him mention Clough and he said, 'We'll do the deal.' By that time I'd been clued in on the first call – literally they were only 15 minutes apart during lunch – and he said to me, 'You don't want to know what it is, but he wants – he's upped the price and he wants something for himself.'

For a long time Venables would not accept that he even had lunch with Berry, let alone any conversation, and the circumstances surrounding it would be so disputed that it became the subject of court affidavits, besides being examined in detail by the Premier League inquiry. Venables' contention was that it was not lunch but dinner, and it was not at Langan's but at Scribes, a restaurant Venables owned with a business partner. The Premier League inquiry saw receipts which proved there was a lunch at Langan's between the two men on that date, and this was supported by Philip Hale, the Langan's waiter who served them at Table 1, a window table.

The Premier League inquiry concluded that the lunch did take place, but they could not judge whether the conversation took place as Berry narrated it. "On that we are left with word against word."

That Saturday Tottenham played Crystal Palace at home, and earned their first home point, but the day was significant for an intriguing scene that Sugar claims he witnessed. He recalls seeing a door closing on what appeared to be a secretive meeting in Venables' office at Tottenham attended by Venables, his assistant Eddie Ashby, Frank McLintock and someone else he could not identify. When Sugar asked Venables, his reply was that it was a meeting to do with the Sheringham transfer. However, in court Venables denied that any such secretive meeting with McLintock ever took place.

On the other hand, when Ashby came to give evidence, he agreed a meeting had taken place but denied it had any significance.

On 25 August Tottenham played a midweek match at Elland Road where, led by a rampant Eric Cantona, Leeds won 5–0. Sugar, back at White Hart Lane, watched the match on the big screen and left before the end, not happy with his team.

It was two days after this, on 27 August 1992, that the most crucial moves in the Sheringham transfer took place. Here we need to pause and remind ourselves of the principal actors in this drama and where they were that day. As ever, Venables was at Tottenham's training ground at Mill Hill. Colin Sandy, Tottenham's finance director, began the day at his tenth-floor office in Brentwood, the headquarters of Alan Sugar's Amstrad empire, and just down the corridor from Sugar. Sandy was due at Tottenham later that day, but this was very much the normal pattern for him: the morning at Brentwood, the afternoon at White Hart Lane. Ashby was at Mill Hill. He says he was there all afternoon, but did go to Tottenham later. McLintock was also at Mill Hill before going to Tottenham later.

According to Venables, the deal was finally done when he rang Fred Reacher direct and told him it was now or never – he came back within an hour and it was now. The only thing to be decided was Sheringham's personal terms. McLintock and Sheringham went to the training ground and his personal terms were quickly agreed.

Interestingly, Venables' autobiography does not mention the presence of Ashby. The point is important because Ashby's witness statement in a court action clearly says he was there. Also, more than three years later, a handwritten sheet of notes emerged. It contained cryptic words such as, "Player – 100k, further 100k, 30k car not 20k, invoice by 1.00pm., check last regd time, medical 1.00pm", and a mobile phone number surfaced – 0836 353980. The notes were allegedly in Ashby's handwriting and, along with other papers, were submitted in a court case, where it was further alleged that they had been found on Ashby's desk at Tottenham. Ashby contested the evidence and told the police and the Premier League they were all forgeries. We shall see in due course whether or not this was the case.

The absence of Ashby from the account in Venables' autobiography is significant because we now have two entirely different versions of one of the most crucial phases of the day: the demand that Tottenham pay £50,000 to McLintock's company First Wave. Who made that request?

Venables in his book says he made the call to Sugar and Sandy, explaining that the money was needed because McLintock had insisted he be paid that day. Tottenham owed his company that money, had not paid him for months, and this deal was an irresistible chance for him to get it.

Yet all the other evidence indicates that Venables did not make the initial call, although he did speak to Sandy later. Anis

The Bung/Used Five-Pound Notes and Motorway Cafés

Rahman, Tottenham's then-credit controller, remembers receiving a call from Ashby saying Venables had authorized a payment of £50,000 to McLintock. It had to be cash, and he ordered him to organize it. Ashby, who was at Venables' side making notes of the transfer and has never disputed making that call, apparently then rang Rahman to ask for the money.

Rahman, unnerved that such a large amount of cash was required, rang Sandy. Sandy knew the money was for the Sheringham deal, but having to pay it in cash raised his hackles and he stormed into Sugar's office.

"Talk to Terry," said Sugar, quite calm about it, or at least much calmer than Sandy.

"I telephoned Mr Venables," Sandy says in his affidavit, "and asked for an explanation. He told me that no other method of payment, not even a bank draft, would do, and if we did not do it this way, the Sheringham deal would fail. I said I would arrange for the cash but that I would not authorize its release unless I received a VAT invoice."

Venables' recollection of that phone conversation is very different:

Frank McLintock insisted on having the money before he would let Mr Sheringham sign the contract. He wanted the money that evening or the contract would go off. Accordingly, I told Mr Sandy that Frank McLintock had to have the money that night, but I never said that it must be in cash. Mr Sandy did not query the request and I certainly never told him to mind his own business. Mr Sandy knew that the money was in connection with the Sheringham transfer, and that Frank McLintock wanted it that night, but if he did not get it that night the deal would be off. Mr Sandy did not query why a banker's draft would not be sufficient and I never specifically requested cash. What I believe must have happened is that Mr Sandy must have discovered that a banker's draft could not be made available in time. I cannot recall whether Mr Sandy mentioned a VAT invoice. The deal which I did with Frank McLintock was £50,000 inclusive of VAT, although he submitted an invoice for the £50,000 exclusive of VAT which was paid by Mr Sandy in cash.

Sandy rang Rahman, asking him to collect £58,750 in cash – £8,750 being the VAT on £50,000 – but not to hand over the money without Sandy's authority. It was in fury that Sandy got into his car and drove to Tottenham. He arrived to find that Rahman had not yet returned from the bank.

Rahman was not finding it that easy to get the cash from Tottenham's local branch of the Midland Bank. It did not have such a large sum in cash and Rahman had to go to the Midland's Aldwych offices. He returned accompanied by a security guard. When he got back, Sandy was not in his office. Rahman put the money in the cupboard in his office and left.

Meanwhile Ashby had returned from Mill Hill. The Tottenham security log says he arrived at about 3.30pm. At this point another character appears who took no part in the transfer but claims to have heard and seen things in Ashby's office that day that would later be the subject of sensational revelations in court. If true, they put an entirely new light on the whole affair.

That character is Jeff Fugler. He had been involved in doing PR and marketing for both Tottenham and Scribes West. He came to Ashby's office to discuss payments due to him from Scribes. In the course of this conversation, Ashby showed him several invoices. They were all addressed to Ashby at Tottenham, they were all for the same amount – £50,000 – and the wording was identical. However, they were from different companies. One, dated 25 August, was from Silver Rose International Ltd (Export), a naughty-knickers, Ann Summers-style company based in London's Finchley Road. This said that the invoice of £50,000 was: "For the assistance in arranging distribution and merchandizing network on behalf of T.H.F.C. in the U.S.A. to include travel and all consultancy work involved in the project."

Later investigation has established that there was much that was odd about this company. In the first place it claimed to be a member of the British Chamber of Commerce, something no firm can be, since that is a parent chamber, whereas a company can only belong to a local chamber such as the London Chamber. Also, no listing for such a company has been found in this country or the Channel Islands. It could be a trade name, and it is certainly odd to find words coming after 'Ltd' on a company invoice. A previous incarnation of this company, with a similar name, has been in

The Bung/Used Five-Pound Notes and Motorway Cafés

liquidation since 1987. When I spoke to Jeffrey Silver, who is again trading under the name Silver Rose in Finchley Road but a few hundred yards from the address on the invoice, he said he knew nothing about the invoice but could not be sure if he had ever traded under that name.

There was more than one copy of this invoice. One, addressed to Eddie Ashby at Tottenham, had been faxed at 11.56am on that very day. Another, again addressed to Ashby at Tottenham, and bearing the name and fax number of a B.S. Berrick, had been faxed from Monaco at 5.13pm that day. Bernard Berrick is a British expat who lives in Monte Carlo. He is a fervent Tottenham supporter whose son Steven is married to the daughter of Jeffrey Silver and had done some work for First Wave. Bernard Berrick, when asked, could not work out why and how his fax number appeared on a copy of the invoice.

There was also an invoice from First Wave. It asked for the same amount, £50,000, and had the same wording except that the abbreviations 'T.H.F.C' and 'U.S.A.' were written in full. Dated 27 August, two days after the Silver Rose invoice, it too appeared to have been faxed.

What were these invoices for? Were they meant to launder money out of Tottenham? Was the Silver Rose invoice the first draft, as it were, and the First Wave invoice the second? Fugler told the court he had no doubt the other invoices were bogus.

When Fugler made these allegations in a court case seeking nearly £20,000 from Scribes, Ashby went into the witness box to deny them. He denied he had seen Fugler that day at Tottenham. However, the security log shows Fugler was there, arriving at 6.13pm, an hour after a copy of the Silver Rose invoice was timed as having left Berrick's fax number in Monaco. What is more, Fugler arrived before McLintock. Fugler says that while sitting in Ashby's office he looked out of the window and saw McLintock drive in, and that the security man buzzed Ashby to tell him of his arrival. Ashby asked Fugler to leave and he left.

Some time after Fugler won his case against Venables and Scribes West, Scribes West moved an application to have the judgement set aside on the grounds that Fugler had perjured himself and had supported his own allegations with a forged invoice. It was not suggested in the application that the Silver Rose invoices were forged. The judge granted the application, set aside the judgement and ordered Fugler to pay costs.

The Premier League inquiry, after considering all this, concluded:

While the evidence given by Mr Fugler must naturally attract great suspicion, it is agreed by Mr Ashby that the page of notes which was produced by Mr Fugler together with the Silver Rose invoices is a genuine page of Mr Ashby's notes. This lends some credence to an otherwise unconvincing story by Mr Fugler. It does not, however, eliminate the possibility that the documents could have been given to Mr Fugler at some later stage by someone at Tottenham who wished to harm the cause of Mr Ashby and, through him, of Mr Venables. We are of the view that the faxes are not forged. However, the evidence is insufficient to enable us to form any view as to who sent them. We are however confident that the faxes were sent with a view to assisting in the making of an improper payment in relation to the Sheringham transfer even though they were not in the event used for that purpose.

Now let us return to 27 August 1992 and White Hart Lane.

The money Rahman had collected from the Midland Bank and put in Sandy's cupboard was now handed over. The money was given to Ashby and McLintock in Sandy's office. As soon as they got the money, Ashby and McLintock left. Sandy, keen to get his invoice, followed them to Ashby's office, where McLintock gave him a First Wave invoice. This had the same wording as the other First Wave and Silver Rose invoices and also asked for £50,000 but, unlike the other invoices, this one had VAT added to it. Again unlike the other invoices which Fugler saw on Ashby's desk, this one was signed, the signature being that of Venables.

For two and a half years after Sugar's allegations made these events public Venables said nothing about the signature on this invoice, despite the fact that he spoke of this transaction on various occasions, notably in court affidavits, in his autobiography and at the Premier League inquiry.

Then, in the last week of November 1995, just after the police had dropped an investigation into his complaint that there was a criminal conspiracy against him, he alleged that his signature was a forgery and that he did not how it got there.

On 26 November, the *News of the World* reported Venables as saying, "That invoice was used as a stick to beat me with because my detractors claimed it was proof that I had engineered a bung for Forest manager Brian Clough and was looking for a cut out of the deal myself."

Venables claimed he had never seen the invoice, that he did not know how his signature got there and that it would have physically impossible for him to sign, since he was at Mill Hill and the invoice was never faxed to him at the training ground. As we have seen, however, Ashby was at Mill Hill, and so was McLintock. Both later went to White Hart Lane, and they could very easily have brought the invoice back there with them. Venables' talk of the invoice not being faxed to him is mystifying. Unlike the Silver Rose and previous First Wave invoices, the later First Wave invoice was not faxed anywhere. The original, still with Tottenham, clearly indicates that. Why he should make this claim after such a long time is a mystery. In any case it is hard to see how it makes any difference, because he authorized the payment – indeed, if his autobiography is to be believed, he asked for it.

In Ashby's room on that August evening the participants seemed to have no doubt about the invoice. Sandy got McLintock to sign it as well, to show that he had received the money. Sandy was intrigued that McLintock separated the money into two piles, one for £50,000, another for £8,750, as if the VAT had nothing to do with the £50,000. It is worth stressing that although this transfer generated three invoices, this was the only invoice Tottenham paid in this transaction. The other two invoices did not surface until more than three years after the transfer took place.

At some stage in the evening McLintock drove off. He picked up Sheringham and they drove to the Post House Hotel in Luton, where they met Ronnie Fenton. What did the three men discuss? Sheringham says he does not know, as he never left the car. McLintock says that far from giving Fenton anything, he received something from Fenton – an envelope containing the transfer forms.

Why Fenton should drive some 90 miles to Luton from Nottingham for the purpose of handing over transfer forms is a mystery. It would be more usual for such forms to be faxed between the clubs concerned. Here we have another little twist.

As secretary of the football club, Peter Barnes should have dealt with these administrative details. However, he was on holiday. Barnes recalls, "I had not taken any holiday that year and Terry was very keen I take one. He seemed particularly keen for me to go and kept telling me I was knackered, so I went for a few days."

Barnes, a great cricket enthusiast, went to Scarborough to see Pakistan play – they had their own worries, with the ball-tampering row at its height. His holiday was paid for by Jonathan Crystal, a barrister, a long-standing friend of Venables and at that time a Tottenham director. Crystal told the Premier League inquiry that he had paid for the holiday as a personal and private gesture to Barnes and had not been reimbursed by Tottenham or anyone else. It has never been made clear why Crystal, who was not particularly close to Barnes, should suddenly provide him and his family with a holiday.

The Sugar–Venables court case in May 1993 which first brought these matters to light saw McLintock and his partner Graham Smith indignantly deny that they were acting as bag-carriers for Clough. They said the money had gone into their company. Although Smith had a limited company called First Wave Sports Management, this money supposedly went into the partnership of the same name that he had with McLintock. The First Wave invoice that Tottenham paid and the one that Fugler claims to have seen on Ashby's desk both had the word 'Limited' crossed out.

In his first interview, Smith told the Premier League he had used the money to pay his builder. The builder, when contacted, confirmed that he had received some money, but this was in July, more than a month before Tottenham paid the money. Subsequent investigations by the Premier League established that although the £50,000 was paid into the First Wave partnership, this did not happen until after the affair had been made public by Sugar. The company also submitted a late VAT return. This seems very odd, and suggests that the £50,000 may have gone to another person or group of people. But who?

Clough has always indignantly denied any involvement. When Sugar first made the bungs allegations in the summer of 1993, he asked Sugar to repeat these allegations outside the privilege of the courtroom so that

The Bung/Used Five-Pound Notes and Motorway Cafés

his lawyer could deal with them. For him, the allegations that he wanted a bung were preposterous. "A bung? Isn't that something you get from a plumber to stop up the bath?"

By the turn of 1993, when the FA was considering appointing a successor to Graham Taylor, Clough came out in favour of Venables and suggested they appoint him straight away.

Fugler says that Ashby told him at their meeting on 27 August that the money was for Venables. Ashby denies seeing Fugler on that day and says that his story of the invoice is a complete fiction, so it must follow that this claim, from Ashby's point of view, is also nonsense. However, it is interesting that in his *News of the World* interview Venables denied rumours he had got "a cut out of the deal", although it is not clear who has ever made such a claim.

Venables has triumphantly pointed to the fact that the cheque was signed by Sandy and Sugar as proof that they must bear responsibility. In fact, a similar bank authorization was also signed by Venables, but it took longer to get to the bank from the Tottenham training ground. By the time it did, the Tottenham accounts department had already acted on the Sugar authorization.

The VAT invoice was to provide the final twist to this story. Venables was furious when he found that, as a result of Sandy demanding the VAT invoice, Tottenham had paid an extra £8,750. Two days later, on 29 August, Venables rang McLintock, who agreed to return the VAT. On this visit to White Hart Lane – he was such a regular that Venables

Dodgy deals: Teddy Sheringham's transfer to Spurs left Terry Venables in a heap of trouble.

had given him his own parking space – he saw Peter Barnes, who counted the money, put it an envelope and locked it in his safe.

Venables has pointed to the return of the VAT as proof that he had no designs on the money. "If I had wanted to steal that money I would have said, 'Bring it back to me'. Instead I told him [McLintock] to go to the club and give it back...I thought no more about it until my court action against Tottenham a year ago when I was told that £8,750 was apparently still in the safe. I have no idea why Barnes did not pass it directly to the accounts department."

Barnes has said that Venables had given him instructions to keep the money in the safe and he did just that. There it stayed for another nine months, until June 1993. Then it was that Sugar and Sandy discovered what happened to the VAT on £50,000.

The story does not finish there. When Sugar raised the wording of the invoice with Venables, his explanation was that this was necessary because it was improper and illegal to use agents for the transfer of players. In any case, he reassured Sugar, it was all above-board and Sandy had a VAT invoice. "Don't insult my intelligence," said Sugar. "This whole thing stinks. I know damn well where some of that money is going. I want nothing to do with it if the whole affair comes out."

Some days later Sugar, still bristling with rage and concern, mentioned it to Crystal, who appeared surprised. Sugar made it very clear to Crystal that he didn't like the deal and again said the whole thing "stank". In his capacity as a barrister Crystal should be concerned. Crystal, says Sugar, made some meaningless remarks. Crystal denies all this.

So the mystery remains unsolved. A public company made a cash payment; a whole series of invoices, one from a very dodgy naughty-nighties company, was raised – all of them with the same wording and for the same amount –yet people associated with these events disclaim knowledge.

The Premier League inquiry concluded:

> On the evidence which has been presented to the Inquiry our position is as follows:
>
> The various accounts of events relating to the transfer differ to an extent beyond that which can reasonably be attributed to the results of fading memories, differences of perception or differences of recollection. We are satisfied that several witnesses have attempted deliberately to mislead the inquiry in their evidence.
>
> Mr Clough played little or no direct part in the negotiations relating to Mr Sheringham's transfer, other than in relation to his discussions with Mr Sheringham concerning Mr Sheringham's signing-on fees and the £30,000 ex gratia payment.
>
> On Tottenham's side, initially Mr Buxton conducted negotiations on the instructions of Mr Venables. Subsequently Mr McLintock acted on behalf of Tottenham in negotiating with Forest. On Forest's side Mr Fenton (taking instructions from Mr Clough) conducted negotiations. Mr Reacher and (in relation to administrative matters and the player's ex gratia payment) Mr White became involved in the arrangements for the transfer. Of the intermediaries, First Wave acted not only, through Mr McLintock, on behalf on Tottenham but also on behalf of the player. Mr McLintock undertook most of the work required in the transaction, although Mr Smith was also involved. Mr Venables and Mr Reacher spoke only on 27 August, when the deal was effectively concluded.
>
> At the Tottenham end of the transfer, Mrs Zolnierowicz [Tottenham personnel officer] prepared the necessary paperwork. In doing so she acted on information received from Mr Crystal, and on advice given by telephone by Mr Barnes from Scarborough. At the Forest end the documentation was prepared by Mr White [secretary at Nottingham Forest].
>
> The payment made to Mr McLintock by Tottenham on 27 August 1992 was not an amount agreed at the last minute on 27 August as Mr Venables and Mr Ashby suggested. It had been agreed before that date in discussions to which Mr Venables, Mr Smith, Mr McLintock and possibly Mr Ashby were parties.
>
> The payment was made by Tottenham in cash at the request of Mr Ashby and Mr Venables. The reason for that method of payment is not explained by any necessity to pay Mr McLintock on the day of the transfer. We do not accept the suggestion that payment in cash was demanded by Mr McLintock as a prerequisite of his allowing the transfer to go through. Mr Sheringham was keen to move to Tottenham and in his

capacity as Mr Sheringham's agent there was nothing Mr McLintock could do once Mr Sheringham had agreed personal terms.

After the conclusion of the transfer Mr Sheringham paid First Wave for their services by cheque in the sum of £5,000. First Wave also invoiced Forest in the sum of £5,875, but that invoice was never passed to Forest's accounts department and never paid and First Wave was never forced to write it off as a bad debt.

The evidence does not substantiate the claim that First Wave had outstanding unpaid work for Tottenham (even including work on the Sheringham transfer) which justified payment of a sum of £50,000, or that Tottenham's history of paying First Wave's invoices was unsatisfactory. All invoices submitted to Tottenham by First Wave before 27 August 1992 had been settled by that date. The most recent had been settled as late as 15 August 1992. Mr Smith told the Inquiry that First Wave had not previously submitted an invoice in respect of a number of items of outstanding work because they were "ongoing". Of the work which the Inquiry was informed had been undertaken for Tottenham by First Wave, however, only one item is reflected on the narrative of the invoice paid on 27 August 1992, and that work was on the evidence of Mr Smith and Mr Venables itself not completed before 27 August 1992.

Although there was a practice of disguising invoices which related to payments which might be in breach of FA or FA Premier League rules, several of the outstanding pieces of work referred to by Mr McLintock as being unpaid (for example the provision of videos of players to Mr Venables) would not have constituted an infringement of the rules and therefore the existence of the rules did not constitute a reason why First Wave would need to falsify the narrative of the invoice.

Mr Venables' evidence at various times and in different places concerning the amount of the First Wave fee attributable to the Sheringham transfer, and the point at which he became aware that cash was being paid to Mr McLintock, is self-contradictory. In our view Mr Venables knew of the cash payment long before it was referred to on the Panorama television programme. His subsequent adoption of this account in the Fugler action was not the consequence, as Mr Ashby suggested, of a misunderstanding arising out of Mr Venables' hurried signature of a witness statement in the Fugler action, nor the consequence of a lapse of memory, but a deliberate attempt to distance himself from the payment in cash made to Mr McLintock.

Of the £58,750 paid to Mr McLintock by Mr Ashby and Mr Sandy, £8,750 was returned to Tottenham. We are satisfied that neither Mr Venables nor anyone else at Tottenham or elsewhere had any intention of misappropriating that money following its return to the club.

Of the remaining £50,000, the account given by Mr Smith of what he did with the money is not credible. So far as Mr McLintock is concerned, we have no reason to doubt that he spent the money of which he told us. We cannot, however, accept that that expenditure represents his use of £25,000 from the money paid to First Wave from the Sheringham transfer. References to the invoice and to those moneys were only entered in First Wave's accounts at a much later date (probably at around the time of the "voluntary disclosure of error" on 26 May 1993). We are satisfied that this was not because the invoice was mislaid, but because it was only at a later date (following press coverage of Mr Sugar's affidavit containing allegations in relation the transfer) that Mr Smith and Mr McLintock felt it was going to be necessary for the money to be shown as having passed through First Wave's books.

The meeting which took place (at Luton's Post House Hotel) on the evening of 27 August 1992 was attended by Mr Fenton, Mr McLintock and Mr Sheringham. All of those persons deliberately omitted to make any mention of the meeting with the intention of misleading the Inquiry. Even when driven to admitting that the meeting took place we are satisfied that all three of these witnesses gave accounts which did not accord with what actually occurred at the meeting.

We are satisfied that at the meeting on 27 August 1992 Mr Fenton signed the transfer agreement on behalf of Forest and handed it over to Mr McLintock and that Mr Sheringham signed the Deed of Release/Waiver (his signature being witnessed by Mr Fenton). Two members of the Inquiry (Mr Parry and Mr Reid) are satisfied that at the

> meeting Mr McLintock handed over to Mr Fenton at least a substantial part, if not all, of the £50,000 which he had received earlier that day from Tottenham and that Mr Fenton returned to Nottingham with the money from Mr McLintock. Mr Coppell is not satisfied of this, and by extension the conclusions set out in paragraphs 21.15 and 21.16 are those of Mr Parry and Mr Reid and not Mr Coppell.
>
> Mr Fenton has denied receipt of that money. Mr Clough has denied receiving any money as a result of the transfer. We have heard evidence that payments were made in cash to members of the Forest staff arising out of the transfer, but we do not have evidence on which we can determine at whose instance those payments were made. We are satisfied that cash payments were made from the £50,000 to members of staff at Forest. We think it likely though we cannot be sure that part of the cash was used by Mr Fenton to pay for his daughter's wedding reception on 6 September 1992.
>
> We are satisfied that Mr Venables did not believe that the £50,000 which he authorized on 27 August 1992 to First Wave was simply a payment to First Wave in respect of services by First Wave to Tottenham, whether in relation to Mr Sheringham's transfer or otherwise.
>
> Mr Sandy considered his duties were simply to ensure that the paperwork in relation to the payments to First Wave was properly completed. He was content to rely upon obtaining the authorization from Mr Venables and Mr Sugar for payment. So far as Mr Sugar is concerned it is singularly unfortunate that his customary acuity should have apparently deserted him at the time that he signed, together with Mr Sandy, the authorization which was eventually acted upon by the bank to raise the moneys. He had been aware, on his own evidence, of earlier conversations with Mr Venables on the subject of "bungs" in relation to this transfer. And again, on his own evidence, he considered very shortly after the payment in cash had been made that the payment was for an improper use and had considered the case with Mr Crystal.
>
> The evidence available to us would not substantiate any claim that Mr White or Mr Reacher knew the details of what was occurring in relation to the transfer, in particular what happened to the payment made to First Wave. In our view this was because the control over the manner in which business was conducted at Forest was wholly inadequate. Mr Clough and Mr Fenton were allowed to conduct matters without proper supervision or control by the board. The fact that Mr Fenton was allowed to sign the transfer agreement on behalf of Forest, although he had no authority to do so, is something which Mr White should never have allowed to happen. In our view Mr Reacher was careful to avoid interfering in the way in which the club's management was conducted by Mr Clough and Mr Fenton.
>
> The Silver Rose invoices were in our view bogus invoices raised with a view to facilitating the payment of the £50,000. Although they are addressed to Mr Ashby we are unable to say on the evidence before us that they were procured by him. It is equally possible that they were raised by some third party with a view to their being used in the Sheringham transfer, without reference to Mr Ashby. On the material we have had made available to us we are unable to say who was responsible for the sending of either invoice: either that which was apparently faxed out to Monaco or that which was faxed back to Tottenham from the flat of Mr Berrick Senior.
>
> Whilst the conduct of Mr Venables cannot be justified, it should be borne in mind that, in our view, he regarded the obtaining of Mr Sheringham's services as being essential for the good of the Tottenham team. He did not make or intend to make any personal benefit from the payment of £50,000. In our view he regarded that payment as being an essential prerequisite of obtaining Mr Sheringham's transfer and therefore something which could properly be done on behalf of the club.

As was only to be expected, as soon as the inquiry reported various people criticized in it, particularly Venables, said that they felt vindicated, claiming that the inquiry had "cleared" them. It had done nothing of the sort. What the lengthiest inquiry into any football transfer in the history of the game, and one headed by an eminent QC, had demonstrated was that the old football story of bungs had taken a

The Bung/Used Five-Pound Notes and Motorway Cafés

new and more complicated form. So in 1992 – in the very season that saw the birth of the Premier League, widely advertized as the richest and most successful league in the world – a public company had made a cash payment of £50,000 in relation to the transfer and this was in all probability handed over in a hotel car park, very nearly in the way Sugar alleged Venables had told him it was.

On receiving the report, the FA decided to charge four individuals and one club: Brian Clough, Ronnie Fenton and Nottingham Forest, as well as George Graham and Steve Burtenshaw of Arsenal in a separate investigation (see Chapter 9).

Clough's illness led to the charges against him being dropped, and football, which still nourished warm memories of the man, comforted itself with the picture of a folk hero who behaved rather like a modern-day Robin Hood; taking money, it is true, but then distributing it to others, sometimes to his players or his coaching staff.

The other people involved inspired less sympathy and their stories had different endings.

Finger of guilt: despite denying all knowledge of bungs, Brian Clough faced charges – later dropped – from the FA.

Paul Gascoigne
Daft as a Brush

Paul Gascoigne is the most gifted footballer to emerge from these islands in the last 20 years or more. Yet personal flaws also made him the most self-destructive sportsman since George Best. This combination of immense ability with a football and sad lack of ability as a human being has, in the end, proved too much for Gascoigne, and the 1990s were punctuated by his acts of self-destruction.

It is fair to say that there has been more than one Paul Gascoigne. There was Gascoigne the precocious teenager who never seemed to lose his fondness for childish pranks; who, for example, when he transferred from Newcastle to Tottenham at the age of 21, sounded the fire alarms at the temporary hotel he was being housed at by his new club; and who, when he arrived at White Hart Lane, decided to climb into the old condemned press box – and was lucky not to fall and break his neck.

The antics of this Paul Gascoigne, the boy who never grew up to be a man, could make him lovable. Once, after the then-England manager Bobby Robson had called him "as daft as a brush", he arrived the next day at training with a brush under his jersey. Then there was the occasion when room-mate Chris Waddle was served a cup of tea made with washing-up liquid.

While he could be full of charm and tricks, he also had a dark side. This was the Gascoigne who could be a hopeless drunk, a wife-beater and a foul-mouthed misfit who was so lacking in any social graces, manners or intelligence that he could insult whole nations just for the fun of it.

In some ways, Gascoigne has been lucky to stay out of jail. He came close to it when he punched railway signalman John Beach. In an out-of-court settlement in March 1995, he agreed to pay Beach £5,000 in damages and £2,500 in costs. Beach had been punched twice and knocked to the ground by Gascoigne after accidentally stumbling into his sister Lindsay in Newcastle. At the time of the original incident Gascoigne had pleaded guilty and was conditionally discharged.

It was in 1990 that the various contradictory strands in Gascoigne's life were revealed to the public. Having moved from his native Newcastle to Tottenham two years earlier for a fee of £2.1 million, he was then in his prime as a footballer, as he demonstrated when he played a crucial part in England's impressive 1990 World Cup campaign in Italy. Then the power and beauty of Gascoigne's football, along with that of Gary Lineker and David Platt, helped England reach the semi-finals. It was the greatest achievement by an England team since 1966, and their best-ever performance away from home.

In the semi-final against Germany, moreover, Gascoigne shed tears, a sight that moved the nation and showed that here, at last, was an English football player who could not only play but also cry, something only Latins and other strange continentals were supposed to do. Almost instantly he was converted from a fat northern git into a national hero.

What caused the tears was his realization, after he was booked, that he would now miss the final if England were to go through. As it turned out, they did not. The tears were to prove profitable as they started the "Gazza" hype of the 1990s that converted Gascoigne from just another player into a megastar. But his tears were genuine enough, and showed his humanity underneath all the toughness and skill of the professional footballer. They also brought Gascoigne the World Cup star closer to ordinary footballers who played on parks up and down the country and who knew they

Tears of a clown: Gazzamania breaks out after England lose the 1990 World Cup semi-final.

would suffer the same emotions if they ever found themselves similarly deprived of a great honour.

That has always been Gascoigne's ability: he can strike up a rapport with the ordinary fans, even with the wider public whose knowledge and awareness of the game are limited. The problem lies with the hooligan inside him who is incapable of recognizing the very fine but distinct dividing line between acceptable and unacceptable behaviour. After the World Cup, Gianni Agnelli of Fiat summed up the effect of Gascoigne when he described him as "a dog of war with the face of a child".

Gazzamania now swept the country, so much so that when a judge asked counsel whether Gascoigne could be more popular than the Duke of Wellington in 1815, the barrister replied, "I have to say I think it's possible."

As the 1990–91 English season opened, there were high expectations of what Gascoigne might achieve and, while he could never match the hype, that season Gascoigne's football was touched by magic. As always, however, there was the fear that he could self-destruct, as he was eventually to do in the last match of the season.

In the early days it was often Gazza the lovable child who was on view, as in Tottenham's opening match of the FA Cup campaign. They travelled to Blackpool on a cold, blustery day in January, and although Gascoigne did not score – Paul Stewart did – he dominated the match both on and off the field. Before the match, as the Spurs coach made its way to the ground, he had acted as an impromptu guide, and as the coach passed a nightclub called Rumours, he said,

"On the left-hand side there is the famous nightclub Rumours and, let's be honest, there's plenty of those going round Tottenham at the moment", a witty reference to the financial problems that eventually led to the club being sold.

During that FA Cup run Gazza took hold of matches in a way no British player had done since the days of Best, and he was able, almost single-handedly, to guide Tottenham to Wembley. His majestic free kick in the semi-final against Arsenal – by a player who had just come back from a hernia operation – remains one of the great goals of the competition, and showed the sort of fantasy his feet could produce.

Yet always bubbling underneath was the dark side, which very nearly meant that Gascoigne did not play in the Cup Final.

Just days before the final the Tottenham players were invited to a lunch at Scribes, the drinking club that Terry Venables, the then-Tottenham manager, had acquired with his partner Paul Riviere.

Riviere recalls that lunch, which was a near-disaster. "Just before the Cup Final Terry said to me, 'I'm going to have the lads down for lunch. Let's have a few people around at lunchtime.' We never usually had big lunch crowds at Scribes. I'd gone down the previous week and I'd met this girl, Nicky somebody, who was a flower-girl of Frank Warren: she came down. The players had lunch. Paul Gascoigne had been doing an advertising thing up in Birmingham and came down and was behind all the others, from the point of view of not having had a drink, and got into the drink."

Gascoigne had arrived at 4.30pm and the first thing he did, recalls Gavin Hans-Hamilton, a director of Scribes, was to go to the bar. "And he was ordering quadruple Drambuies. I didn't realize what was happening and I was bloody angry with the guy who served him. Gascoigne had about four of these, which equals about half a bottle of Drambuie, before you could bat an eyelid, and I don't think he'd eaten, so of course it went straight to his head. Then the stupidity started. It just degenerated into a mess."

According to Riviere, "Gascoigne said something to Nicky, which was obviously something she didn't like. She'd had a few and she went to throw her glass of champagne at him and some champagne went over his head. I said to the barman that that was the last drink he could have because he'd obviously had a few drinks. I think he was drinking something like Drambuie and ice. He threw some at her, missed her and hit a friend of mine. The friend then went to have a go at Gazza and all hell started to break loose. Ray Clemence and the guys then took him off. It was one of those things that happened at Scribes."

Until Clemence intervened, Hamilton and the others could not help but feel that this was a disaster waiting to happen. "It was clear there was going to be a big punch-up. Gascoigne was basically hustled out of the place by about four of them who grabbed hold of him and took him out, and that more or less ended the evening. It could have been ridiculous because the guy he was going to hit was a man much bigger than him anyway. He could well have found himself in a situation where he had a broken nose or whatever and in the week of the FA Cup Final."

If Gascoigne avoided disaster at Scribes, he could not avoid it in the Cup Final, billed in advance as "his" match. It was less than 20 minutes old when he made a horrible tackle on Nottingham Forest's Gary Charles which showed the dark side of the man.

The challenge resulted in a free kick from which Forest scored, and for a long time it looked like as if this might win them the Cup before two goals took Tottenham to victory. Worse, however, was the fact that in making the tackle Gascoigne snapped the cruciate ligaments in his right knee, was carried off and was never the same player again.

Gascoigne was hyped up for the final, and afterwards there was criticism of the referee for not booking him for an earlier tackle which was just as bad as the one on Charles. Yet the demons lay within Gascoigne. Two years earlier, soon after his move to Tottenham, he was accused of breaking bottles, glasses and furniture during a Christmas drinking binge at a hotel, where an assistant manager alleged that Gascoigne was legless. Stan Seymour, the Newcastle chairman who had sold him to Tottenham, said at the time, "He's like George Best without brains."

Gascoigne was to prove this yet again when, four months after his horrible tackle at Wembley, he fractured his right kneecap during a brawl in a Newcastle drinking club and had to have another operation.

In the years since then, while on the field

he never quite regained the heights he had reached in the 1990–91 season, off the field his dark moods seemed to increase in intensity.

In 1992, when a Norwegian TV crew covering the England–Norway match asked him for a pre-match comment, his reply was "Fuck off, Norway". By this time he was playing for Lazio in Italy, where his belching on a TV programme led to a fine of £9,000 and questions in the Italian parliament.

This lack of any sense of how to behave has become more pronounced over the years. So, after transferring to Rangers from Lazio, he totally ignored the religious divide in Glasgow and on three occasions made a gesture that was bound to inflame the religious feelings of rival Celtic.

This was to mimic a man playing the flute, something considered provocative by Celtic's Catholic supporters as it recalls the Protestant Apprentice Boys as they march each year in celebration of the victory of Protestants over Catholics in Ireland in the seventeenth century. Gascoigne first performed this party piece when playing for Rangers against Steaua Bucharest in 1995.

Reckless: Gascoigne's career was never the same after his lunge at Forest's Gary Charles in the 1991 FA Cup Final.

Then he repeated it in 1998 when Rangers played Celtic.

This caused a tremendous furore, but Gascoigne claimed he had done it not knowing the history of the action or that it would cause offence. However, on 2 March 1999, by which time he had finished at Rangers and should have been well aware of the religious feelings in the city, he did it again. He was playing in a testimonial for Rangers' Alan McLaren when he was asked by the crowd to perform the flute trick again, and sure enough he obliged. However, he still insisted he was innocent and not intending to cause trouble, but merely pretending to take a photograph.

This pattern of unacceptable behaviour followed by attempts at apology and promises to behave in the future has characterized Gascoigne.

His relationship with Sheryl Kyle, a mother of two, after Gascoigne had ditched his long-standing girlfriend, offered a vivid illustration.

He proposed to Sheryl in the extravagant sort of way that you expect from a pop star – driving to the restaurant in a limousine strewn with red roses and producing a heart-shaped cake iced with the message: "Will you marry me?" She accepted, but then discovered the dark side to his nature as he beat her black and blue.

Gascoigne would afterwards confess to a reporter from the *News of the World* that he had struck Sheryl, "grabbing her very hard by the arms, putting my head against her, pulling her head back, grabbing her head". Gascoigne added he had done so for no reason, and was all contrition.

"Yes," he said, "I've been a violent bastard and a coward and I want the world to know it."

Yet such confessions always seem to be for public consumption, never for the inner man, and with hindsight it now seems inevitable that what looks like being the final chapter of Gascoigne's international career was even then being written.

For weeks before England went to France 98 the big question was: would Glenn Hoddle, the then-England manager, pick Gascoigne? Hoddle was not convinced he was fit, and just before the team assembled for England's final pre-World Cup preparations Gascoigne was caught by the tabloid press partying it up with his media friends Chris Evans and Danny Baker. He was once pictured eating a kebab at two in the morning.

Such activities did not please Hoddle, but he felt Gascoigne might still make it. However, by the time the warm-up matches had finished it was clear that Gascoigne was not fit enough. Hoddle gathered the England team at La Manga in Spain for his final pre-World Cup camp, where he had decided that the players who were not going to make it to France 98 should be called individually to his room. He left Gascoigne till last.

When Hoddle told him he was not fit enough to go to France, Gascoigne seemed at first to take it well, saying, "I don't believe this, gaffer; my career is finished." He then wished Hoddle well, but Hoddle could see he was drunk, and suddenly Gascoigne flipped. He let fly with a full-blooded kick at a chair and, given that he had bare feet, he was lucky not to break anything.

Hoddle would later write in his diary, "He was a different person now. He had snapped... He was like a man possessed, totally different from the person who had been shaking my hand a minute ago... I thought he was going to hit me. There was a lamp to my left, to his right, and he just punched it. The glass shattered all over the room."

For days the nation seemed to talk of little else as they debated whether Hoddle was right not to take Gascoigne to France. If the *Sun* is any barometer of opinion, then it seemed he was right.

In an exclusive for the newspaper, Gascoigne revealed how he had written to the other England players to say: "I feel I have let you down because of two nights out with pals. But I can't see how one kebab can be the difference between beating one or three men or running from box to box or scoring a goal. I say this because the press have talked about it for weeks. Bloody hell, in Scotland I had haggis and won the Double."

His agent Mel Stein, not surprisingly, blamed the media, saying they had brainwashed Hoddle into dropping him. Others feared that Hoddle had now condemned Gascoigne to a fate worse than death. These fears seemed to be realized when in the 1998–99 season Gascoigne found his old friend the booze again.

On 13 October 1999 the *Sun* devoted its entire front page to describing a Gascoigne night out in a Newcastle pub the previous month. The headline said: "What Gazza

Drank in Just One Night" over a picture of a large array of bottles. The *Sun* reporter wrote: "Gazza, 31, downed about 100 units of alcohol in seven hours – nearly four times the recommended maximum for a week. His massive binge in Newcastle included 20 bottles of Hooch alcoholic lemonade and 40 measures of Archers peach schnapps. He finished off with two mind-blowing cocktails containing Pernod, Bailey's, tequila, Galliano and Sambucca."

The reporter went on to describe how during Gascoigne's seven-hour drinking binge at the Mean Fiddler pub in Sunnyside, Newcastle, which began at 4pm, he pawed and pestered a 20-year-old girl called Kelly Preston, whose parents owned the pub. He tried to lure her to bed, gawping at her breasts and saying, "Are they real? I want your breasts in my face." Gascoigne also grabbed her by the arm in the corridor and said, "I want to fuck the tits off you."

Kelly Preston would tell the *Sun* how horrified she was. In addition to telling the story, she also posed for the paper's photographer in the classic Page Three girl posture – she was pictured topless with her arms crossed in front of her breasts, giving millions a glimpse of what had driven Gascoigne so wild. According to Kelly, Gascoigne alternated between leering and crying. At one stage he told her, "I hate playing football. At times I just want to curl up in a ball and hide. I don't want to be famous – I just want to be normal...I'd prefer to be a normal person with a normal job and a normal family. I want to get away from it all."

After this inglorious episode Gascoigne did get away from it all, if only for a time. He checked into a drying-out clinic, The Priory, for therapy and counselling about his drinking. He also returned to football, but his sobbing confession to Kelly Preston still sums up this, the most gifted footballer of his generation. When he allowed his football to do the talking, he could fulfil every childhood fantasy. But the devils were always lurking within him, ready at any moment to tempt him into doing wrong.

Stir it up: Gascoigne celebrates after scoring for England *(below left)* and at Rangers.

The Bung/Fishing Trawlers off Hull and Bars in Park Lane

When the word "bung" was first brought to the public's attention by Alan Sugar, Brian Clough asked, "Bung; isn't that something you get from a plumber to stop up the bath?" Clough, in his characteristic way, was trying to use humour to get out of a tricky situation; but over the next few years, as Clough himself, his assistant and other figures in "the people's game" found themselves involved in the bungs scandal, the humour came not from what those involved said but the bizarre ways in which they are said to have received their bungs including, in one case, allegedly collecting it from a fishing trawler, and in another being invited to receive a Christmas gift in a West End hotel, only to find a briefcase stuffed with £50 notes in plastic envelopes totalling £140,500.

The man who allegedly went to Hull to find the fishing trawler bearing his bung was Ronnie Fenton. He is now out of the game, and although he was charged by the FA his case has still to be decided.

As we have seen, two of the three members of the Premier League inquiry concluded that Fenton had received some or all of the £50,000 from the Sheringham transfer.

The inquiry found something very similar in another transfer that had taken place before the Premier League was set up in 1992. This was the transfer of Thorvalder Orlygsson from the Icelandic

Fall guy: Arsenal manager George Graham paid a heavy price for accepting "unsolicited gifts".

club Knattstsprunufelag Akureyrar to Nottingham Forest in December 1989.

The question here was how much Forest paid and whether anyone there got a bung. The inquiry found that in the application for a work permit for the Icelandic player, made in October to the Department of Employment, Forest said that the transfer was agreed and the fee payable was £150,000.

The application, copies of which were sent to the League and the FA, also contained details of the player's wages. However, when the deal was finally done Forest paid £174,000. Why was the extra £24,000 paid?

Fenton, who had travelled to Iceland to sign the player after a trial, told the inquiry the deal had not been concluded before his visit, and that when he got there the club wanted more money. He had spoken to Clough on the telephone and it was agreed. Fenton denied bringing any money back from Iceland. All he had brought back, he said, were two small artificial Christmas trees, one of them for Clough.

However, the inquiry heard from Allan Clarke, who worked as a general factotum at Forest, that Fenton had gone to Hull to collect £45,000 in a fish-box from a trawler. This was common gossip at Forest, and Clarke's version was supported by two other officials, coach Archie Gemmill and physio Graham Lyas. Fenton denied ever receiving any such money either in Iceland or in England.

The inquiry concluded that the transfer gave cause for concern. This was because the transfer agreement was signed by Fenton, who was not authorized to sign it. The inquiry was also concerned that there were different signatures on the engrossments of the transfer form, although the form presented to the English authorities had the correct, authorized signature.

To add to its concern about why the transfer fee increased from £150,000 to £174,000, the inquiry also noted the persistence of stories that Fenton had collected cash from the transfer. Then there were the similarities between this case and that of the Sheringham transfer. As in the later case, it was Fenton who signed the transfer document; Fenton made a trip carrying the document; and the central allegation was that he received cash from the deal. But the inquiry could not come to a conclusion about whether he had or not.

However, if the inquiry found this suspicious but inconclusive, it had no doubts about the roles of Fenton and Clough in the transfers of Anthony Louglan and Neil Lyne from non-league Leicester United to Nottingham Forest in August 1989. Because these transfers took place before the Premier League's formation in 1992, the inquiry did not examine them exhaustively as it had with the Sheringham transfer, but it did look at copies of the working files held by Forest.

Forest were supposed to pay Leicester United £15,000 but ended up paying £61,000, the payments being made on three separate occasions. The question was why Forest paid so much more and to whom this extra money went: Fenton? Clough?

The inquiry had no doubts, concluding: "...there is direct evidence of a fraudulent arrangement by which Mr Clough and Mr Fenton acquired a substantial sum of money from the two transfers."

It was foreign transfers involving the Norwegian agent Rune Hauge which provided the most fruitful area for the inquiry and led it to conclude that managers and coaches were getting kickbacks from transfer fees paid by clubs.

One of them was the transfer of Alf-Inge Haaland to Forest from the Norwegian club Bryne. The initial agreement to transfer him took place in October 1992. However, there were problems with paperwork, and it was December 1993 before the Department of Employment granted a work permit. The player agreed personal terms in January 1994, and the transfer documentation was registered with the Football League and the FA that same month.

On 20 January 1994 Bryne invoiced Forest for the sum of £350,000, and on 27 January the money was transferred to Bryne's account. But, as always when bungs are involved, the money Forest paid Bryne did not all remain with Bryne: some of it went to others.

What Forest did not know, but the Premier League inquiry found out, was that Bryne had an arrangement with InterClub, the company owned by Rune Hauge, Haaland's agent. Under this agreement the club would pay InterClub any money received over and above £150,000.

So who received the extra money? The inquiry had no doubt that some of it went to Fenton. He had known Hauge since 1990,

Kickback: Alf Inge Haaland's transfer proved profitable for Ron Fenton, seen here with Brian Clough.

when Hauge had visited the Forest ground. After that, according to Fenton, Hauge had rung him persistently, wanting to find out what players the club wanted. Hauge was an agent for a number of Norwegian players whom he was keen to sell to English clubs.

Fenton had made a number of recommendations regarding players who would be useful in England and introduced Hauge to English club managers. Fenton had spoken to Alex Ferguson, the Manchester United manager, prior to the club signing Peter Schmeichel from Brondbyernes IF, and had arranged for Ferguson to take a call from Hauge. Fenton had also made a similar arrangement for Graeme Souness, when he was manager of Liverpool, to contact Hauge, and he had introduced Hauge to Mick Walker, then manager of Notts County. Fenton once told Hauge that Dave Bassett, then at Sheffield United, was looking for a centre-half.

"That's all I was doing with Rune," Fenton told the inquiry, "just, you know, 'So-and-so is looking for a goalkeeper, and so-and-so is looking for a full-back, so-and-so is looking for a centre-forward, if you have got anything', and then he used to come and say, 'Well, if you're coming to this particular game, will you look at so-and-so and just tell me whether you think they're good enough?', and that's what the arrangement was."

After the transfer of Haaland, on 5 March 1994, Allan Hill, who held various posts at Forest and was then assistant manager, met Fenton at a match between Watford and Oxford at Vicarage Road. Hill was assessing the form of Oxford, whom Forest were to play in the League in a few weeks' time. Fenton, who by this time had left Forest, was at the match with his wife, and sat four seats away from Hill.

At half-time both men went downstairs for a cup of tea. Hill told the inquiry: "Ronnie came up to me at half-time and said, 'Did you get anything out of the Haaland deal?' I said, 'What are you talking about?' He said, 'I agreed with Rune some money', but he did not tell me how much, and I said, 'I don't know anything about it', and just left it at that."

In another statement to the inquiry Hill described the conversation somewhat differently. He said Fenton had asked if Hill had received any money from Hauge for Haaland. Fenton went on to say that he needed money and asked if he could have £5,000, stating that he had agreed it.

When the inquiry asked Fenton, he accepted that he had met Hill but was not sure it was at the Watford match. According to Fenton, he asked Hill, "Did you get anything from the Haaland deal?" or "Did you get a drink out of it?" Fenton explained that he had asked the question facetiously and was insinuating to Hill that there "had been something in it" for him because there had been no renegotiating after the problem over the work permit. Fenton denied asking Hill for £5,000.

Hill returned to Forest after the Watford game and claims he reported the conversation to Frank Clark, who by then had succeeded Clough as the Forest manager. Clark asked him to check with Hauge, who told Hill that he had an "agreement with the past management for the payment of money to him for the transfer" (the words are from the statement Hill made to police on 12 January 1996).

On 15 March 1994, the day Arsenal played Torino and some ten days after he had met Hill, Fenton drove to London to meet Hauge at the Royal Lancaster Hotel. According to Fenton he had been rung up by Hauge, who said he wished to see him and that it would "be to your advantage".

Fenton gave two contradictory explanations of what happened at the London meeting. The first was that Hauge told him he wished to pay Fenton £45,000 as commission for help that Fenton had given him over the previous four or five years. Fenton said the payment "came out of the blue". However, in a later statement Fenton accepted that Hauge told him that the £45,000 was, in part, commission for the Haaland transfer.

Hauge told Fenton he should contact a certain Lisa Davey, an employee of Saffrey Champness Management International Limited, which was then acting for Hauge's company InterClub Ltd.

On 22 March 1994 Hauge wrote a letter to Davey, headed "Re: Transfer of Alf-Inge Haaland: payment of other commission. Our conversation." In the letter he asked Davey to find a practical way of making sure Fenton received £45,000. Hauge also wanted to pay another £45,000 as commission on the deal, although it is not clear who was to receive this money.

Fenton told the Premier League inquiry

that he told Davey how he wanted the money: £5,000 by cheque, £10,000 to be transferred to him from the Inter Club account, and the remaining £30,000 to a French bank account held in St Tropez. He also told them that he spent some of the money on a holiday and retained the rest. On another occasion Fenton said he received the final £10,000 in two payments of £5,000 each. Fenton refused to provide the inquiry with copies of his correspondence with Saffrey Champness and his relevant bank records, saying they were with the Inland Revenue, which was conducting its own inquiry.

The inquiry were well aware that there was tension between Hill and Fenton, and that this could colour what Hill said. However, even after taking that into account it came to the conclusion that "Mr Fenton's evidence to the Inquiry is largely unreliable." It also concluded:

The payment received by Mr Fenton was a benefit deriving from the sums received by InterClub Limited from Bryne, originating initially from the transfer fee paid by Forest to Bryne for the transfer of Haaland. We are satisfied that Mr Fenton was aware that this was the case.

The irresistible inference is that Mr Fenton and Mr Hauge had agreed that out of the monies received by Mr Hauge from the transfer a substantial sum would be paid to Mr Fenton.

On the evidence [the Inquiry] has seen Mr Clough did not benefit from the transfer and he was, until relatively recently, unaware that Mr Fenton received any payment form InterClub Ltd. We are unable to say whether the original intention was that some or all of the £45,000 should be passed on to Mr Clough.

Another man who had featured briefly in the Haaland story was Steve Burtenshaw, then the chief scout at Arsenal. Although Burtenshaw was a paid employee, he did not have a written contract. He also had an arrangement with Proman A/S, one of the companies controlled by Hauge, to undertake certain activities in relation to Hauge and certain Scandinavian players.

According to Hill, a week after the Watford match, at which he had his conversation with Fenton, he got a call from Burtenshaw asking for Fenton's number. The inference here is that Burtenshaw wanted Fenton's number to give to Hauge. Shortly afterwards Fenton, while on a visit to Forest, saw Hill and expressed concern that Hill had given Burtenshaw his number. Fenton pointed out that Hill should be aware that Hauge was under investigation by the Norwegian Fraud Squad – an investigation which did not lead to any charges.

Whatever the reason for Burtenshaw wanting Fenton's number, his links with Hauge were close and would cause him to be investigated by the Premier League inquiry. They looked in particular at the transfer of four players to Arsenal: Anders Limpar, Pal Lydersen, John Jensen and Stefan Schwarz.

The agreement between Burtenshaw and Proman A/S, which was not dated but was meant to come into existence on 1 July 1989, said that if a player moved from a continental club to a British club on the recommendation of Burtenshaw he would receive a fee out of the amount Proman collected and this would not be more than 25 per cent of Proman's fees.

The agreement also had a clause stating, "The fee will be smaller according to the number of 'paybacks' which are involved."

The Premier League inquiry was struck by the word "paybacks". Burtenshaw's lawyers could not help. Burtenshaw was asked about it in court during an Norwegian investigation into Hauge. He was asked: "Does 'paybacks' mean 'palm-greasers'?" Burtenshaw replied, "You could say that. Yes, introductions, perhaps."

Some time in May 1990 Burtenshaw, who was in Dublin on business, walked into a city-centre branch of the Allied Irish Bank and asked, "Can I as an Englishman open an account here?" An account was opened and on 14 May 1990 Proman A/S transferred £20,284.62 into that account.

On 17 July 1990 Anders Limpar was transferred from the Italian club Cremonese to Arsenal for a fee of DM4,150,000 (about £1.4 million). Hauge told the Premier League inquiry that he sent a video of Limpar to Arsenal and, after talking to Burtenshaw over the telephone, he knew Arsenal were ready to do business about the player. Burtenshaw has tried to suggest that his role was minimal. George Graham, the Arsenal manager, told the inquiry that Burtenshaw had negotiated the transfer along with Ken Friar, the Arsenal chief executive. Burtenshaw denied this.

Proman had an agreement with Cremonese whereby it was due to receive just over £450,00 for the transfer of Limpar. This payment – £451,639 – was made by Cremonese on 30 September 1990.

Just over ten weeks later, on 19 December, Burtenshaw's Dublin account received some more money – £13,474. Was this or the earlier payment connected with any transfer activity on Arsenal's behalf?

That was the question asked by the Premier League. Its conclusion was that the first payment to Burtenshaw "did not derive from any fee paid to Mr Hauge or his companies in connection with a transfer to Arsenal".

What about the second payment?

"As to the second payment, Proman A/S had received payment from Cremonese on 30 September 1990, who had in turn received the transfer fee from Arsenal. It was therefore in funds to pay Mr Burtenshaw in respect of the transaction on 19 December. There is no conclusive evidence as to whether this payment arose from this transfer or was for some other (unidentifiable) reason. However there is no evidence of other payments from Proman A/S (as opposed to InterClub, another of Hauge's companies) to employees of a purchaser club."

On 6 November 1991, Pal Lydersen was transferred from the Norwegian club IK Start to Arsenal. Burtenshaw made the first moves, watching the player first for his club and then his country. After the club match he went up to Lydersen on Hauge's instigation and said, "Pal; good game", indicating someone from England was there. Burtenshaw then found out the approximate transfer fee IK Start would want.

But after that, according to Burtenshaw, he played no part in the negotiations, which were conducted by Graham and IK Start. However, Arsenal have maintained that Burtenshaw would have "started the ball rolling with Hauge to see if he could get a price". Arsenal also described Burtenshaw, along with Graham and Friar, as the prime movers in the transfer negotiations. Burtenshaw denied this.

On 14 July 1992, John Jensen was transferred to Arsenal from the Danish club Brondby IF. According to Burtenshaw, Arsenal became interested when they received a fax from Hauge. Burtenshaw then saw Jensen play both for his club and for his country, notably in the 1992 European Championships.

Initially Burtenshaw was not impressed, but in the European Championships, which Denmark unexpectedly won – having been a last-minute replacement for Yugoslavia – Jensen performed very well. Burtenshaw told Hauge that Graham would now take over any contacts necessary to transfer the player, and Burtenshaw said he played no part in the negotiations.

Graham's recollection is that he and Burtenshaw together decided that Arsenal should pay £1.5 million for Jensen, but Burtenshaw rejects this, saying that when he first saw Jensen playing for his club he thought he was worth £750,000 but then, after the European Championships, he thought he would be worth £1–1.2 million and he informed Graham about this. He did not fix the price of £1.5 million with Graham.

On 19 September 1992 Burtenshaw received his third payment from Hauge. But this time the money, £35,000, did not go into his Dublin account but was paid into an overseas client account held for Burtenshaw in Guernsey by Saffrey Champness Management International Ltd, acting for Hauge's Interclub Ltd.

The Premier League inquiry was able to trace the accounts of InterClub Ltd. These showed that it received £749,433.48 from Brondby IF on 7 August 1992, clearly marked as a payment received in connection with the Jensen transfer. The accounts also showed that on 9 September 1992 InterClub made a payment of £35,000, describing it as "Trf to S. Burtenshaw Personal". The money remained in the Saffrey Champness account, earning interest, until 26 October 1994, when a total of £39,142.76 was transferred to Barclays Bank, Muswell Hill, where Burtenshaw had a joint account with his wife.

Burtenshaw's legal advisers got into a terrible tangle in trying to explain to the Premier League inquiry how the money was brought to this country. It had first written to the inquiry saying the account was closed on 30 June 1994. However, the Premier League learned from Saffrey Champness that the account was not closed until 26 October 1994.

The advisers then wrote to the inquiry saying, "There was no intention to mislead the Inquiry as to when the account had been closed. When giving the information it

Capital gains: John Jensen's transfer provided George Graham with a dubious "gift".

appears that [the adviser] was looking at a statement of account which covered interest paid up to 30 June 1994. There was a simple error in referring to it as a closing balance. It is quite true that the closing balance was transferred on 2 October 1994 some four months later."

Indeed, Burtenshaw received the last bit of interest from this account on 1 March 1995, a payment of £119.01.

Burtenshaw told the inquiry that he did not even know he had an account at Saffrey Champness until some time in September 1994. He claimed that he did not know why £35,000 was paid to this account in his name. Hauge was to tell him that this was because of "various good contacts he had made" but, says Burtenshaw, Hauge never identified the names of any of the contacts.

The Premier League inquiry had no doubt what the £35,000 was for:

"In the case of the payment of £35,000, we are satisfied that the payment credited from InterClub Ltd to Mr Burtenshaw's account at Saffrey Champness, and later transferred to Mr and Mrs Burtenshaw's joint account in England, derived directly from the transfer fee paid by Arsenal FC to Brondby IF in connection with the transfer of John Jensen."

The FA finally held its hearing in September 1998. Appearing before the three-man inquiry, Burtenshaw admitted that the £35,000 he had received was an illegal payment, and apologized.

The FA spokesman Steve Double said, "The unauthorized payment is outside FA rules. It was accepted by the FA Commission that the payment was not solicited and counsel representing him [Burtenshaw] said that other than this incident he had an unblemished five-year record in football. He added he was guilty of misjudging, for which he was deeply sorry."

Burtenshaw was eventually fined £7,500 and asked to pay £2,500 in costs. He is still in football as the chief scout at Queen's Park Rangers.

But what about the man Burtenshaw worked for during his time at Arsenal, George Graham?

Graham is a man whose achievements as a manager are beyond dispute. In 1986 he was made manager of Arsenal, having been a highly-successful player with the club and part of the Double-winning team of 1970–71. In his first year as manager he won the League Cup for Arsenal. Then, in 1989, thanks to a dramatic last-minute goal from Michael Thomas at Liverpool, he won Arsenal their first championship since the Double triumph 18 years earlier.

He followed this up with another championship in 1991, and then a feat still unique in English football: both cups, the FA Cup and the League Cup, in 1993. In 1994 came the Cup Winners' Cup. In eight seasons he won six trophies, and along with the legendary Herbert Chapman he remains the club's most successful manager.

He was also the most high-profile victim – indeed perhaps the only victim – of the bungs inquiry.

Graham's downfall came earlier than Burtenshaw's and involved two of the transfers in which Burtenshaw was involved: those of Pal Lydersen and John Jensen. Although the whole affair started with the bung for Jensen, it was the payment he received over the Lydersen transfer that cost him his job.

As we have seen, Burtenshaw scouted Lydersen. The detailed transfer negotiations were handled by Graham. Three directors of IK Start later gave statements to the Premier League inquiry that the original fee they agreed with Graham for Lydersen was £215,000. However, Arsenal paid £500,000 and Graham flew to Oslo in September 1991 to conclude the deal. Graham denies he lied to Arsenal about the transfer money or that he flew to Oslo to increase the transfer fee from £215,000 to £500,000 so as to get some of this money for himself. Instead, he says, he flew to Oslo because there was a personality clash between Hauge and one of the Start officials involved in the negotiations.

Graham's version flatly contradicted what the Start directors told the Premier League inquiry team. Peter Hill-Wood, the Arsenal chairman, would later describe what happened:

Graham had told us he was going to Copenhagen merely to rubber-stamp the deal. It did seem odd because he normally did not do that. He told us, "It was a done deal. I didn't negotiate. I wasn't even in the same room." Three Start directors all said he spent three hours haggling with them. You don't take three hours if you are just discussing where you are going for dinner. What was interesting about the evidence of the Start directors as given to the Premier League was that it was all slightly different, which as Robert Reid said meant they hadn't cooked it up.

Lydersen confirmed Graham's role, unintentionally, because he was waiting in the Oslo hotel wondering if the deal was going through, and the Start directors kept coming back reassuring him.

So, from the £500,000 IK Start received from Arsenal, they kept the £215,000 and the rest of Arsenal's transfer money for Lydersen went various ways, with Graham receiving £140,500.

This was paid to him on 23 December 1991. The previous day Hauge had phoned him to say that he was coming to London and had "a Christmas present for you." Hauge laughed as he said this, and the two met at the Park Lane Hotel, curiously an hotel owned by one of the Carr brothers, both of whom are Arsenal directors.

According to Graham, Hauge came into the bar carrying a holdall. The two men ordered a drink and Hauge said, "I have something here for you, George." Hauge opened the holdall, brought out several plastic envelopes and, giving them to Graham, asked him to put them in his briefcase. According to Graham, Hauge said, "It's my appreciation for all that you have done to help me open up doors here in England."

Graham said he got home to find the envelopes were full of £50 notes. He deposited the cash at the Allied Irish Bank in Berkeley Square. According to Graham, depositing it with an Irish bank was not trying to hide a bung but simply good old-fashioned Scottish housekeeping. Allied were paying a higher rate of interest on special deposit. Graham later transferred it to the Jersey branch of the bank and set up a trust for his children Nicole and Daniel. All the while Graham insisted it was not money from the Lydersen deal and he did not know why Hauge had paid him. On the advice of a tax consultant he described it as an "unsolicited gift". This meant it was not in any way related to the transfer money Arsenal had paid, and was an important phrase in connection with his Inland Revenue negotiations – Graham had not paid tax on it and the Revenue were on to him.

The other part of the "unsolicited gift" also came from Hauge and amounted to £285,000. It arose in connection with the Jensen transfer.

As we have seen, Arsenal paid Brondby £1.5 million for Jensen in September 1992. Brondby had an arrangement with Hauge's company InterClub to pay him, and on 7 August 1992 transferred £749,433.48 to InterClub's account.

On 12 August 1992 InterClub sent a bank draft to George Graham. The entry in InterClub's books reads: "Bank Draft to George Graham JJ" and comes under an account entitled "J Jensen Management 92–I".

Graham admitted he had received the money and credited it to his Jersey account, but said he did not ask for it and did not know it was related to the Jensen transfer. "It no doubt sounds like a bung, and looks like a bung, but it was a gift", Graham claimed.

Arsenal discovered what had happened to their money quite by chance. Hamburg, who had a 20 per cent interest in Jensen, asked Arsenal how much the club had paid, but Arsenal could not help them as their contract was with Brondby, and they asked Hamburg to get the information through the German FA.

Even before this Arsenal were beginning to have doubts. Hill-Wood says, "There had been a book in Denmark, and prior to that I had seen doubts cast on the transfer in the newspaper. It did seem strange and I couldn't work out where they had got their figures. We had paid Brondby £1.5 million and thought that was the end of it."

In October Brondby went to Arsenal, having been drawn against them in the Cup Winners' Cup. David Dein, the Arsenal vice-chairman, asked the Brondby chairman how much they had kept from the Jensen transfer and was told £900,000, which surprized Arsenal.

By this time the Inland Revenue had also begun investigating undeclared payments received by Graham and Burtenshaw. On 22 April the Revenue had written to Kidsons Impey, Arsenal's accountants, saying they had "evidence...of a concrete nature, that clearly demonstrates that certain players and coaching staff have received payments or [that] monies are held by other parties as nominees, which have emanated from the transfer fees paid by [Arsenal]."

Like many clubs, Arsenal had been

subject to an investigation going back six years but, what is more, the Revenue had access to the Norwegian inquiry then being conducted into Hauge.

Ken Friar called a meeting at Highbury. Present were representatives of Kidsons Impey, Arsenal's lawyers, and Graham and Burtenshaw since, as Friar would put it to the Premier League inquiry, "They were the only two individuals at Arsenal who were involved in any way in the transfer of players to and from Arsenal."

They all looked blankly until finally Burtenshaw spoke up, saying it might have something to do with him, and that he had received money from Hauge. Graham remained silent. Following the meeting Graham told Friar that Burtenshaw was "a bloody fool" to have accepted the money. Graham denies saying this.

But soon Graham was to feel the Revenue heat himself. By August 1994 he was having meetings with his own financial advisers. The Norwegian authorities investigating Hauge had found a slip of paper bearing Graham's name and a sum of money paid to him.

On 26 August 1994, Graham was told by his financial advisers that he must declare the money to the Revenue, wind up the trusts he had set up for his children and bring the matter to the attention of Arsenal.

Within weeks, on 19 September, Graham was coming to see Hill-Wood. "He told me he had been silly and had some money which he had not declared to the Inland Revenue. I felt, 'What an idiot; he has got the Inland Revenue on his back.' It never crossed my mind it might have anything to do with transfers. He did not say that, not the first time round."

Graham was more forthcoming when he next met Hill-Wood, who recalled: "When I met him second time round I asked, 'Please give me more details. How much is it; how did you get it?' He couldn't remember the date and he couldn't remember the exact amounts. Then a week or two later he came forward with the information."

Graham's memory of these meetings is somewhat different. He suggests Hill-Wood was initially very relaxed about his Revenue problems and did not even ask him about the exact amounts. Graham kept insisting they were unsolicited gifts.

In the weeks and months that followed there were several discussions with Arsenal. The Arsenal board thought of sacking Graham, but also discussed a deal whereby Graham would be allowed to leave at the end of the season, Arsenal would pay him compensation of £500,000 and give him a testimonial worth £250,000.

Graham told Hill-Wood he could no longer motivate the players. Graham believes he had a firm agreement about how he would depart from Highbury. Hill-Wood says nothing was finalized, and in any case it was conditional on Graham telling them the whole truth. "If the story was not true then the deal was off."

Hill-Wood says, "We knew there was a Premier League inquiry and they seemed better qualified to look into it. I am not sure it is right to sack someone unless you have the evidence. We took the view that we would wait and see what the evidence showed before taking any decision. With hindsight we probably should have sacked him then."

Publicly, Arsenal were so supportive that Graham was allowed to spend £4 million on two new players, John Hartson and Chris Kiwomya.

There were other pressures on Graham. His advisers had received a letter from the Inland Revenue saying they were preparing a report for the Inland Revenue Board as to whether Graham should face criminal charges, and soon the Premier League inquiry was looking into the transfers. It was this investigation that produced the testimony of the three IK Start directors and revealed why Graham had gone to Oslo in connection with the Lydersen transfer.

By this time Graham, on counsel's advice had paid back the money he had received, including interest, a payment of £465,500 being made on 1 December 1994.

But on 10 February 1995 it all changed. At the start of the day, Arsenal were still committed to Graham; indeed, he was given permission to buy Glen Helder for £2 million.

But some time that day the Arsenal directors went to the offices of Denton Hall, the lawyers to the Premier League, and were shown the Premier League report on Graham. It contained the damning evidence from the IK Start directors on Graham's visit to Oslo, and the die was cast.

Arsenal's board considered prosecuting Graham: says Hill-Wood, "It was our money and we took counsel's advice.

Counsel waved his arm in the direction of the window and said, 'The police have a lot on their plate.'"

Prosecution or no prosecution, Arsenal decided Graham had to go, and on Tuesday, 21 February 1995 he was summoned to Highbury and sacked. Graham noted bitterly that whereas it had taken him eight and a half years to win six trophies, it had taken two and a half minutes to be sacked.

Following the Premier League inquiry the FA charged Graham under Rule 26, the catch-all one of bringing the game into disrepute. In July 1995 the three-man FA commission met for a hearing that lasted 18 hours spread over three days. Brian Leveson, the man who had led the Crown's case against serial killer Rosemary West, tried hard to prove that the £425,000 Graham had received from Hauge did come from the Lydersen and Jensen transfers. Graham maintained the line given to him by his advisers that he had received "unsolicited gifts".

Normally such FA hearings are, like civil cases, decided on the balance of probabilities. But this one had the higher standard used in criminal trials, where the case has to be proved "beyond reasonable doubt". Graham was defended expertly by Anthony Aldridge, and despite Leveson's best efforts he failed to convince the three-man FA commission that Graham had conspired with Hauge to siphon away Arsenal's transfer money.

But if the FA commission would not accept a Graham–Hauge conspiracy, they were nonetheless convinced he had to be punished for taking his "unsolicited gifts".

They decided that "Mr Graham gave evidence about the payments being unsolicited. However, even if this is right, as a respected manager...we find that he must have known how serious a matter it was for him to be receiving this amount from an agent. Mr Graham did not tell anyone connected with Arsenal about the payments until a meeting with Messrs Friar or Hill-Wood on 19 September 1994."

Graham was banned for a year and required to pay a share of the FA's legal costs, which came to about £50,000. FIFA extended this ban world-wide, and Graham believes that the year-long ban, plus waiting five months for the FA hearing, cost him £2 million. Burtenshaw was fined £7,500 with £2,500 costs.

When Graham was sacked and then charged he made noises suggesting that while now he was alone in the dock, soon it would be very crowded. But it has not got crowded, and it is a measure of how football handles such issues that Graham is not only fully rehabilitated but once again, as manager of Tottenham, one of the leading lights of football.

If the subjects of these sorry sagas exemplify what could be called sport's Arthur Daley tendency – raising the question of whether you would buy a used car from them – sport also provides plenty of examples of the other side of the coin: the sportsmen who end up buying a used car from the Arthur Daleys of this world and then repent at their leisure. The classic example of this was the footballer Peter Shilton.

In his prime Shilton, one of England's greatest-ever goalkeepers, earned more than £250,000 a year, owned three luxury homes and bred racehorses. But a series of ill-judged investments – many on cards and horses – plunged him into debt to the tune of more than £500,000.

Debts caused by the liquidation of his company Bridge Promotions, mortgage rate rises and the collapse of property prices drove him into rented accommodation and to the verge of bankruptcy. Creditors included banks, building societies, a former team-mate, his parents and even his players' association. As he commented ruefully, "Investments I have made have failed and left me with substantial personal liabilities that I am not able to meet. I do not have any material assets of significant value. My properties have all been repossessed."

In 1996 Shilton was still playing for Coventry City reserves at the age of 46, and hoping to go on doing so in an attempt to raise money to pay off some of his debts. It is a sad end to a distinguished 30-year career which included a record 125 caps for England.

It also indicates why sport has so many dark stories of bent players and officials. For all the thrills, excitement, wonder and brilliance it provides, it can also be so uncertain, so transitory, that many sportsmen and officials feel that if they do not seize the moment they may never get another chance.

In that sense, the very wonder of sport contains its own seed of destruction.

Dennis Wise

Dennis the Menace

Dennis Wise epitomizes a certain kind of modern footballer. Every club he plays for swears by him, and he is idolized both by his fellow-players and by the supporters. To them he quickly becomes an icon, valued for his playing skills. Unwilling to hear a word against him, they treat any criticism of him as ill-founded, and cast him in the role of misunderstood imp – his only crime being that he wants to love the world, but that the world somehow converts this to hate.

However, those outside this myopic, charmed circle have a very different view of Wise. They find it impossible to ignore his violence both on and off the field, which makes him not Dennis the Loveable but Dennis the Menace, the man whose very presence on the field of play raises questions about what has happened to a game originally founded on Corinthian principles of good sportsmanship.

This was best illustrated during the 1998–99 season when Chelsea played Real Mallorca in the first leg of the Cup Winners' Cup semi-final at Stamford Bridge. While Chelsea lacked incisiveness, Wise, their captain, was all too ready to bare his teeth. In the second half he became entangled with Marcelino, the Real Mallorca defender. As the centre-back threw an arm round Wise and seemed to scratch him, Wise retaliated by biting Marcelino high on his arm. The exchange, unnoticed by Dick Jol, the referee, was caught by television cameras.

Immediately one of Wise's former colleagues, now a television commentator, tried to excuse it by saying it had been provoked by Marcelino. As it happened UEFA did not take any action and it was fortunate for Wise that Marcelino was relaxed about the incident. "It was nothing," he said.

Chelsea are all too used to sheltering Wise from controversy. Since August 1990, when Wise transferred to Chelsea from Wimbledon where he was part of the so called "Crazy Gang", he has been sent off seven times, and his misdemeanours are becoming more frequent. In the 1998–99 season he was shown the red card on four occasions. This was despite his declared determination to mend his ways after he was dismissed in a pre-season match against Atletico Madrid. Two months after that, he made another early departure following a two-footed tackle on Darren Byfield when his team were beating Aston Villa comfortably. In November, two bookings against Everton brought an abrupt conclusion to his return from suspension. He was also sent off in February 1999 for two yellow cards against Oxford United.

Wise's behaviour against Real Mallorca arose partly, no doubt, from the frustration of finding such difficulty in overcoming their defence. Yet it is less and less easy to find excuses for Wise's behaviour, although his admirers have always tried hard to do so – even when he faced a three-month jail sentence for assaulting a taxi-driver.

The incident took place in October 1994 during a night out at Scribes, the Kensington drinking club and restaurant owned at the time by Terry Venables. Venables was then the England coach, and Wise one of the men he was keen to see playing for England. Wise emerged from Scribes with three friends and hailed a cab to go to Boston Manor, more than six miles away. Cab driver Gerald Graham refused, as he was entitled to do. Wise, who Graham would later describe as the most violent customer he had ever had, flew into a rage, kicking the cab and punching the door. Graham flinched and his foot slipped off the brake, making the cab lurch forward. The door caught the arm of

Moody blue: Dennis Wise shows his combative nature against Arsenal (left) and with Engonga of Real Mallorca.

Wise's girlfriend, who screamed in agony. Wise, says Graham, went berserk and shouted, "You've hurt my girl's arm."

According to Graham, then aged 65, Wise leapt into the cab, smashed a glass partition inside it and punched him. Wise hit Graham a couple of times round the head, knocked his glasses off, and then had his hands round his neck when a police car came along. The police freed Graham and handcuffed Wise before arresting him.

At Horseferry Road Magistrates' Court, Wise accepted that he had smashed the glass partition of Graham's taxi with his fists and then held the driver by the neck, but claimed he did so in order to bring the taxi to a halt. Magistrate Geoffrey Breen dismissed Wise's explanation. Mr Breen said he was satisfied that the cab was stationary when Wise got in. His motives were to get at the cab driver. Wise had reacted like a bully, said Mr Breen, convicting him of the charges. He also told him that a prison sentence was the only punishment to fit his crime.

When it came to sentencing a Mr Fulford, representing Wise, tried hard to convince Mr Breen that Wise should not be sent to jail. He said that since his conviction Wise had suffered a truly "devastating experience" which had affected him, his family and his girlfriend. The footballer, he said, was keenly aware of his position in sport and how his conviction had damaged its reputation. He had also suffered a poison-pen campaign from the outraged public, which had upset him. Mr Fulford described the incident as spontaneous and wholly unpremeditated and pleaded: "Neither precedence nor justice demands he be put in prison."

Mr Breen was not convinced. As Wise stood in the dock, nervously knotting his fingers behind his back, Mr Breen said to him: "You were found guilty of assaulting a 65-year-old taxi driver late at night in quite disgraceful circumstances. Whilst you may have been annoyed at his refusal to take you where you wanted to go, he was quite within his rights and any reasonable person would have accepted that position. Your reaction was that of a bully. When he made it clear he was not going to bow to your demands you resorted to violence." Mr Breen also said that had it not been for the police, Wise would have carried out further violence, and although the driver had no physical injury he was clearly quite terrified by what occurred, and suffered shock and distress.

Wise had been convicted seven years earlier of criminal damage for kicking a vehicle during an argument, but Mr Breen decided to disregard that conviction. He added: "In my view these two offences are so serious only a custodial sentence is justified. I am aware of your considerable status as a professional footballer, and one who has had the honour, of representing his country, but that doesn't entitle you to special treatment."

Wise was jailed for three months He was also ordered to pay £965.14 compensation to Graham for damage to his taxi, £169.95 for damage to his spectacles and £100 for shock and distress, as well as £370 prosecution costs.

As the sentence was read out, Wise slumped in his seat and put his hands between his knees below the dock rail, presenting a picture of utter desolation.

Wise's legal team and advisers were equally stunned, his agent Eric Hall saying he was "monster, monster shocked". His barrister immediately went to Southwark Crown Court where, 90 minutes later, he won bail for Wise pending an appeal. Judge John Rodgers, who heard the bail application in camera, took only a few minutes to free Wise, and his legal representatives confirmed that Wise would appeal against both sentence and conviction.

Hall caused further controversy when he predicted how Wise would be welcomed in the Chelsea dressing-room before that night's European Cup Winners' Cup match against Bruges, which Wise was missing because of injury. Hall said, "He is a popular player, and I expect he will get a hero's welcome at the club. He will be in the changing-room trying to gee up the lads before the game."

The judge's decision brought accusations from the police of special treatment. A senior police source said: "It is almost beyond belief that Wise can be put forward as a hero figure when he has been convicted and gaoled for assault. The fact that he has been granted bail pending an appeal also hints at special treatment because of who he is. Most people are remanded in custody pending the appeal, and this brings the law into further disrepute – in other words one law for the rich and famous and one for the rest of us."

When Wise's appeal was heard in June 1995, his conviction was overturned and the gaol sentence quashed. Southwark's senior judge, Gerald Butler QC, sitting with two magistrates, felt that the case against Wise had not been proved "beyond reasonable doubt". However, he said the decision had been reached "with no enthusiasm". The judge strongly criticized Wise, saying, "Even on his own account Mr Wise's conduct was quite disgraceful and does him no credit at all." As far as costs were concerned, he said: "We are satisfied that to a considerable extent this appellant brought this prosecution upon himself. In these circumstances we make no order as to costs."

His conviction overturned, Wise was now a free man, even if he had hardly come out smelling of roses. However, that was now how his fans saw it. Indeed it is Chelsea's treatment of Wise and their reaction to the whole affair that is the most interesting aspect of it. Following the taxi incident, the then-Chelsea manager Glenn Hoddle had withdrawn the captain's armband, only to restore it a few weeks later, citing Wise's good "attitude and example".

As the Wise case came up before the magistrates, Chelsea chairman Ken Bates and managing director Colin Hutchinson both wrote to the court supporting Wise and highlighting his work for charity, in particular for sick children. Outside the court, Hutchinson confirmed that the club were standing by their man, who would also continue to captain the side. "We don't condone what Dennis did, but it's non-football-related and the punishment will come through the courts."

The Chelsea-supporting Labour MP Tony Banks, who had also provided a character reference for Wise, declared that Mr Breen's decision to gaol Wise was outrageous and

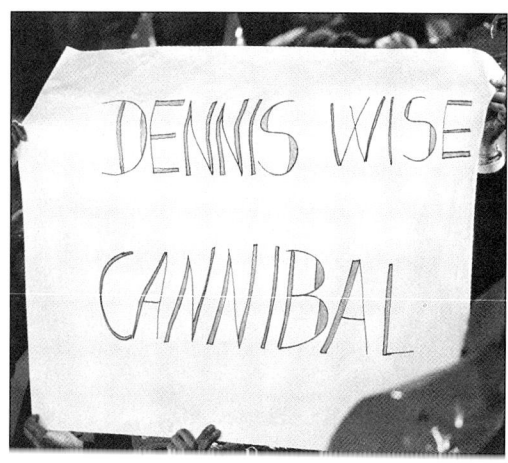

Real Mallorca fans' message to Dennis Wise.

out of all proportion to the offence.

Banks, MP for Newham North-West, and still some years away from becoming sports minister, said: "There were mitigating circumstances which the magistrate has clearly chosen to ignore. The delay between the original appearance in court and sentencing was excessive and represented double jeopardy. I get the feeling the magistrate has been trying to make a name for himself like some ham actor. The refusal of bail makes me feel the magistrate is more interested in self-publicity than justice."

After Wise's sentencing a more dispassionate approach was shown by Tom Pendry MP, who was then the Opposition spokesman on sport and was expected to become Labour's sports minister before Banks suddenly got the job. "I am sure the court took everything into consideration," said Pendry. "I hope it's a lesson to anyone who might be tempted to go down the same road."

Since then Wise has no shown no tendency to go down that particular road again, but he remains a player whose intensity makes him a popular figure with the crowd and with his employers, but one hated by almost everyone else. Gianluca Vialli, the current Chelsea manager, has steadfastly refused to strip Wise of the captaincy. As the Chelsea side has been built up from a rootless, cosmopolitan band of players, Wise has retained his place, performing with a passion that harks back to a former time. It is a commitment that has kept him at the heart of the club, but the question is always been asked: is he the sort of icon the club, or for that matter football, can any longer afford?

Chastened: Wise emerges from court.

Dennis the Menace's Record

Dennis Wise missed ten of Chelsea's first 28 games in the 1998–99 season through suspension and is no stranger to controversy, as his disciplinary record reveals:

- May 1990: Fined £200 and given one-year driving ban after refusing to give a breath specimen.
- August 1990: Sent off in only his second game for Chelsea.
- October 1993: Only weeks after being appointed Chelsea captain, he is sent off for a two-footed tackle and stripped of captaincy. Banned for three games.
- September 1994: Sent off against Newcastle for foul and abusive language to a linesman.
- February 1995: Convicted of assault and causing criminal damage to a taxi. Withdrawn from England squad to face Ireland.
- March 1995: Sentenced to three months in prison; released on bail.
- June 1995: On appeal, sentence quashed "with no enthusiasm" by the judge.
- February 1998: Receives 11th yellow card of season after being booked against Manchester United. FA give him a two-match ban.
- August 1998: Sent off against Atletico Madrid for stamping in a pre-season match. Banned for three games.
- October 1998: Dismissed for two-footed tackle on Darren Byfield in the Worthington Cup tie against Aston Villa.
- December 1998: On his return from a four-match ban, Wise is sent off after 37 minutes at Everton for two bookable offences. Faces three-match ban.
- February 1999: Sent off in Chelsea's FA Cup fourth-round replay against Oxford.

10

The Rings of Deceit

Modern sport is big business. Thanks to the power of television, sport is the ultimate marketing tool, offering the the great consumer companies a means of reaching millions across the world. Of all sporting events, the biggest and most international are the Olympics.

The 1996 Games in Atlanta were seen by an estimated 3.2 billion viewers out of a possible 3.5 billion world-wide. The Games provide prodigious commercial opportunities: for multinational companies through advertizing and sponsorship, for television companies, and for the cities which host the games.

Meanwhile the Olympic movement, led by Juan Antonio Samaranch, President of the International Olympic Committee, still claims to enshrine the lofty principles of Pierre de Coubertin, founder of the modern Games: that, because the participants compete not for prize-money but for medals and glory, the Games are above such petty considerations as filthy lucre. Such is the Olympics' lure that highly-paid athletes from Michael Jordan to Steffi Graf are indeed happy to forget about money for a couple of weeks and to compete "purely" for Olympic glory. Doubtless their commercial associates are happy too.

Yet the IOC is the world's richest sports organization. This is Samaranch's greatest contribution: selling the Games to TV and to sponsors such as Coca-Cola, McDonald's, IBM, Panasonic and Samsung, known as

Trading up: Juan Antonio Samaranch has increased the IOC's TV income 20 times since 1980.

TOP sponsors, who under his expert tutelage have come to see the Games not as a sports event but a global marketing bazaar.

Since 1980, when Samaranch became President, the IOC's television income has increased by 20 times. In 1980 TV paid the IOC just $122 million. The TV rights for the forthcoming Sydney Games will themselves generate $1,246 million ($1.3 billion), on top of another $512 million from the 1998 Nagano Winter Games. The TOP sponsors will bring in a further $350 million.

While the IOC generates huge revenue, however, Mammon is always clothed in the garb of a higher morality. So the IOC boasts that no money is taken from spirits or tobacco companies, and that the Games are the only sporting event where advertizing on hoardings or athletes' uniforms is banned (this is also true, however, of the US Masters in Augusta). Much is also made of the fact that most of this cash goes back to the national Olympic bodies and the cities which host the Games. However, the IOC does retain some seven per cent, which amounts to a colossal sum and funds the first-class travel and expensive hotel suites of the IOC members.

The IOC is a self-elected oligarchy. Its 115 members are not voted on, but join by presidential invitation; and, while they come from different countries, once on the IOC they are supposed to forget their national origins and try to be high-minded Olympians whose only pursuit is the ideal of free competition. They remain for life, and are not subject to any democratic checks such as elections.

To be fair to Samaranch, the Olympic movement has always been an oligarchy: in many ways Avery Brundage, the American who ran it for decades, was even more of a dictator. However, under previous presidents the Olympic organization was much more homogenous, composed mainly of wealthy men from the West but also minor nobility from other parts of the world. Under Samaranch it has become more populist, with members ranging from Princess Anne at one extreme to small-scale businessmen and military officers in the developing world.

This change in the composition of the IOC – over a period which has seen a vast increase in the Games' commercial value, and therefore in the temptation to bend the rules in order to win the right to host them – has been largely responsible for bringing the IOC into its current state of ignominy.

The Olympic Charter declares that "Olympism" is based on "respect for universal fundamental ethical principles". The IOC members take an oath to keep themselves free from any "commercial influence". These principles are never more severely tested than when IOC members have to decide which city is to hold the Olympic Games.

Selecting a bid city is not an exact science, or even based purely on merit. IOC members may favour a city from their own country or continent. They may even trade votes, promising to support a certain city in exchange for a reciprocal commitment in the next bid cycle. However, these political realities are fundamentally different from, and do not justify, an IOC member profiting personally from his or her voting privileges.

Similarly, the movement does not ban payments by bid cities to Olympic organizations – indeed, encourages assistance to athletes, particularly those in developing countries. But payments to IOC members, on the pretext that they will be used for athletes, violate the common ethic of both the IOC and the communities where the Games are held.

A certain level of diplomatic gift-giving is accepted and is common in international relations. However, excessive gifts, let alone payments which virtually amount to bribes, are not sanctioned by IOC guidelines.

At the end of 1998 it suddenly emerged that inducements had not only been offered by bid cities wishing to procure votes, but eagerly accepted by a number of IOC members. Indeed, such a web of bribery and corruption was revealed at the heart of the organization that for a time the very future of the movement seemed to be in doubt.

The storm broke unexpectedly on the afternoon of Saturday, 12 December 1998, at a routine meeting of the IOC Executive Board in Lausanne, Switzerland, to prepare for a world conference on drugs it was to host there two months later. To the surprize of journalists Marc Hodler, one of the IOC's two most senior members, spilled the beans in a series of unscripted, impromptu briefings. Hodler, the 80-year-old head of a Swiss law firm, has been on the IOC since 1963, and held almost every senior post.

Normally the IOC works hard to control the flow of information. But now, as bemused journalists moved round the conference hall Hodler huddled with them, an old man apparently seeking to relieve himself of an enormous burden he had borne for many decades. In the process he tore away the pretence, so studiously maintained up to that moment, that there was no corruption in the Olympic movement, and confirmed suspicions which had long existed but always been denied.

Hodler alleged, among other things, that the successful bids by Atlanta for the 1996 Olympic Games, Sydney for the 2000 Games, Nagano for the 1998 Winter Games and Salt Lake City for the 2002 Winter Games were not clean; that IOC members' votes could be bought; that there were agents specializing in such deals; and that one agent was himself an IOC member. Hodler also described as a bribe a $500,000 scholarship fund set up by Salt Lake City during its bid process, which benefited IOC members' relatives.

The IOC tried hard to stifle these astonishing allegations. At one stage, as Hodler was talking to the press, IOC secretary-general Françoise Zweifel came on to the rostrum and shepherded him away, as if Hodler was a sick man. The allegations resulted in such unparalleled confusion and chaos that for a time it seemed Samaranch and his executive board might be losing control. Indeed, the IOC can be said never to have regained control since. It lost its innocence that weekend, and its claim of clean sport for all, where everyone had a level playing-field, was exposed as a fraud.

The drama reached its climax on Sunday afternoon when Hodler failed to take his place on the podium for a press conference about Salt Lake City and the 2002 Winter Games. As chairman of the co-ordinating commission for the Games, he should have been there.

It later emerged that Hodler had been ordered by Samaranch himself not to go. Hodler confirmed this when he emerged for lunch. Asked if he had been silenced, he made a motion across his lips like a zip being closed and said, "Exactly. I have been muzzled [using the German word *maulkorb*, the muzzle put on guard-dogs]." Then he added, "Apparently I said too much."

What had prompted Hodler to say "too much" was the leaking of a document in the United States two weeks before the IOC Executive Board meeting, which lifted the lid on the bribery and corruption used by Salt Lake City to win the 2002 Winter Games. This was a letter, drafted by the deputy head of the Salt Lake City Bid Committee, to Sonia Essomba, daughter of an IOC member, informing her that the Bid

Marc Hodler: spilling the beans on corruption.

Committee intended to stop paying for her tuition. Nobody in the outside world had known such payments were being made.

Twenty-four hours before Hodler blew the whistle, the IOC set up an *ad hoc* commission to investigate the Salt Lake City scholarship. Dick Pound, a Canadian QC and an IOC vice-president, was put in charge. Of Hodler's allegations, he said: "We are aware that there are agents; we are aware of the identity of some of them. What seems to be developing is a professional class of Olympic agents offering services for bidding committees." Pound also confirmed that even before Hodler made his comments the IOC, concerned about agents, had warned cities bidding for the Winter Games in 2006 to tread very carefully.

Hodler having opened the can of worms, others were soon testifying to corruption. But Atlanta, Sydney and Nagano all vigorously denied any wrongdoing during their successful bids. Sydney confirmed they had received an offer from an unnamed agent to buy African votes, but said they had turned it down.

The biggest repercussions from the Olympic corruption story were felt in Salt Lake City, where the Board of Ethics commenced its work on 18 December 1998. It interviewed several witnesses, including officers, employees and trustees of the Bid Committee and the organizing committee.

While the Board of Ethics had no power to compel witnesses to attend, most persons invited to meet it did so. Others made unsolicited offers to appear. However, one important witness, Craig Peterson, the Chief Administrative Officer of the Bid Committee throughout the entire bid period, declined to attend on the advice of counsel.

The Board's report ran to more than 300 pages and was a devastating indictment of the corruption in the Olympics.

It shows how sport can be corrupted in the name of altruism, and how those who have made themselves leaders of sports can use them to make money in a way that the commercial world would never tolerate.

The Salt Lake City Bids

Salt Lake City's bid for the 2002 Olympic Winter Games was not its first: it had been trying for more than 30 years. In 1966 the city lost to Sapporo in Japan, which held the 1972 Winter Games. In the 1980s a joint Salt Lake City/State of Utah task force was formed to reconsider the feasibility of hosting future Olympic Winter Games. In November 1989 Utah voters supported a tax referendum to fund the building of Olympic venues. Following this, the US Olympic Committee's nomination was officially extended to Salt Lake City, enabling it to bid for the 1998 Games. But once again, the Japanese were in the way.

The bid for the 1998 Winter Games was to be decided at an IOC meeting in Birmingham, England. Salt Lake City had 18 months and a budget of $5 million. Two men – Tom Welch, volunteer president of the Bid Committee, and vice-president David Johnson – were at the heart of the operation.

They saw their mission as "marketing" the city, likening it to a political campaign. Shortly before the 1989 referendum, Welch and Johnson had consulted Samaranch on how to run a successful bid. He advized them to become personally acquainted with as many IOC members as possible and to become part of the "Olympic family".

This phrase, much used in the Olympic movement, is meant to convey a relationship of trust, mutual support and commitment which embraces IOC members, staff, national Olympic Committees, international sports federations and individual athletes.

In order to join the "family", individuals associated with the Bid Committee travelled to meetings attended by IOC members, met representatives of successful Olympic bid cities, visited IOC members in their own countries and invited them to visit Salt Lake City. These visits allowed the Bid Committee not only to showcase Utah's Olympic venues and natural beauty, but also to demonstrate the state's hospitality to the Olympic family.

It quickly became clear that the family put strong demands on this hospitality, as some IOC members expected to be treated on a lavish scale including first-class air travel and the finest hotels, meals, gifts and entertainment, all at the bid city's expense.

Through 1990–91 the lobbying effort consisted mainly of attending IOC meetings and hosting some IOC members, though not a majority of the voters, in Salt Lake City. The Bid Committee also presented gifts to some visiting IOC members, typically local souvenirs such as clothing with the Salt Lake Olympic logo and jars of Utah honey. On a similar 'hometown' theme, the committee presented IOC members with its "bid book", detailing the technical merits of the city's bid, in a leather saddlebag.

Salt Lake City's bid for the 1998 Winter Games had been conducted in what could be called the old style, before big money came in and brought large-scale corruption in its wake. Throughout the bidding process, many Utah residents graciously provided hospitality to IOC members; others travelled around the world, sometimes at their own expense, to visit IOC members in their home countries or at various Olympic meetings.

Salt Lake City's campaign culminated in June 1991 at the three-day IOC site selection meeting in Birmingham in England. Like the other bid cities, including Nagano, Salt Lake City sent a large contingent of both paid staff and local business and government leaders for one last lobbying effort. Each Bid Committee hosted parties, delivered last-minute gifts and made final personal appeals to IOC members. By all accounts Nagano outdid Salt Lake City in each of these areas. Exposure to Nagano's well-oiled bid machine, and to the excessive demands of certain IOC members, would prove to be a watershed which shaped the approach of Welch and Johnson to the campaign for the 2002 Games.

Several witnesses described Nagano's bid effort as more sophisticated and extravagant than Salt Lake City's. Nagano gave IOC members video cameras: Salt Lake gave them disposable cameras as part of a personalized "welcome package". Shortly before the meeting Japanese companies made large donations, reported to be in excess of $15 million, to the IOC Museum in Lausanne.

The behaviour of some IOC members was an eye-opener as well. The night before the vote, Welch was approached by at least two individuals acting on behalf of IOC members and asking for cash in exchange for votes. Bid committee personnel refused these requests. On 15 June the vote went to Nagano by a narrow margin of 46–42.

The details of what Nagano did will never be known: the Japanese burnt 90 books of account of the Nagano Bid Committee and, when this emerged in the wake of the Salt Lake scandal, claimed it was the Japanese way. Having seen the Japanese way, the Americans tried to copy it.

The Board of Ethics report observed that, after the vote, Salt Lake City's Bid Committee personnel, trustees and several business leaders from the bid contingent met to analyse the defeat and discuss how to improve their approach next time. They decided that for the 2002 Winter Games the Bid Committee should increase its focus on winning the "hearts" of IOC members by developing personal friendships with them and their families, and particularly by bringing more of them to Salt Lake City.

The group also discussed the behaviour of the Nagano Bid Committee and the solicitations for cash made on behalf of certain IOC members. According to their own statements, several Salt Lake City business leaders, including trustee Verl Topham (who shortly thereafter joined the Bid Committee's executive), told Bid Committee personnel, Welch and Johnson among them, that they had consistently refused to succumb to bribery in their international business dealings, and likewise would not "buy the Olympics".

With nearly four years to go until the IOC met in Budapest to select the site of the 2002 Winter Games in June 1995, few IOC members wanted to visit Salt Lake City in 1991–92. Instead, Bid Committee personnel continued to visit them at home and at international Olympic meetings.

In some cases, the relationships became very close. For instance, in November 1991, the wife of Seiuli Paul Wallwork, an IOC member from Western Samoa, wrote to Welch asking to speak to him on "a matter of great urgency". In a follow-up telegram dated 12 November, Mrs Wallwork requested his assistance "to help a friend in a serious situation" by remitting US$30,000 to her account in Auckland, New Zealand. The telegram stated that the loan had "nothing to do with Paul [Mr Wallwork] or bid city but [is to be] regard[ed] as [a] business arrangement between you and me".

Welch authorized a $30,000 wire transfer from his children's personal trust account. The loan was eventually repaid.

At the same time, Welch and other senior Bid Committee officials embarked on a programme to provide assistance to relatives of other IOC members. During 1991–92, at least four relatives or associates of IOC members received tuition fees and/or help with living expenses. This has been widely described as a "scholarship program", but in reality the payments bore little resemblance to traditional scholarships.

While the existence of a "scholarship program" was not acknowledged in any Bid Committee documents until January 1992, a summary budget for Fiscal Year 1992 (1 July 1991–30 June 1992) presented to the executive committee included $30,000 for a "NOC Assistance Program" out of a total budget of approximately $540,000. It appears some of the payments made on behalf of relatives of IOC members came from this "NOC Program" budget.

Poisoned chalice: a representative of Salt Lake City is handed the Olympic flag by Juan Antonio Samaranch at Nagano in 1998.

From early 1993, Welch and Johnson appear to have abandoned any pretext of following the "scholarship" criteria, and began to pay for IOC members' relatives to attend colleges outside Utah and, in some cases, send cash to IOC members' relatives.

During 1993–94, more IOC members visited Salt Lake City. David Johnson estimated approximately 70 were welcomed over the course of the two bid campaigns.

In February 1994, at the Olympic Winter Games in Lillehammer, the IOC adopted "guidelines" to limit the expenses incurred by bid cities on gifts and travel for IOC members. Introduced by Marc Hodler, these "Hodler Rules" started a two-phase bid procedure. During Phase I, all nominated cities are considered as candidates. In Phase II, six months prior to the final site selection, the IOC narrows this field to four finalists.

IOC members and their relatives may visit only the four finalist cities, for no more than three days. Gifts to IOC members during Phase I are limited to $50; during Phase II, to $150. However, no enforcement measures accompanied these guidelines, and Salt Lake City, now little more than a year away from its crucial date in Budapest, carried on merrily trying to bribe IOC members.

The Bid Committee paid for IOC members and their relatives (sometimes more than one) to fly first-class to Salt Lake City (often more than once), and sometimes paid for their travel to other Olympic events. While in the city, IOC members were given extensive planned itineraries, including trips to the venues and to other local sites and dinners in restaurants and private homes.

Some IOC members enjoyed additional stays, again at Bid Committee expense, at locations other than Salt Lake City. On several occasions the committee paid for IOC members to stay in New York, Paris and London for extended periods both before and after visiting Salt Lake City. While some IOC members may conceivably have needed a few days in Paris or London to arrange US visas, SLOC records clearly show many of these stays either had no relation to obtaining travel documents or were far longer than necessary.

Presenting gifts to members of the "Olympic family" is a long-established tradition. Bid cities customarily exchange gifts with IOC members, government representatives and others in the Olympic movement.

Some gifts, particularly those with a Utah theme, were given uniformly to each visitor: others were personalized for individual IOC members. Several prominent guests received personalized gifts in recognition of their positions within the Olympic family, ranging in value from $200 to $9,000.

IOC President Samaranch was given a $9,000 limited-edition pistol donated by arms manufacturers Browning. Norwegian IOC member Jan Staubo was presented with a replica model of the Spitfire he flew as a fighter pilot during the Second World War. Stein Erickson, brother of a former comrade of Staubo who lost his life in combat, presented the model to him. These gifts were intended to strengthen ties between the recipient and the Salt Lake City campaign.

Other gifts were not so personalized. Some IOC guests expressed an interest in shopping trips for themselves or their companions. While some of this shopping was paid for by the visitors, a Bid Committee representative was often present who would pay for the purchases on a personal chargecard and subsequently be reimbursed by the Bid Committee.

Entertainment of IOC members in Salt Lake City ranged from private dinners at the homes of local residents to sports events, such as Utah Jazz basketball games, cultural performances and recreational excursions. Some group activities were conducted in full view of the public. For example, large numbers of IOC members were honoured during half-time breaks at Utah Jazz games and were presented with Jazz collectables.

Like the gifts, some of the entertainment was more personalized. Many IOC members were taken ski-ing, and others were taken on trips to Moab, Yellowstone Park, Las Vegas and even Florida for the Super Bowl.

The IOC investigation

The detailed evidence of corruption in the Board of Ethics report sowed panic among IOC members, clearly unprepared to have their individual financial dealings with the Salt Lake City Bid Committee laid bare. Indeed, the IOC Commission's Report into the conduct of its own members, presented to the IOC executive in Lausanne on 11 March 1999, criticized the report on the grounds that "IOC members were publicly named, based on information that was acknowledged as incomplete, and that many of the IOC members named were given no opportunity to comment upon the contents before it was made public".

The Commission also rejected what it described as "the more general and extreme characterizations" contained in the report of the US Olympic Committee into the Salt Lake City bid. This suggested the IOC itself had contributed to a "flourishing culture of improper gift-giving" in the bidding process for major Games.

The IOC Commission report was an attempt to pass the buck to the USOC for the corruption of Salt Lake City. "Many of the excesses which occurred on this occasion might have been avoided had the USOC been more active in discharging its responsibilities, including the bringing of any violations of the rules to the attention of the IOC," it loftily pronounced.

The report then went on to defend the Commission's decision to impose penalties short of expulsion on several IOC members on the basis that their improper gains from the Bid Committee had been unsolicited. In many cases, it said, "members were led to believe that invitations, gifts or liberalities were personal favours or courtesies between friends, unconnected with the bid process, and were surprized to find that they had been charged or reimbursed by SLBC to the purported donors."

Finally, it sidestepped the whole question of "improper gift-giving" by introducing a plea of cultural relativism: one man's improper gift is another man's traditional token of reciprocal friendship. "In many societies, these exchanges are viewed as an honourable tradition and are not corruption," the IOC report said.

Not surprisingly, the IOC Commission failed to comment on most of the key recommendations of the USOC report regarding democratization and open accounting of the IOC. Among other proposals, USOC recommended that:

● IOC members and leaders should be subject to periodic re-election with appropriate term limits;
● the IOC should engage an independent auditor and disclose publicly, at least yearly, the IOC's audited financial statements;
● the meetings of the IOC and its committees should be open to the public;
● the IOC should require members to disclose promptly to the Office of Compliance all gifts (whether in the form of money, goods, or services) offered to the member, whether accepted or declined, by anyone acting on behalf of candidate cities, host cities or NOCs.

Finally, the USOC report suggested that the IOC should the IOC "take the steps necessary to designate the IOC a 'public international organization' pursuant to the Organization for Economic Co-Operation and Development's recommendation on combating bribery in international transactions, and pursuant to the Foreign Corrupt Practices Act (FCPA) of the USA". This move "would make bribery of an IOC member a crime under the FCPA".

In response to these recommendations, the IOC Commission recommended only that they be "studied" along with several others, and underlined that the IOC should do nothing to restrict its ability "to act autonomously in the best interests of the Olympic movement as a whole".

Nevertheless, the weight of evidence against many IOC members was so overwhelming that the IOC could not avoid expulsions. The Commission drew a distinction between members who violated the guidelines on free travel and gifts – here it was keen to pin a large part of the blame on the Salt Lake City bid officials – and those who had received economic benefits beyond gifts and travel. The former got away with a slap on the wrist – in the IOC's Commission's words, "a graduated series of warnings, from warning to serious warning to most serious warning".

Six IOC members were expelled: Agustin Arroyo (Ecuador), General Zein El Abdin Ahmed Abdel Gadir (Sudan), Jean-Claude Ganga (Congo), Lamine Keita (Mali), Sergio Santander Fantini (Chile) and Paul Wallwork (Western Samoa). Another, Charles Mukora (Kenya), resigned, pre-empting any further action against him.

Nine IOC members received various degrees of "warning": Phil Coles (Australia), Louis Guirandou-N'Diaye (Ivory Coast), Willi Kaltschmitt (Guatemala), Un Yong Kim (South Korea), Shagdarav Magvan (Mongolia), Anani Matthia (Togo), Austin Sealy (Barbados), Vitaly Smirnov (Russia) and Mohamed Zerguini (Algeria).

Three IOC members, Henry Adefope (Nigeria), Ashwini Kumar (India) and Ram Ruhee (Mauritius), were exonerated of all the allegations made against them.

Agustin Arroyo

The Commission found that Arroyo's stepdaughter, Nancy Rignault Arroyo, received benefits totalling $10,468.83 from the Bid Committee. Although Arroyo admitted asking Tom Welch to help find her employment in Salt Lake City, he denied all knowledge of any payments made to her.

Arroyo also admitted he, his family and some friends had visited Salt Lake City between 20 December 1994 and 2 January 1995 for a ski-ing holiday, and that the Bid Committee had paid $6,991.42 to cover the rental of a condominium for his party.

Of the money received by Nancy Arroyo two cheques, for $3,000 and $2,500, were made payable to her and marked "NOC Program". Arroyo said his stepdaughter had moved back to Texas in October 1992, and queried records showing she had received money for "living expenses" in Salt Lake City after this date. However, the Commission discovered none of the cheqes paid to her after October 1992 was necessarily tied to her presence in Salt Lake City: among them were sums to cover an American Express bill ($193.49), a Holiday Inn bill ($529.69) and rent ($295.67). Arroyo was expelled from the IOC.

General Zein El Abdin Ahmed Abdel Gadir

Gen. Gadir, the IOC member for Sudan, first contacted Welch in December 1993 asking for help in sending three Sudanese athletes to train in the USA. Welch contacted Harvey Schiller, then executive director of the USOC, pointing out that the USOC's International Assistance Fund should treat the proposal favourably because "this is the first opportunity [the Bid Committee] has had to make progress with Gen. Gadir".

Then on 10 October 1994 SLBC vice-president David Johnson received a fax from one of its consultants, Muttaleb Ahmad, the director general of the Olympic Council of Asia – who had been engaged to facilitate introductions to IOC members – asking the committee to send $1,000 per month to the "daughter" of Gen. Gadir. Ahmad's fax stated: "On a personal level: [General Gadir] has a daughter in UK. Help may be extended. He expects $1,000 only a month to ZEMA GADIR. Act #18154530 National Westminster Bank. Brompton Square. London. W3." The same day, Johnson replied: "We will organize support for Zema Gadir in London."

On 24 October 1994, $1,000 was wired to this account and six identical payments were made until 7 June 1995, one week before the site selection meeting in Budapest.

Gen. Gadir later admitted to the IOC that he had no daughter named Zema, and this was a pseudonym for Gadir himself. He was expelled from the IOC.

Jean-Claude Ganga

One IOC member was marked for special attention in the Ethics Board's report – Jean-Claude Ganga from the Congo. Many witnesses described Ganga as the IOC member who took greatest advantage of the Bid Committee's and the city's generosity; Salt Lake City appears to have spent a total of $250,000 on the Ganga family.

Starting in August 1993, Ganga became a frequent guest in Salt Lake Cty. While it is typical for an IOC member and a companion to make one visit to a bid city, Ganga went at least half a dozen times, variously accompanied by his wife Eugenie, his son Jean-Jacques and his mother-in-law Pauline Biyendolo. Since 1990, the total spent by the Bid Committee and the SLOC on travel for Ganga and his family amounted to more than $115,000; meals and lodging for the Gangas cost the Bid Committee $13,900.

During their many visits, Ganga and his relatives received extensive medical care. Ganga was treated for hepatitis, his mother-in-law underwent knee replacement surgery and his wife cosmetic surgery. Some expenses were covered by insurance; others were paid directly by the Bid Committee. However, the bulk of the bills were borne without charge by health care providers. Welch arranged free medical care with doctors and hospitals. The precise value of the health care received by Ganga and his family could not be calculated from the financial records of the Bid Committee, though one firm, Intermountain Health Care, has publicly reported the treatment it donated was worth around $28,000. The Bid Committee directly paid $17,172.37 for health care expenses for Ganga.

Welch had also formed what the Ethics Board termed an improper business relationship with Ganga via a partnership called Claudet Investments. According to the partnership agreement, dated 14 May 1994, its purpose was to "invest in real and personal property, including bank notes, paper, mortgages and real property": its place of business was Welch's home. Each would contribute $1,000 to the partnership. On 14 July 1994, Welch and Ganga opened a bank account at West One Bank called the Claudet Account. Welch never revealed this partnership to the Board; in fact, he told them he had opened a bank account with Ganga solely in order to be of local banking assistance while Ganga was in the Congo.

In late 1994, the Bid Committee's *largesse* to Ganga extended beyond expensive gifts, lavish entertainment and expensive travel and lodging to include unexplained direct payments to Ganga himself. These totalled $70,010.48.

According to Welch, Ganga often solicited assistance for amateur athletics programs in the Congo. Some time in 1992 or 1993, Welch said, he had promised Ganga $50,000 from the Bid Committee for this purpose. The record does not mention any such payments in 1992 or 1993. However, on 25 October 1994, the SLBC issued a $10,000 cheque to First Security Bank on Ganga's behalf. It was endorsed "for deposit only" by Rod Hamson, a Bid Committee employee, and deposited in an account which had been opened in the name of Ganga and his wife on 11 April.

On 20 January 1995 the Bid Committee issued a $20,000 cheque payable to the "Jean-Claude Ganga NOC Program", and on 27 March 1995 a $30,000 cheque was issued to the same payee. There is, however, no documentation regarding this putative NOC program. Questioned about these cheques, Welch said they fulfilled his pledge of $50,000 for amateur sport in the Congo. Both were again endorsed for deposit only by Hamson, and deposited in Ganga's private account at First Security Bank. Welch denied any knowledge that the cheques were paid into Ganga's account.

Hamson told the Board he was sceptical about the funds' destination and suspected they were diverted to Ganga's personal use. This belief, he said, was based on a conversation with Welch shortly before the trip to Budapest, in which Welch complained that he was being "squeezed" by Ganga for money. However, without access to First Security Bank records, the Board of Ethics could not determine for certain whether Ganga used the $50,000 himself.

According to Johnson, on at least two occasions he had returned from trips overseas carrying envelopes containing large sums of cash which Ganga asked him to deposit to his account at First Security Bank. Ganga had told him, Johnson explained, that these monies had been received from the IOC as reimbursement for travel expenses. At least one of these deposits was carried by hand by SLOC employee Van Alford from Johnson to First Security Bank. Another SLOC employee, Sharon Kingman, said Alford had shown her an envelope containing the cash. In her interview with the Board, Kingman said she examined the cash and counted one hundred $100 bills. Alford's recollection is that the amount may have been less than this. Ganga's expulsion from the IOC was confirmed.

Jean-Claude Ganga: expelled from the IOC.

Lamine Keita

Payments to relatives of IOC members continued long after the vote was taken on 16 June 1995 to award the 2002 Winter Games to Salt Lake City. One of these, Moriba Keita, son of Lamine Keita, the IOC member for Mali, received payments until February 1997. Lamine Keita's expulsion from the IOC was confirmed.

Sergio Santander Fantini

In December 1993 and January 1994, two direct payments were made from Bid Committee funds to Sergio Santander Fantini, IOC member for Chile, who also served as president of the Chilean National Olympic Committee throughout the bid period. Both cheques, totalling $20,050, lack proper documentation and the Bid Committee's files contain no information relating to the reason for these payments.

Santander made a site visit to Salt Lake City in 1995. He was accompanied by his wife, his friend Christian Rodriguez, who served as the general secretary of the Chilean NOC, and Rodriguez's wife. Initially Tom Welch offered no explanation to the Board of Ethics for the payments to Santander, but later recalled that they had been a political contribution to Santander at the request of Rodriguez, his campaign manager.

When Santander was asked to explain the payments he admitted he had indeed received a political contribution, but claimed that he understood it to have been a purely personal contribution by Welch and his wife.

The expulsion of Sergio Santander Fantini from the IOC was confirmed.

Phil Coles

Phil Coles, the IOC member for Australia and a member of the Organizing Committee for the 2000 Olympic Games in Sydney, faced a series of allegations connected with visits made to the United States at Salt Lake City's expense. The Board of Ethics suggested there were five in total, with two only four months apart in 1995, and that they included a trip to the Super Bowl in Miami with his family during which he did not visit Salt Lake City.

Records gathered by the IOC Commission pointed to an additional trip to Salt Lake City by Coles's daughter and son-in-law from 2-10 January 1995.

Coles insisted he had in fact visited Salt Lake City on the occasion of his trip to the Super Bowl, and outlined the six visits made by himself and/or members of his family:

Trip No. 1: 12–20 February 1993. Coles and a guest travelled to Salt Lake City for an informal visit as guests of Tom Welch. All expenses, including air fares, lodging, car rental, ski-ing and ski lessons were paid by the Bid Committee.

Trip No. 2: 28 January – 4 February 1995. Coles and a guest travelled to the Super Bowl in Miami, before visiting Salt Lake City. Coles insisted Tom Welch had assured him that CBS and Delta Airlines were financing the Super Bowl portion of the trip. In fact, the Bid Committee met virtually all Coles's expenses.

Trip No. 3: 21 December 1995 – 4 January 1996. Coles, a guest and two of their children visited Salt Lake City for a holiday, six months after Salt Lake had won the bid to host the 2002 Games, staying in an apartment at Deer Valley. Coles said when he asked for the bill at the end of the holiday, he was told, "There is no bill." He volunteered to repay any expenses incurred by the organizing committee for this trip.

Trip No. 4: 1–9 February 1997. Coles and a guest travelled to Salt Lake City for a ski holiday. The organizing committee booked them into Trailsend Condominiums in Deer Valley and provided the party with free ski lessons and ski lifts.

Coles said it was his understanding that the condominium belonged to a friend of either Welch or David Johnson and that the organizing committee had incurred no cost for his stay. He volunteered to reimburse any costs incurred by the organizers. The SLOC records show that the cost of Coles's accommodation amounted to $6,051.

Trip No 5: 19–31 March 1998. Coles and a guest came to Salt Lake City for a ski-ing holiday. SLOC provided him with a car for the trip and two gold passes for ski-ing.

Trip No. 6: January 2–10 1995. Coles's daughter and son-in-law spent a holiday in Salt Lake City, paying their own transport costs. Coles admitted he had asked Tom Welch to arrange some accommodation for his family, assuming they would pay for it when they left. When his daughter and son-in-law left, the bill was met by the SLOC. Coles said he did not learn about this until they returned to Australia.

The IOC Commission accused Coles of a failure of judgement in his repeated acceptance of benefits from representatives of Salt Lake City. In particular, he should have warned his daughter to ensure that any expenses paid by the Bid Committee during her stay were properly reimbursed.

The Commission recommended that Coles be given "the most serious of warnings", and that, should similar facts ever emerge again, such repeated lack of judgement would expose him to expulsion.

In fact, three months later, Coles was in further trouble after it was revealed that he and his companion Patricia Rosenbrock had compiled dossiers on IOC members which had been passed to the Salt Lake City bid committee.

The dossiers, compiled to further the Sydney bid for the 2000 Games, contained assessments of how IOC members might vote as well as information "of a somewhat personal nature on IOC members –and in some cases their spouses –such as details about their likes and dislikes and about their personalities".

He was found guilty of serious negligence but not corruption by the IOC's executive, meeting in Seoul in June 1999. Though there was a narrow majority in favour of expelling him from the IOC, the split vote won him a reprieve. The Commission recommended that in addition to his "most severe warning", the IOC should "add a reprimand...for serious negligence". Nor should he serve as a member of any IOC commission or working group for the next two years. Coles immediately resigned from the Sydney 2000 Organizing Committee.

Louis Guirandou-N'Diaye

Louis Guirandou'N'Diaye, the IOC member for the Ivory Coast, faced three allegations: that he had received a payment of $5,000 in cash from the SLOC itemized as "NOC Program – Guirandou"; that in June 1995 SLOC had given him an air ticket from Abidjan to Budapest for his wife, Simone, worth $3,314; and that he and his daughter Gazelle had received gifts worth $972 during their visit to Salt Lake City in April-May 1995.

Guirandou-N'Diaye produced a letter in his defence on the first charge from Koffi Guipro, treasurer of the Ivory Coast NOC, confirming Guirandou-N'Diaye had passed him the $5,000 to benefit Ivory Coast sport.

The Commission accepted Guirandou's explanations, and also noted that the offer of an air ticket from Welch for Simone Guirandou-N'Diaye had been unsolicited. Likewise, although the gifts accepted by Guirandou-N'Diaye and his daughter in Salt Lake City exceeded the IOC guidelines, this was not incompatible with his position as an IOC member. However, Guirandou-N'Diaye was issued with a serious warning.

Willi Kaltschmitt

Willi Kaltschmitt, the IOC member for Guatemala, faced similar allegations to those against Phil Coles. The Board of Ethics suggested he had made four visits to the United States, travelling with his family and the family of Phil Coles, at the expense of the Bid Committee, with two visits only four months apart in 1995, and that one visit included a trip to the Super Bowl in Miami but not to Salt Lake City.

In his defence, Kaltschmitt insisted that he had made only two visits to Salt Lake City; that the first trip was not an official IOC visit; and that he had gone on to Salt Lake City after attending the Super Bowl with his wife and daughter as a guest of Tom Welch in January 1995. At no time was he advized that any expenses associated with his attendance at the Super Bowl would be paid by the Bid Committee.

The IOC Commission decided that Kaltschmitt had allowed a conflict of interest to arise by allowing the Bid Committee to pay for his expenses during his first visit, and by letting his daughter accompany him as a guest of the Bid Committee on the second visit. Kaltschmitt received a warning from the IOC.

Dr Un Yong Kim

The main allegation against Dr Kim, the IOC member for South Korea and a long-term favourite to succeed Samaranch as IOC president, concerned the convoluted employment arrangements of his son.

Some time in the spring of 1992 Welch, using Bid Committee funds, arranged for Dr Kim's son to begin working for a Salt Lake City telecommunications company by reimbursing all the costs associated with his employment. According to Welch, Dr Kim had contacted him and explained that his son Jung Hoon, known as John Kim, was being laid off from his job in New York City and needed to find alternative work in the United States to retain his green card. Because John Kim had some experience in the telecommunications industry, Welch contacted David Simmons, the former chief executive of Keystone Communications, a satellite telecommunications company based at that time in Salt Lake City. With Welch's assistance, Keystone hired John Kim.

Welch told Simmons that Kim was working for the TV network NBC Sports in New York, but was about to lose his job in a cutback. Welch also mentioned that Dr Kim, John's father, was a member of the IOC and the chairman of the IOC's Radio and Television Commission.

Simmons met John Kim, was impressed and believed Keystone could use his skills to aid its expansion into Asian markets. But Keystone was only in a position to pay him commission. Welch reassured Simmons that the Bid Committee would be willing to pay Kim's salary over and above any commission he earned. On this basis Keystone agreed to hire Kim with the title of Director of Marketing for International Sales.

However, Simmons first wanted to ensure that both the Bid Committee and Dr Kim were in agreement with the arrangement. According to Simmons, he met Welch and Johnson and received their approval. Simmons also recalls speaking to Dr Kim while on a visit to Seoul, where Dr Kim told him that he knew from Welch of the agreement which had been reached and that he approved of it. Simmons also recalls meeting Dr Kim on two other occasions, and believed that he still understood the arrangement that had been made for his son. In fact, John Kim never earned any commissions at Keystone. Since he lived in New York, Keystone was unable to monitor his work and Simmons became dissatisfied with the relationship.

In the spring of 1993, Kim agreed to end his employment with Keystone. Keystone felt it had not had its money's worth and demanded reimbursement from the Bid Committee. Keystone received the full costs of John Kim's employment, amounting to between $75,000 and $100,000.

In addition, John Kim is alleged to have received a $20,000 consulting contract from the Bid Committee via Komar International Inc., a firm belonging to John Kim.

It was also claimed that Dr Kim used his influence over the Bid Committee to secure professional performance engagements for his daughter, the pianist Hae Jung Kim, on 24 and 25 March 1995 with the Utah Symphony Orchestra, which would have learned of her through the Bid Committee.

Furthermore, Dr Kim was accused of using his influence to secure a college scholarship at the University of Utah for Ekaterina Soukhorado, the daughter of a Russian businessman who was the head of Melodiya, a Moscow firm which had produced records made by Hae Jung Kim. Soukharado had been a student at the University of Maryland on a foreign exchange in the spring of 1991. An extensive correspondence took place between Dr Kim, David Johnson and Soukhorado in October and November 1991, indicating that Dr Kim was helping to handle her arrangements with the Bid Committee.

In response to the first allegation, DrKim and his son John Kim denied all knowledge of an arrangement by the Bid Committee to pay Keystone for John Kim's salary. It was, they insisted, a "secret deal" to which neither of them were a party.

John Kim also denied all knowledge of a consulting agreement between the Bid Committee and Komar International. As to a cheque for $20,000 dated September 30 1992 made payable to Komar Inc., John Kim insisted that the cheque was issued to 'Kobee Inc.', a company based in New Jersey, not to Komar, and that "the Kim family had no knowledge of anyone or any firm with this name". The documents which suggested a contract existed between the Bid Committee and Komar "appear to have been manufactured in an attempt to damage the Kim family reputation".

On the second allegation, Dr Kim claimed that it was his daughter's agent, IMG Artists, who negotiated her performance engagements in Salt Lake City.

As regards the scholarship at the University of Utah for Ekaterina Soukhorado, Dr Kim insisted he had been asked by fellow-IOC member Vitaly Smirnov of Russia to recommend Ms Soukhorado to an American college. This he did, through the Bid Committee. He denied all knowledge of payments being made to Soukhorado by the Bid Committee.

The IOC Commission concluded an agreement did exist between Keystone and the Bid Committee for the reimbursement of John Kim's salary. On 1 July 1992 a consulting contract had been entered into between the Bid Committee and Keystone according to which Keystone, "having knowledge of and access to certain members of the IOC", was to provide consulting services to the Bid Committee.

On the cheque for $20,000 dated 30 September 1992 which was signed by Tom Welch, the name of the beneficiary, which had been typed, had been covered by a portion written in ink which read "Kobee".

The commission characterized the movement of cheques and payments between Welch, Komar, Keystone and John Kim as "unusual". It was "highly unlikely" Dr Kim would have been unaware of arrangements made by SLBC and Tom Welch in favour of his son. "Should the allegations be fully established," the Commission continued, "the Commission would consider that such behaviour by an IOC member would justify expulsion".

Furthermore, the Commission felt Dr Kim had created "very serious appearances of conflict of interest" in the timing of Hae Jung Kim's concert engagements in Salt Lake City and in his role over the university scholarship for Ekaterina Soukhorado and the payments made to her by the SLBC. He received "the most serious of warnings".

Shagdarav Magvan

It was alleged that Bold Magvan, son of Shagdarav Magvan, IOC member for Mongolia, had received help from the SLBC in obtaining employment at First Security Bank of Utah in Salt Lake City; that the Bid Committee had paid $762 to the University of Utah in April 1992 so he could attend an economics course; and that the committee had also paid $4,792.95 for his airfare from Mongolia, plus expenses totalling less than $1,000 during his stay in Salt Lake City.

It was also alleged that Shagdarav Magvan asked the SLBC to provide assistance towards English language study

Tom Welch: "improper gift-giving".

for B. Gansukh, secretary general of the Mongolian NOC, and that the Bid Committee had paid for an eye examination and new glasses for Magvan.

In his defence Bold Magvan said the SLBC had paid the fees for the evening lectures because he could not afford them.

The Commission found Shagdarav Magvan received care, including medication and new glasses, at SLBC expense during a visit in 1995. Bold Magvan received medical expenses totalling $1,559 in 1992. This, it said, had created a conflict of interest.

The eye care received by Shagdarav Magvan during his visit to Salt Lake City in 1995 had not resulted from an injury or illness during his visit, so he should have met the full cost himself. Shagdarav Magvan received a "serious warning".

Anani Matthia

Anani Matthia, IOC member for Togo, faced allegations that the Bid Committee paid for: his wife's airfare from Lome to Budapest, which cost $2,891, to attend the IOC session in June 1995; purchases worth $435.86 made by Mrs Matthia during her visit to Salt Lake City with her husband in February 1993; and a Paris hotel bill for $3,925.61 run up by Matthia and his wife during a stopover on that same trip.

Matthia said that some weeks before the IOC session in Budapest, at the end of a visit to Salt Lake City, Tom Welch took Mrs Matthia to one side and slipped her a sealed envelope which he asked her not to open until she was on the plane. It contained a business-class Lome-Budapest return air ticket with Sabena.

Matthia also said that he was reluctant to make his second visit to Salt Lake City in 1995, having already visited the city on the occasion of an NBA event there in 1993, but the intervention of the US Ambassador to Togo, Johnny Young, appealing to him to change his mind, convinced him to go.

The Commission concluded that by accepting the plane ticket and by paying two visits to Salt Lake City, Matthia was in breach of IOC guidelines. However, given the intervention of the US Ambassador, his behaviour did not mean he was unworthy to serve the Olympic movement. He, too, received a "serious warning".

Austin Sealy

Between February 1992 and October 1995, the SLBC maintained a consulting relationship with a body called ARCA, which was affiliated with Alfredo La Mont, then the USOC's director of international relations and protocol. The Bid Committee made six payments to ARCA during that period, totalling $18,185.90.

However, with regard to this money, ARCA wrote to Tom Welch stating that it would be making monthly payments of $3,000 to Austin Sealy, the IOC member for Barbados, "for his services in assisting in developing relations and information to better serve NOCs in the Caribbean and the NOC members of the Commonwealth Games Association".

Sealy wrote in his defence that La Mont had first invited him to work for ARCA in June 1995, but that he had not cashed ARCA's first cheque for $3,000 because he had not yet received a written business proposal from La Mont. On 18 October 1995 he had written to La Mont saying that none of the areas outlined by La Mont was "the kind of activities for which I would seek a retainer". Sealy added: "I do not want to become involved in any conflict of interest situation or indeed in any form of activity which might raise questions."

Although Sealy declined to enter into a relationship with ARCA, his son agreed to work for ARCA starting in November 1995. La Mont agreed the first $3,000 cheque should be negotiated by Sealy's son as payment for his services for the months of November and December 1995. Sealy denied any knowledge that the work for ARCA was linked with Salt Lake City's bid.

The IOC Commission concluded there was no evidence that Sealy had received any money from ARCA other than the August 1995 cheque for $3,000, which was ultimately passed on to his son. Nor did it find any evidence Sealy was aware that ARCA had any affiliation with Salt Lake City. However, it ruled that accepting the cheque under any circmstances may have created an appearance of a conflict of interest; he should have returned the cheque immediately he received it. Sealy was given a "warning" by the IOC.

Vitaly Smirnov

It was alleged Smirnov, IOC member for Russia, was instrumental in obtaining free medical care for a former ice-hockey player, Alexander Ragulin, from Salt Lake City Intermountain Health Care in 1991. He was also said to have accepted excessive gifts, namely a Browning rifle in March 1991 and "bathroom fixtures" to the value of $1,488.

Furthermore, he reportedly helped a young Russian student, Ekaterina Soukhorado, obtain a £12,644 scholarship from the SLBC to the University of Utah.

In addition, David Johnson alleged that, on the eve of the 1991 election for the 1998 Games, a man named Goran Takatch offered him Smirnov's vote for $35,000.

Smirnov explained Ragulin was suffering from serious cardiovascular disease and risked losing his legs without proper treatment, which was not available in Russia. Smirnov considered he was acting more as president of the Russian NOC than as an IOC member, and asked Welch to help "as a gesture of Olympic solidarity".

He also claimed he refused the Browning rifle and left it in the United States. When it was delivered to him a year or so later he donated it to a sporting group, who produced a letter confirming receipt.

As to Ms Soukhorado's scholarship, he had merely consulted Un Yong Kim about how to gain entry to a US university. Any further actions for the girl were carried out on the sole initiative of the SLBC.

The Commission ruled that although Smirnov believed he was acting for humanitarian reasons regarding Alexander Ragulin, he should have realized his request would lead SLBC to believe it might be to its advantage to assist, thereby creating the appearance of a conflict of interest. The same applied to Ms Soukhorado's scholarship: Smirnov had been told SLBC was sponsoring in a letter of 4 August 1993.

It accepted his explanation regarding the rifle, and found that the materiality of the allegations regarding the gift of "bathroom fixtures" and the conversation between Takatch and Johnson were not established. Smirnov was given a "serious warning".

Mohamed Zerguini

The Board of Ethics alleged that regular payments were made by the Bid Committee to Raouf Scally, on the recommendation of Mahmoud El Farnawani, a Toronto-based consultant engaged by the SLBC to make contact with IOC members from the Mediterranean. According to Johnson, El Farnawani said Scally was a relative of Mohammed Zerguini, the Tunisian member.

The Board also claimed the SLBC had covered the expenses of a trip by Zerguini's son, Dr Yacine Zerguini, to Las Vegas and Zion National Park, comprising hotel bills, meals, water- and jet-ski rentals, shopping and entertainment to the value of $1,980.

Furthermore, in summer 1994 Dr Yacine Zerguini and his son Zaki travelled throughout the US, with all airfares (totalling $14,300) covered by Delta Air Line certificates at the request of the Bid Committee and the purchase of gifts (a Gameboy, games and a Nintendo machine worth $1,073.27) paid for by the SLBC.

In February 1996 Dr Yacine Zerguini flew to a convention for orthopaedic practitioners in Atlanta. The SLBC allegedly paid the airfare ($5,015.11) and the convention registration fees ($400).

Mohamed Zerguini said he had no knowledge of Raouf Scally, who was not a relative. He had been too ill to accept the SLBC's invitation himself, but Welch had insisted two members of his family should take his place and sent him two tickets. Dr Yacine Zerguini travelled to Salt Lake City in September 1994, while his grandson Zaki stayed with Welch's family to learn English in June 1994. He denied the SLBC had paid for Dr Zerguini's trip in February 1996: the Commission found no evidence that it had, nor that Scally and Zerguini were related.

However, the Commission said that by sending his son and grandson to Salt Lake City instead of himself Zerguini had created an appearance of improper conduct and he received a "serious warning" from the IOC.

Charles Mukora

In late 1993 the Bid Committee began a series of direct payments to Charles Mukora, an IOC member from Kenya. Welch insists the first was for a Kenyan NOC programme, but acknowledges that the other payments were for Mukora's personal use, including the cost of a civil lawsuit in Kenya. Between November 1993 and May 1995, these totalled $$29,450.

Mukora's defence was that the funds had been used to support amateur athletics in Kenya, and he produced literature about the "Charles Mukora Sports Foundation" but made no mention of his request for personal financial assistance from Welch. Mukora subsequently resigned, and the Commission decided to take no further action.

Rene Essomba

In August 1993, the Bid Committee entered into one of its most expensive relationships: a series of payments to Sonia Essomba, daughter of Prof. Rene Essomba, then the IOC member from Cameroon. They were meant to support her as she attended American University in Washington, DC. Records show that from August 1993 until November 1996 payments for her rent, tuition and expenses totalled $108,350.

Sonia Essomba apparently understood the relationship to be long-term, as she sent two letters asking SLBC to confirm it would take responsibility for her expenses in the USA. Essomba said she needed this to renew her visa and on 29 January 1996 SLBC sent a letter confirming the relationship. Additionally, on 7 July 1994, Welch wrote a letter assuming personal liability for Sonia Essomba's financial support during a visit to Paris from 10 July to 14 August 1994.

Rene Essomba was considered so important to Salt Lake City's bid that the Bid Committee went out of its way to help his daughter. Two officials flew to Washington to help her move her furniture to a new apartment. Welch also acted as her attorney, sending letters to help her terminate her tenancy at an apartment complex.

Since Rene Essomba died before the IOC Commission reported, it took no action.

In many ways the most astonishing aspect of the story was that some people did turn down bribes, clearly seeing them as such. One honest man among the thieves was Dr Andrei Siperco, son of Alexandru Siperco, an IOC member from Romania.

After some earlier correspondence, Johnson wrote to Alexandru Siperco on 27 November 1996 to say he had found Andrei a position at Brigham Young University. Johnson advized Siperco the University "has not budgeted for this position, but the SLOC has budgeted to assist Andrei with airline tickets, housing and a modest living expense, as part of our approved grant program."

On 1 December 1996, Dr Siperco responded, thanking Johnson for his help, but going on to write:

Please remember that never came under discussion the matter of an financial help of any kind from the Salt Lake organising Committee for the Olympic Winter Games of 2002. Through my entire correspondence with Jason Gull and yourself was discussed only the possibility that I might have to participate at the American academic life. As you certainly remember Jason Gull himself was the one that approached me and gave me to understand that the University of Utah or B.Y.U. could be interested to enlist my services, on the subject of my doctorate dissertation...That's the reason why I've sent to the University of Utah the proper documents (resumé, brief summary of the doctorate dissertation, etc.) and I've applied for a teaching position or scholarship. Please believe, dear Mr Johnson, that if I had the slightest idea that all will come down to offer some financial help from the organizing committee of the Winter Olympic Games, I would not even mentioned to you my interest. I want to thank for you generous offer that I have to decline because I consider that it is not appropriate for me to take any advantage of member of family of a member of I.O.C in my relations with people involved in any Olympic activity.

Unfortunately, few in this story had Dr Siperco's integrity or his sense of what the Olympics mean, and so Salt Lake City went on bribing, comfortable in the belief that this was the way to Olympic glory.

The expulsions of IOC members made no difference to the destination of the 2002 Winter Games. On June 16 1995 the efforts of the Bid Committee were rewarded when IOC president Samaranch announced that Salt Lake City had been selected as the site for the Games. Having lost in 1991 to Nagano by four votes, Salt Lake City now beat the three other finalists by a landslide, 54-14-7-7. Salt Lake City may indeed have been the best choice, given its winter sports infrastructure, large population base and impressive record of hosting successful sporting events. But the bribes and extensive corruption had made doubly sure.

And despite all the rhetoric about the IOC's willingness to reform and change itself, it remains a feudal organization where favours count more than anything else. There was a brutal reminder of this when the IOC executive met in the South Korean capital, Seoul, on 19 June 1999 to elect the host city for the 2006 Winter Games.

The strong favourite before the vote was the Swiss city of Sion, and it caused momentary incomprehension when it was revealed that Turin in Italy had in fact won. It made more sense when one considered that the IOC member for Switzerland, and the prime proponent of Sion's candidacy, was none other than Marc Hodler, the man who had brought about the biggest crisis in IOC history by attempting to expose the 'gravy train' culture of the IOC members. It was the revenge of the freeloaders.

Samaranch may promise reform, but even his modest proposals have drawn fire from IOC members. In dismissing the scandal as a small affair, he shows his failure to appreciate the problem – and an amazing lack of understanding of how his beloved Olympic rings have been corrupted.

Countdown to Olympic Corruption – Four Months That Shook the World

1998

24 November
A leaked letter written by an official of Salt Lake City's Bid Committee for the 2002 Winter Games reveals the committee had a scholarship fund to bribe relatives of IOC members. This is the tip of the iceberg.

11 December
Bruce Baird, Australian Federal MP and former New South Wales minister in charge of Sydney's bid, says he was approached by an agent in Acapulco who offered to secure African votes for the Sydney bid. He refused.

12 December
Marc Hodler holds a series of briefings at IOC headquarters in Lausanne, making allegations. The IOC Executive Board dissociate themselves from the allegations and Samaranch says that only he and IOC director general François Carrard can speak for the IOC.

Crisis: Dick Pound and François Carrard.

13 December
Salt Lake City apologizes for its scholarship fund and says it should not have been part of its bid programme. The IOC says Salt Lake won on merit, but it will continue to investigate what may or may not have been inappropriate conduct on the part of some of the members of the Bid Committee. Hodler emerges to say he has been muzzled and might be expelled.

18 December
Salt Lake City's Board of Ethics starts its investigation.

1999

18 January
Sydney is revealed to have operated a fund to help two African countries and met officials from the countries the night before the vote in Monte Carlo, where Sydney beat Beijing for the right to stage the 2000 Games. Sydney claims it was intended to assist athletes in the two countries and not a bribe like Salt Lake City's.

24 January
The IOC announces that six members are to be expelled, four others have resigned and three others are still being investigated. In addition, the process whereby cities are selected for Games is to be reformed.

2–4 February
The IOC holds its doping conference in Lausanne, where government ministers including Britain's Tony Banks call for the IOC to clean up its act and become more democratic, hold elections, open its books and be more accountable. There is an internal revolt against Samaranch about reform. IOC members complain they are being neutered.

9 February
The Board of Ethics issues its report on Salt Lake City, and ten more IOC members are accused of corruption.

27–28 February
The IOC Executive Board hold a secret session in Lausanne, where the ten members facing corruptino allegations are allowed to present their case.

1 March
The Ethics Board of the United States Olympic Committee calls for the IOC to reform and become a more democratic, accountable organization.

17–18 March
The IOC meets in emergency session to expel corrupt members, and vote on reforming procedure for selecting cities for Games.

Roll of Dishonour

The following table contains a selection of the gifts and entertainment provided to visiting IOC members, as shown on Salt Lake City Bid Committee expense reports.

The table represents only a few of the many instances where the Bid Committee paid for shopping trips; supporting documents of expenses did not always include sufficient detail to identify the IOC member who received the item purchased.

Item	Amount	Item	Amount
Luggage and clothing	$5,189	Ski clothing	$810
Letterhead for NOC	$4,891	Door-knobs	$673
Draperies and hardware	$3,117	Violin	$524
Refrigerator and other appliances	$2,600	Ski lessons ≠ child student	$414
		Golf clubs	$403
Clothing	$2,630	Lawn equipment	$268
Shipping of goods	$2,258	Furniture rental for child	$250
UPS ≠ to ship letterhead	$2,043	NFL Super Bowl trip to Florida (3 couples)	$19,991
Glasses, luggage, etc	$1,732	New York City trip with family	$3,395
Bathroom fixtures	$1,488	Las Vegas trip	$1,791
English language training	$1,390	River-running trip	$1,702
Mattress and other bedding	$1,282	Niagara Falls trip	$1,591
Video games/recreation	$1,171	Moab trip	$1,312
Computer ≠ child student	$1,168	Disneyland trip	$1,202
Dogs ≠ retrievers	$1,010	Yellowstone trip	$926
HealthRider exercize machine	$793		

Index

Note: Pages numbers in *italics* refer to illustrations.

A

Abou, Samassi 19
Adams, Tony 13
Adefope, Henry 209
Agassi, Andre 39
Ailton 67
Albertosi, Ricky 140
Alcock, Paul 18, 19, 20
Ali, Muhammad 112, 113, 114, 115, 146
Allemandi, Luigi 140
Alvarez, Wille Pato 37
Amritraj, A.J. 37
Amritraj, V.J. 37
Anderson, Willie 30
Angus, Ronald 89
Arbeit, Ekhart 83
ARCA, Inc. 215
Ardiles, Osvaldo 166
Aristizabal, Victor 25
Armfield, Jimmy 138
Armstrong, Chris 110
Arroyo, Agustin 208, 209
Ashby, Eddie 169, 170, 171, 172, 173, 175, 176
Asprilla, Faustino 25
Astle, Jeff 51
Aston, Ken 22
Ata-ur-Rehman 153
Atherton, Michael 11, 31
Athey, Bill 32
Autuori, Paulo 67
Azharuddin, Mohammed 151, 152, 153
Azzini, Gianni 140

B

Bacher, Ali 121
Back, Neil 28
Baggio, Dino 65
Bailey, David 44
Baird, Bruce 218
Baker, Danny 182
Ball, Alan 138
Bangerter, Hans 53
Banks, Gordon 138
Banks, Tony 19, 81, 198–99, 218
Barber, Shane 20
Barin, Ljubomir 142
Barlow, Eddie 121
Barnes, Peter 172, 174
Barnes, Randy 89, 91
Barthe, Stéphane 92
Basile, Alfio 21
Bassett, Dave 188
Bates, Ken 53, 198
Batista, José 23
Batson, Brendan 108
Battiston, Patrick 23
Batty, David 19, 109, 110
Beach, John 178
Beatrice, Bruno 95
Beldham, William "Silver Billy" 149
Benaud, Richie 31
Berbick, Trevor 112
Berg, Elandre van der 30
Berkovic, Eyal 16–17
Bernes, Jean-Pierre 142
Berrick, Bernard 171, 176
Berry, Tony 168, 169
Best, George 41, *100*, 101–02, 103, 108, 178, 180
Bevilacqua, Antonella 90
Bez, Claude 142
Birch, Paul 65
Bizot, Hervé 142
Blair, Tony 77
Blastow, Diddie 36
Blinker, Reggi 14
Bolanios, Amelia 67
Bonetti, Ivano 20
Borg, Bjorn 37
Borras, Omar 23
Bossi, Miguel 23
Boszik, Joszef 22
Botha, François 114
Botham, Ian 103, 121
Bowen, Mark 13
Bowyer, Lee 110
Boycott, Geoffrey 41, 121
Breen, Geoffrey 197–98, 200
Bremner, Billy *15*, 134–35
Breuer, Grit 84
Bright, Mark 106
Browing, John 134
Brown, Kerrith 88
Brownlie, Cyril 27
Bruin, Erik de 86
Brundage, Avery 202
Bruno, Frank 112, *147*
Bryson, Bob 48
Buchanan, Ken 39
Budd, Zola 30
Buford, Bill 56
Burge, Peter 31
Burki, Javed 150, 151, 154
Burnett, David 27
Burns, Kenny 16
Burtenshaw, Steve 177, 189, 190, 192, 193, 194
Butcher, Terry 17
Butt, Nicky 15
Buxton, Ted 167, 168, 174
Byfield, Darren 196, 199

C

Caccitori, Massimo 140
Calderwood, Colin 166
Calhoun, Cameron 65
Califano, Christian 30
Callaghan, James 121
Callard, Jon 29, 30
Campbell, Sherwin 72
Campbell, Sol 80
Cantona, Eric 11, 40, 96, 126–29, 169
Capel, David 32
Capobianco, Dean 90
Cardona, Roberto 67
Carlos, John 118
Carr, Darren 18
Carson, Willie 94
Cartwright, Tom 120
Cecil, Henry 161
Chandler, Dean 110
Chandrachud, Mr Justice 152
Chang, Michael 37
Chapman, Herbert 164, 192
Chappell, Greg 31, 33
Chappell, Ian 33–34
Chappell, Trevor 11, 31
Charles, Gary 180, *181*
Chauhan, Chetan 32
Chilavert, Jose Luis 25
Chilcott, Gareth 27
Chisholm, Sam 7
Christie, Linford 80, 82, 124–25
Cicotte, Eddie 132, 133
Clarke, Allan 186
Clarke, Ben 30
Clark, Frank 188
Clarke, Nigel 37
Clegg, Charles 164
Clemence, Ray 167, 180
Clohessy, Peter 30
Clough, Brian 11, 16, 128, 143, 167, 168, 172–74, 176–77, 185–89
Cochell, Earl 37
Cockerill, Glen 13
Cole, Andy 123
Coleman, David 22
Coles, Phil 208, 211–12
Collymore, Stan 20, 41, 106–08
Columbo, Felice 140
Comiskey, Charles 131–32, 133
Common, Alf 164
Compton, Denis 101
Coney, Jeremy 31
Constant, David 69
Coppell, Steve 167, 176
Coubertin, Pierre de 201
Couecou, Didier 142
Cowie, James 29
Cowlings, Al 73
Cox, Neil 18
Crocker, John 65
Croker, Ted 52, 53
Crystal, Jonathan 172, 174, 176
Cucchi, Enrico 95
Cunningham, Laurie 108
Curd, Richard 21
Curi, Renato 95
Cyril the Swan 21, *22*

D

Dalglish, Kenny 42
Dallaglio, Lawrence 8,

Index

104–05
Dallas, Hugh 49, *50*
D'Amato, Cus 115
Davey, Lisa 188–89
David, Mario 22
Davies, Kevin 18
Davis, Paul 13, 14
Dawe, Graham 27
De Avila, Anthony 24–25
de Freitas, Phil 122
De Glanville, Phil 29–30
Decker, Mary 30 (see also Slaney, Mary)
Dein, David 14, 193
Del Piero, Alessandro 95
Delgado, Pedro 92
DeMont, Rick 89
Denya, Kazi 140
Devereux, Simon 29
Di Canio, Paolo 18, 19, 20
Dispatches 166
Dixon, Lee 13
Docherty, Tommy 40
D'Oliveira, Basil 120–21
D'Onofrio, Licio 142
Dooley, Wade 27
Doshi, Dilip 34
Double, Steve 17, 110, 192
Douglas, James "Buster" 112, 113, 145, 146
Dourthe, Richard 30
Drake, Ted 21
Dreschler, Heiki 83
Dublin, Dion 108
Duckenfield, Ch. Supt. David 59, 60
Dufaux, Laurent 93
Duleepsinhji, K.S. 119, 122
Duran, Roberto 39
Durani, S.K. 32
Durkin, Paul 108
Dwyer, Bob 30
Dying to Win (Houlihan) 79, 91

E

Edwards, Paul 88
Elder, Lee 123
El Farnawani, Mahmoud 216
Electra, Carmen 97, 98
Elleray, David 18
Ellis, Arthur 22
Emburey, John 121
Emerson, Ross 32, *33*
Engineer, Faroukh 32
England, Mike 108
Escobar, Andres 23, *24*
Essomba, Rene 216–17
Evans, Chris 182
Evans, David 58
Evans, Lee 119
Eydelie, Jean-Jacques 141

F

Fakruddin Ibrahim 151, 156
Farndale, Nigel 144
Farrar, Vince 166
Faschet, Eric 65
Fashanu, John 135, 136, 138
Fashanu, Justin 110
Fenn, Simon 28, 29
Fenton, Ronnie 167–68, 172, 174–77, 185–89
Ferdinand, Les 128
Ferguson, Alex 12–13, 126, 127, 129, 188
Ferguson, Duncan 11, 16, 17
Ferrier, Marc 66
Ferrini, Giorgio 22
Findlay, Donald 49
Fitzpatrick, Sean 29, 30
Foreman, George 113, 146
Fortunato, Andrea 95
Foster, Robin 29
Fowler, Robbie 108, *111*
Francis, Trevor 129
Francisco, Silvino 95
Frandsen, Per 17
Franke, Malcolm 123
Fransson, Stefan 38
Freeman, Ron 119
Friar, Ken 14, 189, 190, 194, 195
Fugler, Jeff 170, 171, 172, 173, 175

G

Gadir, General Zein El Abdin Mohamed Ahmed Abdel 208, 209
Gadir, Zuhair 212
Galeone, Giovanni 66
Gandil, Chick 132, 133
Ganga, Jean-Claude 208, 209–210
Gardner, Paul, *Nice Guys Finish Last* 8
Gascoigne, Paul 42, *45*, 96, 178–183
Gatting, Mike 11, 31, 32, 121–22
Gauld, Jimmy 134
Gavaskar, Sunil 32, 33, 34
Gear, Tim 43
Gemmill, Archie 186
Giles, Johnny 15
Givens, Robin 115
Glanville, Brian 57, 140, 143
Goehr, Marlies 83
Goldman, Ronald 75
Gomez, Hernan Dario 24
Gooch, Graham 121
Gordon, John 143
Gough, Darren 32
Gower, David 121
Graf, Steffi 73, 201
Graham, George 13, 14, 15, 177, *184*, 189, 190, 192–95
Graham, Gerald 196–98
Grant, Charlie 118
Gregory, John 107–08
Griffith-Joyner, Florence 82–83
Grobbelaar, Bruce 18, 60, *130*, 135–36, 138
Guirandou-N'Diaye, Louis 208, 212
Guliyev, Zafar 90
Gullit, Ruud 42, 123

H

Haaland, Alf-Inge 14, 106, 186, *187*, 188, 189
Hagler, Marvin 147
Hain, Peter 121
Hair, Darrell 32
Hall, Douglas 105
Hall, Eric 198
Halsey, Mark 65
Hamilton, Gavin 134
Hammond, Frank 36
Hamson, Rod 210, 214
Hans-Hamilton, Gavin 180
Hansen, Alan 138
Hapgood, Eddie 22
Harding, Tonya 73
Harkness, Steve 106
Harris, Ron 14
Harry, Richard 29
Hart, Paul 143
Harte, Ian 14
Hartson, John 16–17, 18, 20, 194
Hardwick, George 164
Hauge, Rune 186, 188–190, 192–95
Healey, Austin 28–29
Helder, Glen 194

Hemmings, Eddie 32
Hendry, Colin *50*
Heng Suan Lim 135, 136, 138
Henman, Tim 37, 94
Hervé, Pascal 93
Hicks, Tom 89
Hidegkuti, Nandor 22
Higgins, Alex 103, 104–05
Higuita, Rene 25
Hilditch, Steven 26, 27
Hill, Allan 188, 189
Hill, Damon 12, 34
Hill, Richard 27
Hill-Wood, Peter 14, 15, 16, 192–95
Hillier, Brian 165, 166
Hillier, David 110
Hilman, Jack 133
Hoddle, Glen 182, 198
Hodler, Marc 202, *203*, 206, 207, 217, 218
Holyfield, Evander 11, 113, 114, *145*, 146
Hookes, David 154
Hooper, Clay 118
Hope, Lord 16
Horne, John *145*
Horner, Chris 93
Horton, John 27
Houlihan, Barry, *Dying to Win* 79, 91
Hughes, Mark 13
Hunter, Norman 15–16
Hutchinson, Colin 198

I

Igoe, Sammy 65
Illingworth, Ray 31, 70, 122
Imran Khan 150
Ince, Paul 108, 123
Intikhab Alam 150
Issajenko, Angella 90

J

Jackman, Robin 122
Jackson, "Shoeless" Joe 13
Jadeja, Ajay 152
Jalabert, Laurent 92, 93
James, Larry 119
James, Tony 18
Jardine, Douglas 69
Jenkins, David 81
Jenner, Terry 70

Index

Jensen, John 189, 190, *191*, 192, 193, 195
Jensen, Knut 91
Jensen, Murphy 37
Jesus, Uriel de 23
Johansson, Lennart 143
Johnson, Ben 81–82, 87, 88, 90
Johnson, David 204, 205, 207, 209–212, 214, 215, 216
Johnson, Magic 114
Johnson, Peter 16
Johnstone, Mo 49
Jones, Alan 121
Jones, Dean 111
Jones, Jimmy 48
Jones, Mick 18
Jones, Tanya 41, 42
Jones, Vinnie 17, 40–45, 61, 96
Jonsson, Ulrika 40, 106–07
Jordan, Michael 93, 96, 98, 115, 201
Julian, Brendon 72
Juninho 108

K

Kaltschmitt, Willi 208, 212
Kapuscinski, Ryszard, *The Soccer War* 68
Kay, Tony 134, *135*
Keegan, Kevin 12–13, *15*
Keita, Lamine 208, 210
Kenyon, Don 31
Killy, Jean-Claude 92
Kim, John 210, 213–14
Kim, Un Yong 208, 212–14
King, Don 112, 113, 114, 115, 144–47
King, Howard 142–43
Kiwomya, Chris 194
Knott, Alan 70
Korda, Peter *94*
Korneyev, Andrei 90
Krabbe, Katrin 84, 85
Krieger, Heidi 84
Kumar, Ashwini 209
Kumble, Anil 122
Kyle, Archibald 134
Kyle, Rollo 143
Kyle, Sheryl 182

L

La Mont, Alfredo 215
Lambert, William 149
Landa, Honorino 22
Lander, Steve 28
Lascubé, Gregoire 26, 27
Latif, Rashid 152, 153
Lausanne Declaration on Doping in Sport 81
Law, Brian 107
Lawrence, David 122
Lawry, Bill 71–72
Laws, Brian 20
Layne, David 134
Le Roux, Johan 29
Le Saux, Graeme 108, 109, 110
Leake, Alec 133
Leblanc, Jean-Marie 93
Lee, Francis 15–16
Lefèvre, Patrick 93
Legeay, Roger 93
Lenglen, Suzanne 36
Lennox, Bobby 21
Lewis, Carl 82, 83
Lewis, Lennox *145*, 146
Lillee, Dennis 33–34, 72
Lima, Dias 67
Limpar, Anders 13, 14, 189, 190
Lineker, Gary 178
Linton, Arthur 91
Livermore, Doug 167
Livingston, Jason 88
Lloyd, Clive 72
Lobo, Francisco Marques 143
Logan, Richard 18
Lomas, Steve 19
Lorz, Fred 89
Louglan, Anthony 186
Lucas, Gavin 21
Lyas, Graham 186
Lydersen, Pal 189, 190, 192, 193, 195
Lyne, Neil 186

M

McAlinden, Kevin 48
Macari, Lou *165*, 166
McCann, Sean 48
McClair, Brian 13, 108
McDonald, Malcolm 54
McEnroe, John 12, 36, 37, 38
McGraw, John 118
McGwire, Mark 91
McIlvaney, Hugh 53
Mackenzie, Colin 88–89
McLaren, Alan 102
McLintock, Frank 168–176
McMahon, Steve 42, 60
McStay, John 16

Madonna 98
Magvan, Shagdarav 208, 214
Malam, Colin 53
Malcolm, Devon 122–23
Mamiit, Cecil 39
Mandela, Nelson 121
Mannion, Wilf 164
Maradona, Diego 128
Marcelino, 196
Maris, Roger 91
Marshall, Supt. Roger 59
Martin, Edward 65
Martini, Bruno 129
Masback, Craig 90
Maschio, Limberto 22
Massi, Rodolfo 92
Matthews, Stanley 164
Matthia, Anani 208, 215
Mauge, Ronnie 18
May, Tim 150, 151, 154
Meads, Colin 28
Meek, Nigel 29
Meier, Armin 93
Mellor, David 110
Meredith, Billy 133, *162*, 163
Merson, Paul 106
Meszoly, Kalman 142
Miandad, Javed 33–34, 153
Michel, Henri 129
Milburn, Dick 39
Miller, Keith 101
Mitchell, Dennis 90
Mitford, Mary Russell 150
Modahl, Diane 87, 88
Moeller, Silke 84
Mohan, Ramaswami 151
Monserrate, Angel 39
Monti, Luis 21
Mooney, David 134
Mora, Bruno 95
Morrisson, Ed 25
Moscato, Vincent 27
Mottin, Yves 91
Mronz, Alexander 38
Mujic, Muhamed 23
Mukora, Charles 208, 216
Muldoon, Robert 31
Munro, Frank 134–35
Muralitharan, Murali 32, 33
Murdoch, W.L. 68
Murless, Sir Noel 160, 161
Muro, Guruceta 143
Murray, David 50
Murray, Supt. David 60
Mushtaq Ahmed 153
Mushtaq Mohammed 153, 156–57
Muttaleb Ahmad 209

N

Nastase, Ilie 36
Navratilova, Martina 36
Nepia, George 119
Nestor, Daniel 39
Nice Guys Finish Last (Gardner) 8
Nicholson, Shane 111
Nivel, Daniel 65
Norgrove, Frank 164
Norman, Paul 14
Norris, Sir Henry 164
Notley, Jay 111
Novacek, Karel 94

O

O'Brien, Vincent 160, 161
Offiah, Martin 124
Oldfield, Bert 69
Oliver, Ted 40
Ondarts, Pascal 27
O'Neill, Jimmy 164
Orlygsson, Thorvalder 185
Orwell, George 8
Oviedo, Leon 25
Owens, Jesse *116*, 118

P

Paisley, Bob 54
Panorama 166
Pantini, Marco 93
Parry, Rick 167, 175–76
Parsche, Gunther 73
Parsons, John 36
Pavone, Christian 95
Peate, Edmund 68
Pendlebury, Richard 63–64
Pendry, Tom 199
Pennington, Jesse 134
Peper, Bram 66
Perez, Sebastian 108
Pescante, Mario 95
Peterson, Craig 204
Petit, Emmanuel 15, 19
Picpornie, Carlo 66
Piggott, Lester 158–161
Pinheiro 22
Pitarelli 67
Platt, David 178
Pleat, David 14, 58
Pohmann, Hans-Joachim 36
Pohrebnyak, Yuri 23
Pollock, Graeme 121
Pollock, Jamie 18
Pollock, Peter 121
Ponting, Ricky 157

Index

Poole, Thomas Gibson 133
Popplewell, Mr Justice 54
Poulain, Richard 18
Pound, Dick 203, *218*
Powell, Jeff 65
Pozzi, Humbert 22
Prabhakar, Manoj 151, 152
Pressman, Kevin 60
Preston, Kelly 183
Priem, Cees 92
Princess Michael of Kent 40
Probyn, Jeff 29
Procter, Mike 121
Prost, Alain 12, 34, 35
Puskas, Ferenc 22
Putt, Kevin 29
Pycroft, James 149, 150

Q

Qayyum, Justice Malik Mohammed 153, 154, 156
Quiniou, Joel 23
Quinn, Niall 13
Quiroga, Ramon 139

R

Rahman, Anis 169, 170, 171
Raju 152
Ram Ruhee 209
Rana, Shakoor 11, 31, 32
Ranatunga, Arjuna 32, *33*
Ranjitsinhji, K.S. 122
Reacher, Fred 168, 169, 174, 176
Rebeuh, Bruno 38
Redknapp, Harry 17
Reed, Mike 16
Regis, Cyrille 108
Reid, Robert 167, 175–76
Reinisch, Rica 84
Reverie, Paul 180
Revie, Don 51, 134
Reynolds, Harry "Butch" 89
Rice-Davies, Mandy 102
Richards, Barry 121
Richards, David 150, 154–55
Richards, Sir Gordon 160
Richards, Viv 122
Richardson, Richie 122
Rickey, Branch 118
Rijckaert, Eric 92
Riley, Mike 14
Ringer, Paul 27
Rix, Graham 8

Roberts, Graham 165
Robins, Debbie 21
Robinson, Andy 28
Robinson, Jackie 117, 118
Robinson, Jason 124
Robson, Bobby 178
Rocastle, David 13, 14
Rodber, Tim 30
Rodgers, Judge John 198
Rodman, Dennis 96–99
Rodriguez, Gilberto 24
Rodriguez, Miguel 24
Rogers, Bob 29
Rojas, Roberto 67
Roosevelt, Theodore 9
Rossi, Paolo 140
Rothstein, Arnold 132
Roumat, Olivier 30
Rous, Sir Stanley 21
Roussel, Bruno 92
Roux, Laurent 93
Rowan, Lou 70
Royle, Joe 16
Ruddock, Razor 112
Ryan, Elizabeth 36

S

Sacchi, Arrigo 66
Saeed Anwar 156
Saiz, Manolo 93
Salim Malik 32, *148*, 150, 151, 152, 153, 154, 155–56
Sallai, Sandor 142
Samaranch, Juan Antonio 81, 85, *200*, 203–07, 212, 215, 217, 218
Samuel, Martin 61–62
Samways, Vinny 57
Sanchez, Leonel 22
Sandy, Colin 169, 170, 171, 172, 173, 175, 176
Santander Fantini, Sergio 208, 210
Santos, Nilton 22
Saunders, Dean 167
Savage, Dave 60
Schmeichel, Peter *10*, 14, 188
Schmidt, Roland 84
Scholar, Irving 58
Schumacher, Harald 23
Schumacher, Michael 11, 12, 34
Schwarz, Stefan 189
Sealy, Austin 208, 215
Segers, Hans 135, 136, 138, 139
Seles, Monica 72, 73
Senna, Ayrton 12, 34, 35

Seymour, Stan 180
Shackleton, Len 164
Shankly, Bill 102, 140
Shayler, James 63
Shearer, Alan 44
Sheldon, Jackie 134
Shepherd, Freddie 105
Sheppard, Simon 61
Sheringham, Teddy 44, 167–70, 172, 174–76, 185, 186
Sherwood, Tim *109*
Shevchenko, Vadym 23
Shilton, Peter 102, 195
Siddhu, Navjot 152
Silver, Jeffrey 171
Simmons, David 212–13
Simmons, Matthew 126–27, 128
Simoes, Rene 23
Simpson, Billy 48
Simpson, Nicole 73
Simpson, O.J. 8, 74–77
Simpson, Tommy 91
Sinclair, Frank 20
Siperco, Andrei 217
Slaney, Mary (née Decker) 30, *78*, 89–90
Smirnov, Vitaly 208, 214, 215–16
Smith, Alan 13
Smith, Graham 168, 172, 174, 175
Smith, John 54
Smith, Michelle 86
Smith, Tommie 118
Snow, John 32, 70
The Soccer War (Kapuscinski) 68
Soccer's Hard Men (video) 17, 40
Sohail, Amir 153
Solti, Deszo 140, 142
Sosa, Sammy 91
Soukhorado, Ekaterina 212–13
Souness, Graeme 49, 188
Southgate, Gareth 108
Spinks, Michael 112
Stanislaus, Roger 111
Staubo, Jan 207
Steels, Tom 93
Stein, Jock 49
Stein, Mel 182
Stepanovic, Dejan 14
Stern, David 96–97
Stevens, Kirk 95
Stewart, Alec 32
Stewart, Bobby 115
Stewart, Paul 179
Stiles, Nobby 21, 134

Stock, Roger van den 143
Storey, Peter 103
Storrie, Peter 17
Strachan, Gordon 23
Strauss, Astrid 90
Street, Colin 102
Street, Tina 102
Straw, Jack 60
Stuart, Jamie 111
Subba Row, Raman 72
Suddell, William 163
Sugar, Alan 166, *167*, 168–76
Suggett, Colin 51
Swain, Kenny 143
Swan, Peter 134
Sylvester, Martin 21

T

Tapie, Bernard 141–42
Tarango, Benedicte 37, 38
Tarango, Jeff 37–39
Tarantino, Quentin 42
Taylor, Gordon 17–18, 110
Taylor, Graham 173
Taylor, Mark 154
Taylor, Martin 61
Taylor Report 55, 60
Tendulkar, Sachin 72, 122
Terrados, Nicolas 92
Thatcher, Margaret 53, 55
Thomas, Michael 13, 14, 192
Thornley, Irving 164
Tillekaratne, H.B. 32
Tillman, Henry 115
Tinkler, Ray 51
Topham, Verl 205
Topley, Don 150
Toth, Mihaly 22
Tracey, Simon 65
Trevino, Lee 123
Tucker, Tony 112
Turnbull, Sandy 134
Tyson, Mike 11, 12, 41, 112–15, 145, 146

U

Underwood, Derek 121

V

Vainio, Martti 89
Vandenbrouck, Frank 93
Van Heerden 29

Index

Venables, Terry 61, 166–176, 180, 196
Verbruggen, Hein 93
Vialli, Gianluca 95, 199
Viana, Eduardo 143
Vicenze, Guido 95
Vieira, Patrick 17, 18–19
Villa, Ricky 166
Vincent, Christopher 135–36, 138
Viola, Dino 140
Virenque, Richard 92, 93
Viswanath, Sadanand 34
Vivas, Nelson 15
Voet, Willy 92, 93
Vogel, Renate 83
Volley, Paul 28
Vorster, John 120–21

W

Waddle, Chris 17, 178
Walcott, Clyde 154
Walker, Andy 133
Walker, Dougie 87
Walker, Harry 48
Walker, Mick 188
Wallwork, Seiuli Paul 205, 208
Wallwork, Mrs Seiuli Paul 205
Wariso, Solomon 88
Warne, Shane 150, 151, 154, 155, 156, 157
Warren, Frank 145, *147*, 180
Washington, Diane 113
Wasim Akram 153
Waugh, Mark 150, 151, 154, 155, 156, 157
Waugh, Steve 72
Weaver, Buck 133
Welch, Tom 204, 205, 207, 209–212, 213, 214, 216, 217
Wenger, Arsène 13, 14–15
West, Enoch "Knocker" 134
West, Graeme 124
Wilander, Mats 94
Wilkinson, Howard 12, 128, 129
Williams, Rex 95
Wilson, Bob 138
Wilson, Danny 19
Winner, Michael 74
Winstanley, Eric 18
Winterburn, Nigel 13, 14
Wise, Dennis 196–99
Woodfull, Bill 69
Woods, Tiger 123, *124*
World in Action 166
Worrell, Sir Frank 120, 123
Worthington, Frank 102–03
Wright, Ian *10*, 14, 18, 80, 106, 123

Y

Yates, Kevin 28
Yorath, Terry 52
Young, Donna 94

Z

Zeman, Zdenek 95
Zerguini, Mohamed 208, 216
Zuelle, Alex 92
Zweifel, Françoise 203

The publishers would like to thank the following sources for their kind permission to reproduce the pictures in this book:

Action Images PLC 127l, cr
Allsport UK Ltd. 7, 35, 43r, l, 98, 99, 127tr, 129, 141, 177, 181, 184, 196, 199l/Al Bello 113l, tr, 145l, T. Blackburn 145tr, Shaun Botterill 62, 136, 148, Simon Bruty 73, 86, David Cannon 26, 46, 124, Phil Cole 183r, Jonathan Daniel 97l, Tony Duffy 2, 38, 78, 125, Stu Forster 3, 33, 183l, J. Gichigi 147, Steve Grayson 97r, Mike Hewitt 88, 191, Hulton Getty 116, 120, Jed Jacobsohn 113c, Ross Kinnaird 111, 187, Alex Livesey 22, 199r, 200, Clive Mason 155, Gray Mortimore 84, 85, Steve Morton 173, Adrian Murrell 105, Mike Powell 24, Gary M. Prior 94, Ben Radford 71, 152, Ezra O. Shaw 145cr, Paul Spinelli 75l, Billy Stickland 179, Todd Warshaw 113tl
Allsport Historical Collection 100, MSI 159/Chris Cole 160
Colorsport 10, 15, 59, 162, 165
Corbis/Bettmann 132/UPI 75r, Omega 77, Larry White 76
Empics Ltd. 29, 50, 64/Andy Heading 109, Steve Morton 57, Neal Simpson 19
Ronald Grant Archive/ Lock Stock and Two Smoking Barrels 1998, Polygram/Starfilms 41
Hulton Getty 135
Mark Leech Photography/Michael Craig 5
Mirror Syndication International 4, 45
PA News Photo Library 9r, l, 69, 161/AFP Photo/George Frey 216, Sean Dempsey 130, EPA Photo AFP/Pascal George 214, EPA Photo AFP Files/Kazuhiro 208, EPA Photo/Keystone/Fabrice Coffrini 202, 205, 218, Rebecca Naden 201, John Stillwell 167

Every effort has been made to acknowledge correctly and contact the source and/or copyright holder of each picture, and Carlton Books Limited apologises for any unintentional errors or omissions which will be corrected in future editions of this book.